REF

E

i

i

Bolden, Tonya

W9-BFC-810

STRONG MEN KEEP COMING

The Book of African American Men

Tonya Bolden

Foreword by Herb Boyd

John Wiley & Sons, Inc.

New York • Chichester • Weinheim • Brisbane • Singapore • Toronto

*For the first black man in my life and the first reason
why I can't help but love black men. For my father,
Willie J. Bolden, who over the years made tremendous
sacrifices for me, who embraced and braced me during
my struggles and my stumbles, and who in word and
deed supported me mightily in my desire to be a writer.*

This book is printed on acid-free paper.

Copyright © 1999 by Tonya Bolden. All rights reserved
Foreword copyright © 1999 by Herb Boyd
Published by John Wiley & Sons, Inc.
Published simultaneously in Canada

No part of this publication may be reproduced, stored in a retrieval system or transmitted in any
form or by any means, electronic, mechanical, photocopying, recording, scanning or otherwise, except as permitted under Sections 107 or 108 of the 1976 United States Copyright Act, without either
the prior written permission of the Publisher, or authorization through payment of the appropriate
per-copy fee to the Copyright Clearance Center, 222 Rosewood Drive, Danvers, MA 01923, (978)
750-8400, fax (978) 750-4744. Requests to the Publisher for permission should be addressed to the
Permissions Department, John Wiley & Sons, Inc., 605 Third Avenue, New York, NY 10158-0012,
(212) 850-6011, fax (212) 850-6008, E-mail: PERMREQ @ WILEY.COM.

This publication is designed to provide accurate and authoritative information in regard to the subject matter covered. It is sold with the understanding that the publisher is not engaged in rendering professional services. If professional advice or other expert assistance is required, the services
of a competent professional person should be sought.

Library of Congress Cataloging-in-Publication Data:

Bolden, Tonya.
    Strong men keep coming : the book of African American men / Tonya
Bolden : foreword by Herb Boyd.
        p.   cm.
    Includes bibliographical references and index.
    ISBN 0-471-25202-6 (cloth : alk. paper)
    1. Afro-American men—Biography.   I. Title.
E185.86.B65   1999
920.71'08996073—dc21   98-41699

Printed in the United States of America

10 9 8 7 6 5 4 3 2 1

CONTENTS

Part II: Sons of the Dawn   121

FOREWORD

BY HERB BOYD

With several impressive books to her credit, Tonya Bolden is rapidly carving a niche as a resourceful writer in the realm of black history and culture. If she had nothing more on her résumé than *The Book of African American Women*, her place at the table of scholars on this topic would be secured.

She will command additional space with the publication of *Strong Men Keep Coming: The Book of African American Men*, which in many respects balances her previous research on black women crusaders, creators, and uplifters. While the bulk of the men she profiles are quite notable, and she certainly presents a handsome lot of the expected giants—W. E. B. Du Bois, Booker T. Washington, A. Philip Randolph—there are a dozen or more who will be unknown for even the most diligent of our historians. And these rather obscure, but fascinating, men make the book vibrate with the common touch. In her own special, provocative language, she gives a voice to the voiceless, a name to the nameless. How many of you recall the oft-used photo of a black man with his back hideously scarred with massive welts. Through meticulous research, Tonya tells us who this man actually was, giving life and substance to the symbol.

Given her witty commentary and choice anecdotes, even such mythical black men as Stagolee, John Henry, and High John the Conqueror are provided an almost human aspect. On the other hand, real men of the West, such as Jim Beckwourth and Nat Love, take on legendary stature.

Tonya's profiles are also enriched by a variety of approaches. She may interrogate her entry, frame him within a fictional motif, or merely itemize the man's accomplishments. These changing formats, along with a shifting writing style that can be captious or flip, are a relief from the typical way books of this kind are shaped. It is an innovative, experimental leap, and for the most part, she succeeds.

Anyone who ventures on such a project as this can expect a barrage of why his or her favorite black man was not included. From my own list are Paul Robeson, Langston Hughes, and John Coltrane. Tonya's tactic of invoking many icons—as she does with Robeson—is not direct, but through her discussion of their fathers or mentors. Again, though the method is risky, most readers should be satisfied. I am.

There are two more points to be made and I'll shut up and let you get to the book. After her remarks on a main entry, Tonya has attached other men in the category, field, or discipline for further reading. The process works extremely well when two men with similar names are paired, most notably on the abolitionist William Still and the composer William Grant Still. And throughout the book, there are pleasant little gems of discovery. For example, very few of us are aware that during the attack on Fort Wagner in the midst of the Civil War, the Fifty-fourth Regiment included the grandson of Sojourner Truth and the sons of Martin Delany and Frederick Douglass—another fact the movie *Glory* failed to reveal.

Revelations abound in *Strong Men Keep Coming,* and as Tonya relates in her introduction, this is her own singular take on the endless parade of black men who have fought, sung, cajoled, tricked, worked, written, or roped their way into the American experience. Yes, there are times when her perspective may seem a bit quirky, but at the end of the day, she has assembled a most rewarding cast, a phenomenal coterie of role models and phantoms, and she has done a splendid job of telling her stories.

New York City
September, 1998

ACKNOWLEDGMENTS

To have an editor who is as passionate about a project as you are is a writer's dream. To have an editor who is open-eyed, open-minded, intelligent, and curious is a writer's delight. I was fortunate to have all this in my editor on this book, Chris Jackson. I shall forever be grateful to Chris for saying yes to the idea, and for being wonderful to work with.

Huge gratitude also goes to my friend and fellow writer Elza Dinwiddie-Boyd—gracious enough to listen to my angst and anxieties and my bad ideas from beginning to end; giving enough to read the manuscript when she was crazy-busy with her own projects and all the good works she's always doing.

As for others who were there for me during this journey, there's the once-upon-a-time New Yorker with the lightning mind, editor, journalist, and nonpareil poet Judy Simmons, at present of Anniston, Alabama, who let me read portraits to her over the phone (often on her nickel) and gave me permission to take chances. Ronda Racha Penrice was a great help with some of the research. Wise beyond her years, clear about the power of knowing history, Mississippi/Chicago-rooted Ronda helped me put my hands on things (and put many things *in* my hands) I did not know I was looking for but definitely needed. William Jelani Cobb, one of our present-era race men, gave me feedback, useful debate, and good tips. Thanks also to Sharon M. Howard at the Schomburg Center for Research in Black Culture. Invariably, when I got stymied on a point of research, Sharon came to my rescue.

As always, I must give thanks to my agent, Marie Dutton Brown, who championed me when I had not a single byline, nor a clue about how to become a real writer, just a lot of desire.

And what would I do without my sister and best friend, Nelta, who reads everything I write, helps me think so much through, rejoices in my discoveries, knows when to let me be, and cheers me all the time, especially when I'm tired.

For the strength and the hope and light in the dark times, I thank God, the source.

INTRODUCTION

These portraits of men from the seventeenth century to the present are borne of my love of history and my love for black men.

I am the daughter of a black man in America, granddaughter of black men in America, great-great-granddaughter of black men in America. I am a niece, cousin, sister, and aunt—and have been a wife and lover—of black men in America. How can I not want to know about their journey?

Out of shackles or a cramped antebellum freedom, out of blasted Reconstruction dreams, out of Jim Crow's grip, out of that moment when there was some overcoming and some expectancy that freedom would truly ring—through tempests and trials and a straining for the dawn—black men in America have endured so much, have achieved so much. How can I not want to contribute a little something to the telling of their story? It is, indeed, a story of varied experiences in bondage and freedom, of a breadth of strivings—in the arts, politics, education, business, sports, the sciences—of different philosophies and strategies for liberation and uplift.

My selection of subjects considered was not scientific. I tried that route—ten percent artists, ten percent entrepreneurs, ten percent activists, ten percent scientists, ten percent athletes, et cetera, et cetera. I found that approach too cumbersome and unfun, however. I ended up taking a chance, going with my gut: That is, I chose from among the men who have tickled, baffled, intrigued, inspired, mystified, encouraged, and warmed me. This still meant making tough choices.

"People might think you're ignorant," advised one friend, when I said that there was no entry on Romare Bearden. Richard Allen, William Wells Brown, Paul Laurence Dunbar, Langston Hughes, James Baldwin, Miles Davis, Adam Clayton Powell Jr., Muhammad Ali, Spike Lee, and, yes, Sterling Brown, whose soulful poem inspired this book's title—these are some of the scores of chiefs, champions, and celebrated ones I've not sketched in this book. I really hope you don't think I'm ignorant and that I don't cherish such men. I hope you understand that were I to attempt profiles of half the noteworthy black men in America from the seventeenth century to the present, I would still be writing. (And how many people would buy a 5,000-page book?)

The thing is, I never set out to do a book about just the brightest lights, the tallest talents because I felt that there are many readers who would appreciate a book that is not entirely focused on the great ones.

I believed that many know that if we revisit the familiar only, we will not grow. (However, careful readers will discover that many of the greats not sketched do have a presence in this book.)

Nevertheless, this book has its share of familiars—Attucks, Douglass, Du Bois, Booker T. Washington, Malcolm and Martin, and Jesse Jackson, among others. There are also many more who are not as talked about today as when they walked the world—Josiah Henson, the alleged model for Harriet Beecher Stowe's Uncle Tom; Philadelphia's "merchant prince," James Forten; photographer J. P. Ball; the intrepid, high-strung William Monroe Trotter; founder of the Piney Woods School, Laurence C. Jones; Newspaper publisher Carl Murphy; American Communist Party official Benjamin J. Davis Jr.; architect Paul R. Williams; astronaut Robert Lawrence Jr.—heroes true and true, men who call us all to persevere in treasuring our talents, in doing good works, and in doing when *don't* prevails.

Had I limited my subjects to the canonized history makers, it would have meant essentially denying the existence of those ordinary fellows, champions to their children and wives and friends, men who are representative of the integrity, grit, and wisdom of millions of yesteryear and today, but whose stories are rarely deemed worthy of inclusion in a history book. These are the kinds of men who have peopled my world. For example, there's Dave Dinwiddie, a small-business owner in the all-black town of Taft, Oklahoma; in his quiet, steady way, he was a master builder of his community, and in his stern way, he raised his children to be credits to the race. Or take the man with the pseudonym Jackson Jordan, Jr., whose thoughts on race strike me as more sensible and honest than the discourse of many exalted present-era public intellectuals. In and around the well-known and little known men are a few men who aren't real men—John Henry, Stagolee, Blood—but who are men so many of us know or have known. Could I ignore the history of crazy outrages and most chilling white violence after the days of the captivity? I didn't think so, and, hence, my profiles of men about whom we must never forget, such as the would-be West Pointer Johnson Chesnutt Whittaker, lynch victim Robert Charles, the falsely accused Scottsboro Boys, and the Black Panther Fred Hampton.

Telling the story: That's what I have reached to do in a small space, and the moral is that despite the bondage, despite the postbellum oppression, despite the wretches and the traitors to the race, strong black men—thinkers, creators, builders, fighters, givers of good things—they have kept and will keep coming. And I say, Thank you, Lord.

Note: In some entries, you will come across another man's name in **boldface** type, denoting that there's an entry on him in this book.

PART I
FOREFATHERS

They were clear. In the seventeenth, eighteenth, and late nineteenth century, they were clear about where they stood. Captivity permits no illusions. Freeborns knew the deal, too. They knew that their lives—family, home, livelihood, person—could be abused, destroyed, stolen, and there'd be no universal hue and cry. Supreme Court Justice Roger Brooke Taney's proclamation in the **Dred Scott** decision told the story: "The black man has no rights that the white man is bound to respect."

Yet, there was so much overcoming. So many survived enslavement with bodies bruised but souls intact and minds made up to be men. So many freeborns surrendered all notions of leisure time and put their lives on the line to help others get free. So many achieved so much—plied a trade with pride; started an enterprise; made a farm, or a book, or a family; went on wild adventures; thought a thought; delivered a tough speech; slapped the white man back.

So many free, freed, and self-liberated spent their time, their talents, their money on raising the race—through churches, societies, schools. There were giants in those days: men righteous, men so strong, so long on courage. There were geniuses back then, too.

Not every black man in early America was a genius, was a prince. There were also those who were punks, snitches, selfish people. Being that way had to be tempting: It was the safest thing to be if you wanted to stay alive. The ignoble ones make the men who did noble, risky, reaching things all the more epic—and all the more a strengthening for the seekers and sojourners of today.

☼ Jiro

In August, when the shadows are long on the land and even the air oppresses, the furies of fate hang in the balance of Black America. It was in August, in the eighth month of the year, that three hundred thousand men and women marched on Washington, D.C. It was in August that Watts exploded. It was in August, on a hot and heavy day in the nineteenth century, that **Nat Turner** rode. And it was in another August, 344 years before the March on Washington, 346 years before Watts, and 212 years before Nat Turner's war, that "a Dutch man of Warr" sailed up the river James and landed the first generation of black Americans at Jamestown, Virginia.

LERONE BENNETT, JR., *The Shaping of Black America* (1991)

Yes, we know that sons of sub-Saharan Africa came before Columbus and that a few even came *with* the Spain-sponsored Italian explorer. However, we who regard ourselves as a separate, unique tribe, as aware of the African in us as we are of our Americanness—we who call ourselves African Americans—we trace our beginnings to that late August day in 1619, when Captain Jope docked at the twelve-year-old British settlement with twenty "negars" in the hold of his ship, merchandise pirated from a Spanish frigate bound for the West Indies.

So much more than the twenty pieces of human cargo lay in the hold of that Dutch man-o'-war, the name of which is today a mystery. As Lerone Bennett, Jr., mused in *The Shaping of Black America,*

In the hold of that ship, in a manner of speaking, was the whole gorgeous panorama of Black America, was jazz and the spirituals and the Funky Broadway. **Bird** was there and Bigger and **Malcolm** and millions of other X's and crosses, along with Mahalia singing, Gwendolyn Brooks rhyming, Duke Ellington composing, James Brown grunting, Paul Robeson emoting, and Sidney Poitier walking. It was all there in embryo in the 160-ton ship.

The ship that sailed up the James on a day we will never know was the beginning of America, and, if we are not careful, the end. *That* ship brought the black gold that made capitalism possible in America; it brought slave-built Monticello and slave-built Mount Vernon and the Cotton Kingdom and the graves on the slopes of Gettysburg. It was all there, illegible and inevitable, on that August day. That ship brought the *blues* to America, it brought *soul,* and a man with eyes would have seen it, would have said that the seeds of a Joe Louis are here, would have announced that a **King** was coming and that a **Du Bois** would live and die.

Jiro. He was among the men down below in Jope's mystery ship. Jiro. That is all we know of him, this hint of his aboriginal name.

A painting of Africans unloaded from a Dutch man-o'-war at Jamestown Landing in 1619. (Courtesy of the Library of Congress)

How did he resist a rechristening to Anthony or Peter or William? How did he keep a trace of his name?

Had he been a prince among his people? A member of the warrior class? Artisan? Tender of crops or herds?

Who wailed when he became booty, loot, a swap—a mother, a father, many sisters and brothers, one or two wives, how many dark and darling daughters and sons? To what god did he pray during that queer trans-Atlantic journey? Did he weep much? Did he yearn for a long sleep? Was it fear or disgust that coursed through his soul when he first set foot on that Jamestown land, on that puny island of marsh and mosquito and pale people?

Did Jiro rage?

Like the other "negars," Jiro was not made a slave, but an indentured servant, who probably labored alongside Brits cast in the same class.

Jiro never imagined the millionsmillionsmillionsmillions who would be crammed into perpetual servitude—and thereby fated for a long resistance. Never could he have foreseen that out of the vortex of these contending forces would arise a new people, a new tribe: we African Americans who wonder about him as we ponder our beginnings.

Anthony Johnson

Aboard the Dutch man-o'-war that hauled the historic twenty to Jamestown in 1619 were three men renamed Anthony, but this Anthony was not one of them. This Anthony arrived in Virginia in 1621, aboard the *James* out of London, listed on the ship's manifest as "Antonio a Negro."

This man's new home was in Warresquioake (later Wariscoyack in Isle of Wight County). There, he worked in the tobacco fields of a plantation belonging to an Englishman, Edward Bennett. We do not know who changed Anthony to Antonio—Bennett, one of his deputies, or the hapless African himself. Nor do we know how Anthony came into the surname Johnson. Also, there is debate as to whether Anthony Johnson was a slave or an indentured servant. Whatever his status was at the start of his European experience, by the 1640s, he was definitely his own man with his own land. "Now I know myne owne ground and I will worke when I please and play when I please." This is what Johnson allegedly told a court clerk in 1645 after negotiating a land matter with a Captain Philip Taylor.

Anthony Johnson's property was some distance from Warresquioake: north and across the Chesapeake Bay, in Northampton County. Johnson raised livestock, along with corn and tobacco on his own ground.

Helping him in his life of independence was his wife. "Mary a Negro" was how this woman was itemized on the manifest of the *Margrett & John*, which brought her from England to Virginia in 1622. Like Anthony, Mary also labored on the Bennett plantation, where they became mates, eventually having four children for certain, but perhaps more.

In 1651, Anthony Johnson increased his holdings in Northampton through the land-grant scheme designed to build up the colony: the "headright" system that gave farmers fifty acres for every person they imported into the colony to work the land in an indenture. Johnson received 250 acres on the banks of the Pungoteague Creek because he filed for five headrights.

Anthony Johnson's plantation was the seed of the second black settlement in the colonies (New York boasts the first). This community eventually amounted to about a dozen stout homesteads, two of them belonging to other Johnsons: In 1652, Anthony and Mary's son John purchased 450 acres close by his father's land, and their son Richard bought 100 acres in 1654.

Life was not total bliss for Anthony Johnson (for one, in 1653, a terrible fire ravaged his plantation), but life was real and it was his own. Based on the records of his business dealings, Anthony Johnson was treated no differently than any other landowner (paying taxes like the rest), and he received his fair share of respect from many of the Europeans in whose midst he lived. Black life in this part of the New World could be a good thing, it seemed. In a few years time, however, that would change.

In Virginia, tobacco was becoming king, with more labor sorely needed, and the greedy quickly seeing that the cheaper the labor, the better. Thus, in 1661, the Virginia legislature legalized perpetual slavery for all blacks in servitude; and it wasn't unheard of for a free black person to be enslaved on a European's say-so. The inflow of enslaved Africans increased sharply a decade later when Virginia commenced importing black souls directly from Africa, rather than routing them through England or Spain. By then the Johnson family was no longer in Virginia. In the mid-1660s, Anthony Johnson packed it in and went north to Somerset County, Maryland. There, he leased a 300-acre plantation he named "Tonies Vineyard." His sons made the move to Maryland, too.

Anthony Johnson died not long after he became a Marylander, and Mary carried on with the lease of the land, managing to get the lease stretched to ninety-nine years (with one ear of Indian corn her yearly rent). Mary Johnson died in 1672 (the year she made out her will) or shortly thereafter.

"The story of the Johnson family concludes strangely," we read in *"Myne Owne Ground": Race and Freedom on Virginia's Eastern Shore, 1640–1676,* by T. H. Breen and Stephen Innes (1980). "Around the turn of the century, the clan dropped out of the records." One of the last traces of the family is the 1677 purchase of forty-four acres in Somerset County by one of Anthony Johnson's grandsons, John, Jr., who named this modest bit of his own ground "Angola." This Johnson died in 1706, apparently with no heirs, and hence, with no one to pass down whatever he knew about the origins and original name of the man who started the clan.

Coffee

Unless he was renamed after the bean, Coffee's original name probably meant "male child born on Friday." Kofi, Cuffie—either one would have been a better transliteration, but this involuntary New Yorker went down in history as Coffee and as a Coromantee, a name with various spellings applied to a group of Africans from the Gold Coast (now Ghana). In *Black Cargoes* (1962), written with Malcolm Cowley, Daniel P. Mannix suggests that the Coromantees were either Fanti or Asante. "No other group of slaves aroused so much controversy," Mannix wrote. As evidence, he cited several eighteenth-century sources on how troublesome the Coromantee were. A ship's captain wrote that they "despise punishment and even death itself, it having often happened that on their being any ways hardly dealt with twenty or more have hang'd themselves at a time." In *History of Jamaica* (1774), Edward Long described them as "haughty, ferocious, and stubborn." In reports on several revolts, the authorities in Jamaica claimed that "these disturbances" had been "planned and conducted by the Coromantin Negroes who are distinguished from their brethren by their aversion to husbandry and the martial ferocity of their dispositions."

What Coffee did some time around midnight on the sixth day of April 1712 certainly bears out the characterization: He lit the fuse that signaled the start of a radical act of resistance undertaken by some two dozen Africans and two Native Americans. According to Governor Robert Hunter's report, Coffee and his conspirators were intent on destroying "as many of the Inhabitants as they could," having "resolved to revenge themselves for some hard usage they apprehended to have received from their masters."

It was not a spontaneous happening; it was a thing plotted, a thing the participants were weaponed up for in advance—"some provided with fire arms," wrote Governor Hunter, "some with swords and others with knives and hatchets."

Nobody was ever happy about bondage, but at least when the Dutch were in control, slavery in New Netherland wasn't as bad as it could get. Things changed when the British took over in 1664 and New

Netherland became New York and New Amsterdam, New York City. The British were intent on making slavery as profitable in the north as it was for them in the southern colonies, which meant making it as brutal up north as it was down south. In 1709, at the foot of fabled Wall Street, a "proper" slave market was up and running. By 1712, among the roughly 6,100 people living in New York City, approximately 1,100 were black, with the majority of them enslaved. They say that Coffee the Coromantee was among the recent arrivals from Africa.

According to the governor's report, Coffee helped set fire to an outbuilding on the property of his owner, Peter Vantilburgh, located around present-day Maiden Lane, forcing many "Inhabitants" out into the night to battle the blaze. With the trap sprung, Coffee and company set upon the whites, killing about nine and wounding several others, and planning to do more damage, no doubt.

Did they think that legions of others enduring "some hard usage"— black, white, and Native American—would join them? Did they think they could flatly conquer that stretch of Manhattan and make of it a free land? Perhaps they thought they could strike out into the wilderness and maroon. Whatever their plans, whatever their hopes, all was dashed when Governor Hunter dispatched the colonial militia.

We do not know whether Coffee was among the six who preferred suicide to a trial. If he wasn't, then he was among the twenty-one who were "forthwith brought to their tryal before ye Justices," condemned to death, and executed posthaste. "Some were burnt," Governor Hunter reported, "others hanged, one broke on the wheele, and one hung a live in chains in the town."

"Coffee's Rebellion" was the first major slave revolt of the colonial period, but it was not the first time enslaved Africans engaged in organized resistance. We have record of about half a dozen plots in Virginia (between 1663 and 1730), of two in the Massachusetts Bay Colony (1638, 1731), and several in South Carolina during this era. There is reason to believe that colonists, north and south, were confronted by lots of angry black men (and women) on many more occasions.

NEWS BITS

In 1712, the year of Coffee's Rebellion . . .

- All blacks, mulattoes, and Native Americans in New York were forbidden to carry firearms.

- Pennsylvania enacted a law prohibiting the importation of slaves, but Britain vetoed it.

- The Rhode Island legislature enacted measures that made the importation of slaves more costly.

- Following the lead of several other colonies, South Carolina instituted Slave Codes (revised in 1739 after the Stono Rebellion). Of the ten clauses of the 1712 code that Charles M. Christian lists in *Black Saga* (1995), the following three are good indicators that the enslaved were not complacent, not to mention how vile slavery had become by the early 1700s: (1) "Slaves are forbidden to leave the owner's property without written permission, unless accompanied by a white person." (2) "Every white person in the community is charged to chastise promptly any slave apprehended without such a pass to leave the owner's property." (3) "Any slave absconding or successfully evading capture for twenty days is to be publicly whipped for the first offense, branded with the letter *R* on the right cheek for the second offense, and lose one ear if absent thirty days for the third offense; and for the fourth offense, a male slave is to be castrated, a female slave is to be whipped, branded on the left cheek with the letter *R*, and lose her left ear."

 Broteer (c. 1729–1805)

"I was bought on board by one Robertson Mumford, steward of said vessel, for four gallons of rum and a piece of calico, and called Venture, on account of his having purchased me with his own private venture." But his father had named him Broteer. We know so because he told us in his autobiography, one of the earliest accounts of a once-African life in America: *A Narrative of the Life and Adventures of Venture, a Native of Africa: But Resident above Sixty Years in the United States of America. Related by Himself.* Broteer dictated his story to Elisha Niles, a Connecticut schoolteacher.

"I was born at Dukandarra, in Guinea, about the year 1729," Broteer's narrative begins. "My father's name was Saungm Furro, Prince of the Tribe of Dukandarra." Of his heritage, Broteer recalled, "I descended from a very large, tall, and stout race of beings, much larger than the generality of people in other parts of the globe, being commonly considerable above six feet in height, and every way well proportioned." His people were not fractious, not greedy, not thievish—but others were.

When he was close to seven years old, there descended upon Broteer's people a band of marauders led by one Baukurre, thugs "instigated by some white nation who equipped and sent them to subdue" other Africans. Broteer's village could escape a savage sacking, Baukurre's henchman announced, if they paid tribute: "a large sum of money, three hundred fat cattle, and a great number of goats, sheep, asses, &c." Broteer's father met the demand, only to find that he had been duped, only to see his village assailed.

Men of the tribe of Dukandarra attempted defense, but their arrows were no match for the weapons in the hands of Baukurre's band, and the stand of tall reeds to which women and children fled proved a feeble hiding place.

> They then came to us in the reeds, and the very first salute I had from them was a violent blow on the head with the fore part of a gun, and at the same time a grasp round the neck. I then had a rope put about my neck, as had all the women in the thicket with me, and were immediately led to my father, who was likewise pinioned and haltered for leading. In this condition we were all led to the camp.

Broteer's father was interrogated about his cache of riches but refused to divulge any information. His son witnessed the price he paid for his obstinacy.

> He was instantly cut and pounded on his body with great inhumanity. . . . All this availed not in the least to make him give up his money, but he despised all the tortures which they inflicted, until the continued exercise and increase of torment obliged him to sink and expire. . . . The shocking scene is to this day fresh in my mind, and I have often been overcome while thinking on it. He was a man of remarkable stature. I should judge as much as six feet and six or seven inches high, two feet across his shoulders, and every way well proportioned. He was a man of remarkable strength and resolution, affable, kind and gentle, ruling with equity and moderation.

Baukurre's band plundered other villages during their march to the sea, eventually getting their comeuppance from inhabitants of Anamaboo, who were also willing to traffick in black souls for the free-labor lust of the New World order.

"I was then taken a second time," Broteer recounted. "All of us were then put into the castle, and kept for market." Soon, he and more than two hundred others were loaded onto a ship that sold the majority of its cargo to planters in Barbados and then set sail for its base in Rhode Island. It was on this vessel that steward Robertson Mumford purchased Broteer for some booze and cloth and renamed him Venture.

This eight year old, who would never again hear his true name called, carded wool until very late at night, rapidly pounded four bushels of corn ears during daylight, and carried out various other tasks. He grew up to be, like his father, a man of "remarkable strength"—toting a barrel of molasses on his shoulders for two miles without pause. Also like his father, he became a man of great "resolution"—snatching a club out of one master's hand before the devil could deliver a second blow. (True tales and tall tales of his strength so abounded during and after his life that he has been dubbed the "Colonial **John Henry**.")

By the time he was thirty, this son of royalty had lived in Narragansett, Rhode Island, and on Fisher's Island in New York, and was being sold for the third time to a Colonel Smith of Hartford, Connecticut, the man from whom he bought himself and whose surname he took.

From early on in his captivity, in and around the forced labor, Broteer had snaggled up all kinds of odd jobs, putting bits of money aside for his freedom. In 1765, at about age thirty-six, after nearly three decades of bondage, Broteer, at last, became master of himself, for seventy-one pounds two shillings. He promptly quit Connecticut to make a life on Long Island.

Freedom meant working immeasurably harder than he had ever done before because Broteer had a goal: To buy his family out of bondage—a family that included wife Meg, daughter Hannah, and two sons, Solomon and Cuff. For this cause, Broteer was a lumberjack, was a farmer, was a whaler, was a fisher, was a trader, was a worker worker worker at whatever he could get his hands on.

By the time he was forty-seven, Broteer's family was free. Shortly thereafter, he and his family left Long Island and settled in East Haddam, Connecticut. There, by dint of more tough and tremendous labor, he accumulated land. He did this despite misfortunes that dogged his every plan—a son running off to sea, his daughter getting sick unto death, friends defrauding him, and strangers cheating him. Still, the brave, stalwart Broteer worked. Still, Broteer saved. Still, Broteer built.

By 1798, the year his narrative was published, Broteer, nigh unto seventy, was "possessed of more than one hundred acres of land, and three habitable dwelling houses." All the toil, first for others and later for himself, had definitely left its mark on the man.

> Though once strait and tall, measuring without shoes six feet one inch and an half, and every way well proportioned, I am now bowed down with age and hardship. My strength which was once equal if not superior to any man whom I have ever seen, is now enfeebled so that life is a burden, and it is with fatigue that I can walk a couple of miles, stooped over my staff. . . . My eyesight has gradually failed, till I am almost blind, and whenever I go abroad one of my grandchildren must direct my way; besides for many years I have been much pained and troubled with an ulcer on one of my legs.

Embittered and bilious Broteer was not. He was quick to count his blessings, noting that "amidst all my griefs and pains I have many consolations"—among them that "Meg, the wife of my youth, whom I married for love, and bought with my money, is still alive." To this, Broteer added, "My freedom is a privilege which nothing else can equal."

"Privilege?" we who've known only liberty are tempted to scream. "Don't you mean freedom is a *right?"* we might correct Broteer if we could—or maybe not. Maybe we wouldn't ruffle the elder, but reflect on the humbling effect bondage can have—and count our own blessings instead.

SOME OTHER EIGHTEENTH-CENTURY NARRATIVES

- *A Narrative of the Uncommon Sufferings and Surprising Deliverance of Briton Hammon, a Negro Man—Servant to General Winslow of Marsh-field, in New England; Who Returned to Boston, after Having Been Absent Almost Thirteen Years* (1760): The "uncommon sufferings" of this man included shipwreck on the coast of Florida during a return voyage from Jamaica (a voyage from which General Winslow was absent); capture by Native Americans, then escape aboard a Spanish schooner; and Spanish imprisonment in a dungeon in Havana for five years. Hammon's very brief narrative is the first published piece of prose by a black person living in what became America.

- *A Narrative of the Most Remarkable Particulars in the Life of James Albert Ukawsaw Gronniosaw, An African Prince* (c. 1770): When he was a boy, this grandson of a king in the northeast section of present-day Nigeria decided to accompany a merchant to the Gold Coast because the man had told him he'd behold wonders: "He told me that if I would go with him I should see houses with wings to them walk upon the water, and should also see the white folks." Long story short: the kid ended up the slave of a very rich Dutch family in New York, and later of a Dutch Reformed minister of Raritan Valley in New Jersey, who freed the prince shortly before the minister died. In the early 1760s, during the Seven Years' War, Gronniosaw joined Britain's Twenty-eighth Regiment, thereby getting a whiff of Barbados, Martinique, and Cuba. He settled in England with a weaver, for what turned out to be a life of extreme poverty. His little narrative was a fundraiser for him.

- *The Interesting Narrative of the Life of Olaudah Equiano, or Gustavus Vassa, the African. Written by Himself* (1789): This son of an Igbo chieftain only spent a brief time in America (in Virginia). His truly interesting narrative, covering his snatch from Africa through his British bondage, is the first full-length (and textured) English-language memoir by an African.

✸ Crispus Attucks (c. 1723–1770)

For generations, Attucks was the first black hero we heard about: the man who was the first to die in the skirmish between colonists and their keepers, on Boston's King Street. He was one of the most hosannaed heros of a revolution that was five years away. Of this event, later known as the Boston Massacre, President John Adams proclaimed, "Not the Battle of Lexington or Bunker Hill, not the surrender of Burgoyne or Cornwallis were more important events in American history than the Battle of King Street on the 5th of March, 1770."

Once upon a time, by candlelight and in classrooms, blacks relished the retelling of Crispus Attucks's role in that historic day. They told how when word reached this seafarer and others milling around Dock Square that a British sentry had assaulted a barber's apprentice, people got riled because they didn't see it as some isolated tiff, but as yet another example of British tyranny. Taxation without representation, quartering troops in their midst, a Redcoat clobbering a kid—it was all one and the same.

They told about how in this crowd of discontent, Attucks rose up to say, "The way to get rid of these soldiers is to attack the main guard! Strike at the root! This is the nest!"

They told about how he led the charge down to King Street. "Do not be afraid," he told the people when they reached the Custom House where the guilty sentry stood. "They dare not fire," he shouted, as Redcoats rushed to the sentry's aide.

They told how someone threw a stick, how a nervous private fired, how Attucks fell from musket shots to his chest—at close range—and how the crowd, emboldened, surged to give the Redcoats what-for.

Blacks reveled in recounting how white people honored him: how when time came for the funeral and burial, Crispus Attucks received the same royal treatment as the white men the British killed right after him. What a famous day, with Boston merchants closing their shops and the city's bells tolling for the martyrs. In time, there were songs and monuments with the name of Crispus Attucks just as prominent as those of the white heroes of the Boston Massacre.

Many, many years later, the tale became stale.

Well, now, some reasoned, the short, knock-kneed mixed man (black, white, and red) wasn't all that "political" and was maybe riding on the tide of too much ale. What in the world was a runaway slave doing messing in white-folks business anyhow? True, he'd been twenty years long gone from Framingham, where he'd been the property of a William Brown, but still, shouldn't he have kept a low profile? Who but the foolhardy stands in front of a scared soldier with a loaded musket and proclaims, "They dare not fire on us!"?

Is being honored by white people for dying something in which we should delight? So it is that some late twentieth-century cynics would throw Crispus Attucks away. Are they justified?

There are those who say, "No"—not if you consider that doing so disrespects such historians as **William C. Nell,** who worked hard to keep Attucks's name in the history books and in the nation's collective memory. These historians have known that someone of African descent playing a role in a historic event is actually thousands of people of African descent crying out, *"I am."* This is why many still tell the story, albeit without runaway praise, but at least without mockery. Those who vote to bounce Crispus Attucks from the canon of black heroes also do a disservice to black youths: Attucks makes an interesting entry point for study of the uprising that spawned this nation.

 # Salem Poor (c. 1758–?)

In early December 1775, a group of officers in the Continental Army wrote to "the Honorable General Court of the Massachusetts Bay," petitioning for official acknowledgment of the valor of Salem Poor, a freeborn from Andover.

> The Subscribers begg leave to Report to your Honble. House, (which Wee do in justice to the Caracter of so Brave a Man) that under Our Own observation, Wee declare that A Negro Man Called Salem Poor of Col. Fryes Regiment. Capt. Ames. Company—in the late Battle at Charlestown, behaved like an Experienced officer, as Well as an Excellent Soldier, to Set forth Particulars of his Conduct Would be Tedious, Wee Would Only begg leave to say in the Person of this sd. Negro Centers a Brave & gallant Soldier. The Reward due to so great and Distinguisht a Caracter, Wee submit to the Congress.

Poor was credited with taking down a British officer in the "Battle of Charlestown," that famous fight of June 17, 1775, on Breed's Hill, long since called the Battle of Bunker Hill. That battle resulted in a great lift to the Patriots' morale because although they did not win the day, they did give the Loyalists' attempt a bruising.

In this battle, Poor was not the sole black soldier. Peter Salem, Prince Estabrook, Grant Cooper, Caesar Brown, George Middleton, and Prince Hall (future founder of the Black Masons) were among the sons of Africa who fought bravely that mid-June day. You can imagine how these men and other black Patriots smarted when, shortly after taking command of the Continental Army, George Washington banned the recruitment of blacks, and then, in mid-November 1775, banned black reenlistment. Yes, Washington reversed himself, but only after the British began recruiting the slaves of Patriots, promising them freedom in exchange for their service.

By war's end, some five thousand black men had served in the Continental Army. They were freeborns and freedmen. They were bondsmen sent as substitutes for their owners or owners' sons. They were runaways from Loyalists. Whatever their status, they supposed that if the Patriots were victorious, the Patriots would make black freedom the law of the land. With this hope, black men served as scouts and spies, as laborers and servants, as sailors and, like Salem Poor, soldiers.

Salem Poor reenlisted after Washington lifted the ban. All we know about his service from this point on is that he survived the Continental Army's bashing at the Battle of White Plains in October 1776 and the horrible hunger at Valley Forge in the winter of 1777–1778.

We do not know what happened to Salem Poor after the American Revolution, or whether he even lived to see the thirteen colonies fully recognized as a nation. As for that petition of December 1775, there is no record that Congress granted him any special honor or commendation. However, this "Brave & gallant Soldier" received some posthumous praise from the government two hundred years after the Battle of Bunker Hill: In 1975, the United States Post Office issued a Salem Poor stamp.

 Amos Fortune (1710?–1801)

His epitaph, chiseled on gray slate, below a sketch of an urn and a spray of willow, could not say it all, but it did say a lot:

> SACRED
> to the memory of
> Amos Fortune,
> who was born free in
> Africa, a slave in America
> he purchased liberty,
> professed Christianity
> lived reputably, &
> died hopefully.
> Nov. 17, 1801

After fifteen years of bondage in Boston, Amos Fortune was sold to a tanner, Ichabod Richardson of Woburn, Massachusetts, who trained him in his trade. Having purchased his own freedom by 1770, at age sixty, Fortune was a free man. Several years later, he purchased a woman named Lydia and married her, but within months of their wedding, she died. Again, he purchased a woman, and with her he was to have a sweet life. Her name was Violate Baldwin, and her young daughter Celyndia was included in the sale.

In 1781, the Fortunes moved to Jaffrey, New Hampshire, where Amos made a fine living at his trade, apprenticing both blacks and whites. The money he made was meant for more than hoarding, the old tanner believed, and so he shared. More than a few times, he came to the rescue of a son or daughter of Africa in dire financial straits (including buying some their liberty). Amos Fortune also contributed to projects for the common good. One was the little library established in 1796, for which he gave three dollars (two days wages for some men) and rebound library books for free (including the leather). The Social Library, which became the cornerstone of the Jaffrey Public Library, was very dear to Fortune because books were very dear to him. He had learned to read and write in his youth and was one of the most literate citizens of Jaffrey.

Amos Fortune had Jaffrey's welfare on his mind when he made out his will. Except for a few items he bequeathed to his adopted daughter, his legacy (including upward of $800) went to Violate, with the stipulation that if any money remained in the estate after her death, it should go toward the support of the town's church and school. Fortune also requested matching gravestones for himself and Violate, composing the epitaphs himself, we believe.

Violate died a year after Amos (leaving a hefty sum in the estate). Her epitaph reads,

SACRED
to the memory of
Violate,
by sale the slave of
Amos Fortune, by Marri-
age his wife, by her
fidelity his friend and
solace, she died his widow
Sept. 13, 1802.

The gravestones of the New Hampshire artisan and humanitarian and his wife are resting in peace in the graveyard of the Old Meeting House where the couple worshiped with their fellow Quakers.

☀ Andrew Bryan (1737–1812)

"[They] were inhumanly cut, and their backs were so lacerated that their blood ran down to the earth." This quote is from a sympathizer's report on one of the beatings laid on Andrew Bryan and his brother Sampson. The punishment was not for sassing a white man, not for slacking at work, not for attempting escape. Their offense was worshiping God.

After the beating, the brothers were thrown in jail. There's no telling what they might have suffered at the hands of their keepers had their owner not come to the rescue. He, Jonathan Bryan, not only secured their release and swore that they were up to nothing untoward, but also informed the authorities that he was going to let Andrew Bryan hold services in a barn on his plantation. Bryan's flock was one of the earliest black Baptist congregations in America, the First African Baptist Church in Savannah, Georgia. It was on January 20, 1788, that a white Baptist minister ordained Bryan and certified him as this congregation's pastor.

This servant of the Lord was born in slavery in Goose Creek, South Carolina, roughly sixteen miles from Charleston. No one knows when he was brought to Savannah, but it was in Savannah, during the upheaval that gave birth to this nation, that Bryan became a Christian. His shepherd was the dynamic preacher George Leile (Liele in some sources), who founded First African on December 7, 1777, and baptized Bryan and his wife Hannah, in 1782. Not long after this, Leile, a freedman who had worked for a British officer, shoved off with the British when they evacuated Savannah, and he eventually settled in Jamaica, West Indies, where he founded another church. After Leile's departure, Bryan became the leader of Leile's former followers. Bryan's owner had no problem with Bryan's calling and gave his blessing on the erection of a place to worship—a small, rough-wood structure, which some viewed as a huge threat. Fearing that Bryan was out to stir up within their human property something more than a love for God, some slaveholders organized and participated in the harassment of worship services at the rough-wood structure. The nearby swamps then became the congregation's sanctuary. Bryan, like his members, was fully aware that detection would mean a whipping or some other intense punishment.

Blessed are they which are persecuted for righteousness' sake . . . No doubt this beatitude had extra-special significance for Bryan, who did not lift his hand from the plow, did not turn back from the call, but persevered by what else but faith. *Watch and pray.* Surely, this was another scripture in the forefront of Bryan's mind as he ministered to his congregation in the deep dark of night.

Bryan might have thought persecution would end once he had the imprimatur of a white Baptist official, but such was not the case. It was after his ordination that he and his brother (one of the church's deacons) "were inhumanly cut, and their backs were so lacerated that their blood ran down to the earth." The account of this beating noted that "while under this torture," Bryan "declared to his persecutors that he rejoiced not only to be whipped," but would "freely suffer death for the cause of Jesus Christ."

The persecution did stop, and First African Baptist Church grew mightily. Its first substantial building went up in 1794, funded by members and a few white well-wishers. Around this time, Bryan's owner died, and Bryan was permitted to purchase himself. He subsequently purchased his wife and then property: a house, land, and eight black people, "whose education and happiness," Bryan wrote in a letter dated December 23, 1800, to a benefactor in England, "I am enabled thro' mercy to provide." Were these eight souls slaves on paper only? Was Bryan waiting for some special time or circumstance to legally grant them liberty? We can only hope so, and that the right time came soon.

In this same letter to his English benefactor, Bryan stated that his church was doing quite nicely and that his congregation was worshiping, "not only without molestation, but in the presence, and with the approbation and encouragement of many of the white people." By now, the church had seven hundred members. The congregation continued to grow. The overflow formed Second African Baptist Church and Third African Baptist Church, now First Bryan Baptist Church.

If Andrew Bryan was lucid right before he went to be "present with the Lord," undoubtedly he prayed for the survival of the church he shepherded for nearly twenty-five years. The "Amen" is now at 23 Montgomery Street, the present location of First African Baptist Church, not just the oldest black Baptist church still in existence, but the oldest black church in the United States, and the place where several months before the March on Washington Martin Luther King, Jr., first delivered his "I Have a Dream" speech.

Benjamin Banneker (1731–1806)

His lineage is almost as interesting as his life: One grandmama was an Englishwoman named Molly Welsh, who was accused of stealing a pail of milk and, for this, was sentenced to seven years of indentured servitude in Maryland. Not long after she became free, she had a farm and two African men, both of whom she one day freed, and one of whom, around 1696, she wedded—the one they say was the very bright one, the literally princely one from Senegal. Bannka (or Bannaka) was his name, which became his family's surname, eventually spelled Banneky.

Daughter Mary married a full-bloodied African named Robert, a freedman who preferred his bride's last name to that of his former owner. Whether it was he who amended that name to Banneker, no one knows, but we do know that one day, Robert acquired twenty-five and then one hundred acres of land about ten miles west of Baltimore. With its main crop of tobacco, eventual fruit trees, cattle, poultry, and busy bee hives for rich honey, this farm became a robust one, providing good soil for Robert and Mary's four children, the oldest of whom was the wunderkind Benjamin.

Benjamin's mind took fast to the three R's at the one-room Quaker school he attended. His aptitude for mathematics and anything mechanical was apparent early on. His prodigious intellect kept growing right along with the rest of him, as he was becoming a proud black man—"I freely and Chearfully acknowledge, that I am of the African race, and in that colour which is natural to them of the deepest dye"—and becoming a genius.

Definitely, he was a night person; the stars were his delight. Stretched out on his back, with a crude telescope or only his mind's eye, he wandered the night sky. With a sweet fatigue that comes of marveling at the celestials and pondering their mysteries, he would usually head for bed after dawn peeked in.

At around age twenty-two, having closely observed a pocket watch, this genius made a wooden clock that was the marvel of the region for the nearly fifty years it tick-tocked. This genius also had a predilection for poring over scientific texts—Ferguson's *Astronomy,* Mayer's *Tables,* and Leadbetter's *Lunar Tables.* Nor was he too shy to question the luminaries. We find one such example in a note from Banneker to neighbor George Ellicott:

> It appears to me that the wisest men may at times be in error; for instance, Dr. Ferguson informs us that, when the sun is within 12° of either node at the time of full moon, the moon will be eclipsed; but I find that, according to his method of projecting a lunar eclipse, there will be none by the above elements, and yet the sun is within 11° 468' 11" of the moon's ascending node. But the moon, being in her apogee, prevents the appearance of this eclipse.

Hmmmm.

Banneker's ruminations were not lost on George Ellicott, who was himself a mathematician and astronomer. It was he who had lent Banneker those books and astronomical instruments. It was with him that Banneker, for years, engaged in enlightening conversations about lots of lofty things.

Banneker enjoyed a good relationship with the entire Ellicott family, Quakers who, in the early 1770s, built flour mills near the Banneker farm, then a store, and more, leading to the designation of their corner of the sky Ellicott City. For their various enterprises the Ellicotts purchased supplies from the Banneker farm, which had become Benjamin's after his father's death in 1759. When this genius decided that farming was not for him, it was to the Ellicotts that he sold his property for an annuity on which he could live happily, in a cabin on the land—home and workshop both for this bachelor man.

The celebrity of this genius increased in the spring of 1791 when word got out that he had been appointed to the team charged with the task of configuring a new national capital out of big patches of Maryland and Virginia. Banneker's appointment to the survey team for the District of Columbia was made by the overseer of the project, George Ellicott's cousin Major Andrew Ellicott. When the Georgetown *Weekly Ledger* ran a notice of the project in March, 1791, the newspaper mentioned Banneker's involvement, referring to him as "an Ethiopian, whose abilities, as a surveyor, and astronomer, clearly prove that Mr. Jefferson's concluding that race of men were void of mental endowments, was without foundation." And best of all, this sable genius developed a knack for constructing the critical part of an almanac.

Prior to his work with the survey team, Banneker had constructed an ephemeris: Based on his calculations of heavenly bodies, he had forecast a variety of natural phenomena for 1791, from sunrises and sunsets to the ways of the weather. He sent his findings to a printer, who declined to publish the work. By the time Banneker finished his work with the survey team, he was close to completing another ephemeris, and this one was published: *Benjamin Banneker's Pennsylvania, Delaware, Maryland and Virginia Almanack and Ephemeris for the Year of Our Lord 1792, Being Bissextile, or Leap-Year, and the Sixteenth Year of American Independence, which commenced July 4, 1776.*

That genius had the forethought to let his ephemeris do double duty, offering it up as evidence of the glory, not of himself, but of his people. Banneker sent his ephemeris, along with the legendary letter of August 19, 1791, to that most peculiar philosopher–politician, then Secretary of State, Thomas Jefferson, who had given the official okay to Banneker's appointment to the survey team for D.C.

Like other conscious black folks, Banneker was peeved with Jefferson for promoting the notion of black inferiority. Jefferson, whose slaves included several of his own children, had expressed such sentiments most memorably in his *Notes on the State of Virginia:* "I advance it, therefore, as a suspicion only, that the blacks, whether originally a distinct race or made distinct by time and circumstance, are inferior to the whites in the endowments of both body and mind." Banneker begged to differ, in writing and with a most poised, fluid penmanship. Early in the letter came this:

> I suppose it is a truth too well attested to you, to need a proof here, that we are a race of Beings who have long laboured under the abuse and censure of the world, that we have long been looked upon with an eye of contempt, and that we have long been considered rather as brutish than human, and Scarcely capable of mental endowments.

Following the flow of his intrinsic elegance, Banneker played on Jefferson's perception of himself as a thoughtful, sensitive man, as one "measurably friendly and well disposed towards us." If what he had heard of Jefferson were "founded in truth," then

> I apprehend you will readily embrace every opportunity to eradicate that train of absurd and false ideas and opinions which so generally prevail with respect to us, and that your Sentiments are concurrent with mine, which are that one universal Father hath given being to us all, and that he hath not only made us all of one flesh, but that he hath also without partiality afforded us all the Same Sensations, and endued us all with the same faculties, and that however variable we may be in Society or religion, however diversified in Situation or colour, we are all of the Same Family, and Stand in the Same relation to him.
>
> Sir, if these are Sentiments of which you are fully persuaded, I hope you cannot but acknowledge, that it is the indispensable duty of those who maintain for themselves the rights of human nature, and who possess the obligations of Christianity, to extend their power and influence to the relief of every part of the human race, from whatever burden or oppression they may unjustly labour under.

In his quiet, but barbed, way, Banneker appealed to the sage of Monticello to truly promote those glorious words he had penned—"We hold these truths to be self-evident, that all men are created equal"—and to unequivocally renounce and denounce slavery.

As tangible evidence of black ability, Banneker sent Jefferson a copy of his ephemeris. He was also shrewd enough to give the Virginian no out for doubt that the work was original to his black mind: "and altho you may have the opportunity of perusing it after its publication, yet I chose to send it to you in manuscript previous thereto, that thereby you might not only have an earlier inspection, but that you might also view it in my own hand writing."

To his credit, Jefferson promptly responded to Banneker, in a letter dated August 30, 1791. However, his reply reveals that he simply

The title page of Banneker's fourth published almanac had a variant spelling of his surname. The woodcut engraving of Banneker in the Quaker garb he regularly wore is the only known likeness of him. (Courtesy of the Maryland Historical Society, Baltimore)

didn't get it: "No body wishes more than I do, to see such proofs as you exhibit, that nature has given to our black brethren talents equal to those of the other colors of men," Jefferson claimed, adding, "and that the appearance of a want of them is owing merely to the degraded condition of their existence both in Africa and America. I can add with truth that no body wishes more ardently to see a good system commenced for raising the condition both of their body & mind to what it ought to be, as fast as the imbecility of their present existence, and other circumstances which cannot be neglected, will admit."

Huh?

We do not know what Banneker made of Jefferson's tap dance. Ditto on Jefferson's mention that he had sent Banneker's almanac to the Secretary of the Academy of Sciences in Paris "because I considered it as a document to which your whole colour had a right for their justification against the doubts which have been entertained of them."

One can imagine Banneker shaking his head over Jefferson's obtuseness, as if it were up to the French to give liberty to the nearly 700,000 people enduring American bondage and to cease and desist from oppressing the 60,000 free blacks in the United States at the time.

The Banneker–Jefferson correspondence didn't make it into the

1792 almanac as Banneker had wished, but it was reprinted in the 1793 edition which—like all Banneker's almanacs—was prized (especially by farmers) in the mid-Atlantic states. As was the custom, Banneker's almanacs carried ancillary material such as recipes, remedies, poems, and proverbs. Much of this material was not from the hand of Banneker, but some of it was, such as the table on the impact of the twelve zodiac constellations on the human body, provided in his 1795 almanac. The last Banneker almanac to be published was the one for 1797. He also constructed several more ephemerides, which never reached the public.

Benjamin Banneker spent his last years on earth being his inquisitive self: studying the stars by night and nature (especially bees) by day and making notes of all he surveyed, observed, and pondered. He pretty much kept to himself, but he was not an absolute recluse. "He seemed acquainted with every thing of importance that was passing in the country" recalled a clerk in the Ellicotts' store. This clerk remembered that after Banneker finished his shopping, he often "went to the part of the store were George Ellicott was in the habit of sitting, to converse with him about the affairs of our Government and other matters."

His was a quiet death, but it wasn't while savoring delights of the night sky, as some later claimed. It was less romantic than that. The white-haired genius was a month away from his seventy-fifth birthday, when, during a morning walk, he felt some dis-ease. He tucked into his cabin for a nap, from which he never awoke.

 ## Tom Molineaux (c. 1784–1818)

Early on, black men had a hand in just about every hot sport, including the one many rank high among the most barbaric—boxing. The first who "could have been a contender" was Tom Molineaux, who literally used his fists to get up and out from slavery on a plantation in Georgetown.

His father, Zachariah (or Zachary), whom some credit with starting boxing in the United States, taught Tom and his brothers this sport. The Molineaux brothers were often pitted against bondsmen from nearby plantations—and often the stakes were quite high. In volume one of *A Hard Road to Glory: A History of the African-American Athlete,* **Arthur Ashe** tells us just how high: "The average price of a healthy, male, field-hand slave around 1800 was roughly a thousand dollars. But the Molineaux boys could command a premium of nearly a hundred percent in a bout if the right deal were struck."

One can't help but conclude that Tom was the best of the Molineaux boys, for it was to him that in 1809 Master Algernon Molineaux made a most enticing offer: Beat another slave–boxer, Abe, and be a free soul, with a hundred bucks. Maybe this fellow Abe was not offered as appetizing an incentive, or maybe Molineaux was simply the better boxer. Either way, it wasn't long before Tom Molineaux bid adieu to the South.

He bounced about New York for a while (porter, stevedore, back-alley boxer) until the prospect of boxing for bucks beckoned him to Britain. There, he became a protégé of Bill Richmond, a freeborn from Staten Island, New York, whose boxing ability had earned him a ticket to Britain in the late 1770s, and who made a strong name for himself as a boxer ("the Black Terror") and then as a trainer and manager (with a tavern on the side). Under Richmond's tutelage, Molineaux engaged in rigorous, vigorous training, and racked up a string of wins.

Molineaux's big chance came in the winter of 1810, in a bout with the Brit Tom Cribb, who had secured the heavyweight title in 1807 and then retired. To draw Cribb out of retirement was a coup for Richmond: Back in 1805, Cribb had "beat him without hurt" as one reporter put it. For Molineaux, it was a chance absolutely to do his mentor–manager proud—and more: to become the first black world-prize fight champ.

It was reported that on that rainy-cold mid-December day, some ten thousand spectators were in attendance at Copthall Common in Sussex for the much-ballyhooed battle between the Toms. In *A Hard Road to Glory*, we find this recap of the match:

> As the fight began, Molineaux quickly established his dominance, but Cribb held his ground. After twenty-seven rounds the bout was still in doubt.
>
> In the twenty-eighth round Molineaux suddenly caught Cribb with a hard right. The Englishman went down, and [the referee] started his count of thirty seconds. (A fighter had thirty seconds to "toe the mark" after a knockdown. A round ended when any fighter went down.) When Cribb failed to "come to scratch," Molineaux and Richmond began a gleeful victory dance. But Joe Ward, Cribb's aide, leaped into the ring in clear violation of the rules and accused Richmond of hiding weights in Molineaux's hands. All the while the timekeeper . . . kept yelling *"Time! Time!"*
>
> Incredibly, [the referee] waived the rules and allowed Cribb a full two minutes to revive. He went on to win sixteen rounds later over a dejected Molineaux.

Richmond refused to accept dejection and defeat; he demanded a rematch. As it is doubtful that Molineaux was literate, it was probably Richmond who ghosted his formal challenge, a letter that appeared in the *London Times* several days after the bout, with the hard-hitting statement, "I cannot omit the opportunity of expressing a confident hope that the circumstance of my being of a different color to that of a people amongst whom I have sought protection will not in any way operate to my prejudice."

To the challenge, Cribb gave the back-century Brit equivalent of "You're on." The rematch was set for September 28, 1811, at Thistleton Gap outside London.

Molineaux may have been beaten more badly in the first fight with Cribb than anyone imagined. Maybe that referee's bold-faced bending of the rules in Cribb's favor left him convinced that no man his hue could get a fair fight if he challenged a great white hope. Or it could be that Molineaux was simply addled from one hundred too many rounds of bare-knuckle boxing sans TKOs. In any event, Molineaux gave Cribb the victory before he stepped into the ring: He got sloppy and cocky and quarrelsome with Richmond. They say, too, that Tom Molineaux got a little belly-heavy right before the bout, with a quart of ale and a whole chicken. Whatever the cause, he got trounced by Cribb, whose powerful pummeling left Molineaux with a broken jaw in round nine, and out cold in the eleventh, this time before a crowd of twenty thousand.

The rest of Molineaux's story is, unfortunately, an all too familiar tale. After a few comeback attempts (and a spot of wrestling), he took up with a boxing troupe that toured the British Isles, and he died on one of them (Ireland) a pauper alcoholic.

 # Bilali Mohammed (?–1859?)

This from a great-granddaughter of Bilali Mohammed:

> Belali Mohomet? Yes'm, I knows bout Belali. He wife Phoebe. He hab plenty daughtuhs, Magret, Bentoo, Chaalut, Medina, Yaruba, Fatima, an Hestuh.
>
> Magret an uh daughtuh Cotto use tuh say dat Belali an he wife Phoebe pray on duh bead. Dey wuz bery puhticluh bout duh time dey pray an dey bery regluh bout duh hour. Wen duh sun come up, wen it straight obuh head an wen it set, das duh time dey pray. Dey bow tuh duh sun an hab lill mat tuh kneel on. Duh beads is on a long string. Belali he pull bead an he say, "Belambi, Hakabara, Mahamadu." Phoebe she say, "Ameen, Ameen."

This remembrance is found in an interview with Katie Brown, granddaughter of Bilali Mohammed's daughter Margaret. The interview was conducted during the Depression by a fieldworker in the

Savannah Unit of the Federal Writers Project and was published in *Drums and Shadows: Survival Studies among the Georgia Coastal Negroes* (1940). Katie Brown was born and raised on Sapelo Island, where her great-grandfather spent most of his life.

"She tell me Belali wuz coal black, wid duh small feechuhs we hab, an he wuz bery tall." This is some of what a great-grandson, Shadrach Hall, recalled of the Fula from Timbo in present-day Guinea. The "she" Hall referenced was his grandmother, Bilali Mohammed's daughter Hester.

Bilali Mohammed was kidnapped when he was a teenager. He may have been captured while in prayer, since some sources maintain that his Qur'an and prayer rug made the journey with him. If true, one wonders why these items were not confiscated—or perhaps this indicates his strong will and the modicum of respect he commanded from his captors. Or perhaps he came upon a Qur'an and prayer rug in the Bahamas, which is where he was first deposited (which would also say a lot about his fortitude in holding onto his identity).

It was also in the Bahamas that he acquired one of his wives, Phoebe. While it's known that Bilali Mohammed had more than one wife, it's unclear how many he had and whence they came. What is clear is that by the early 1800s, this man was in Georgia, with Phoebe and their children. The family was the property of Thomas Spalding, who purchased four thousand acres of land on the southern tip of Sapelo Island around 1802. Rice, sugar, and cotton were among the plantation's principal crops. "It was Spalding's plan to treat his slaves like serfs," wrote Allan D. Austin in *African Muslims in Antebellum America: Transatlantic Stories and Spiritual Struggles* (1997). What did this mean? As Austin went on to explain, "Each had his own land to work; labor for the master was limited to six hours a day; and slaves worked by the task system—a fairly common practice on the islands off Georgia, where slaves significantly outnumbered freemen." Spalding broke up his plantation into villages, and each had its head man. Spalding had no white manager for his "villagers," who some say numbered around four hundred and others, close to one thousand. The overseer was Bilali Mohammed, whom Spalding trusted without pause—so much so that at one point during the War of 1812, when Spalding had to go away, he made Bilali, in essence, his minister of defense, entrusing him with eighty muskets in the event of a British assault on Sapelo Island. "This appears to have been the only instance in which slaves were given guns in Georgia during the antebellum period," observed Austin.

Along with being the overseer, Bilali Mohammed was also the Imam of the other Muslims on Spalding's plantation. In this capacity, he produced a thirteen-page manuscript believed to be a guide for right living, and given the English title, "First Fruits of Happiness." The manuscript proved a challenge for would-be translators because the text, it seems, is a mix of Arabic and Fula, written in Arabic letters. Only snatches of the manuscript had been translated by 1998. Presumably, once the task is complete, we will know more about Bilali Mohammed, one of the tens of thousands of African Muslims forced to call America home, and the one who captured the imagination of Toni Morrison (Balaly in *Song of Solomon*) and Julie Dash, who fast-forwarded him to the 1860s, with the name Bilal Muhamed, in her film about a South Carolina–Georgia sea-island family, *Daughters of the Dust.*

 # Abraham Camp

In the early nineteenth century, many of the roughly 200,000 free blacks in America had hope that this nation could and would be a good home. They hoped, too, that soon, very soon, it would become a land of liberty for the roughly 1.5 million men, women, and children enslaved.

At the same time, a minority believed the chances were slim that America would ever be a beneficent place for a black person, so they wanted to leave it. Among the deeply discontented was Abraham Camp of Wabash, Illinois. We know this because of a letter dated July 13, 1818, and collected in *The Mind of the Negro as Reflected in Letters Written during the Crisis, 1800–1860* (1926) by **Carter G. Woodson.** The person to whom Abraham Camp wrote was Elias B. Caldwell, Secretary of the American Colonization Society:

> I am a free man of colour, have a family and a large connection of free people of colour residing in Wabash, who are all willing to leave America whenever the way shall be opened. We love this country and its liberties, if we could share an equal right in them; but our freedom is partial, and we have no hope that it ever will be otherwise here; therefore we had rather be gone, though we should suffer hunger and nakedness for years. Your honour may be assured that nothing shall be lacking on our part in complying with whatever provisions shall be made by the United States, whether it be to go to Africa or some other place; we shall hold ourselves in readiness, praying that God (who made man free in the beginning, and who by his kind providence has broken the yoke from every white American) would inspire the heart of every true son of liberty with zeal and pity, to open the door of freedom for us also. I am, &c.
>
> Abraham Camp

Camp wrote this letter two years after the American Colonization Society (ACS) was formed for the express purpose of settling free and freed blacks far away from America. The ACS was made up of prominent white Northerners and Southerners, but it was Southerners who wielded the most power: future Vice President John C. Calhoun of South Carolina, future Secretary of State Henry Clay of Kentucky, and the Virginian who was president when Camp wrote his letter, James Monroe. Such men had the most to gain from black emigration. By ridding America of free and freed blacks, they would be ridding it of a lot of agitators: people who petitioned the government for civil rights and abolition, who worked to persuade ambivalent whites to support these efforts, who rallied the enslaved to revolt, who conspired in escapes and gave runaways refuge, and who just by their very presence in America increased the yearning for freedom among the enslaved. The ACS was, at bottom, about divide and conquer.

Abraham Camp couldn't see that far—or if he could, he had no desire to stay in the fight, had not the will to bear up under the indignities and expect a brighter coming day.

We do not know whether Camp and his family and neighbors in Wabash were among the group the ACS shipped to Cape Mesurado in January 1822. The group's landing led to the founding of the town that became Monrovia, in the territory that became Liberia, which became an independent republic in 1847, and where, by 1885, the ACS had settled some sixteen thousand people who, like Abraham Camp, had grown sour on America.

Perhaps, instead, Camp never made the journey to Africa or anywhere else. Maybe he ended up staying in America, bearing a "partial" freedom along with the rest of the free blacks.

NEWS BITS

- In 1818, the year Abraham Camp wrote to the ASC, . . . Illinois abolished slavery but also disenfranchised blacks.

- Connecticut disenfranchised blacks.

- The Georgia legislature prohibited manumission.

 James Forten (1766–1842)

A year before **Abraham Camp** wrote to the American Colonization Society about wanting to leave America, James Forten was leading a protest against the ACS, as chair of a meeting held at Bethel Church in

Philadelphia. In times past, Forten had not opposed the effort to send free and freed blacks back to Africa. On one occasion, he had even given money to the ACS. He had also supported Paul Cuffee, the successful shipbuilder and sea captain from Massachusetts who sailed thirty-eight people to Sierra Leone in 1815. Subsequently, Forten had changed his mind, however, having come to see the ACS as nefarious, and having become one of the fiercest opponents of re-Africanization. He was certainly a coauthor, if not the author, of the resolution unanimously adopted by the crowd of three thousand assembled at Bethel in January 1817. This classic document of black protest reads in part

> Whereas our ancestors (not of choice) were the first successful cultivators of the wilds of America, we their descendants feel ourselves entitled to participate in the blessings of her luxuriant soil, which their blood and sweat manured; and that any measure or system of measures, having a tendency to banish us from her bosom, would not only be cruel, but in direct violation of those principles, which have been the boast of this republic.
>
> Resolved, That we view with deep abhorrence the unmerited stigma attempted to be cast upon the reputation of the free people of color, by the promoters of this measure, "that they are a dangerous and useless part of the community." . . .
>
> Resolved, That we never will separate ourselves voluntarily from the slave population of this country; they are our brethren by the ties of consanguinity, of suffering, and of wrong; and we feel that there is more virtue in suffering privations with them, than fancied advantages for a season.

This was not Forten's first act of protest. Back in 1800, he was among the signers of a petition to the U.S. Congress calling for the abolition of the slave trade and the modification of the Fugitive Slave Law of 1793. In 1813, he authored a pamphlet, *A Series of Letters by a Man of Color,* opposing a Pennsylvania Senate bill that restricted black immigration into the state, often the first refuge for freed people, as well as for runaways.

Forten's protest against the ACS in 1817 was also not his last investment of energy on behalf of his people. In 1818, he cofounded the Augustine Society, the mission of which was "the establishment and maintenance of a Seminary, in which children of colour shall be taught all the useful and scientific branches of education." In 1830, he helped organize the first National Negro Convention held in Philadelphia, a coming-together of prominent men from more than half a dozen states for the purpose of strategizing on how to ameliorate their people's plight. Among the ideas advanced was support of black emigration to Canada (but not to Africa) and a boycott of slavemade products.

It was in Forten's home that, in 1833, William Lloyd Garrison organized the American Anti-Slavery Society. Forten was one of the society's most stalwart supporters. The same was true when it came to Garrison's newspaper *The Liberator:* Forten did tremendous fundraising for its launch and made substantial donations for years. Forten's home was also a way station on the Underground Railroad, and over the years, he purchased many people out of slavery, including once an entire family.

These are just some of the ways Forten gave of his time and resources for the uplift of free blacks and the liberation of those enslaved. In just about every one of his early endeavors, he was working closely with two other formidable Philadelphians. One was Richard Allen (1760–1831): cofounder of the first black self-help organization, Free African Society (1787), and founder of the Bethel Church, the cornerstone of the African Methodist Episcopal Church (1816). The other was the much older Absalom Jones (1746–1818): coauthor, with Richard Allen, of a searing testimonial on the great good that black Philadelphians did during the yellow fever epidemic of 1793; cofounder of the Free African Society; and founder of The African Church (1794), which became St. Thomas Episcopal Church, which is where Forten worshiped.

These two men were close friends and major mentors of James Forten, a gentle, regal soul who was committed to sticking it out in America because he truly felt it was his country as much as it was any white man's. After all, he was born in America. Too, he had rallied behind this nation during two of its wars. When he was a lad, Forten had served the Patriots' cause as powder boy aboard the *Royal Louis,* during which time he spent seven months as a British prisoner of war, in the underbelly of the wretched prison ship *Jersey.* During the war of 1812, he had helped raise a black regiment to defend Philadelphia against the British.

Forten's sense of obligation to the enslaved was a consequence of his sterling character, as well as his family history: The only reason he was a freeborn was because his paternal grandfather, who had been born in captivity, had worked overtime on the side to come up with enough money to purchase his and his wife's freedom.

James Forten was himself a very hardworking man. He had accumulated an estimated $100,000 by the early 1830s, and he would have had far more money had he not been so generous. He had made his fortune in the very place his father had worked: the sail-making enterprise of the white Philadelphian Robert Bridges. James Forten began his apprenticeship with Bridges when he was twenty years old, and within a few years, he was foreman of this sail loft where blacks worked alongside whites. Bridges was so impressed with Forten's skills and diligence that when, in 1798, he decided to retire and sell his business, not only was he willing to sell it to his 32-year-old foreman, but he also had a hand in helping Forten secure the loan to do so. Forten had no problem repaying the loan; nor did he have a problem keeping content the roughly forty men in his employ, about half of whom were white. Forten's business grew and thrived, in large part because he designed a sail that made it easier to steer ships. This invention brought beaucoup contracts to Forten's shop, which, by the way, would not do business with ships involved with the slave trade.

With his wealth, Forten was able to build an exquisite red brick home at 92 Lombard Street for his family. This brings us to another contribution he made to society (with no small assistance from his wife Charlotte): namely, his children. His daughters Margaretta and Harriet (expert organizers and fundraisers) and Sarah (a writer, as well as an organizer) were steadfast in their abolitionist work, primarily as members, like their mother, of the Philadelphia Female Anti-Slavery Society. So impressive were they that John Greenleaf Whittier, the poet laureate of the antislavery movement, celebrated them in a poem: "To the Daughters of James Forten." Two of the Forten sisters married into an activist family: Harriet married Robert Purvis, and Sarah married Robert's younger brother, Joseph.

The Forten boys—James, Jr.; William; and Robert—were also involved in the antislavery movement, early on as members of Philadelphia's Young Men's Anti-Slavery Society; and it was Robert who sired educator and reformer Charlotte Forten Grimké.

When James Forten died, he left behind an exemplary family, a sizable fortune, and a legacy of philanthropy and activism that inspired generations of black Philadelphians.

Thomas L. Jennings (1791–1859)

There has always been and always will be multitudes of great men never publicly proclaimed "hero," "role model," or any such thing as that. They live strong, stand tall, do their duty for their family, and, in and around their everyday lives, find time to support the larger strivings of the race. Such was Thomas Jennings, a successful New York City clothier whose shop was on Nassau and Chatham Streets.

Generally, nowadays, mention of this man is slight, other than highlighting that he was among the first blacks to receive a patent: his innovation, a dry-cleaning process. Thomas Jennings should be extolled for being more than an early inventor, however. The only thing that saved the larger truths about him from oblivion was that someone happened to write a short sketch that appeared in the April 1859 issue of *The Anglo-African Magazine*. That someone was **Frederick Douglass.**

> Mr. Jennings was a native of New York, and in his early youth was one of the bold men of color who, in this then slave State, paraded the streets of the metropolis with a banner inscribed with the figure of a black man, and the words, "AM I NOT A MAN AND A BROTHER?" He was one of the colored volunteers who aided in digging trenches on Long Island in the war of 1812. He took a leading part in the celebration of the abolition of slavery in New York in 1827. He was one of the founders of the Wilberforce Society. When in 1830 Wm. Lloyd Garrison came on from Baltimore, Mr. Jennings was among the colored men of New York . . . who gave him a cordial welcome and God-speed, and subscribed largely to establish the *Liberator*. . . .
>
> He was a leading member of the first, second and third of the National Conventions of colored men of the United States, held in New York and Philadelphia in 1831–4. He was one of the originators of the Legal Rights' Association in New York city, and President thereof at the time of his death. His suit against the Third Avenue Railroad Company for ejecting his daughter from one of its cars on Sabbath day, led to the abolition of caste in cars in four out of the five city railroads. He was one of the founders, and during many years a trustee of the Abyssinian Baptist Church.
>
> In his boyhood, Mr. Jennings served an apprenticeship with one of the most celebrated of the New York tailors. Soon after reaching manhood, he entered business on his own account, and invented a method of renovating garments, for which he obtained letters patent from the United States.* Although it was well known that he was a black man "of African descent," these letters recognize him as a "citizen of the United States." This document, in an antique gilded frame, hangs above the bed in which Mr. Jennings breathed his last, and is signed by the historic names of John Quincy Adams and William Wirt, and bears the broad seal of the United States of America. . . .
>
> Mr. Jennings had a large family, whom he educated carefully and successfully, both in intellectual and moral training. He taught all his children some useful trades, and accustomed them betimes to rely on themselves for their support. His son William died twenty years ago, a successful business man in Boston; Thomas was until lately, one the most skilful dentists in New Orleans; his daughter Matilda is one of the best dress makers in New York City, and Elizabeth the most learned of our female teachers in the city of New York. . . .
>
> This is a noble picture of a noble man. Born in a slave state, and of a race held in slavery, living in the midst of all the crushing influences which human prejudice and caste could heap upon him, he yet fulfilled all the purposes of an upright man, a useful citizen, and a de-

---

*Jennings received this patent on March 3, 1821.

voted Christian. . . . Not gifted with extraordinary talents or endowments, he made full use of such as it had pleased God to give him.

Mr. Jennings was one of that large class of earnest, upright colored men who dwell in our large cities. He was not an exception, but a representative of his class, whose novel sacrifices, and unheralded labors are too little known to the public.

 Devany

Item 93 in Jeffrey C. Stewart's *1001 Things Everyone Should Know about African American History* is something many might prefer not to be reminded of: "Many rebellions were thwarted because slaves told their masters about plots," we read under the subhead "Slaves Betraying Slaves." Stewart tells of Devany, who snitched on what might have been the largest revolt ever: the plot of Denmark Vesey, the Methodist preacher who had purchased his freedom and earned a living as a carpenter in Charleston, South Carolina.

Vesey had begun laying plans for an uprising in the winter of 1821. The revolt was scheduled for mid-July of the following year. As the day drew near, he had thousands of free and enslaved people committed to this freedom fight. This fellow Devany (also known as Peter), a house servant of Colonel J. C. Prioleau (or Privoleau) was not one of them.

It was a late May day in 1822, and Devany had finished his marketing for his mistress. He was strolling along the wharf when he was approached by a man who tried to recruit him for the insurrection. "I was so much astonished and horror struck at this information," Devany later testified, "that it was a moment or two before I could collect myself sufficient to tell him I would have nothing to do with this business, that I was satisfied with my condition, that I was grateful to my master for his kindness and wished no change." After taking his leave of the man, Devany consulted a free black man, who advised him to tell his master about the encounter. Posthaste, Devany did just that.

The authorities had suspected that something was afoot. Devany's disclosure was the nail in the coffin. When Vesey discovered that the plan was in jeopardy, he did not abandon it but instead pushed the date up to mid-June—but it was no use. The authorities went after the plot in earnest, scouring Charleston for information. After a few more blacks gave up some informational goodies, troops arrested hundreds of prospective insurgents and numerous innocents, and trials began.

Vesey and five coconspirators were hanged on July 2, 1822. In days to come, thirty-eight more blacks were executed, and forty-three were deported. For their crime of "inciting slaves to insurrection," four whites were punished with a fine and a short imprisonment.

As for Devany, he received his freedom and an annual pension of $50, which was raised to $250 in 1857.

BOOK MARK

- *American Negro Slave Revolts* by Herbert Aptheker (1943)

- *Insurrection in South Carolina, The Turbulent World of Denmark Vesey* by John Lofton (1964), who followed up on the subject with *Denmark Vesey's Revolt: The Slave Plot That Lit a Fuse to Fort Sumter* (1983)

- *The Trial Record of Denmark Vesey,* edited by John Oliver Killens (1970), who wrote a fictionalized biography of Vesey, *Great Gettin' Up Morning* (1972)

 # Ira Aldridge (1807–1867)

Nearly a century before Paul Robeson riveted London theatergoers at the Savoy with his portrayal of that ill-fated fellow who "loved not wisely but too well," Ira Frederick Aldridge made news with his rendition of the Moor at London's Theatre Royal at Covent Garden. The year was 1833, and for the next three decades, Aldridge would capture high praise for his acting abilities, going down in history as one of the finest Shakespearean actors of the nineteenth century. The accolades were as much for his portrayal of Macbeth, Shylock, King Lear, and others from the Bard as for his signature role, Othello.

His 1833 performance of Othello was not Aldridge's debut on the English stage. That had occurred eight years earlier, in 1825, at the Royal Coburg Theatre, where he played lead roles in several plays, including *The Revolt of Surinam, or A Slave's Revenge,* based on Thomas Southerne's *Oroonoko,* and *The Slave* by Thomas Morton. His performance was not a case of art imitating life, for Ira Aldridge was born free.

He grew up in New York City, where his mind was nourished and his talents cultivated in the African Free School #2. Shortly after leaving school, around age fifteen, Aldridge began performing with the African Grove Theater Company, located in the section of Manhattan now known as SoHo.

Founded in 1821, to present plays "agreeable to Ladies and Gentlemen of Colour," the African Grove's repertoire included a number of

Given that the thespian's name is rendered in Cyrillic, this portrait of Aldridge as Othello was, presumably, created in Russia, perhaps during his first visit in 1858, when he was made an honorary member of the Imperial Academy of Fine Arts. (Courtesy of Photographs and Prints Division, Schomburg Center for Research in Black Culture, The New York Public Library, Astor, Lenox and Tilden Foundations)

Shakespeare's plays, among them *Richard III, Hamlet,* and *Othello.* As a member of this company, Aldridge no doubt received much audience appreciation, for the African Grove offered handsome productions. Many performances were before a packed house, with ticket prices ranging from twenty-five to seventy-five cents (hardly chump change at that time). Undoubtedly, this theater would have become a strong, rich institution had it not been for both the harassment by the police and the antics of local yokels, who were sorely displeased with Negroes not knowing their place—presumably, minstrelsy and such.

One might assume that the travails of the African Grove (which closed in 1829) and other cruel realities of black life in America convinced Aldridge that he could never pursue a serious acting career in his native land. Certainly, that's a reasonable assumption; however, the truth is far more mundane: It was Aldridge's father who ran him out of town. This straw vendor and lay Presbyterian minister was not at all pleased with his son's thespian adventures and thought that a change of air—an education at the University of Glasgow—would worm the acting bug out of young Ira.

Daddy was wrong. Ira did go to Scotland, and he did take some classes at the University of Glasgow, but those studies didn't last long. So it was that in 1824, seventeen-year-old Ira Aldridge landed in England, soon to debut at the Coburg, to tour the provinces, to open at Covent Garden, to do more touring of the provinces, and then to triumph on grand stages all over the world—in Ireland and Scotland, in Switzerland and the Netherlands, and in Austria, Prussia, and Russia, among other European nations. Honors and awards galore attested to how well he was received in Europe—such as the White Cross of Switzerland, the Grand Cross of the Order of Leopold presented by the Emperor of Austria, and membership in the Prussian Academy of Arts and Sciences and in the National Dramatic Conservatoire of Hungary.

"Ira Aldridge is without a doubt the greatest actor that has ever been seen in Europe," wrote a critic in Vienna. "It may well be doubted whether Shakespeare himself had ever dreamed for his masterpiece, *Othello,* an interpretation so masterly, so truly perfect." A St. Petersburg correspondent for *Le Nord* observed, "From his appearance on the stage the African artist completely captivated his audience by his harmonious and resonant voice, and by a style full of simplicity, nature, and dignity." Adding to the allure of Aldridge, who early on billed himself as the "African Roscius" (after the illustrious Roman actor Quintus Roscius Gallus), was the fabulous identity he concocted: that he had been born in Senegal and descended from royalty. We do not know how Aldridge was going to handle that tale when he toured America, which was the very thing he was planning when he died in Poland.

Patrick Henry Reason (1816–1898)

This native New Yorker, born to a father from Guadeloupe and a mother from Saint-Domingue, made a name for himself in art. One piece of evidence of his early ability is a drawing he made when he was thirteen. It was of the school he attended on Mulberry Street, the African Free School #2, where many history makers received their early education, including actor **Ira Aldridge,** physician **James Mc-Cune Smith,** and activist–ministers Alexander Crummell, Samuel Ringgold Ward, and **Henry Highland Garnet.** Another of Patrick Reason's schoolmates was his older brother Charles, who made history in 1849 as the first black professor at a white school, New York Central College.

Thirteen-year-old Patrick Reason's drawing of this legendary school served as the frontispiece to Charles C. Andrews's 1830 book, *The History of the African Free Schools.* This honor may have been what made Reason enter an apprenticeship with a white engraver, thus making a way for him to earn a living as an artist.

Much of Reason's work was associated with the antislavery cause. His best-known piece in this regard is the engraving of a young woman in manacles and on bended knee, usually accompanied by the words,

From the frontispiece to *The History of the African Free Schools.* The African Free Schools project was started by the New York Manumission Society in the late 1780s. In 1834, the African Free Schools were absorbed into what became the New York City Public School System. (Courtesy of Photographs and Prints Division, Schomburg Center for Research in Black Culture, The New York Public Library, Astor, Lenox and Tilden Foundations)

"Am I Not a Woman and a Sister?" This emblem, created in 1835, echoed the "Am I Not a Brother and a Man?" emblem (the Kneeling Slave), designed by Josiah Wedgewood in 1787 and widely used by an English antislavery association. (See also **Frederick Douglass**'s sketch of **Thomas L. Jennings.**) Reason's sister emblem was just as popular among American abolitionists, appearing on coins, broadsides, and other items. Among Reason's many portraits of activists is one of Britain's Granville Sharp and two of Henry Bibb (one of which served as the frontispiece to *The Narrative of the Life and Adventures of Henry Bibb*, published in 1848).

Reason's relative prominence as an engraver was not based solely on his work for the antislavery movement. Critical to the success of his business were jobs from the United States government, the most famous of which was the coffinplate for Daniel Webster, who was Secretary of State at the time of his death in 1852.

 William Henry Lane (c. 1825–c. 1852)

This freeborn originally from Rhode Island made a name for himself with his feet. His stage name became "Master Juba" because at the root of his footwork was Juba, the Americanization of *giouba* (or *djouba*), a complex step dance of West Africa, with tantalizing rhythms, loose body moves, and hands hamboning away. To this, Lane added elements of clog dancing and the jig, which he picked up hanging out in the Five Points section of New York (now South Street Seaport) with the city's low white men on the totem pole: the Irish. He also received some smooth tutoring from the great jig and reel dancer Jim Lowe. When he put it all together, Lane stepped up with the granddad of tap.

By the mid-1840s, having triumphed in contest after contest, Lane was the "King of All Dancers" as far as northeasterners were concerned. His fame grew when he began touring with white minstrels over whom he had top billing. Lane then decided to chance it abroad.

Lane left no diary or memoirs, but in present-era writer Wesley Brown's novel *Darktown Strutters* (1994), we find room to speculate about what was on Lane's mind and what kind of man he was. In this scene, Lane visits the novel's hero Jim, a former slave turned dancing phenom who has a permanent grin slashed on his face by whites enraged by his refusal to perform in blackface. Jim is in his dressing room in Cincinnati when he's told that he has a visitor.

"Come on, if you comin!" Jim said.

The door swung all the way open and a man the color of brand-new copper stood in the doorway. His unbuttoned waistcoat gave way to a vest that blossomed into a fluffy shirt and a head of curly hair held down by a hat shaped like an overturned flower pot. The man's legs swelled inside his pants, looking like they were the offspring of a tree trunk.

"I'm William Lane," he said.

Jim couldn't believe it! He was in the same room with the great Master Juba—the man many said was the greatest dancer that ever was and the first black dancer to get top billing in an all-white minstrel show.

"Come in," Jim said, getting up and putting his hand out. "Mister Lane. I was hopin I'd meet you one day. Please, sit down."

Lane sat down, crossed his legs, took off his hat, and held it in his lap.

"I came to find out if what they say about you is true."

"What's that?" Jim asked.

"That you the best thing to hit the ground on two feet since me. . . . After seein you tonight, I knew we'd met before. . . . Not face to face. But in another way that counts for more."

"So what you think?" Jim asked, not wanting to pass up the chance to be praised by the great Master Juba.

"If you need me to tell you what you already know, then I guess we both wrong about you."

The words stung and Jim tried to change the subject.

"You ever go up against Jack Diamond?"*

"Jack Diamond's the best jigger that ever was. I never outdanced him. I just outlasted him."

Lane stared across the room like he was remembering something.

"But that time's gone. . . . There's a fuse burning in this country and it's connected to slavery. And I don't wanna be here when it blows."

"Where you gonna go?"

---

*Jack Diamond was a renowned white minstrel dancer.

"I been invited to England. The money's better than anything I'd make if I stayed here. And if I had any doubts about leavin, seein you dance convinced me that I made the right decision."

"What did I do?"

"It ain't what you did. It's how you went about doin it. You didn't show me nothin dancewise that I didn't expect to see. What I wasn't sure about was somethin else that burned inside a me when I was your age. I knew you had it the moment I saw you. It made me feel good, but I was sorry too cause it's a blessing and a curse."

"I don't understand."

"There's a power in you that's got nothin to do with wantin it. A lot of our people have it. But when you live in a country where people got so much hate in them, you can find yourself turning away from the power inside you and wanting the power others have over you. I don't want that to happen to me. But if I stay here, it will."

"You sayin, I wanna be like the ones that done this to me?" Jim said, pointing at his scar.

"I'm sayin, sometimes you can lose your way."

"You ever been in slavery, Mister Lane?"

"No."

"Maybe if you was, you'd know it ain't so easy talkin about losin your way when you ain't never had your own way to begin with."

Lane got up from his chair, put his hat on his head, patted the top with the palm of his hand, and reached out to shake Jim's hand.

"I'll tell you what," Lane said. "I know I'm right about me. But if I come back, you can tell me if you was right about you."

In 1848, Lane was touring England with the troupe Pell's Ethiopian Serenades, and the reviews were raves. "The style as well as the execution is unlike anything ever seen in this country," remarked one English critic. "The manner in which he beats time with his feet and the extraordinary command he possesses over them can only be believed by those who have been present at his exhibition."

Wesley Brown's Jim never had the chance to tell Master Juba whether he was right about himself because his idol never returned to America, dying in England.

 # Robert the Hermit (c. 1769–?)

Life *seriously* made Robert holler, and he threw up both his hands.

The most we know about him comes from a thirty-six-page book published in 1829, and priced at twelve-and-a-half cents: *Life and Adventures of Robert Voorhis, the Hermit of Massachusetts, Who Has Lived 14 Years in a Cave, Secluded from Human Society. Comprising an Account of His Birth, Parentage, Sufferings, and Providential Escape from Unjust and Cruel Bondage in Early Life—and His Reasons for Becoming a Recluse. Taken from His Own Mouth, and Published for His Benefit.* Robert's amanuensis and publisher was Henry Trumbull of Providence, Rhode Island, who lived in the vicinity of Robert's "cave."

Several area residents had tried to pry from the "strange and mysterious being" the story of his life, but he never obliged until Trumbull came along. Trumbull struck him as someone out for more than a lark. Too, Trumbull told the recluse that if his life story were published, he would "reap a benefit thereby." It seems the fellow wasn't so otherworldly that he'd shun a chance for some cash. So it was that Robert the Hermit recounted his story.

His griefs began when he was born in Princeton, New Jersey, for he was born a slave. His father was an English gentleman, his mother, one of this man's slaves. When Robert was very young, his father–owner gave him to his daughter on the occasion of her marriage to a German named John Voorhis. When Robert was about four, the Voorhises moved to Georgetown, and that was the end of Robert's contact with his mother and siblings.

When Robert was about fifteen, he was apprenticed to a shoemaker. When he proved not so sharp at this craft, he was put on garden duty. It wasn't until Robert was coming up on twenty that a little splendor entered his life: He fell in love with a free woman named Alley Pennington, who loved him back but would not consent to be his wife as long as he was a slave. Bummer.

Robert thought himself blessed when James Bevins, a white man he regarded as something of a friend, consented to help him out. The deal was that Bevins would purchase Robert and keep him as his slave on paper only until Robert repaid the debt. Bevins did indeed pay the asking price of fifty pounds, and forthwith, Robert and Alley married and began making a family, with Robert paying Bevins back bit by bit.

For about three years, life was pretty good for Robert. Then came that terrible night when Bevins, armed with his henchmen, jammed into Robert's home and claimed him as his slave. Bevins denied he'd ever received a farthing from Robert, denied they'd ever had a deal. In front of his wife and babies, Robert was dragged from his house.

Then came a three-day journey of chains and scraps of moldy bread; then, an auction block in Charleston, South Carolina; then, Sold! Then— miraculously—he escaped right quick after the sale and stowed away on a vessel bound for Philadelphia. Then he was recaptured in Philadelphia and returned to Charleston, where he was sold to another man.

After about a year and a half with his new owner, Robert escaped and again stowed away in the hold of a ship, this one bound for Boston. For five long days, he didn't even have moldy bread to eat. When the hunger and thirst became unbearable—"I seized a fragment of a hoop, with which I crawled to and commenced thumping upon a beam near the hatchway, at the same time hallooing as loud as the strength of my lungs would admit of." Lucky for Robert, the captain of the ship was a practicing Quaker, and therefore opposed to slavery.

Robert ended up in Salem, Massachusetts, where he signed on with a ship headed for India. For the next ten years, he made his living as "a common hand" on ships sailing to Europe and the East. Though he had zesty times while at sea (and got jolly with the best of them when back at home port), Robert frequently fell into depressions, a consequence of lingering too long on what might have been with his wife Alley and the kids.

Eventually, Robert married again. His "angel" was a daughter of the widow in whose home he lodged when he wasn't away at sea. Then came Robert's return from a very long time at sea, and his discovery that his wife had been "transformed to a demon!" who told him that had he never come back, she'd have been "the last to lament it!"

Robert sulked around Salem for close to a year until he decided to sneak a trip South, in hopes of finding his first wife and kids. To his profound sorrow, he discovered that not long after that terrible night when he was captured, Alley had killed herself, and his children had died soon thereafter. "I then felt but little desire to live, as there was nothing then remaining to attach me to this world—and it was at that moment that I formed the determination to retire from it—to become a recluse, and mingle thereafter as little as possible with human society." Though distraught, Robert had the presence of mind to keep gettin' up—that is, out of the South.

Once back in New England, he settled in Providence, Rhode Island, where he built himself a hut and stayed for several years, "until annoyed and discommoded by the youth of the town, and by labourers employed in levelling the hill in the neighborhood of my dwelling." Robert moved farther from town and into a thick pine grove, where he constructed a squat stone house. A crude fireplace, a bed of rags and straw, a block of oak wood that did double duty as chair and table, a piece of iron for a knife, a few pieces of cracked earthenware, and a very aged sea bucket: This is just about all there was inside Robert's hermitage, where he spent almost all the hours of all his days for years.

He lived off what nature had to offer, some of which (potatoes, corn, beans) he cultivated in a patch of ground close by his rude dwelling. The only thing Robert did that might be reckoned a pastime was to read; mostly what he read was the Bible. The only time he left his "rocky cavern," as he called it, was to pick up a few odd jobs or a few (a very few) necessities in town.

Whenever he was out and about, he hardly went unnoticed. As Trumbull reported at the end of Robert's narrative, this nearly six-foot-tall man had "a thick and curly beard, of a jet black, and of uncommon length." Then there was the matter of his attire: "His garments (or many of them)," wrote Trumbull, "are of his own manufacture, and whenever a breach appears in any one article, it is either closed by him in a bungling manner, with needle and twine, or a patch is applied without regard to the quality or colour of the cloth. The tattered surtout coat commonly worn by him, in his excursions abroad in winter, in imitation of the military, he has fancifully faced with red."

And he had a cap to match.

 # David Walker (1785–1830)

"I will stand my ground. *Somebody must die in this cause.* I may be doomed to the stake and the fire, or to the scaffold tree, but it is not in me to falter if I can promote the work of emancipation." This was David Walker's response to his wife Eliza and their friends' urging that he flee to Canada after word came that a group of Georgians had vowed to kill him and that there was a price on his head—one thousand dollars if dead, ten thousand if alive.

His offense was the pamphlet *David Walker's Appeal in Four Articles; Together With a Preamble, to the Coloured Citizens of the World, but in Particular, and Very Expressly, to Those of the United States of America*. His preamble began,

> Having travelled over a considerable portion of these United States, and having, in the course of my travels, taken the most accurate observations of things as they exist—the result of my observations has warranted the full and unshaken conviction, that we, (coloured people of these United States), are the most degraded, wretched, and abject set of beings that ever lived since the world began.

Such was the tone and timbre of Walker's roundly radical call for black liberation on all levels.

Walker covered a lot of territory in his *Appeal*. With his fevered prose, he recounted the horrors of slavery and predicted that fire and brimstone would be the lot of those who enabled it, from slave traders to slaveholders. Walker vilified as apostate those Christians who sanctioned slavery. He warned of traitors: those who set up their black brothers and sisters for enslavement. Walker also sought to light a fire under the complacent among the free:

> Do any of you say that you and your family are free and happy and what have you to do with the wretched slaves and other people? . . . If any of you wish to know how FREE you are, let one of you . . . go through the southern and western States of this country, and unless you travel as a slave to a white man (a servant is a slave to the man

whom he serves) or have your free papers, (which if you are not careful they will get from you) if they do not take you up and put you in jail, and if you cannot give good evidence of your freedom, sell you into eternal slavery, I am not a living man.

Walker lashed out against the work of the American Colonization Society,* deeming it a devilish scheme of slaveholders to keep those in bondage "secure in ignorance and wretchedness, to support them and their children." Walker went on to explain why slaveholders wanted free blacks out of the way: "For if the free are allowed to stay among the slave, they will . . . learn the slave *bad habits*, by teaching them that they are MEN, as well as other people, and certainly *ought* and *must* be FREE." Speaking of freedom, Walker strongly urged those in bondage to revolt. Another thing this self-taught man advocated was education—"for coloured people to acquire learning in this country, makes tyrants quake and tremble on their sandy foundations."

As James Turner remarked in his introduction to Black Classic Press's reissue of the third edition of Walker's pamphlet, the *Appeal* was "the most seminal expression of African American thought to come forth in the early nineteenth century." It was also, observed Turner, "the first sustained critique of slavery and racism in the United States" by a black person—and this, at a time when the organized abolitionist movement was in its infancy.

David Walker spent his infancy in Wilmington, North Carolina, where he was born to a free woman and an enslaved man who died before David was born. At around age thirty, fed up with the South, fed up with witness after witness of horrors heaped on his people, Walker traveled to other parts of the country, finding thick evidence of how widespread oppression was.

In 1826, Walker settled in Boston, where he became proprietor of a shop on Brattle Street, which sold new and used clothing. When not tending to his business, Walker was studying history and other subjects, then writing down his analyses and musings, some of which were published in *Freedom's Journal*,[†] where a brief version of the *Appeal* appeared in December 1828.

Walker regularly attended local antislavery lectures and meetings. He also worked with the Underground Railroad, which may be how he

---

*See entries on **Abraham Camp** and **James Forten**.

[†]*Freedom's Journal*, founded in March 1827 by John B. Russwurm and Reverend Samuel E. Cornish, was the first black weekly in America. Its motto was "We Wish to Plead Our Own Cause." The paper ceased publication in the spring of 1829, when Russwurm joined the American Colonization Society's settlement in Liberia. Cornish restarted the paper as *The Rights of Man*, but it did not last long.

met the woman he married in 1828 because it is believed that Eliza Walker was among its passengers. (Another of Walker's small attacks on slavery was his contribution to a fundraiser for the liberty of **George Moses Horton.**)

By 1829, Walker had completed his full-length *Appeal,* self-publishing it in the fall of that year. Though it scared the dickens out of many free blacks, his pamphlet was manna to the militant. Maria Stewart, the first American woman political speaker, was among those who acknowledged the debt they owed to Walker for expanding their consciousness (but Stewart neither confirmed nor denied that her husband James Stewart, a shipping agent, helped Walker smuggle his *Appeal* into the South and thereby into the hands of the enslaved).

As one would expect, Walker's *Appeal* was an abomination in the eyes of slaveholders and their sympathizers. The powers that be did their utmost to suppress the work (the Georgia legislature, for example, banned its circulation), but word of the *Appeal* spread, and people continued to read it. By 1830, Walker had released a third, revised edition. And that would be his last. Before the year was out, David Walker's dead body was found near the door of his shop. Poison was, and still is, believed to have been the cause of his death.

Walker's work lived on, thanks to such brave hearts as **Henry Highland Garnet,** who in 1848 reprinted the second edition of the *Appeal* with his own incendiary "Call to Rebellion." Walker's work lived on in another sense, too: His son, Edward Garrison Walker. Born a few months after his death, he grew up to be a successful entrepreneur and lawyer. He became a member of the Massachusetts General Legislature in 1866 and a force in black political activity in New England.

NEWS BITS

In 1829, the year David Walker's *Appeal* first appeared . . .

- South Carolina's Governor, Stephen Miller, declared before the state legislature: "Slavery is not a national evil; on the contrary it is a national benefit."

- Riled about the increase of free blacks in their city, in August 1829, white mobs in Cincinnati attacked black folks and their property. At the end of a three-day race riot, more than a thousand blacks left Cincinnati for New York, for Pennsylvania, for Michigan, and for Canada.

- Georgia prohibited the education of slaves and free blacks, and several states were to do the same in a few years.

Nat Turner (1800–1831)

Sir,—You have asked me to give a history of the motives which in-
duced me to undertake the late insurrection, as you call it—To do so I
must go back to the days of my infancy, and even before I was born.
from *The Confessions of Nat Turner*

He was an infant when his father escaped captivity on the farm of Benjamin Turner. This same man owned Nat Turner's mother and the
grandmother who raised him, hopefully, carefully, and with mystical
expectations.

An extremely bright child he was: learning to read and write with
such ease that he had "no recollection of learning the alphabet";
speaking on events that happened before his birth; telling of things to
come. Early on, he was struck with a hunger for knowledge of the Holy:
he fasted and prayed, fasted and prayed. With the passage of time, he
was taken with a blessed assurance of what the elders had said of him:
"That I was ordained for some great purpose in the hands of the
Almighty."

So obedient was he to a calling from on high that after a successful
escape from his owner (then Joseph Travis), he returned to captivity because, he claimed, the Holy Ghost had commanded such. It was
around this time that he had one of his great and terrible visions: "I saw
white spirits and black spirits engaged in battle, and the sun dark-
ened—the thunder rolled in the heavens, and blood flowed in streams."
Was it a prophecy of the Civil War, or a foreshadowing of the uprising he
would engineer in Southampton County Virginia in 1831?

Many stress **David Walker**'s *Appeal* as the catalyst for Turner's act.
That could be—but we cannot ignore that Turner himself credited the
Holy Ghost.

And on the 12th of May, 1828, I heard a loud noise in the heavens,
and the Spirit instantly appeared to me and said the Serpent was loos-
ened, and Christ had laid down the yoke he had borne for the sins of
men, and that I should take it on and fight against the Serpent. . . .
And by the signs in the heavens that it would make known to me when
I should commence the great work, and until the first sign appeared I
should conceal it from the knowledge of men; and on the appearance
of the sign (the eclipse of the sun, last February), I should arise and
prepare myself, and slay my enemies with their own weapons.

Immediately after the solar eclipse of February 1831, Turner con-
fided in four black men (Henry, Hark, Nelson, and Sam) and began laying plans to actuate his vision. Before dawn on August 22, 1831, Nat

Richland Community College
Decatur, IL 62521

Turner's Rebellion began—in a place where blacks greatly outnumbered whites (about 9,500 vs. 6,500).

Turner's owner and the owner's family were the first to die a bloody death. On to one neighboring house after another after another, Turner's midnight troops moved "with neither age nor sex to be spared." The number of insurgents rose to about seventy angry black men amassing more axes, more guns, more swords, more cudgels, more scythes with which they would murder some sixty white people.

Turner never thought the wild killing would go on and on. The Baptist preacher envisioned that such a great fear and trembling would strike the whites after that first lightning assault and the establishment of a stronghold that the women and children and unresistant men could be spared. Once slavery was surrendered, the killing would cease.

So it was that beyond daylight, Turner and a corps of his forces set out on the road to the county seat, Jerusalem, to seize the arsenal. Unfortunately for them, however, the alarm had been sounded, and the militia was out. The soldiers did their duty with a vengeance, killing willy-nilly some one hundred people, littering the landscape with black heads on poles.

Nat Turner eluded capture for more than a month. His day of reckoning began on October 30, when he was seized in swampland about five miles from his owner's farm. He was not summarily lynched by a frothing mob, but put in jail to await a trial. Two days after his arrest, calmly and resolutely, he dictated his "confession" to Thomas Ruffin Gray, his court-appointed attorney (who mounted no defense at all). A little over a week later, Nat Turner was hanged.

His corpse was skinned, his flesh made into grease, and his bones became a doctor's trophy.

Not surprisingly, in the wake of Nat Turner's Rebellion, the largest and bloodiest ever seen, black folks throughout the South caught more hell than ever. There were indiscriminate beatings and killings. Tighter reins were put on the movements and assembly of those in captivity. Teaching an enslaved man, woman, or child to read and write became a much more serious crime. The Bible was viewed as bad news in black hands, and black preachers became anathema.

Turner's Rebellion also almost put an end to slavery in Virginia, for its legislature debated a proposal for emancipation that carried with it the deportation of all blacks from the state.

Henry Highland Garnet (1815–1882)

A descendant of a Mandingo chieftain, he claimed. "Let your motto be resistance!" he proclaimed.

Henry Highland Garnet (circa 1881) in his midsixties, about a year before he died. (Courtesy of the National Portrait Gallery, Smithsonian Institution/Art Resource, NY)

He knew bondage on Maryland's Eastern Shore until the age of nine, when his father spirited the family away to New York.

Let your motto be resistance!

He knew fear and loathing as a young man when, upon his return from sea, he found his family gone—forced into hiding by slavehunters. Young Henry went scowling about the streets of New York City, ready to defend himself with a knife, until friends whisked him away to Long Island for safekeeping.

Let your motto be resistance!

He knew that learning was one of the most liberating things a black man could have, and he was determined to get all he could. As a boy, he had attended the African Free School on Mulberry Street and, later, the Canal Street High School run by two of the most prominent black New Yorkers, the Reverends Theodore S. Wright and Peter Williams, Jr. In 1835, at the age of twenty, along with Thomas S. Sidney and Alexander Crummell, Garnet journeyed up to Canaan, New Hampshire, to enroll in the heretofore all-white Noyes Academy. Opposition to the presence of these three young men peaked when a mob descended upon the school with a brigade of oxen and dragged the school's main building into a swamp. It wasn't just their blackness that had riled the neighboring farmers: Garnet and Crummell had engaged in antislavery talk at a local church.

Let your motto be resistance!

Garnet continued his education at Oneida Theological Institute in Whitesboro, New York, graduating in 1839. The next year, he began pastoring a Presbyterian church in Troy, New York, which Garnet made extremely socially useful: It had a grammar school, it served as a station on the Underground Railroad, and it was home for other anti-slavery activities that came with the territory of Garnet's membership in the Liberty Party.

Let your motto be resistance! He was serious about this motto. It was his main point in what became his most famous speech: "An Address to the Slaves of the United States of America," delivered in August 1843 at the National Negro Convention in Buffalo, New York. Garnet's address, known as "A Call to Rebellion," began,

> Brethren and Fellow Citizens:
>
> Your brethren of the north, east, and west have been accustomed to meet together in National Conventions, to sympathize with each other, and to weep over your unhappy condition. In these meetings we have addressed all classes of the free, but we have never until this time, sent a word of consolation and advice to you. We have been contented in sitting still and mourning over your sorrows, earnestly hoping that before this day, your sacred liberties would have been restored. But, we have hoped in vain. . . . While you have been oppressed, we have also been partakers with you; nor can we be free while you are enslaved. We therefore write to you as being bound with you.
>
> Many of you are bound to us, not only by the ties of a common humanity, but we are connected by the more tender relations of parents, wives, husbands, children, brothers, and sisters, and friends. . . .
>
> Two hundred and twenty-seven years ago, the first of our injured race were brought to the shores of America. They came not with glad spirits to select their homes, in the New World. They came not with their own consent, to find an unmolested enjoyment of the blessings of this fruitful soil. The first dealings they had with men calling themselves Christians, exhibited to them the worst features of corrupt and sordid hearts; and convinced them that no cruelty is too great, no villainy and no robbery too abhorrent for even enlightened men to perform, when influenced by avarice, and lust.

Further along, Garnet expressed why he could have no faith in moral suasion, no faith that slaveholders would come to do the right thing out of change of heart. He reminded his people how men like **Salem Poor** had been duped.

> The colonists threw the blame [for slavery] upon England. They said that the mother country entailed the evil upon them, and that they would rid themselves of it if they could. The world thought they were sincere, and the philanthropic pitied them. But time soon tested their sincerity. In a few years, the colonists grew strong and severed themselves from the British Government. Their Independence was declared, and they took their station among the sovereign powers of the earth. The declaration was a glorious document. Sages admired it, and the patriotic of every nation reverenced the Godlike sentiments

which it contained. When the power of Government returned to their hands, did they emancipate the slaves? No; they rather added links to our chains. Were they ignorant of the principles of Liberty? Certainly they were not. The sentiments of their revolutionary orators fell in burning eloquence upon their hearts, and with one voice they cried, LIBERTY OR DEATH. O, what a sentence was that! It ran from soul to soul like electric fire, and nerved the arm of thousands to fight in the holy cause of Freedom.

Garnet exhorted those in bondage to do likewise. After a few words on slavery's desolation of the black body, mind, and spirit, we gather from the typography that Garnet shouted these next words:

TO SUCH DEGRADATION IT IS SINFUL IN THE EXTREME FOR YOU TO MAKE VOLUNTARY SUBMISSION. . . . NEITHER GOD, NOR ANGELS, OR JUST MEN, COMMAND YOU TO SUFFER FOR A SINGLE MOMENT. THEREFORE IT IS YOUR SOLEMN AND IMPERATIVE DUTY TO USE EVERY MEANS, BOTH MORAL, IN-TELLECTUAL, AND PHYSICAL THAT PROMISES SUCCESS.

Garnet went on to recall some of those who led rebellions, men he deemed blessed—Denmark Vesey (see **Devany**), **Nat Turner,** Joseph Cinque, and Madison Washington. He rallied the enslaved to cherish and draw on the courage of these souls, and in closing, he urged,

Let your motto be RESISTANCE! RESISTANCE! RESISTANCE!—No op-pressed people have ever secured their liberty without resistance. What kind of resistance you had better make, you must decide by the circumstances that surround you, and according to the suggestion of expediency. Brethren, adieu. Trust in the living God. Labor for the peace of the human race, and remember that you are three millions.

Garnet's address scared a lot of people, among them **Frederick Douglass,** one of the delegates at the convention who voted "no" to the resolution that the speech be distributed.

We'll never know how many copies of the speech were smuggled into the slave states. We'll never know how many acts of resistance it in-spired: how many foiled revolts were ignited, how many slaveholders were discreetly poisoned, how much work was subversively monkey-wrenched.

Garnet's address reached more ears in 1847 when he delivered it at the convention in Troy, New York. It reached more eyes when he pub-lished it with the *Appeal* by **David Walker** in 1848. Clearly, with this speech, Garnet was not merely rallying the enslaved to resistance. He was also rallying the free to work harder for the abolition of slavery. For the remainder of his days, he never stopped working for the free-dom of his people.

In the early 1850s, Garnet lectured in England to raise support for the boycott of foods and other goods produced with slave labor, the free-produce movement. In the late 1850s, he served as president of the African Civilization Society, whose members would include Martin Delany. This organization's purpose was to establish a focused emigration to the Niger Valley for the making of a new nation that would not just be a place where blacks could breathe free but would be dedicated to producing goods to compete with slave-labor products.

Garnet's activities left little time for either of his wives: neither his wife Julia, whom he married in 1842, nor the woman he married after Julia died, women's rights activist Sarah Thompson Garnet, sister of one of the first female physicians in America, Susan McKinney Steward. Neither of Garnet's wives could have been unaware of what they were getting when they hitched up with him, however; even early on, he was solely a man on a mission, for whom personal life was secondary. After all, even though he had developed a strange swelling on his right leg, which left him a "cripple" as a young man and later an amputee, his physical limitations didn't stop him from being a man of action.

The Civil War brought Garnet a new hope for America. The African Civilization Society shifted its focus to helping freed people who flocked north. Garnet also recruited black New Yorkers for the Union Army— even after the draft riots in New York City, where whites expressed their displeasure at being summoned to fight for blacks by running amok on black life and property, including Shiloh Presbyterian Church of which Garnet was pastor at the time.

Garnet was involved in relief efforts for the thousands of freed people who rushed to the nation's capital after the war, where he was by then pastor of Fifteenth Street First Presbyterian Church. In 1865 he made history as the first African American minister to deliver a sermon in Congress. The occasion was the commemoration of the passage of the Thirteenth Amendment, the most important part of which was Article XIII, which abolished slavery in the United States (as it upheld prison labor): "Neither the slavery nor involuntary servitude, except as punishment for crime whereof the party shall have been duly convicted, shall exist within the United States, or any place subject to their jurisdiction." What a hallelujah Garnet must have raised when he heard these words.

"Emancipate, enfranchise, educate, and give the blessings of the gospel to every American citizen." This is a snippet of his sermon before Congress, delivered on February 12, 1865.

Garnet died on that very day seventeen years later. At the end of his life, he was a very tired and embittered man. After the failure of Reconstruction, he abandoned all hope of America ever being a just nation. In 1881, he found a way out: appointment as Minister to Liberia, where he died and was, as he wished, buried.

Josiah Henson (1789–1883)

An incident that occurred when he was three or four years old was his earliest memory of his Maryland captivity. It was the day he saw his father, property of a Mr. Francis N., "with his head bloody and his back lacerated." Henson's father's right ear had been "cut off close to his head," and the man had received one hundred lashes on his back. This was the price Henson's father paid for standing up for his woman, who belonged to a Dr. Josiah McP. As Henson recalled,

> He had beaten the overseer for a brutal assault on my mother, and this was his punishment. Furious at such treatment, my father became a different man, and was so morose, disobedient, and intractable, that Mr. N. determined to sell him. He accordingly parted with him, not long after, to his son, who lived in Alabama; and neither my mother nor I, ever heard of him again. He was naturally, as I understand afterwards from my mother and other persons, a man of amiable temper, and of considerable energy of character.

Henson's second major memory was of the day he, his mother, and his siblings, like all of the deceased Dr. McP.'s holdings, were put up for auction. Henson was five or six.

> My brothers and sisters were bid off one by one, while my mother, holding my hand, looked on in an agony of grief, the cause of which I but ill understood at first, but which dawned on my mind, with dreadful clearness, as the sale proceeded. My mother was then separated from me, and put up in her turn. She was bought by a man named Isaac R., residing in Montgomery county, and then I was offered to the assembled purchasers. My mother, half distracted with the parting forever from all her children, pushed through the crowd, while the bidding for me was going on, to the spot where R. was standing. She fell at his feet, and clung to his knees, entreating him in tones that a mother only could command, to buy her *baby* as well as herself, and spare to her one of her little ones at least.

How did Mr. R. respond? The man disengaged himself from Henson's mother "with such violent blows and kicks, as to reduce her to the necessity of creeping out of his reach, and mingling the groan of bodily suffering with the sob of a breaking heart."

Fortuitously, little Josiah fell strangely ill shortly after his purchase—quite possibly fatally ill, feared his new master. In an effort to cut his losses, the new master persuaded Mr. R. to buy little Josiah "at such a trifling rate that it could not be refused." Little Josiah (and maybe little trickster?) soon recovered.

He grew up to be strong and strapping and full of force. By his own admission, he also grew up to be what whites would regard as a model slave: supremely obedient and exceptionally hardworking. All this earned Henson the underjob of overseer, and according to him, he was a great boss, eliciting greater productivity from his fellow captives. How did he achieve this? By fright? By might? The fact that from time to time, by Henson's hand, a sheep, a pig, or some other edible of Mr. R's went missing and into the bellies of his slaves may have been a factor.

Henson's gleanings went unnoticed, in part because Henson was smooth, but also because Mr. R. was pretty much a fool: "Coarse and vulgar in his habits, unprincipled and cruel in his general deportment, and especially addicted to the vice of licentiousness" is how Henson quick-sketched the man.

What kept Henson dutiful was, by his own account, his most powerful adult experience: his acceptance of Jesus as Lord and Savior. The human agent of his conversion was a baker from Georgetown who abhorred slavery and probably said as much in his occasional role of preacher. It was after hearing one of this man's sermons that Henson determined "to find out something more about 'Christ and him crucified.'" He did, and as he grew strong in the faith, he became a most affecting expounder of the Word.

Henson's faith was a shield against the soul blows of bondage; it helped him contain his rage over his master's continued dissolution and abuse of black people. Then came the incident—an eerie echo of his first childhood memory—that occurred when Henson was about thirty, something that could have left him a viciously bitter or altogether numbed man.

Henson was attending his master on one of his master's infamous nights of debauchery, when the drunk Mr. R. got into a fight with his brother's overseer, a Mr. L., who was likewise liquored up. When Henson came to his owner's rescue, he accidentally bounced Mr. L., who "treasured up his vengeance for the first favorable opportunity." This came about a week after the incident, when Henson was on errand for his owner.

> I took a short cut through a lane, separated by gates from the high road, and bounded by a fence on each side. This lane passed through some of the farm owned by my master's brother, and his overseer was in the adjoining field, with three negroes, when I went by. On my return, a half an hour afterwards, the overseer was sitting on the fence; but I could see nothing of the black fellows. I rode on, utterly unsuspicious of any trouble, but as I approached, he jumped off the fence, and at the same moment two of the negroes sprung up from under the bushes, where they had been concealed, and stood with him, immediately in front of me; while the third sprang over the fence just behind me. . . . The overseer seized my horse's bridle, and ordered me to alight. . . . I

asked what I was to alight for. "To take the cursedest flogging you ever had in your life, you d——d black scoundrel." "But what am I to be flogged for, Mr. L.," I asked. "Not a word," said he, "but 'light at once, and take off your jacket."

Henson alighted. When he balked at removing his jacket, Mr. L. brandished a stick and Henson's horse took flight. Then . . .

The overseer called upon the negroes to seize me; but they, knowing something of my physical power, were rather slow to obey. At length they did their best, and as they brought themselves within my reach, I knocked them down successively; and one of them trying to trip up my feet when he was down, I gave him a kick with my heavy shoe, which knocked out several of his front teeth, and sent him groaning away. Meanwhile, the cowardly overseer was availing himself of every opportunity to hit me over the head with his stick, which was not heavy enough to knock me down, though it drew blood freely. At length, tired of the length of the affray, he seized a stake, six or seven feet long, from the fence, and struck at me with his whole strength. In attempting to ward off the blow, my right arm was broken, and I was brought to the ground; where repeated blows broke both my shoulder blades, and made the blood gush from my mouth copiously. The two blacks begged him not to murder me, and he just left me as I was, telling me to learn what it was to strike a white man.

Afterwards Henson could not work for five months and was never again able to raise his hands above is head.

A chance to escape all the hell came when Mr. R's finances went from bad to worse. Fearing that his creditors would soon seize his human property, Mr. R. ordered his good and faithful 'Siah to take his slaves, eighteen in all, to a brother in Kentucky.

The Negro caravan, which included Henson's wife and children, set out from Maryland in February 1825. When they arrived in Ohio, a free state, more than a few people urged them to seize the day and take their liberty. As Henson recounted, freedom was more than a notion.

From my earliest recollection, freedom had been the object of my am-bition, a constant motive to exertion, an ever-present stimulus to gain and to save. No other means of obtaining it, however, had occurred to me, but purchasing myself of my master. The idea of running away was not one that I had ever indulged. . . . I had promised that man to take his property to Kentucky, and deposit it with his brother; and this, and this only, I resolved to do.

True to his word, in mid-April 1825, Henson delivered himself and the others to Mr. R.'s brother, possessor of a large plantation and maybe a hundred black souls.

At the outset, Mr. R. said he and his household would soon relo-cate, too, but Mr. R. never went to Kentucky. Three years passed before news arrived that he was definitely staying put. Henson also discovered that Mr. R. was planning to sell some of his slaves. Eventually, with the encouragement and aid of a white Methodist preacher, Henson returned to Maryland to persuade his owner to let him buy his freedom. When Henson arrived in Maryland, he had about $350, a sum raised along the way from preaching, speaking engagements, and just-because donations from well-wishers.

Mr. R. agreed to manumission for $450; however, once he had Henson's money, he claimed the purchase price was $1000. On top of that, he plotted to sell 'Siah down the river, literally—under the ruse of having Henson accompany his nephew, Amos, on a journey to New Orleans to sell meat, produce, and other merchandise.

It was a troubled journey. Weather was not favorable, and sickness beset the crew and Master Amos. Henson remained hale and hearty but felt a transformation coming on one night as he kept watch alone. Reflecting on how his years of faithful service were about to be repaid "turned my blood to gall and wormwood, and changed me from a lively, and I will say, a pleasant-tempered fellow, into a savage, morose, dangerous slave." Soon, Henson was a savage, morose, dangerous slave with murder on his mind and easy access to an axe.

> One dark, rainy night, within a few days of New Orleans, my hour seemed to have come. I was alone on the deck; Mr. Amos and the hands were all asleep below, and I crept down noiselessly, got hold of an axe, entered the cabin, and looking by the aid of the dim light there for my victims, my eye fell upon Master Amos, who was nearest to me; my hand slid along the axe–handle, I raised it to strike the fatal blow,—when suddenly the thought came to me, "What! commit *murder!* and you a Christian?" I had not called it murder before. It was self-defence,—it was preventing others from murdering me,—it was justifiable, it was even praiseworthy.

Henson heeded the still small voice. Amos and the others lived to see another day.

Henson lived to see his family again: Amos's sickness had prevented him from carrying out his uncle's ultimate transaction, and because he was too ill to take care of himself, he had Henson take him home.

Back in Maryland, Henson's owner showed him some gratitude for returning with his nephew, but Henson suspected that Mr. R. soon would be scheming to sell him away from his family. He therefore determined to "make my escape to Canada." Henson would not be going alone; he was taking his famiy: his wife, Charlotte, their two teenage boys, and their two tots. As part of the preparation for the journey, Henson had Charlotte make a large knapsack in which to carry the two small children, and after a day's work, Henson would often "pack the little ones on my back . . . and trot around the cabin with them, and

This engraving of Henson served as the frontispiece for the 1858 edition of his life story. (Courtesy of Photographs and Prints Division, Schomburg Center for Research in Black Culture, The New York Public Library, Astor, Lenox and Tilden Foundations)

go some little distance from it, in order to accustom both of them and myself to the task before us." The Henson family set out in mid-September 1830. With blessings from above and help from some living on the earth, they made their way North.

A most poignant moment of the journey occurred when the family crossed a body of water in Ohio, a moment that reveals how Josiah Henson gave true, deep meaning to "family man":

> I forded it first, with the help of a sounding-pole, and then taking the children on my back, first, the two little ones, and then the others, one at a time, and lastly, my wife, I succeeded in getting them all safely across, where the ford was one hundred to one hundred and fifty yards wide, and the deepest parts perhaps four feet deep. At this time the skin was worn from my back to an extent almost equal to the size of my knapsack.

The Hensons arrived in Canada on October 28, 1830, and eventually made a nice little life there. In time, Josiah felt called to help others do well, too. He became a leader among blacks in the area, and he was able to get them to focus their energies and feeble resources into some steady self-help. This resulted in the settlement of Dawn (near Chatham in present-day Ontario). With donations from several New England philanthropists, Henson went on to found a trade school. For the buildup of both these entities, Henson worked very hard, going on numerous fund-raising missions in Canada, in the northeastern United States, and in England. As if this wasn't enough to keep Henson busy, he also rendered service to those in bondage as a conductor on the Underground Railroad (Kentucky to Canada was his route).

Henson became semifamous with the publication, in 1849, of *The Life of Josiah Henson, Formerly a Slave, Now an Inhabitant of Canada*, dictated to Samuel A. Eliot. His memoir, a valuable fund-raising tool, was quite popular in the 1840s, selling some 6,000 copies in its first three years of publication. Sales increased dramatically in the 1850s, thanks to Harriet Beecher Stowe, author of the most talked-about piece of antislavery literature by a white person: *Uncle Tom's Cabin*.

In *A Key to Uncle Tom's Cabin* (1853), Stowe referenced Henson's narrative among her sources, giving birth to the rumor that became the legend that Josiah Henson was the original "Uncle Tom." For the sake of his work on behalf of Dawn, Henson made use of the publicity. Pretty soon, hype was running amok, and things got pretty comical.

In 1858, the firm that published *A Key to Uncle Tom's Cabin* released a revised edition of Henson's memoirs: *"Truth Stranger Than Fiction": Father Henson's Story of His Own Life*, with an introduction by Stowe. In 1876, a London firm put out the revised and updated *"Uncle Tom's Story of His Life": An Autobiography of The Rev. Josiah Henson (Mrs. Harriet Beecher Stowe's "Uncle Tom")*. Yet another edition—*"Truth Is Stranger Than Fiction": An Autobiography of the Rev. Josiah Henson (Mrs. Harriet Beecher Stowe's "Uncle Tom")*—appeared from a Boston publisher in 1879, with the added attraction of introductory notes by two legendary reformers, orator Wendell Phillips and poet John Greenleaf Whittier.

The expanded editions of Josiah Henson's life story lacked the simplicity of the 1849 edition. The material was not merely expanded, but embellished for more sensational effect.

The last edition of Henson's life story, *An Autobiography of the Rev. Josiah Henson ("Uncle Tom")*, was published in 1881, by which time the man was in his eighties, and his mind was worse for wear, which explains why he was sometimes caught believing himself to be Uncle Tom.

SOME OTHER NINETEENTH-CENTURY MEMOIRS

- *A Narrative of the Adventures and Escape of Moses Roper, from American Slavery* (1838)

- *Narrative of Henry Box Brown, Written by Himself* (1851)

- *The Narrative of Lunsford Lane, Formerly of Raleigh, N.C., Embracing an Account of His Early Life, the Redemption by Purchase of Himself and Family from Slavery, and His Banishment from the Place of His Birth for the Crime of Wearing a Colored Skin* (1842)

- *Narrative of the Life of Frederick Douglass, an American Slave. Written by Himself* (1845); Douglass's other two autobiographies: *My Bondage and My Freedom* (1855) and *Life and Times of Frederick Douglass* (1881)

- *Narrative and Writings of Andrew Jackson, of Kentucky; Containing an Account of His Birth, and Twenty-six Years of His Life While a Slave; His Escape; Five Years of Freedom, Together with Anecdotes Relating to Slavery; Journal of One Year's Travels; Sketches, Etc. Narrated by Himself; Written by a Friend* (1847)

- *Narrative of William Wells Brown, a Fugitive Slave. Written by Himself* (1847)

- *The Fugitive Blacksmith; Or, Events in the History of James W. C. Pennington, Pastor of a Presbyterian Church, New York, Formerly a Slave in the State of Maryland, United States* (1849)

- *Twelve Years a Slave: Narrative of Solomon Northup, a Citizen of New York, Kidnapped in Washington City in 1841, and Rescued in 1853, from a Cotton Plantation Near the Red River in Louisiana* (1853)

- *Autobiography of a Fugitive Negro: His Antislavery Labours in the United States, Canada, and England,* by Samuel Ringgold Ward (1855)

 # James McCune Smith (1813–1865)

If, as a child, he had kept a journal, surely he would have made an extra-long entry for that eventful day in 1824 when his school had a very special guest: France's Marquis de Lafayette, who had thrown in with the colonists and served as a major in the Continental Army, and who was now touring this new nation, America.

What school did this French hero of the American Revolution (and later of the French Revolution) visit? It was New York's African Free School #2,* and it was eleven-year-old James McCune Smith who delivered the welcoming address. Among other things, the bright boy hailed Monsieur Marquis as "a friend of African emancipation." The child was hardly just being polite: Lafayette had founded, in 1788, the French antislavery society *Amis de noirs,* and surely, like so many blacks in America, little Jimmy was aware of Lafayette's wonderful words in a 1786 letter to John Adams: "I would never have drawn my

*See **Patrick Henry Reason.**

sword in the cause of America, could I have conceived that thereby I was founding a land of Slavery."

Clearly, to be chosen to deliver the welcoming address to so noble a man was a great honor, and the selection of James McCune Smith as the student speaker was a sign that this child would become quite an exceptional man—and so he was. In 1837, Smith made history as the first black person in America to earn a medical degree. This he did at the University of Glasgow, where he had earned his master's and bachelor's degrees. Smith did not expatriate, however: After a short internship in Paris, he took his marvelous mind back home and opened a medical practice in New York City. Not long after he established his practice, Smith opened a pharmacy at 55 West Broadway. "There were drilled in this store men who afterward became successful pharmacists, among these George Phillips, Peter W. Ray and Phillip A. White," recalled Smith's godchild Maritcha Lyons, who noted that Smith's drugstore dispensed more than prescriptions. "The store had a back room which became historical," wrote Lyons. For young men and old, this room was "a rallying centre; it had its library and in there were held discussions and debates on all the topics of the day." Those who gathered in the back room of Smith's store "erected a constructive force that molded public sentiment which had much to do in bringing about a more favorable state of things affecting the colored people of New York State."

Later, Smith was to open a second pharmacy, and for a time, he held down the position of Physician at the Colored Orphan Asylum, its only black officer. During all the days of his professional pursuits, medicine was never the only thing on his mind. Smith's concern for black social and political advancement manifested itself in myriad ways. In the 1840s, he was involved in the movement to broaden the voting rights of black New Yorkers, an issue he worked on continually over the years. (He was, for example, one of the leaders of the New York City and County Suffrage Committee of Colored Citizens, which in September 1860 put out the tract "The Suffrage Question.")

In 1850, Smith was a member of the Committee of Thirteen, laboring to raise resistance to the more pernicious Fugitive Slave Law enacted that year (and he also worked closely with David Ruggles in his efforts to thwart "blackbirders," as slave-hunters were called). At the National Negro Convention in Rochester, New York, in July 1853, Smith presented a plan for a national council and then went on to work with **Frederick Douglass** in the establishment of the National Council of Colored People, the first national organization for black empowerment.

Smith was also a powerful advocate for the establishment of a strong black press, an effort he supported by, among other things, contributing articles to publications, including *The Anglo-African Mag-*

azine, the *Colored American,* and two of Douglass's newspapers, the *North Star* and *Frederick Douglass's Paper.* We find further evidence of Smith's intellectual activism in his pamphlets *A Lecture on the Haytian Revolution* (1841) and *The Destiny of the People of Color* (1843) and in the fact that he was asked to provide introductions to two important texts: **Frederick Douglass**'s second autobiography, *My Bondage and My Freedom* (1855); and *Memorial Discourse* (1865) by **Henry Highland Garnet.**

James McCune Smith's most publicized use of mental muscle occurred in 1844, when he took on former Vice President, then Secretary of State, John C. Calhoun. In an official correspondence to the British Minister to the United States, Calhoun had gone to great lengths to show that enslaved blacks were much better off than the free and the freed. According to Calhoun's research (an important piece of which was the 1840 census) in states that had abolished slavery, "the African race has sunk into vice and pauperism." Furthermore, this was "accompanied by the bodily and mental afflictions incident thereto—deafness, blindness, insanity and idiocy." In summing up, Calhoun proclaimed that "the number of Negroes, who are deaf and dumb, blind, idiots, insane, paupers and in prison, in [the free states] is one out of every six."

A group of New York Negroes—which included Theodore S. Wright, **Patrick Henry Reason,** Charles B. Ray, and Philip A. Bell—cried "foul!" On their behalf, Smith drafted a formal response to the United States Senate. In it, Smith astutely revealed the lunacy of Calhoun's claims. He pointed out, for example, that in more than a hundred towns (in Maine, New Hampshire, Vermont, Massachusetts, New York, Pennsylvania, Ohio, Indiana, Illinois, Michigan, and Iowa) where Calhoun reported a total of 186 insane, 38 blind, and 35 deaf and dumb black people, there were no black residents.

Smith's response to Calhoun's proto–*Bell Curve* was only the beginning. He also produced a number of other works, such as the 1846 pamphlet *Influence of Climate on Longevity, with Special Reference to Life Insurance,* which effectively made him a pioneer in the scientific study of race. This study necessarily involved refuting the charge that his people were disproportionately stupid or criminal, or both.

SOME OTHER EARLY MEDICINE MEN

- David John Peck is believed to have been the first black person to graduate from an American medical school: Rush Medical College in Chicago in 1847. In the early 1850s, Peck emigrated to Nicaragua, where he established a strong practice.

- John V. DeGrasse (1825–1868), who received his M.D., with honors, from Bowdoin College in 1849, was the first black member of the Massachusetts Medical Society (1854), and during the Civil War, he served as assistant surgeon in the Thirty-fifth U.S. Colored Troops.

- James Still (1812–1885), an older brother of William Still, was a renowned herbalist in Medford, New Jersey. This man who never apprenticed with an M.D. or set foot in a medical school, was definitely known as "Doctor" Still to the many whom he cured of bad coughs, hemorrhoids, indigestion, scrofula (lymph-node tuberculosis), and erysipelas (febrile disease caused by streptococcus), among other ailments. Those curious about the life and work of James Still had something tangible to work with when *Early Recollections and Life of Dr. James Still* was published in 1877. By this time, two of his sons had followed in his footsteps: Joseph, as an herbalist; and James Jr., the first black graduate of Harvard Medical School (1871), as a bonafide doctor.

Jim Beckwourth (1798–1866)

Near the top of Harold W. Felton's entry on this fellow in *Dictionary of American Negro Biography,* we read, "Narratives of his life, based largely on his autobiography, are still subjects of controversy (as are those of Buffalo Bill, for example). The following account is believed to be as valid as others."

Felton, author of *Jim Beckwourth, Negro Mountain Man* (1966), went on to offer bare-bones information on this man, born James Pierson Beckwourth (or Beckwith) in Virginia: for instance, that he was the son of a white man (a veteran of the Revolutionary War) and a black woman, who may have been free; that at one point during his childhood, his family lived a little south of St. Charles on the Missouri River; that Beckwourth had four years of schooling; that he was apprenticed to a blacksmith; and that he ran away to New Orleans.

Beckwourth served as a scout for the 1823 and 1824 expeditions of General William Henry Ashley's Rocky Mountain Fur Company; these expeditions made Beckwourth among the first non–Native Americans to lay eyes on territory in what became Arizona, Colorado, and Wyoming, and among the first to become a valuable source of information on its people, land, animals, and weather. By this time, Beckwourth was in his mid-twenties. By the time he was in his mid-thirties, Jim Beckwourth had become quite a legendary mountain man—ace trapper, crack shot, swift with a Bowie knife, not bewildered by wilderness, rugged as a rock, and all that. Beckwourth had also become, as Felton put it, "accepted" by two Great Plains tribes: the Blackfoot and the Crow. Some historians consider it pure fabulation that the Crows adopted him and made him a chief, however. How high and mighty Beckwourth was with the Crows is far less important than the fact that he did live and travel in their territory, learning of their culture and additional survival skills.

Beckwourth obviously had no blanket pro–Native American policy. In the early 1840s, after a few years in St. Louis (having grown tired of "savage life"), he was down in Florida working as a scout for U.S. forces engaged in the Second Seminole War. During the war, he established several trading posts. Those he raised on the Arkansas and South Platte Rivers were owned by others. The ones he built in present-day Taos, New Mexico, and Los Angeles, California, were his. Yes, he certainly got around.

Some time in the 1840s, Beckwourth was back into the business of war. He fought for the California rebellion against Mexico in 1846, and he fought the Mexicans in the Mexican War, which began in 1846 as a consequence of the U.S. annexation of Texas and determination to have California. In 1848, the year the war ended, Beckwourth became the chief scout for General John Charles Fremont's expedition to California. In late April 1850, as Fremont's scout, Beckwourth claimed that he discovered the place that bears his name: Beckwourth Pass, the passageway through the Sierra Nevada Mountains between the Feather

Jim Beckwourth (circa 1860) in his early sixties. (Courtesy of the Colorado Historical Society)

and Truckee rivers, just a few miles northwest of what is now Reno, Nevada. Beckwourth also claimed that once the route was opened up, he led the first wagon train through this great gateway to the West, through which thousands rushed in search of gold. Definitely, this passageway was Beckwourth's biggest boast. Yet, as Felton points out, "this most notable achievement of his career is strenuously denied by some writers."

Beckwourth's blackness was "strenuously denied" by the makers of the 1951 film *Tomahawk*, in which the white actor Jack Oakie was cast as Beckwourth. There was something of a precedent for this. Early portraits of Beckwourth pictured him as much lighter than he was. True, he was a mulatto, but he could not have been mistaken for white by those who saw him. As for the pass, if Beckwourth did not discover it, it's amazing that a black man in the mid-nineteenth century managed to get a historic piece of America named after him.

A few years after the discovery of the pass, Jim Beckwourth was running a trading post and hotel in its valley. "My house," he remarked, "is considered the emigrant's landing-place, as it is the first ranch he arrives at in the golden state, and is the only house between this point and Salt Lake." These words are from his memoirs, dictated to Thomas D. Bonner and published in 1856: *The Life and Adventures of James P. Beckwourth, Mountaineer, Scout, and Pioneer, and Chief of the Crow Nation of Indians, with Illustrations.*

What all Beckwourth did in the late 1850s and early 1860s is a puzzlement (and the same holds true for the number of wives he had). What is clear is that in 1866, the U.S. government turned to him when they needed someone to head up a delegation to the Crow. This delegation's objective was to get the Crow to vow neutrality in the wars the United States was waging against other Native American tribes. This task was to be Beckwourth's last frontier, his last mission and mile.

The circumstances of his death are also the subject of controversy. One story is that when he got ready to leave the Crow, they protested something awful because they wanted him to stay and live with them forever. When he would not relent and prepared to pull out, the Crow honored him with a farewell feast, during which they poisoned him, as Felton explained, "so that his body and his powerful medicine would remain in their land."

The other version is that the mighty mountain man did die of poisoning, only it wasn't a consequence of a Crow scheme, but an accidental helping of bad food.

William C. Nell (1816–1874)

In an article in the July 22, 1847, issue of *National Era*, poet and abolitionist John Greenleaf Whittier remarked, "Of the services and sufferings of the colored soldiers of the Revolution, no attempt has, to our knowledge, been made to preserve a record." Whittier went on to lament, "They have had no historian."

Whittier's friend William Cooper Nell decided to change that. It took time, however, because Nell had no research assistant, no grant, no book contract. Not being independently wealthy, he had to work (mostly as a legal copyist). Then, too, his plate was always full.

Since the 1830s, this Bostonian had been involved with the antislavery movement, working closely for a time with William Lloyd Garrison and his newspaper *The Liberator*. The year Whittier bemoaned the neglect of the black soldier, Nell was living in Rochester, New York, sleeves rolled up with **Frederick Douglass,** on the newspaper the *North Star.*

By 1850, Nell was back in Boston recovering from an unsuccessful bid for a seat in the Massachusetts legislature and rendering services to the Underground Railroad—all the while gathering material on black heroes. His project suffered a setback in the winter of 1850, when he became extremely ill. In the spring of 1851, Nell was back in the saddle, pressing on with his labor of love. As it turned out, he not only recounted the exploits of black Revolutionary War heroes, but also chronicled contributions black men made in the 1812–1815 conflict between America and England, a war Nell's father, William G. Nell, had observed up close and personal as steward aboard the *General Gadsden.*

The Services of Colored Americans in the Wars of 1776 and 1812 was the title of Nell's pioneering work. Anyone who questioned his obsession with so narrow a subject found a spry response in Nell's preface:

> There are those who will ask, why make a parade of the *military* services of *Colored* Americans, instead of recording their attention *to* and progress *in* the various other departments of civil, social, and political elevation? To this let me answer, that I yield to no one in appreciating the propriety and pertinency of *every* effort, on the part of Colored Americans, in *all* pursuits, which, as members of the human family, it becomes them to share in; and, among those, *my* predilections are *least* and *last* for what constitutes the pomp and circumstance of War.
>
> Did the limits of this work permit, I could furnish an elaborate list of those who have distinguished themselves as Teachers, Editors, Orators, Mechanics, Clergymen, Artists, Farmers, Poets, Lawyers, Physicians, Merchants, etc., to whose perennial fame be it recorded, that

most of their attainments were reached through difficulties unknown to any but those whose sin is the curl of the hair and hue of the skin. . . .

But the Orator's voice and the Author's pen have both been eloquent in detailing the merits of Colored Americans in these various ramifications of society, while a combination of circumstances have veiled from the public eye a narration of those military services which are generally conceded as passports to the honorable and lasting notice of Americans.

The Services of Colored Americans in the Wars of 1776 and 1812 was a pamphlet, a mere twenty-three pages, but it was gold. Nell put out a revised edition in 1852 and in 1855, a mightily expanded edition: the nearly 400-page book *The Colored Patriots of the American Revolution, with Sketches of Several Distinguished Colored Persons: To Which Is Added a Brief Survey of the Condition and Prospects of Colored Americans.*

This book was "the high-water mark in antebellum black historical literature," said Benjamin Quarles in his 1979 essay "Black History's Antebellum Origins." After acknowledging that the book had its flaws, Quarles captured why *The Colored Patriots* was something special: "The bulk of Nell's information was documented, some of it derived from personal interviews and visits to cemeteries." As Quarles also pointed out, Nell strongly believed in the preservation of the tangibles of history: "At abolitionist meetings he placed on exhibit some of the objects and materials he had collected, including honorable discharge papers of black soldiers, and army flags and banners of companies in which blacks had served."

The Colored Patriots was not Nell's only contribution to the preservation of black history. Among his other endeavors was the rescue from oblivion of **Crispus Attucks,** whose martyrdom had over time been obscured. In 1851, Nell led a small delegation of black Bostonians who petitioned the state legislature to appropriate $1,500 for a monument to the first hero of the Boston Massacre. The legislature said no, but Nell returned to fight another day. In 1857, as part of his protest of the Dred Scott decision, Nell got Crispus Attucks Day underway; the first observance was held on March 5, 1858, in Faneuil Hall, where Attucks had been buried. It was a full day, with exhibitions of relevant artifacts and memorabilia, rousing oratory by leading abolitionists, and song. As was to be the case with subsequent Crispus Attucks Days, the event was not really about one person, but about the strivings of an entire race.

SOME OTHER EARLY HISTORIANS

- William Wells Brown (1814–1884), who escaped slavery in Ohio in 1834, is best known today as an antislavery lecturer and as the author of the bestseller *Narrative of William W. Brown* (1847) and of the first published novel by an African American, *Clotel; Or, The President's Daughter* (1852). In his day, however, Brown was also highly prized for his historical texts: *The Black Man: His Antecedents, His Genius, and His Achievements* (1863); *The Negro in the American Rebellion: His Heroism and His Fidelity* (1867), and *The Rising Son; Or, The Antecedents and Advancements of the Colored Race* (1874). Brown also wrote the first African American travelogue: *Three Years in Europe; Or, Places I Have Seen and People I Have Met* (1852; reprinted in the U.S. in 1855 as *The American Fugitive in Europe*). He also wrote dramas: *Experience; Or, How to Give a Northern Man Backbone* (never published) and *The Escape; Or, a Leap for Freedom* (1858), the first play by an African American to be published. Brown's last book was a history of slavery cum travelogue: *My Southern Home; Or, The South and Its People* (1880).

* William Simmons (1849–1890) was born in slavery in Charleston, South Carolina, and freed by his mother, who escaped with him and his two siblings, eventually settling in Bordentown, New Jersey. Among the things he grew up to be are Union soldier, student at Howard University (B.A. and M.A.), schoolteacher (in Washington, D.C.), pastor of First Baptist Church (in Lexington, Kentucky), editor of *American Baptist,* and president of the State University of Kentucky in Louisville. It was out of his desire to inspire the next generation to achievement that he compiled the biographical encyclopedia *Men of Mark: Eminent, Progressive, and Rising* (1887). Simmons was at work on a book about women of mark when he died.

* George Washington Williams (1849–1891)—a one-time soldier, cleric (Twelfth Baptist Church in Boston and Union Baptist Church in Cincinnati), and legislator (in Ohio)—contributed two very important works of history: the landmark two-volume *A History of the Negro Race in America, 1619–1880* (1882); and *A History of Negro Troops in the War of Rebellion* (1887). This native of Bedford Springs, Pennsylvania, also wrote *An Open Letter to His Serene Majesty, Leopold II, King of the Belgians* (1890), a stout condemnation of the Belgian savaging of the people of the Congo. Williams knew what he was talking about: After attending an antislavery conference in Brussels, in 1890, he went to the Belgian Congo. Williams was in England, at work on a more extensive exposé, when he died.

William Still (1821–1902)

William learned how to keep mum as a child, how not to tell everything he knew, because he understood that running your mouth could have dire consequences.

With neither a playmate nor a friendly stranger did he share the story of how his father, Levin Steel, at age twenty, purchased his freedom on Maryland's Eastern Shore, and trekked to New Jersey, where he waited for a way to be reunited with his wife and four children. Nor did he tell anyone about how his mother, Sidney, escaped captivity in Maryland with two daughters and two sons (all under age eight) and made it to New Jersey—but not to freedom, because slave-hunters caught up with them.

Although it was a story of daring and great drama—something definitely to crow about—little Willie never breathed a word about how a fortnight after her return to bondage, his mother escaped again, only this time, in the interest of the greatest good for the greatest number, she left her two little boys behind—and this time, she was successful.

As an extra precaution, "Steel" became "Still," and "Sidney" became "Charity." With their new identities, Mr. and Mrs. Still went about making a new life on a modest farm near Medford, in Burlington County, New Jersey, where they had many more children—children who would have become slaves if their mother's whereabouts were discovered. Clearly, the baby of the family, William, had a serious incentive not to blab his family's business, and this discipline prepared him for the great work he was to do when he became a man.

In 1844, when he was in his early twenties, William Still moved to Philadelphia. Barely literate, he kicked about earning his daily bread doing this and that, boning up on the three R's in his spare time. In 1847, he applied for a job at the Pennsylvania Anti-Slavery Society. At the bottom rung of the ladder is where he began: part janitor, part clerk. In a few years, he was secretary and executive director of the society's General Vigilance Committee.

Coordinating rescue missions and disbursing funds to Harriet Tubman and other engineers on the Underground Railroad was only one facet of his work. He also had to raise lots of money for the entire operation, establish many safe houses, and train and coordinate lookouts for slave-hunters. Once people made it to Philadelphia (via the Underground Railroad or not), they needed food, clothing, medical care, money, forged free papers, jobs, friends. Those moving on farther North, possibly all the way to Canada, needed provisions, money, contacts. Still also took his work home: He and his wife, Letitia George Still, frequently hid runaways in their home. In innumerable and varied ways, Still helped roughly eight hundred people gain their freedom.

Still was willing to help any black person, runaway or free, such as the forty-something-year-old Peter he met in 1850. The man had purchased himself in Alabama and had come to Philadelphia in search of clues to his family's whereabouts. "Up by the Delaware River"—that's what Peter and his brother had been told by their grandmother, the only family the boys knew during their Maryland bondage. "Up by the Delaware River"—that's what she told them to remember right before they were sold into Alabama. As Still soon discovered, this brief recollection was not all Peter knew about his people.

For one, Peter knew that his father's name was Levin and his mother's, Sidney. Yes, truth can indeed be stranger than fiction; and back in that day, for so many black folks, a family reunion was more than a picnic.

What a joy inexpressible for William to find his brother, to see his mother behold a son for the first time in more than thirty years, to watch Peter get acquainted with siblings he had never known. Precious memories were the only way for Peter to catch up on his father because Levin had died several years earlier.

Peter had other weighty family matters with which William helped. Peter wanted to rescue his wife and children, whom he had left behind in Alabama. First came stealth: A white abolitionist Seth Conklin tried to spirit Peter's family away, but failed, losing his life in the bargain. Next came negotiation: William Still wrote the man who owned Peter's family, asking him to lower the purchase price (from $5,000 to $2,500). When the man refused, William helped his brother mount a fund-raising drive. It took about three years, but another Still family reunion did occur.

In the meantime, Peter's presence in his life had moved William to keep better records of the people his office serviced, so that he might help others reunite. How likely would it be that thousands whom slavery had separated from loved ones would one day have the good fortune to run into a mother, a son, a wife, a brother?

All along, Still had been keeping a journal, but it was spartan, with just the bare facts on expenses, such as $0.31 for "laundry-washing for fugitives," $1.62 for a pair of pants, $2.00 for a coat, $3.00 for six days board. After finding Peter, he started to gather more data on the people themselves: their names, their aliases, their owners' names, details about kin in bondage or already free. This information gathering was the genesis of Still's priceless book, which, as was the custom, came with a very long title: *The Underground Rail Road: A Record of Facts, Authentic Narratives, Letters, &c., Narrating the Hardships Hair-Breadth Escapes and Death Struggles of the Slaves in Their Efforts for Freedom, as Related by Themselves and Others, or Witnessed by the Author; Together with Sketches of Some of the Largest Stockholders, and Most Liberal Aiders and Advisers, of the Road.* The first edition came out in 1872, by which time Still was succeeding in his business of selling coal and stoves, an enterprise he had started during the Civil War.

The Underground Rail Road was not Still's only post–Civil War gift to his people. He also gave money to various social and civic organizations and to needy individuals, and he was adept at getting other people to donate their money, time, and talents to sound causes. An old-folks home, an orphanage, and a YMCA were among the institutions for Philadelphia Negroes he helped get off the ground. He enabled many families to buy homes and other property through the Berean Building and Loan Association. Still started this business in 1888 with another Philadelphia entrepreneur, his son-in-law Matthew Anderson, the second husband of his daughter Caroline, one of the first African American women to graduate from a medical school (in 1878) and practice medicine.

William Still was very proud of his daughter Caroline Virginia Still Wiley Anderson, as he was of his other children. Indeed, in his senior years, Still had a great deal to savor when it came to family matters—things he did not have to keep mum about at all.

ANOTHER WILLIAM STILL

William Grant Still (1895–1978), born in Woodville, Mississippi, and raised in Little Rock, Arkansas, was the most prolific and successful classical composer of the early twentieth century. This William Still was an African American "first" on several scores: the first to have a symphony performed by a prominent American orchestra (*Afro-American Symphony* by the Rochester Philharmonic in 1931), the first to conduct a leading orchestra (the Los Angeles Philharmonic in 1936), the first to have an opera performed by a major orchestra (*Troubled Island* presented by the New York City Opera in 1949), and one of the first to compose for films, radio, and television. In addition to those works already cited, William Grant Still's finest works include the opera *A Bayou Legend;* the ballets *Sadhji* and *Lenox Avenue;* and the compositions *Darker America, From the Black Belt, Symphony No. 2 in G Minor, They Lynched Him from a Tree,* and *Plain-Chant for America.*

 J. P. Ball (1825–1905)

In 1855, aware and progressive Bostonians had something huge to celebrate in J. P. Ball's handiwork: the 2,400-square-foot antislavery photo panorama *Ball's Splendid Mammoth Pictorial Tour of the United States, Comprising Views of the African Slave Trade; of Northern and Southern Cities; of Cotton and Sugar Plantations; of the Mississippi, Ohio, and Susquehanna Rivers, Niagara Falls, &C.* The exhibit, on view at the Boston Armory, was an outgrowth of Ball's antislavery work in Cincinnati.

James Presley Ball, born free in Virginia, set his sights on becoming a photographer in 1845 after a chance encounter with a black daguerreotypist named John B. Bailey. By 1847, Ball was eking out a living as an

J. P. Ball created this photograph when he was doing business in Helena, Montana, on Main Street and 9th Avenue. (Courtesy of the Montana Historical Society)

itinerant photographer, shooting blacks and whites. Eventually, Ball settled down, in Cincinnati, Ohio, where he became one of the most successful photographers in the city, proficient in a range of photographic techniques, including the ambrotype, the tintype, the stereotype, and the one named after Louis J. M. Daguerre, and all the rage by the 1850s, the daguerreotype.

The most lifelike, the most beautiful, the most durable, the cheapest—that's what a Ball advertisement promised the daguerreotype-loving public. Evidently, there was truth in his advertising because Ball's reputation spread beyond Ohio, carrying many visitors to his studio door in Cincinnati. After the 1855 exhibit of *Ball's Splendid Mammoth Pictorial Tour of the United States,* his reputation soared. At one point, he was making about a hundred dollars a day. Over time, his customers included more and more famous folks: Ulysses S. Grant, **Frederick Douglass,** and **Henry Highland Garnet** among them.

Ball's connections might have had something to do with his being appointed, in 1887, the official photographer for various celebrations for the twenty-fifth anniversary of the Emancipation Proclamation. By then, Ball had been living in Minneapolis, Minnesota, for about ten years. In the fall of 1887, he moved to Helena, Montana, where he got involved with the Republican Party and civic organizations. In the next century, Ball moved to Seattle, Washington, where he continued to work as a photographer until 1904, when rheumatism put him out of business. At that point, he moved to Hawaii, where he died.

Ball's Splendid Mammoth Pictorial Tour of the United States did not survive; however, we can view the pamphlet that accompanied it in *J. P. Ball, Daguerrean and Studio Photographer* (1993), edited by Deborah Willis, which contains some two hundred splendid Ball photographs.

⚜ Dred Scott (c. 1799–1858)

Scott was born around the same time as **Nat Turner,** and in the same place, Southampton County, Virginia. Also like Turner, he landed in the history books because of his freedom fight, only his was not an armed struggle.

The little that we know about his early life includes that he was the property of one Peter Blow, whose final home was Missouri. After Blow's death in 1831, Scott was sold for five hundred dollars to John Emerson, a U.S. Army doctor stationed in St. Louis, but soon transferred to a fort up in Illinois, a free state.

Dr. Emerson was reassigned again in 1836 to Fort Snelling, in what is today St. Paul, Minnesota, but was then part of Wisconsin Territory (declared free soil in the Missouri Compromise of 1820). There, in 1836 or 1837, Scott married Harriet Robinson. Her owner was, among other things, a justice of the peace, and he gave the couple the same kind of ceremony accorded free people, and he ended up giving Harriet to Dr. Emerson. When Dr. Emerson moved to St. Louis in the fall of 1837, he left the couple up at Fort Snelling, renting them out, presumably as house servants.

Around about this time, we start to scratch our heads. Scott lived on free soil for several years, yet he never claimed his liberty. Did he not know where he was? Had he never heard about people who had successfully sued for freedom based on the fact that they hadn't merely passed through territory where slavery was prohibited but had actually dwelled there? Maybe he knew all about this but figured that challenging a military man was mad.

We will never know what was in the mind of this chunky, diminutive, all-African man, whose original owner called him Sam. He didn't become Dred Scott until after 1834. In *Dictionary of American Negro Biography,* Paul McStallworth reports on the possibility that Scott's first name evolved from a tease: that soldiers mocked Sam as "Great Scott" after the very tall General Winfield Scott, and "great" in keeping with a Southern black dialect, became "dret," later heard as "dred." Whether through Sam's own choosing or Emerson's, the name stuck.

Dr. Emerson wasn't in St. Louis but a month when he was sent to a fort in Louisiana. There, he married Eliza Irene Sanford, and shortly thereafter, he sent for Dred and Harriet—and they went. Not under guard, but by themselves, they left free soil for a slave state. Again, why? Because they didn't find bondage unbearable, or because they feared that if they weren't faithful to the journey they would have the U.S. Army on their tails?

Louisiana courts often granted freedom to those who proved they had lived on free soil, but maybe Scott was unaware of that. In any event, Louisiana wasn't home for long because Emerson was reposted to Wisconsin Territory's Fort Snelling. During the journey North, Dred and Harriet had their first child, Eliza. By this time, it was 1839.

In 1840, Dr. Emerson was sent to Florida (the Seminoles were "acting up"), and he sent his wife and the Scotts to St. Louis. After his discharge in 1842, the doctor left Dred and Harriet in St. Louis, while he and the Mrs. settled in Iowa. Dr. Emerson died in 1843, with no provisions in his will for Dred and Harriet's manumission. Mrs. Emerson kept the Scotts enslaved, and at one point, she rented Dred to a man in Texas, which entered the Union as a slave state in 1845.

When Scott returned to St. Louis in 1846, he asked Mrs. Emerson to allow him to purchase himself and his family. No was her reply. What had gotten into Dred Scott? Being separated from his family? Maybe Texas was hell, and he suspected Mrs. Emerson would continue to hire him out to cruel taskmasters. Some suggest that contact with abolitionists played a role. Others point to Scott's reacquaintance with the sons of his first owner, Peter Blow, in Missouri. It was these fellows who prompted Scott to pursue his freedom, they say. Whether or not the Blow brothers instigated it, they certainly supported Scott's case going to court.

With lawyers to take his case and the sons of Peter Blow to take care of the legal expenses, Dred Scott filed suit for his freedom in the Missouri circuit court in 1846. Scott's lawyers probably expected a quick victory because Missouri had granted freedom to other enslaved people who had lived on free soil.

Scott v. Emerson began in June 1847, and Scott lost because of a technicality. Another trial was set for December 1847, a trial that hung in the air for more than a year, finally getting underway in January 1850. This time the verdict was in Scott's favor—but then, Mrs. Emerson appealed the decision.

By this time, Mrs. Emerson was living in Springfield, Massachusetts, where she married another physician, a Dr. Chaffee, who was opposed to slavery and had his eye on a seat in Congress. Mrs. Eliza Irene Sanford Emerson Chaffee handed over all matters pertaining to the Scotts, from the case to their rental, to her brother John Sanford.

For about two years, Dred Scott lived in limbo, during a particularly feverish time in the nation. The South had been talking secession for a while because of the North's effort to curb slavery. The Compromise of 1850 was a marker of the tug of war: On the one hand, California was admitted to the Union as a free state, and the slave trade was abolished in the nation's capital; on the other hand, slavery was not prohibited in land the United States had taken from Mexico (later New Mexico and Utah territories). The compromise also carried the new Fugitive Slave Law that improved a slaveholder's chances of seizing a runaway on free soil and made a lot of blacks, always free and fugitive, emigrate to Canada.

Meanwhile, there was Dred Scott suing for freedom. In 1852 he was dealt a blow: The Missouri State Supreme Court reversed the lower court's decision. Legal precedence was trashed. It didn't matter how many times in the past the courts had granted freedom to someone who had lived where slavery was prohibited. What mattered most to this court was not upsetting the South.

Guess what else. Before the decision was handed down, one of Scott's attorneys died, and the other had left the state. Dred and Harriet Scott continued to live in Missouri, as rental property. One of their hires was to an in-law of the sons of Peter Blow, and this man assisted Scott in securing one of his two new lawyers. The case was back in court in 1854—this time, before the United States Circuit Court. Because John Sanford was still Scott's overseer, he was the defendant; and the case that should have been *Scott v. Sanford* became *Scott v. Sandford* because of a clerical error.

Scott lost. Scott's lawyers appealed. Dred Scott was in limbo again, enduring the nastiness proslavery people put in the wind: that he was a dolt; that he was a no-account Negro who wouldn't know what to do with freedom if it landed on his nose; that he was just a tool for Northern agitators, interfering with states' rights and property laws.

There is no reason to believe that Scott was a fool, a joke, or that he would not know what to do with freedom, especially after all he had been through, now nearing age sixty, and now with two children. Bewildered? Wouldn't you be after a decade of hoping, waiting, hoping? Of course, we'll never know the thoughts of Dred Scott, one of the most known black men in America in the late 1850s, about whom we really know nothing. His name, just his name became famous because the outcome of his case signaled new miseries for black people.

When Scott's case reached the United States Supreme Court in 1856, it was definitely the wrong time: The Kansas–Nebraska Act was two years old and had left "bleeding Kansas" in its wake, with proslavery Southerners thinking harder on secession. It was also definitely before the wrong Chief Justice: Roger Brooke Taney, scion of a very rich slave-owning Maryland family (and brother-in-law of Francis Scott

Key). Taney was proslavery to the core. As U.S. Attorney General back in the 1830s, he uttered some scary words for black souls when he waded in on the issue of the legitimacy of laws banning free blacks from slave states. "The African race in the United States, even when free, are everywhere a degraded class," said Taney. He further declared, "They are not looked upon as citizens by the contracting parties who formed the Constitution. They were evidently not supposed to be included by the term *citizens.*" Scott's case gave Taney the ultimate soapbox for his antiblack sentiments.

"The black man has no rights that the white man is bound to respect." This is the most provocative, most quoted line from Taney's opinion in the decision handed down on March 6, 1857, a decision that declared Scott's residence on free soil a nonissue because Congress's prohibition of slavery in federal territories (as in the Missouri Compromise) was unconstitutional. Equally dreadful was the ruling that Scott had no right to sue in the first place because only citizens of the United States could do that, and blacks were not citizens.

"Such a decision cannot stand," thundered **Frederick Douglass** in a speech delivered in New York on May 11, 1857, before the American Anti-Slavery Society. "God will be true though every man be a liar. We can appeal from this hell-black judgment of the Supreme Court, to the court of common sense and common humanity. We can appeal from man to God. . . . All that is merciful and just, on earth and in Heaven, will execrate and despise this edict of Taney."

Like Douglass, many abolitionists, black and white, who once had faith in moral suasion now saw political agitation as the sine qua non. There were other speeches and protests decrying the Dred Scott decision, bringing new blood into the antislavery cause.

Where did Dred Scott end up? After her win, Miz Eliza sold the Scotts to one of the sons of Peter Blow, who promptly manumitted the family. Sadly, Scott never lived long in liberty. He died a little more than a year after he was freed, with the *Dred Scott* decision living on as kindling for a civil war.

 # James Boon (1808–1857?)

His life story might well have been lost had not snippets of his existence been surrendered to the North Carolina Department of Archives and History. And the Boon Papers could have remained dumb matter were it not for the painstaking work of John Hope Franklin: combing through letters and notes and bills and receipts, backtracking more than a century into Franklin County Court records, pondering the proscribed possibilities of life for someone like James Boon, a free man in a slave state.

Franklin's research culminated in the essay "James Boon, Free Negro Artisan," collected in his *Race and History: Selected Essays* (1989), but first published in the April 1945 issue of *Journal of Negro History,* brainchild of **Carter G. Woodson,** one of Franklin's role models. John Hope Franklin did what he did because of his whole-soul outlook on history: "James Boon reminds us once more that the history of a nation is to be found not only in the records of victorious battles or in the lives of the notable personages but also in the lives of the most humbly born, the most consistently despised, and the most miserably improvident."

James Boon, of Louisburg, North Carolina, had only "X" as a signature all his life long. Nonetheless, this freeborn, whose parentage is a mystery, was by no means a dunce. His leg up in life came at around age nineteen, when he became an apprentice to a master carpenter, William Jones, who became something of a protector and, at times, a petit benefactor. At the end of his two-year apprenticeship, Boon began to support himself by his trade, first with bits and pieces of minor repair work, and then with more substantive jobs, such as making major repairs on the County Court House. Eventually, there came a day when this man climbed the ladder to contractor. Free and enslaved men worked for him, for a daily wage that ranged from fifty cents to a whole buck. (Boon's daily hire started at $1.25.)

The repair of doors, window sills, porches, floors, and molding was among Boon's specialties. Making bedsteads, benches, chairs, and stools was something Boon and crew could also do. More than a few times, Boon got contracts for wholesale remodeling jobs on interiors of residential and commercial properties. When work in his trade was skinny, Boon did a little carting and a miscellany of odd jobs, and sometimes he ventured out of Louisburg for work—to Wilmington, Littleton, Halifax, and Raleigh. No doubt about it, when he went into territory where he was an unknown, he was sure to have with him letters from whites with whom he had done business. Franklin cites a few such letters of recommendation. Among them is this February 22, 1842, item from a Mr. R. H. Mosby of Littleton to a Mr. Isaac Fanecon of Halifax:

> This will be handed to you by James Boon a free man who has been in my imployment as a carpenter for some time—At his instance and as an act of justice I write this to say to you or to any other person who may wish to get his services that he is an orderly and well behaved man and attentive to his business. His work is executed better and with more taste than any persons within my knowledge in this section of the country. Should you want his services my impression is you cannot do better than imploy him.

Such a note could not only help Boon get work, but it could also help this free black man in a slave state avoid being harassed, locked up on trumped up charges of vagrancy, or worse. Yes, indeed, a note from a white person was life, was gold, no matter how poorly composed, such as this one by an A. Kornegay, dated March 7, 1848:

> James Boon is a free man and under my protection and wishes to pass about where his business may cale him at eny time unmolested and rec'd fair treatment as a honable man of culer. I hereby recommend him as such.

What must it have been like to need such passes? Did it grate Boon's gristle, or was it so ordinary that it had no sting? Did the fear ever creep into the mind of this illiterate man that some fellow might play a trick, and instead of a note of praise or safe passage, scribble something hazardous such as, "This man James Boon is a fool. Feel free to beat his —" Maybe Boon had someone like his mentor William Jones read the contents of a note, and perhaps then he memorized it.

We do not know what Boon's ambitions were. Did he ever have any expansion plans, or was he just grateful that he was able to live and work another day? Maybe he had no lofty goals for his enterprise, yet he did have some sense of gettin' ahead, for he made little investments: He had some rental property and land with timber he sold from time to time. Whatever his dreams, he never came anywhere near being prosperous, but he did manage to survive, in part because he did high-quality work, and in part because early on, he established himself as a good credit risk with several merchants from whom he purchased tools and supplies and the necessities for his domestic life.

Good credit came in handy during the mean, lean times, when Boon had trouble meeting payroll and paying his bills. Then, he wiggled and waggled every which way. As Franklin tells it, "The schemes Boon devised to remain solvent were almost ingenious for a man who was illiterate and who doubtless enjoyed only a limited amount of legal counsel."

What were some of the ways Boon robbed Peter to pay Paul? By borrowing, by issuing notes with his house as collateral, by filing deeds of trust for his land that would allow the assignee to sell the property if such-and-such debt wasn't paid by so-and-so date, and by instructing those who did or would owe him for a job to pay his fee to one of his creditors (as Franklin points out, it was a particularly shrewd move to have one white man the debtor of another).

These clever adaptations make you wonder what all James Boon might have been had he been born in a different place and time. "There is not a single record among his papers," observed John Hope Franklin, "which does not suggest a rather remarkable aptitude for understanding business and the many transactions in which the businessman engages. One is led to believe that Boon, without any help or advice whatever, could have made a creditable showing as a carpenter and contractor, if he could have led a normal existence as a free, unmolested, and unintimidated human being." Of course, it is possible that had Boon been born in a different era, he might have been, ultimately, his own undoing. Franklin's sketch of the man is not absent of warts. Boon sometimes let liquor get the best of him; there was at least one occasion when he grieved his wife with adultery; and Franklin found that he "seemed especially fond of fine clothes" he could ill afford.

There are other puzzlements about this man Boon, James Boon. As early as 1843 he owned a black person, a man named Lewis, who was documented as part of Boon's property as late as 1852. How Boon came to be a slaveholder and what manner of slaveholder he was—and whether he ever manumitted Lewis—we do not know. Another aspect of his life that underscores how weird life could be for a free black in the antebellum South is that Boon's wife, Sarah, was the property of a resident of Louisburg when he married her. Franklin found no evidence that Boon ever bought Sarah or that her owner ever freed her. He did, however, find correspondence between Mr. and Mrs. Boon, suggesting that their son had a liberty of movement not usually accorded a slave (which is what he would have been born because it was the condition of his mother). Also, why did Boon make Raleigh home in the early 1850s and leave Sarah behind in Louisburg? Had they split up? Was business irresistibly better in Raleigh, but Sarah's owner would not permit so long a leash?

The last record of Boon's activities is dated 1857. This led John Hope Franklin to surmise that Boon did not live long after that: "It is difficult to believe that a man of his vitality and business initiative could have continued to live without intruding his name into the records of the community." Perhaps instead Boon lived long and prospered. Maybe insightful mementos of Boon's post-1857 life were, during his lifetime or years later, intentionally or accidentally rendered trash or ashes and ultimately, one way or the other, dust.

ABOUT THE RESEARCHER

John Hope Franklin (1915–), born in the all-black town of Rentiesville, Oklahoma, earned a bachelor's from Fisk University (1935) and a Ph.D. in history from Harvard University (1941). Franklin enlightened thousands of minds as a professor of history at, among other places, Fisk, North Carolina Central University, Brooklyn College, University of Chicago, and Duke University, where in the early 1980s he became the James B. Duke Professor of history and a professor of legal history at the university's law school. His books include *The Free Negro in North Carolina, 1790–1860* (1943), a biography of the pioneering historian *George Washington Williams* (1985), and *From Slavery to Freedom*, the preeminent black history textbook since its publication in 1947. Over the years, this scholar presided over several organizations, including the American Studies Association, the Southern Historical Association, and the American Historical Association. A recipient of hundreds of major awards and honors, he received the nation's highest civilian honor, the Medal of Freedom, in 1995. In 1997, President Clinton appointed Franklin chair of the advisory for the Initiative on Race and Reconciliation.

Dangerfield Newby (1815–1859)

Based on her letters, we assume that Newby's wife loved him truly. For instance, from her captivity in Brentville, Virginia, came the following letter, dated April 11, 1859:

> Dear Husband:
>
> I mus now write you apology for not writing you before this, but I know you will excuse me when I tell you Mrs. Gennings has been very sick. She has a baby—a little girl; ben a grate sufferer; her breast raised, and she has had it lanced, and I have had to stay with her day and night; so you know I had no time to write. . . . I am well. . . . I have no news to write you, only the children are all well. I want to see you very much, but am looking forward to the promest time of your coming. Oh, Dear Dangerfield, com this fall without fail, monny or no monney. I want to see you so much. That is one bright hope I have before me. Nothing more at present, but remain
>
> Your affectionate wife,
Harriet Newby
>
> P.S. Write soon, if you please.

Dear Dangerfield had been freed by his master–father and was off working at his trade as a blacksmith, saving up to buy his family.

Days must have seemed weeks must have seemed months to Harriet while apart from her Dear Dangerfield, to whom she wrote again before April was out:

> Dear Husband:
>
> I received your letter to-day, and it gives much pleasure to here from you, but was sorry to [hear] of your sikeness; hope you may be well when you receive this. . . . Dear Dangerfield, you cannot imagine how much I want to see you. Com as soon as you can, for nothing would give more pleasure than to see you. It is the grates Comfort I

have in thinking of the promist time when you will be here. Oh, that <u>bless</u> hour when I shall see you once more. My baby commenced to crall to-day; it is very delicate. Nothing more at present, but remain

Your affectionate wife,
Harriet Newby

P.S. Write soon.

Perhaps Dear Dangerfield began working overtime, anxious to see that baby, pained about how delicate the child might be. Certainly he had cause for even greater worry about his wife and seven children when he received Harriet's letter of August 16, 1859.

Dear Husband:
Your kind letter came duly to hand, and it gave me much pleasure to here from you, and especely to here you are better off [with] your rhumatism, and hope when I here from you again, you may be entirely well. I want you to buy me as soon as possible, for if you do not get me some body else will. . . . Dear Husband you [know], not the trouble I see; the last two years has ben like a trouble dream to me. It is said Master is in want of monney. If so, I know not what time he may sell me, an then all my bright hops of the futer are blasted, for their has ben one bright hope to cheer me in all my troubles, that is to be with you, for if I thought I should never see you this earth would have no charms for me. . . .

As before, Harriet Newby signed off with "Your affectionate wife,"

The daring Dangerfield Newby. (Courtesy of the Library of Congress)

and with no idea that exactly two months from the date of this letter, her Dear Dangerfield would join in an epic event: that her man with the prophetic name, her Dear Dangerfield, would be among those who saddled up with John Brown and became his raiders.

Dear Dangerfield—Had the money you saved up for Harriet and the kids been too little? Too late?

The raiders hoped to seize the United States Armory at Harpers Ferry, Virginia (now West Virginia). They planned to seize the huge stockpile of weapons, then they would deliver the weapons to enslaved people, who would wondrously, dynamically, unstoppably swell an uprising that would rush South, freeing as many slaves as possible and thereby gain more strength for the mother of freedom fights.

Dear Dangerfield—Did you get off a letter to Harriet?

The scheme seemed far-fetched to many, the obvious evidence being that John Brown wasn't even able to muster a whole two dozen men, and among those he did convince were three of his own sons. Brown's black comrades were Shields Green, a runaway from South Carolina whose nickname was "Emperor"; Lewis Sheridan Leary, a saddle and harness maker, attending Oberlin; John A. Copeland, a former student at Oberlin and Leary's nephew; Osborne P. Anderson, a freeborn of Pennsylvania who had emigrated to Canada; and of course, Dear Dangerfield.

Dear Dangerfield—Did you have a vision of Harriet and the children being among the first to be liberated?

They seized the armory all right, on the night of October 16, 1859.

Dear Dangerfield—Did you have visions of seeing your baby girl walk, and run, and smile, and your other children grow strong and proud?

John Brown and his raiders needed a miracle to execute the whole of their plan. On the morning of October 17, they were holed up in the armory, battling gunfire from the townsfolk. Once the battle ensued, some enslaved and free blacks did pitch in with pikes and other makeshift weapons, but their efforts were in vain. The whole affair became pitifully futile when President James Buchanan sent in the Marines under the command of future Commander-in-Chief of the Confederate Army Robert E. Lee, with future Confederate calvary commander J. E. B. Stuart as his second.

Dear Dangerfield—"for if I thought I should never see you this earth would have no charms for me."

Some raiders died in the armory. Some raiders escaped only to be quickly caught and killed on the gallows, as was John Brown. Only one black raider survived.

Dear Dangerfield? No, he was killed in the shootout at the armory.

After he was unmistakably dead, the townsfolk riddled his corpse with bullets, then clubbed it, then let the hogs have it—all except the ears, which were taken as souvenirs.

As for Harriet Newby, she was sold into the Deep South, and then lost to history—all except for her letters, which had been found on her Dear Dangerfield's corpse.

George Moses Horton (1797?–1883?)

Was Countee Cullen remembering especially him when he wrote the last two lines of "Yet Do I Marvel"?

> Yet do I marvel at this curious thing:
> To make a poet black, and bid him sing!

Was Paul Laurence Dunbar thinking intensely of him when he penned especially that last stanza of "Sympathy"?

> I know why the caged bird sings, ah me,
>   When his wing is bruised and his bosom sore,—
> When he beats his bars and he would be free;
> It is not a carol of joy or glee,
>   But a prayer that he sends from his heart's deep core,
> But a plea, that upward to Heaven he flings—
> I know why the caged bird sings!

Surely every poet finds his poetry a liberating experience. George Moses Horton felt so, too—only he wasn't being metaphysical.

His cage was first Northampton County, and then Chatham County, North Carolina, as property of farmer William Horton and later of his son James. George Moses Horton came to poetry through—what else—music. Jumpy tunes were his delight early on. Somewhere in there, the sound of reading also caught his ear, sparking him to strain the brain over scraps of a well-worn spelling book, often by "bark or brushlight" in the "pleasant umbrage of the woods." Thus, he learned small words that would prepare him to read and then perchance to write.

He was composing little poems as a youth, poems based on Scripture and rhythmed on Methodist hymns, poems composed only in his head and tucked there for safekeeping because his ability to write was still a ways off.

And Horton kept at it. He began crafting poems aplenty when he was about twenty, when every Sunday he made an eight-mile journey on foot to Chapel Hill to peddle produce at the University of North Carolina. Somehow, live-wire students heard of Horton's way with words (probably from Horton himself) and set about to make a bit of sport with the self-proclaimed slave–orator—but the joke was on them.

Before long, the students were hooked on Horton. Before long, Horton was peddling more poetry than produce. For a love poem or acrostic custom-made for a sweetheart, Horton's price ranged from twenty-five cents to seventy-five cents.

Sometimes Horton worked on his poetry commissions on the way back from the university; sometimes he worked on his orders in and around doing his chores on the Horton farm; and maybe he did the final editing on his way back to Chapel Hill the next Sabbath, where he recited from memory all his orders and was paid upon delivery.

He soon became a local legend: the "Colored Bard of North Carolina" his tag. To help him along his poeticizing way, his University of North Carolina fans gave him not only praise but also books, from a grammar book and a dictionary to volumes by Byron, Homer, Milton, Shakespeare, and other maestros of verse.

Even Joseph D. Caldwell, the university's president, became a patron, as did novelist Caroline Lee Hentz, wife of one of the university's professors. Hentz not only became Horton's scribe, but also his tutor in prosody; and it was she who paved the way for the first publication of Horton's work by sending several poems to Massachusetts's *Lancaster Gazette*. In the late 1820s, this newspaper published two of Horton's poems, one of which was the ten-stanza "On Liberty and Slavery":

> Alas! and am I born for this,
>   To wear this slavish chain?
> Deprived of all created bliss,
>   Through hardship, toil and pain!
>
> . . . .
>
> Come, Liberty, though cheerful sound,
>   Roll through my ravished ears!
> Come, let my grief in joys be drowned,
>   And drive away my fears.
>
> Say unto foul oppression, Cease:
>   Ye tyrants rage no more,
> And let the joyful trump of peace,
>   Now bid the vassal soar.

Caroline Hentz was a part of the small group that launched a campaign to buy Horton's freedom, a campaign the first black weekly, *Freedom's Journal*, joined in by pleading for a penny from each black New Yorker for the buying of the bard in its summer and fall issues of 1828. The fund-raising drive for Horton's manumission (and emigration to Liberia) continued into 1829, more pointedly with the publication of Horton's first volume of poems, aptly titled *Hope of Liberty*. This collection of twenty-one poems was the first book by a black man published in the South, and the third published collection of poems by a black person in the United States.

Horton's hope of liberty was dashed. Not enough money was raised, and historians suspect that his owner James Horton was not willing to part with his slave–bard anyway, even though he found him not the most productive worker. (What did he expect? The man had a Muse.)

Nonetheless, Horton kept at it, kept writing his verse, literally so by the early 1830s. It was also around 1830 that Horton took a wife, with whom he had a daughter, Rhody, and a son, Free.

A little liberty came soon. Horton's owner, having found him, according to one source, "worthless as a farm hand, since his Pegasus resolutely refused to be harnessed to a plow," allowed Horton to hire his time for twenty-five cents a day. In addition to his mainstay as poet-for-hire, Horton worked as a handyman and served the staff and students at the University of North Carolina to earn money.

Was he really any good as a poet? Hit and miss—but really, when you think about whence he came, everything he penned was in a certain light glorious. But no glory came, and in time, despair set in. Some contend that it was the death of the university's president, Caldwell, in 1835 that precipitated Horton's dissipation. Bereft of such a principle patron, Horton drifted into the blues and tried to drown his sorrows in booze.

Eventually, Horton was able to get on a good footing again. By then, his *Hope of Liberty* had seen two more printings: in 1837, under the title *Poems by a Slave*, which was then bundled with the 1838 edition of *Memoir and Poems of Phillis Wheatley*.

In 1843, Horton's owner died, and the bard soon became the property of another Horton: Hall, a tanner, who raised the hire-out fee to fifty cents. Horton still kept at it. He kept working odd jobs, kept writing for his liberty. In his quest for more publicity and help in getting out another volume of verse, he wrote to William Lloyd Garrison. This letter, dated September 3, 1844, began,

> Having of late received information . . . that you are an Editor and a lover of the genious from every tribe and population of the human race, I am necessarily constrained, to apply to your honor for assistance in carrying my original work into publick execution; while I

gratify your curiosity in resolving the problem whether a negro has any genious or not.

In 1845, through no assistance from Garrison but solely through Horton's beating the local bushes for subscriptions, his second book of poetry was published with an early sale price of fifty cents: *The Poetical Works of George M. Horton, The Colored Bard of North-Carolina, to which is Prefixed the Life of the Author, Written by Himself.* If Horton could sell around four hundred copies, perhaps he could be free, for around now, Horton could be purchased for about two hundred dollars.

It seems odd that with all those fans from the university and his celebrity in the area, it was so hard to come up with the money for his freedom. It makes you wonder whether perhaps his fans loved him most as a novelty, a curiosity. Maybe a slave–bard was a better conversation piece than a black man free to sing.

Horton still kept at it. And at it—a tireless self-promoter (and three cheers for him!)—all the more so after Hall Horton informed him in 1852 that he would sell him for sure for $250. On the wings of this news Horton wrote to the reformer and New York *Tribune* founder Horace Greeley and asked him for $175.

Had the bard come up with $75, or, had his owner dropped the purchase price? Either way, Horton must have been anxiously awaiting Greeley's response. Alas, however, Greeley never pondered the proposition of purchasing the poet. As had happened with Horton's letter to Garrison, the person who promised to post this missive did not keep his word. That person was the new president of the University of North Carolina, and the state's future governor, David Swain (whom Horton had asked on at least two occasions to purchase him, once promising Swain two thirds of the proceeds of his next book).

Horton still kept at it and at it, until April 1865, when the occupation of Chapel Hill by the Union Army's Ninth Michigan Calvary made his liberty a done deal. Among Horton's liberators was the man who became his new patron: Captain Will Banks. As Horton followed the captain about until his muster in Lexington, he composed up a storm. By summer's end, he had written a heap of poems—poems about slavery, poems about soldiers' stories, poems about war's dance and death, poems about Yankee and Rebel leaders, poems about poetry itself. In September 1865, Banks compiled and had printed a good share of these poems and some previously published verse, as evidence that "God in his gifts was in no wise partial to the Uuropean, but that he gave genius to the black as well as the white man." *Naked Genius* is the title of this collection of 132 poems, one of the most intriguing of which is the five-stanza autobiographia "George Moses Horton, Myself": which ends with these two verses:

My genius from a boy,
  Has fluttered like a bird within my heart;
But could not thus confined her powers employ,
  Impatient to depart.

She like a restless bird,
  Would spread her wing, her power to be unfurl'd,
And let her songs be loudly heard,
  And dart from world to world.

Horton settled in Philadelphia at some point in 1866, sans his wife and children. (Horton missed when it came to marital bliss.) In Philadelphia, the "Colored Bard of North Carolina" became pretty much a footnote after his attempt to get some support from some brothers. "To receive Mr. George Horton of North Carolina, a poet of considerable genius" was taken from the minutes of a special meeting held on August 31, 1866, by the Banneker Institute, formerly the Young Man's Mutual Instruction Society, founded in 1854. The institute considered publishing Horton but in the end declined, claiming cost to be the prohibiting factor. Some have said the poet was the real problem, that the Philadelphia Negroes found Horton a ball of bombast and conceit, and so, instead of a warm embrace, they gave him the cold shoulder. Considering all that Horton, now around seventy, had been through, it is too bad that the Philadelphia Negroes could not overlook the bard's excesses.

Even after death, George Moses Horton kept at it. His poetry has been included in numerous anthologies. In 1996, he was inducted into the North Carolina Literary Hall of Fame, and the following year, *The Black Bard of North Carolina: George Moses Horton and His Poetry*, edited by Joan R. Sherman, was published.

☀ Gordon

We have seen him hundreds of times—or rather, his back, with its raised crosshatch of scars, the result of the flogging he received on Christmas Day 1862. The photograph of his back is a frequent Exhibit A for the brutalities of slavery. Indeed, a drawing based on this photograph appeared in the July 4, 1863, issue of *Harper's Weekly* as part of its illustration of "the degree of brutality which slavery has developed among the whites in the section of the country from which this negro came."

That would be Mississippi, specifically. It was from there that Gor-

This photograph of Gordon was taken by C. Seaver, Jr. (Courtesy of Photographs and Prints Division, Schomburg Center for Research in Black Culture, The New York Public Library, Astor, Lenox and Tilden Foundations)

don escaped, making his way to a Union Army camp in Baton Rouge, Louisiana, in March 1863. One key to his success was a pocketful of onions. According to the *Harper's Weekly* article, to throw bloodhounds off his scent, "after crossing each creek or swamp he rubbed his body freely with these onions."

"A Typical Negro" was the headline of this article, which contained the drawing of this man's back, captioned "Gordon under medical inspection," and two other drawings: the first, "Gordon as he entered our lines," shows the subject barefoot and in rags; the second, "Gordon in his uniform as a U.S. Soldier."

Gordon served the Yankees as a guide, and while doing his duty, he was captured. Being bound, beaten, and left for dead by Rebels "infuriated beyond measure" was the price Gordon paid. Miraculously, Gordon survived and once again made his way to Union lines.

Perhaps Gordon was among those Sterling Brown had in mind when he composed the poem "Strong Men"—*The strong men keep a-comin' on/ The strong men get stronger.*

Robert Smalls (1839–1915)

"I thought the *Planter* might be of some use to Uncle Abe." This famous understatement was among the first words uttered by Robert Smalls when he handed the Union Navy a prize. The first official notice of Smalls's daring was flag officer S. F. Dupont's dispatch of May 13, 1862, to the Secretary of War.

> Sir,—I have the honor to inform you that the rebel armed gunboat "Planter" was brought out to us this morning from Charleston by eight contrabands, and delivered up to the squadron. Five colored women and three children are also on board. . . . At four in the morning, in the absence of the captain who was on shore, she left her wharf close to the government office and head-quarters, with the Palmetto and confederate flags flying, and passed the successive forts, saluting as usual, by blowing the steam-whistle. After getting beyond the range of the last gun, they hauled down the rebel flags, and hoisted a white one.

After enumerating the *Planter*'s valuable armament, Du Pont spoke on the young man from Beaufort, South Carolina, who had delivered the cache:

> Robert Small[s], the intelligent slave, and pilot of the boat, who performed this bold feet so skilfully, is a superior man to any who have come into our lines, intelligent as many of them have been. His information has been most interesting, and portions of it of the utmost importance. The steamer is quite a valuable acquisition to the squadron. . . . I do not know whether, in the view of the Government, the vessel will be considered a prize; but, if so, I respectfully submit to the Department the claims of the man Small[s] and his associates.

Smalls's share of the reward was $1,500. To this was added the honor of serving as pilot of the *Planter*, which the Union initially used for transport, as the Confederacy had. When the vessel was transformed into a gunboat, Smalls became its captain, adroitly steering it through close to twenty battles. When he wasn't in action, one of the ways Smalls spent his time was learning to read and write. He had ambitions and knew literacy was imperative.

After the war, Smalls returned to Beaufort, where he continued his course of self-improvement, acquiring more education, as well as property and shares in several businesses. In 1868, he embarked on what would be a long, distinguished political career, serving in the South Carolina Legislature and then in its Senate and then, as a U.S. Congressional Representative. Throughout, Smalls was an advocate for the neediest, black and white, pushing for legislation for such things as health care for the poor and more humane prisons. Among the issues he championed that were especially important to blacks was enforcement of the Civil Rights Act of 1875, the passage of which was in part attributable to the eloquent intelligence of his colleague **Robert Brown Elliott.** Given how dangerous it was to stand up for the oppressed,

Robert Smalls's political career required as much courage as did his snatch of the *Planter.*

☼ William H. Carney (1840–1908)

Carney, born in slavery in Norfolk, Virginia, tasted freedom at age four-teen in the mid-1850s. This freedom came for him and his mother upon their owner's death. In 1856, William's father, a free man, decided the South was no place to be somebody. He moved his family North, to New Bedford, Massachusetts. There, father and son worked at sea for a time. Then, in February 1863, at age twenty-two, William H. Carney left the sea to help others get free. He became a soldier, enlisting in the first black regiment that the Union Army raised in the North: the Fifty-fourth Regiment of Massachusetts Volunteer Infantry, commanded by a young white man, son of abolitionists, Robert Gould Shaw.

Four months after Carney enlisted, on July 18, 1863, he made his-tory in one of the epic Civil War battles: the Fifty-fourth's final charge on Charleston, South Carolina's Fort Wagner. In this battle, intended to pave the way for white troops, and in which Colonel Shaw was killed early on, some 250 of the roughly 600 black soldiers were wounded, captured, or killed—and in this battle, it was William H. Carney (not given much screen time in the 1988 film *Glory*) who picked up the flag when a standard bearer was killed.

In his book *Undying Glory* (1991), Clinton Cox chronicled the sur-rounding moments of Carney's courage with this:

> Those soldiers who managed to get into the fort now fought in a des-perate circle around Shaw's body. At first the ferocity of their charge drove the Confederates back, but more and more Rebels attacked the hopelessly outnumbered band with guns, wooden spikes, gun rammers, musket and pistol shot, and anything they could get their hands on.
> The huge cannons from Sumter, Gregg, and James Island tore into the men still struggling across the ditch and up the parapet, falling into shell holes and over the bodies of their comrades.

The grenades, the bullets, the shells, the stinking deaths, and the blood and shattered bodies—but the living turned not from their charge.

> Corporal Peal planted the tattered state flag at the top of the fort, so close to the enemy a Confederate soldier reached out and ripped it from the staff.
> John Wall struggled just past the ditch. The Stars and Stripes he carried was also in tatters, ripped by countless shells, but still he held

it high. Suddenly he was blown into the air, but before the flag could touch the earth it was grabbed by Sergeant Carney.

Carney ran up the slope and planted the flag next to the wall. While the battle raged around them, both Carney and Peal clung to the sand just outside the wall for over an hour, holding the staffs aloft.

The hell and slaughter was all the worse because white troops arrived too late (but better than never). In the confusion that followed the command "RETREAT!"—

Sergeant Carney finally saw what he thought were his comrades. Raising the flag, he stood up and moved through the smoke toward them, then suddenly realized they were Rebels.

Whirling round, Carney ran for the moat, and though two shots hit him he still held the flag up high. A soldier from the 100th New York grabbed his arm and, while stumbling through the moat, Carney was wounded in the head.

Finally the New Bedford seaman staggered back to the field hospital, still carrying the flag. Some of the wounded rose from their straw mats and cheered as he collapsed beside them, saying; "The old flag never touched the ground, boys."

And what if it had? Well, the world would not have spun off axis, and the Fifty-fourth would not have fought less bravely. Keeping the flag aloft was a sign of Carney's courage and commitment to the Union. It was his proof that he was a man in an arena men traditionally regard as *the* place for a true testing of manhood—war. Carney and the tens of thousands of other black men who fought in the Union Army believed that if they proved themselves men in battle, they would be treated as men when peacetime came. Naïve? Foolish? That's how we see it today because we know about the betrayal, the continuous efforts to beat black men down. It is difficult for us to imagine the hope that men like Carney had, that men like all those who fought in the War of 1812 had, and that hundreds of thousands of black soldiers were to have in the Spanish American War and in wars to come.

So Carney held up that flag to prove that he was a man. He held up that flag, knowing that if he perished in the process of keeping a piece of cloth from touching mud, he would be remembered as a hero, a man, and maybe his heroism would induce white men to treat his brothers as men.

This is why the battle of Fort Wagner, though tragic, represented a great day for the Fifty-fourth, a regiment that included the sons of several legends—James Caldwell, grandson of Sojourner Truth; Toussaint L'Ouverture Delany, son of Martin R. Delany; and Lewis and Charles Douglass, sons of **Frederick Douglass,** the most effective recruiter for the "Glory" corps. Carney's heroism and that of the entire regiment showed that black men had the right stuff for sure. This played an important role in the Union's decision to allow more sons of Africa to enlist, to prove themselves men.

As for Carney, he was honorably discharged in 1864 because of his wounds, and he became the first black person awarded the U.S. military's highest honor, a Congressional Medal of Honor, which he did not receive until May 1900.

After his discharge, Carney settled in California, doing what we don't know. Eventually he returned to New Bedford, where he made a living as a mail carrier, retiring from the post office in 1901 and moving to Boston. There, he was a messenger for a time at the statehouse, where, incidentally, that war-weary Stars and Stripes he didn't let touch the ground was put on permanent display.

High John the Conqueror

How they got over—and through—and beyond: Some oldheads claimed this fellow High John the Conqueror played a potent part in how many who endured the nightmare got over and through and beyond.

He was "the source and soul of our laughter and song" said Zora Neale Hurston in her prose ode "High John de Conquer." This piece first appeared in the October 1943 issue of *The American Mercury* and reads in part,

> High John de Conquer came to be a man, and a mighty man at that. But he was not a natural man in the beginning. First off, he was a whisper, a will to hope, a wish to find something worthy of laughter and song. Then the whisper put on flesh. His footsteps sounded across the world in a low but musical rhythm as if the world he walked on was a singing-drum. The black folks had an irresistible impulse to laugh. High John de Conquer was a man in full, and had come to live and work on the plantations, and all the slave folks knew him in the flesh.
>
> The sign of this man was a laugh, and his singing-symbol was a drum-beat. No parading drum-shout like soldiers out for show. It did not call to the feet of those who were fixed to hear it. It was an inside thing to live by. It was sure to be heard when and where the work was the hardest, and the lot the most cruel. It helped the slaves endure. They knew that something better was coming. So they laughed in the face of things and sang, "I'm so glad! Trouble don't last always." And the white people who heard them were struck dumb that they could laugh. In an outside way, this was Old Massa's fun, so what was Old Cuffy laughing for?

Old Massa couldn't know, of course, but High John de Conquer was there walking his plantation like a natural man. He was treading the sweat-flavored clods of the plantation, crushing out his drum tunes, and giving out secret laughter. He walked on the winds and moved fast. Maybe he was in Texas when the lash fell on a slave in Alabama, but before the blood was dry on the back he was there. A faint pulsing of a drum like a goatskin stretched over a heart, that came nearer and closer, then somebody in the saddened quarters would feel like laughing, and say, "Now, High John de Conquer, Old Massa couldn't get the best of *him*. That old John was a case!" Then everybody sat up and began to smile. Yes, yes, that was right. Old John, High John could beat the unbeatable. He was top-superior to the whole mess of sorrow. . . .

He had come from Africa. He came walking on the waves of sound. Then he took on flesh after he got here. The sea captains of ships knew that they brought slaves in their ships. They knew about those black bodies huddled down there in the middle passage, being hauled across the waters to helplessness. John de Conquer was walking the very winds that filled the sails of the ships. He followed over them like the albatross. . . .

Old Massa met our hope-bringer all right, but when Old Massa met him, he was not going by his right name. He was traveling, and touristing around the plantations as the laugh-provoking Brer Rabbit. So Old Massa and Old Miss and their young ones laughed with and at Brer Rabbit and wished him well. And all the time, there was High John de Conquer playing his tricks of making a way out of no-way. Hitting a straight lick with a crooked stick. Winning the jack pot with no other stake but a laugh. Fighting a mighty battle without outside-showing force, and winning his war from within. Really winning in a permanent way, for he was winning with the soul of the black man whole and free.

High John the Conqueror, that Lover of Song and Master of Laughter—said Zora, "Heaven arms with love and laughter those it does not wish to see destroyed"—that Trumpster, Trickster, that Hope-Bringer, that Champion, that Survivor and Winner-from-Within and so a member of the "Be" class, said Zora—"*Be* here when the ruthless man comes, and *be* here when he is gone." That High John the Conqueror, t'aint no wonder he got a root named after him: *Ipomoea jalapa,* in the morning glory family. Since the days of captivity many have sworn that this root can make a mighty mojo for power and prosperity. That this root can help a man charm a woman makes sense, considering how easy it is to fall in love with High John the Conqueror, the pressed-together essence of all the black men who have helped their people get over and through and beyond.

Jourdon Anderson

We have stories of those flatly befuddled by freedom. They had never nerved to run away from bondage. During all the fluxing chaos of the War of the Rebellion, they didn't dare dash for freedom. At war's end, when they had no choice but to be free, they were bereft of inner heft to forge their own destiny.

So many were so bottom-barrel poor, illiterate, maybe severely ailing from years of back-lashed labor. Certainly spirit-broken such souls must have been who decided to stay on with Massa and settle for a new servitude.

There were others, however, troops of others, whose self survived slavery, who at the first full chance made like a bat out of hell from the plantation, the farm, the backside of the cabinetmaker's shop. Such a one was Jourdon Anderson, once enslaved in Big Spring, Tennessee. He flashed away during the war and resettled himself and his family in Dayton, Ohio. Somehow, his former owner, Colonel P. H. Anderson, got wind of his whereabouts and got in touch, asking him to come back home. The former slave must have been a stout worker. Why else would the colonel have wanted him back?

Thankfully, Jourdon Anderson was not a fool, as we see in his letter of reply to the colonel, dated August 7, 1865, and first collected in Lydia Maria Child's *The Freedmen's Book* (1865). The letter's opening was nice enough:

> Sir: I got your letter, and was glad to find that you had not forgotten Jourdon, and that you wanted me to come back and live with you again, promising to do better for me than anybody else can.

Right soon, he spoke directly to the colonel's petition.

> I want to know particularly what the good chance is you propose to give me. I am doing tolerably well here. I get twenty-five dollars a month, with victuals and clothing; have a comfortable home for Mandy,—the folks call her Mrs. Anderson,—and the children—Milly, Jane, and Grundy—go to school and are learning well. . . . Now if you will write and say what wages you will give me, I will be better able to decide whether it would be to my advantage to move back again.
>
> As to my freedom, which you say I can have, there is nothing to be gained on that score, as I got my freedom papers in 1864 from the Provost-Marshal-General of the Department of Nashville. Mandy says she would be afraid to go back without some proof that you were disposed to treat us justly and kindly; and we have concluded to test your sincerity by asking you to send us our wages for the time we served you.

This man was not talking abstraction. When it came to all his years of unpaid labor, he had done a reckoning.

> I served you faithfully for thirty-two years, and Mandy twenty years. At twenty-five dollars a month for me, and two dollars a week for Mandy, our earnings would amount to eleven thousand six hundred and eighty dollars. Add to this the interest for the time our wages have been kept back, and deduct what you paid for our clothing, and three doctor's visits to me, and pulling a tooth for Mandy, and the balance will show what we are in justice entitled to.

One imagines the colonel turning beet red, and there may have been gnashing of teeth at this:

> Please send the money by Adam's Express, in care of V. Winters, Esq., Dayton, Ohio. If you fail to pay us for our faithful labors in the past, we can have little faith in your promises in the future. We trust the good Maker has opened your eyes to the wrongs which you and your fathers have done to me and my fathers, in making us toil for you for generations without recompense. . . . Surely there will be a day of reckoning for those who defraud the laborer of his hire.

After a few more lines of pointed inquiry, Jourdon Anderson brought his letter to a close with this: "Say howdy to George Carter, and thank him for taking the pistol from you when you were shooting at me."

Isaac Myers (1835–1891)

> To understand black is to understand work—and the denial of work.
> —LERONE BENNETT, JR., *The Shaping of Black America* (1991)

Meyers, a freeborn Baltimorean, rose from being an apprentice to an African American caulker to being proprietor of his own shop. Personal prosperity, however, was not enough for him. He felt a burden for his brothers who were underemployed and underpaid.

The event that spurred him to action was a strike by white caulkers in October 1865. Their big grievance was the employment of blacks on the waterfront. When the strikers were successful, Myers spearheaded a movement of independence.

Chesapeake Marine Railway and Drydock was the cooperative Myers helped start, in February 1866, with ten thousand dollars from black investors and another thirty thousand Myers borrowed. Long before the company was a year old, it was employing three hundred workers at what was considered decent wages in those days: three dollars a day. One of the outgrowths of this successful enterprise was the

Colored Caulkers' Trade Union Society, which Myers organized in 1868, serving as its first president.

While deeply into black self-help, Myers, an optimist, believed that in the battle against capital, the greatest good for the greatest number would result from solidarity between black and white workers. Myers's chance to make a public pitch for this came in August 1869. The occasion was the third annual convention of the largest labor union of the time: the National Labor Union (NLU). It was before this huge assembly that Myers, one of the handful of black invitees, said,

> I speak today for the colored men of the whole country, from the lakes to the Gulf—from the Atlantic to the Pacific—from every hill-top, valley and plain throughout our vast domain, when I tell you that all they ask for themselves is a fair chance; that you shall be no worse off by giving them that chance; that you and they will dwell in peace and harmony together; that you and they may make one steady and strong pull until the laboring men of this country shall receive such pay for time made as will secure them a comfortable living for their families, educate their children and leave a dollar for a rainy day and old age.

Myers's handsome words fell on deaf ears. Lip service was all the NLU was going to give when it came to welcoming black workers into its fold. In the face of this defeat, Myers did what untold numbers of blacks have done in the face of exclusion: He started his own association.

With Isaac Myers as its first president, the Colored National Labor Union (CNLU) formed in December 1869, at the first black national labor convention. To Washington, D.C., came some two hundred representatives from twenty-one states to build up organizations that would have, as the CNLU constitution stated, "for their object the amelioration and advancement of those who labor."

The CNLU, which did not discriminate "as to nationality, sex, or color" was not solely concerned with laborers and artisans. It also championed the cause of agricultural workers. In fact, one of its first acts was to petition Congress on their behalf. To mitigate against the rampant exploitation of black agricultural workers in the South, the CNLU proposed that the government help huge numbers of freedpersons become independent farmers by granting them forty-acre tracts of public land (no mule mentioned) in states that had an abundance of such. In states where public land was not plentiful, the labor union proposed that the government offer forty-acre tracts at a modest price and under a reasonable payment plan. The CNLU argued that this would "place the colored agricultural worker's labor beyond the absolute control of artificial or political cause, by lessening the amount of labor *for hire,* and increasing at the same time the demand for that class of laborers." As the demand for farmworkers increased, inevitably so would their wages.

Under Myers's leadership, the CNLU beavered away at organizing state and city auxiliaries and campaigned for new labor legislation and government aid for education. "The servants, the sweepers of shavings, the scrapers of pitch, and carriers of mortars" would be the black man's lot, Myers contended in his efforts to rally workers to organize.

No mountains moved, but the CNLU effected some small gains, especially in the consciousness of many black workers, whom white unions were increasingly locking out of apprenticeships and prime jobs in factories and shops. Unfortunately, by 1872, the CNLU was out of business. Insufficient funds was a major factor in its demise.

Myers still continued to help his people help themselves after the CNLU closed shop. For one, in 1875, he cofounded the Colored Men's Progressive and Co-Operative Union, aiming (1) to secure equal advantages in schools of all grades, from the primary school to the university; (2) to secure full and complete recognition of our civil rights, and to defend by all proper means any abridgement of the same; (3) to use all justifiable means to obtain for our children admission into the workshops of our country, that they may obtain a practical knowledge of all mechanical branches of business; and (4) to labor for the moral and social elevation of our people.

John Henry

Among the treasures in Henry Chase's *In Their Footsteps: The American Visions Guide to African-American Heritage Sites* is an entry on tributes to John Henry in Talcott, West Virginia:

In the 1870s, laborers for the Chesapeake and Ohio Railroad drove a tunnel nearly a mile through the hard red shale of West Virginia's Big Bend Mountain. The tunneling entailed hammering steel spikes by hand into hard rock and breaking it apart preparatory to blasting. Though arduous, it was even more dangerous, and reportedly one in five of the laborers died under the fall of rocks before daylight could be seen clear through the mountain. Legend ascribes the Big Bend Tunnel as the site of John Henry's competition with a steam drill: "The men that made that steam drill / thought it mighty fine; / John Henry drove his 14 feet / While the steam drill made only nine. . . . John Henry was a steel-drivin' man." Even if he was created by Luddite legend, John Henry is representative, for many of the project's laborers were African Americans—and though many may have welcomed a machine that reduced the intensity of their labor, few could have welcomed the resulting reduction of jobs made the more hard to come by because of their race. Today, near the entrance to the tunnel, a John Henry statue, a commemorative marker, and a park pay homage to the man—or in any event, to an authentic American folk song celebrating the physical prowess of a black man.

Indeed, hard work is admirable, and physical prowess has its place, but the rest of John Henry's story reminds us that if not combined with wisdom, it can lead to a dead end, literally, for in besting the machine, John Henry killed himself. While he had a heart attack, the steam drill lived to work another day.

This, too, is representative of the experiences of so many black men in America: those men who, due to unfair wages and shutouts from high-paying jobs, had to work so hard (sometimes two or three jobs) just to make ends meet, and thereby worked themselves into an early grave.

The other moral of the legend of John Henry is that you can't fight progress, and so you need to think ahead if you hope to survive and possibly prosper. For this, mental muscle becomes far more useful than physical strength. Imagine the dividends (not to mention additional years on Earth) John Henry might have reaped if, instead of competing with the steam drill, he had been able to create or invest in a company that manufactured them.

 ## Nat Love (1854–1921)

Billy the Kid, Buffalo Bill, Kit Carson, Bat Masterson, and the James Brothers: These were, Nat Love claimed, some of the legends of the Old West he knew. And his own life story—according to his telling—gives flesh and sweat to all those old notions about the "Wild, Wild West."

Nat Love was born in slavery in Davidson County, near Nashville, Tennessee. He left home in 1869, when he was around fifteen years old, striking out for Kansas, where cattle was becoming King, now that the Ironhorse was gaining ground. Love joined up with cattle rangers from the Lone Star state, after proving himself bully-bronco by riding the rambunctious steed Good Eye. The camp boss named Nat Love "Red River Dick," and outfitted him in everything he'd need to be a real cowboy. With his new saddle, chaps, spurs, and a Colt .45 revolver, Red River Dick was ready to go, and set. He became a grade-A brand reader and known for other things, as well: for his eagle-eye aim in shooting contests, for riding his horse into a saloon and ordering drinks for two, for surviving a buffalo stampede—a "maddened, plunging, snorting,

One of the photographs Nat Love included in his autobiography. His caption was, "In my fighting clothes." (Author's collection)

bellowing mass of horns and hoofs," as he described his four-footed foes—and for riding a hundred miles without a saddle during his escape from Yellow Dog's tribe.

It was in the spring of 1876 that Nat Love came into the name "Deadwood Dick." His outfit had been given the duty of corralling three thousand head of steer up to Deadwood, South Dakota. After the men completed their mission, they naturally were free for a little fun in town. A piece of action was a contest with the town's toughs: who could make the best time in roping, throwing, tying, bridling, saddling, and mounting a wild mustang—the most vicious of which Love claimed fell to none other than him.

With the crisp crack of a .45, the race was on. Twelve minutes, thirty seconds was the time for the fellow who came in second, whereas Love subdued his mustang in "exactly nine minutes from the crack of the gun." How did the townsfolk react to this out-of-towner grabbing the victory? "Right there the assembled crowd named me Deadwood Dick and proclaimed me champion roper of the western cattle country."

After a passel more years of a rough, roving life, Deadwood Dick went domestic in Denver. On the heels of marriage to a gal named Alice in 1889, Love traded in the trails for the rails. His job as a Pullman porter became the new pride of his life, and in it, he was, of course, a marvel.

A kinder, gentler, less wild and woolly Nat Love. (Author's collection)

Love lassoed his outsized cowboy life and his adventures on the railroad into an autobiography, which he published himself in 1907: *The Life and Adventures of Nat Love, Better Known in the Cattle Country as "Deadwood Dick," Written by Himself: A True History of Slavery Days, Life on the Great Cattle Ranges and on the Plains of the "Wild and Woolly" West, Based on Facts, and Personal Experiences of the Author.*

SOME OTHER LEGENDS OF THE OLD WEST

- Bass Reeves (1840–1910) was a six-foot-tall, broad-backed former slave who began a sterling career as a man of the badge in 1875, when he signed on as a deputy marshall in the Indian Territory (later Oklahoma). During his forty years as a law officer, Reeves almost always got his man, more by guile than by gun. In admitting that he shot fourteen men during the course of his duties, he stressed that each one of them had drawn first.

- Isom Dart (1849–1900), whose real name was Ned Huddleton, was a former slave from Arkansas who became a jack of many trades: rodeo clown in Texas and Mexico; prospector and broncobuster in Colorado. The skill he really mastered, however, was cattle rustling. He worked out of Brown's Park, Colorado—first with a Mexican fellow and later with the Gault gang. A hired gun's bullet in Dart's back led to Dart's early retirement from a life of crime.

- Ben Hodges (1856–1929), who was half-Mexican, was a notorious card shark, cattle thief, and con artist, whose base of operations was Dodge City.

 # George Washington (1817–1905)

He did not father a nation, but he did found a town, a pretty impressive feat considering his beginnings. This George Washington, born in Frederick County, Virginia, was the son of an enslaved man and a white woman. Soon after the baby was born, his father (whose name was Washington) was sold far away, and his mother gave him to a childless white couple, James and Anna Cochran, who named the boy George. Both the birth and the adoption remind us that there were a lot of twists and turns and many grays in black–white relations in the past, just as today.

In the early 1820s, the Cochrans and little George moved to Ohio, and a few years later to Missouri. There, George became quite the master of many trades. With strong steady hands and eagle eyes, he was a crack shot. He was adept at spinning, weaving, tailoring, tanning, cooking, and several other arts and trades. The long, tall lad also learned his letters and how to figure, and during his days in Missouri, he became an expert lumberjack and operator of a sawmill.

In 1850, when George Washington was in his early thirties, he and the Cochrans moved farther west, on a wagon-train journey four months long to Oregon Territory. There, after a time, Washington claimed for himself 640 acres close-by where the rivers Chehalis and Skookumchuck meet. Because of the territory's prohibition against blacks owning land, Washington's father had to file the claim. His father didn't have to front for him forever, though: Thanks to a petition sponsored by some white settlers who'd taken a shine to Washington, he was allowed to own the land outright by a special decree of the Oregon Legislature.

Washington got along quite well over the years, taking care of the Cochrans until their dying days. He became a family man in 1869, when he married an octoroon ("three-quarters Jewish") born in Louisiana. Her name was Mary Jane Cooness (or Coonness) and she had a young son named Stacey by a previous relationship. When George and Mary Jane married, he became to Stacey all that the child could want in a father.

The Washingtons prospered through the output of the farm and through other enterprises Washington managed on the side. Washington's land became more valuable in 1872, when the Northern Pacific

Railroad laid tracks across it for its Kalama–Tacoma run. The arrival of the railroad gave Washington—the sharp, capable, industrious old soul, always ready to try his hand at something new—an idea: a town, situated midway between Kalama and Tacoma. Centerville seemed a logical name to Washington, and he moved his idea into a reality in January 1875.

Acquiring more land was no problem, and to attract town dwellers, Washington offered lots at the modest price of ten dollars, provided that settlers build homes worth at least a hundred dollars. In 1876, Centerville had about fifty residents.

To get the town rooted and grounded, Washington donated land and money for a Baptist church (hewing the wood for the rafters himself) and a cemetery. As the town grew in population and geography, Washington did more to make it a proper little town, including developing a town square. To accommodate newcomers not ready to be home owners, he put up small homes for rental (six or seven dollars a month). In 1883, Centerville got a new name, the name it still bears today: Centralia. By the late 1880s, the town was getting fat (population about nine hundred), and Washington was a happy man, who was generous to the misfortunate and merciful to debtors, and whose laughter could be "heard a block away," wrote Herndon Smith in *Centralia: The First Fifty Years* (1942).

In 1889, the same year that Washington's chunk of the Oregon Territory became part of the new state of Washington, some serious sadness came: George Washington's beloved wife died, and not long after her death, Stacey married and started a family of his own. George Washington wasn't a widower but for a minute, though. In 1890, he married the woman who did his washing, Charity E. Brown, a widow with several wee ones. Near the close of 1891, when George was seventy-three, he and Charity had a wee one: a boy, named after his father and Grover Cleveland, whose first term as President had ended in 1889, and who had not shown himself to be a great friend of the Negro. Nonetheless, maybe naming his son after a president made George Washington feel more American, or maybe he was just trying to follow a family tradition of presidential naming. Whatever.

George Cleveland Washington was only months old when Washington found himself a single father in the wake of the dissolution of his and Charity's union. He suffered more trouble in the 1890s. Between the panic of 1893 and the change of the railroad route, Centralia was in jeopardy of becoming a ghost town. To check the exodus, Washington brought in wagon loads of meat, rice, sugar, and other staples, which he distributed to the many needy, and what jobs he could create, he did. In saving the citizens, he saved his town.

The town—from the beginning and always majority white—mourned greatly when George Washington died at age eighty-eight, from injuries sustained in a horse-and-buggy accident. By mayoral decree, businesses in Centralia closed on the day of the town founder's funeral in the church he had helped establish and his burial in the cemetery on land he had donated.

ANOTHER GEORGE WASHINGTON

George Washington, a former slave in Missouri, struck gold in central Idaho's Sawtooth Mountains in the 1860s and then made his money work for him by investing in real estate. Central Idaho's Washington Lake, Washington Peak, and Washington Basin were named after him.

 # Sydenham Porter

The defeated former Rebels were determined to destroy Reconstruction, the promise of a more equitable nation. They were determined to see the Old South rise again. They used force, fraud, and brainwashing—and here, they had help from folks like former slave Sydenham Porter.

One way this resident of Livingston, Alabama, aided white supremacists was with a speech he delivered on July 18, 1868. In it, Porter chastised Negroes for having truck with the Republicans (those "scalawags and carpet-bag politicians"). He exhorted his people to pursue goodwill and peace with white Southerners. This is some of what he said:

> We have turned our backs on those that we have been raised with, and who support us, and followed after strangers who done nothing for us. This is the reason we are no better off to-day, and there is such a bad state of things.
>
> The only way for us to get along and do well is let politics alone and go to work to gather crops that are now growing, and have something to live on. Politics is a thing we know nothing about; and if we did, it is a mighty unprofitable business. . . . Let us respect everybody's opinion, and have harmony and good feeling between all, especially with those who have known us since childhood till the present hour. They are the ones that have helped and assisted us, and all the money I have made since I have been free come from them. We must continue to live together, and unless there is good feeling between us, it is impossible for us to prosper, make money or a living. If we desire peace and prosperity, let us say or do nothing that will stir bad feeling. He who looks back at the past and talks about our bondage does not love peace and har-

mony. We must look ahead and do our duty in the future. We must also recollect if anybody is to blame for our bondage, it is all the people of the United States, and not the southern people alone.

Then let us let politics alone, go to work, and cherish good and kind feeling toward our old friends.

Was Porter an aberration? Not hardly. Just as there are today, in Porter's time, there were folks who were hunky-dory with the status quo, and who purported that if blacks would only be good and prove themselves worthy, white folks would reward them. Of course, the chief early twentieth-century champion of accommodation was **Booker T. Washington,** but he was not the rank sellout that Porter seems to have been, at least judging by his speech and comments by **John Childers,** which suggest Porter was solely out for personal gain.

 # John Childers

Like **Sydenham Porter,** Childers was a resident of Livingston, Alabama, and a former slave. Whether he heard Porter's speech in July 1868, we do not know—but we do know that he was among those who testified in November 1871 before the Congressional Committee investigating, at the behest of President Grant, allegations of Southerners tampering with Reconstruction.

At the top of his testimony, Childers spoke of a punishment his daughter received from a Mr. Jones, whose baby she tended. What had the girl done?

> She had taken the baby out to the front yard among a parcel of arbor vitae; and, being out there, the baby and she together, she was neglectful, so as to leave the baby's cap out where it was not in place when the mother of the child called for the cap, and it could not be found.

For this, Childers's nine-year-old daughter was "awfully badly" whipped and died several days later. "I aimed to prosecute him at the last gone court," Childers testified, "but the witnesses, by some means or other, was run away."

When the subject turned to politics, Childers spoke of the pressure black men were under to make a mockery of their right to vote.

Q: Did you ever hear any threats made by democrats against Negroes of what would be done if they voted the radical ticket?
A: I have had threats on myself. I can tell them.
Q: What kind of threats were made to you?
A: I have had threats if we all would vote the democratic ticket we

would be well thought of, and the white men of the country . . . would protect us; and every struggle or trouble we got into we could apply to them for protection, and they would assist us.

Q: Where did you hear that said?

A: I have heard it often. At the last [governor's] election it was given to me. There was a man standing here in the court-house door; when he started to the ballot-box he told me he had a coffin already made for me, because he thought I was going to vote the radical ticket.

Q: Who was that man?

A: Well, I am afraid to tell his name, sir. . . .

Q: Did you hear any other Negroes threatened?

A: Well, there was so many of them threatened, I could not say. It was just as drinking is for such things as that to be. . . .

Q: I have heard that a great many colored people voted the democratic ticket at the last governor's election.

A: Yes, sir.

Q: What made them do it?

A: For fear. I voted it myself. I voted the democratic ticket.

Q: Were you afraid if you voted the radical ticket you would be harmed?

A: I was, sir; because, as I just stated to you, there was a man told me he had a coffin already made for me. . . .

Q: Do you know this **Sydenham Porter**?

A: Yes, sir; I am well acquainted with him. I have known him for fifteen years.

Q: He votes the democratic ticket, does he not?

A: Yes, sir.

Q: They think a good deal of him?

A: Yes, sir.

Q: Put him up to speak in their political meetings, do they not?

A: Yes, sir, they do. He is something superior to the balance of the colored people in the community.

Q: By whom is he employed; what does he follow for a living?

A: Well, sir, he isn't employed particularly by no one; he was so well helped up that he works his own scales; he has a little shebang of his own running.

Q: What is that?

A: Selling whiskey and other things.

Q: Do the white democrats patronize—go there and drink his whiskey?

A: I don't know whether they do. He is out in the out edge of town; I never go to his house.

Q: Does he seem to have plenty of money and dress well?

A: Yes, sir, he does. . . .

Q: So far as your acquaintance with your people goes, how many of

them do you think would vote the democratic ticket, if left to themselves?

A: Not one, sir. Not a single one. . . .

Q: How many of your people in this country do you think have been
whipped, or otherwise outraged because of their political sentiments?

A: O, hundreds. I could not number them to you, sir.

Q: Can you name any other colored men that voted the democratic
ticket for the same reason you did—prominent colored men?

A: I never questioned them, sir, what was their reasons for voting it,
but I heard of all such threats and inducements that were given to
influence them to vote the democratic ticket. I could not say that
any other man besides myself did it for the same reason I did?

Q: But that is your belief?

A: Yes, sir, that is it. I voted it, and I don't pretend to deny it before
nobody. When I was going to the polls there was a man standing in
the door and says, "Here comes you, God damn your soul, I have
got a coffin already made for you." I had two tickets in my pocket
then; a democratic ticket and a radical ticket; I pulled out the democratic ticket and showed it to him, and he says, "You are all
right, go on."

Would we find Childers a more "all right" guy had he whipped out
his Republican ticket and risked making his wife a widow? Some
would say that even though he bowed to the pressure, Childers is a
hero. At least he had the courage to testify; and surely, were he alive
today, he would be appalled that so many do not exercise their right to
vote when doing so involves no death threats, no jeopardy at all.

 # Robert Brown Elliott (1842–1884)

[He] was to me a most grateful surprise, and in fact a marvel. Upon
sight and hearing of this man I was chained to the spot with admira-
tion and a feeling akin to wonder.
FREDERICK DOUGLASS

Elliott was among the many who disproved propaganda that black Reconstruction politicians were buffoons and worse. He is among the
men (far right) in the famous 1872 Currier & Ives lithograph "The First
Colored Senator and Representatives."

"Elliott was a man of fine personal presence, dark brown in color,
and with a manner that suggested precision and culture," we read in

ROBERT C. DE LARGE, M.C. of S.Carolina.   JEFFERSON H. LONG, M.C. of Georgia

U.S. Senator H.R REVELS, of Mississippi   BENJ. S. TURNER, M.C. of Alabama.   JOSIAH T. WALLS, M.C. of Florida.   JOSEPH H. RAINY, M.C. of S.Carolina.   R BROWN ELLIOT, M.C. of S.Carolina.

THE FIRST COLORED SENATOR AND REPRESENTATIVES.
In the 41ˢᵗ and 42ⁿᵈ Congress of the United States.

NEW YORK. PUBLISHED BY CURRIER & IVES, 125 NASSAU STREET.

(Courtesy of Photographs and Prints Division, Schomburg Center for Research in Black Culture, The New York Public Library, Astor, Lenox and Tilden Foundations)

Benjamin Brawley's *Negro Builders and Heroes* (1937). "He was temperate in his personal habits, though generous to a fault in dealing with his friends. As a speaker he had firm mastery of the principles of organization; he had also a fine conception of style and the special gift of a vein of irony." He was smart, too, and, boy, was he brave, publicly decrying Klan violence, saying nay to amnesty for former Confederate leaders—this in South Carolina, the state that seceded first and was one of the most hellish for blacks in post–Civil War America.

What's more, Elliott was not a South Carolinian himself, not even a Southerner. For the longest time, he was thought to have been born in Jamaica, West Indies, then it was Boston, and now it's Liverpool, England. Some sources say he attended Eton; others say he did not. What is not disputed is that this lawyer was a most erudite man, for whom Boston was home in the mid-1860s.

By 1868, however, Elliott was living in South Carolina. There, in addition to his law practice, he served as associate editor of the *South Carolina Leader* and organized for the Republican Party. He held various political offices from 1868 to 1876: representative of Edgefield City;

assistant adjutant general of the state militia; member of the United States House of Representatives (two terms); and in 1874, he was elected to the South Carolina House of Representatives, serving as speaker until 1876.

Elliott's moment of greatest majesty came on January 6, 1874, when he rose to defend Charles Sumner's Civil Rights Bill. The bill's chief opponent in Congress was the former Vice President of the Confederacy, Alexander H. Stephens, of Georgia.

Elliott opened with this:

> While I am sincerely grateful for this high mark of courtesy that has been accorded to me by this House, it is a matter of regret to me that it is necessary at this day that I should rise in the presence of an American Congress to advocate a bill which simply asserts equal rights and equal public privileges for all classes of American citizens. I regret, sir, that the dark hue of my skin may lend a color to the imputation that I am controlled by motives personal to myself in my advocacy of this great measure of national justice. Sir, the motive that impels me is restricted by no such narrow boundary, but is as broad as your Constitution. I advocate it, sir, because it is right.

Elliott then proceeded to recount the role black men played in the making of the nation:

> In the events that led to the achievement of American Independence the Negro was not an inactive or unconcerned spectator. He bore his part bravely upon many battle fields, although uncheered by that certain hope of political elevation which victory would secure for the white man. The tall granite shaft, which a grateful State has reared above its sons who fell in defending Fort Griswold against the attack of Benedict Arnold, bears the name of Jordan, Freeman, and other brave men of the African race who there cemented with their blood the corner-stone of the Republic. In the State which I have the honor in part to represent the rifle of the black man rang out against the troops of the British crown in the darkest days of the American Revolution.

Elliott also recalled black patriotism during the War of 1812, reminding his audience of the regiment that drove back the British at the battle of New Orleans, a regiment later praised by their general, Andrew Jackson—the nation's seventh president.

Next came Elliott's astute counter to the opposition's primary contention about the bill—namely, that it would trample on states' rights. Said Elliott,

> I cannot assent to any such proposition. The constitution of a free government ought always to be constructed in favor of human rights. Indeed, the thirteenth, fourteenth, and fifteenth amendments, in positive words, invest Congress with the power to protect the citizen in his civil and political rights.

Further on, he said,

> There are privileges and immunities which belong to me as a citizen of
> the United States and there are other privileges and immunities which
> belong to me as a citizen of my State. The former are under the pro-
> tection of the Constitution and laws of the United States, and the lat-
> ter are under the protection of the constitution and laws of my State.
> But what of that? Are the rights which I now claim—the right to enjoy
> the common public conveniences of travel on public highways, of rest
> and refreshment at public inns, of education in public schools, of bur-
> ial in public cemeteries—rights which I hold as a citizen of the United
> States or of my State? Or, to state the question more exactly, is not
> the denial of such privileges to me a denial to me of the equal protec-
> tion of the laws? For it is under this clause of the fourteenth amend-
> ment that we place the present bill, no State shall "deny to any person
> within its jurisdiction the equal protection of the laws." No matter,
> therefore, whether his rights are held under the United States or
> under his particular State, he is equally protected by this amend-
> ment. He is always and everywhere entitled to the equal protection of
> the laws. All discrimination is forbidden; and while the rights of citi-
> zens of a State as such are not defined or conferred by the Constitu-
> tion of the United States, yet all discrimination, all denial of equality
> before the law, all denial of the equal protection of the laws, whether
> State or national laws, is forbidden.

Near the end of his very long speech, Elliott declared,

> Never was there a bill more completely within the constitutional power
> of Congress. Never was there a bill which appealed for support more
> strongly to that sense of justice and fair-play which has been said,
> and in the main with justice, to be a characteristic of the Anglo-Saxon
> race. The Constitution warrants it; the Supreme Court sanctions it;
> justice demands it.

Elliott's eloquence was a major factor in the passage of the bill,
signed into law on March 1, 1875, as the Civil Rights Act, the pinnacle
of which was "that all persons within the jurisdiction of the United
States shall be entitled to the full and equal enjoyment of the accommodations, advantages, facilities, and privileges of inns, public
conveyances on land or water, theaters, and other places of public
amusement." This was to be applicable to "citizens of every race, color,
regardless of any previous condition of servitude." Anyone who violated
this law could suffer a fine of "not less than five hundred nor more
than one thousand dollars," or be imprisoned "not less than thirty days
nor more than one year."

What a great victory for African Americans, but the forces of evil
kept busy: so many white folks violated the law right and left with im-
punity. Elliott, too, kept busy. In 1876, he made an unsuccessful bid
for state attorney general. His continued activity in politics was heroic,

to say the least, considering all the white-hot hatred he incurred, hatred that did not take his life but sorely affected his livelihood: "Utterly unable to earn a living owing to the severe ostracism and mean prejudice of my political opponents" is how he summed up his situation in a letter to Secretary of the Treasury John Sherman. At the heart of his letter was a request for an appointment of some kind. Inspector of Customs in Charleston was Sherman's response.

Another majestic moment came for Elliott in early January 1881, when he served as the spokesperson for a delegation of eleven black Republicans from the South, who went to the nation's capital seeking government help in relieving some of the griefs of their people. The addressee was President-elect James Garfield.

After congratulating Garfield on his "triumphant election," Elliott said, "Although clothed with the rights of citizenship by all the provisions of the Constitution of the United States . . . yet still in all the Southern States we are but citizens in name and not in fact." As an example, Elliott turned to the issue of voting: "Our right to participate in elections for the choice of public offices is not only questioned, but, in many localities, absolutely denied us by means of armed violence, fraud and intimidation." Elliott went on to explain that when it came to voting and other issues, blacks were rarely able to get any redress from the courts, "for to all intents and purposes they are organized against us." Further on in his address, Elliott mentioned "the want of proper educational facilities for our children" and urged the creation of "a national system of education for the toiling masses, under the supervision and control of the Federal Government."

The forces of evil kept busy. Black life in America became no easier. One piece of evidence is that in 1881, the same year Elliott addressed President Garfield, roughly five thousand black people fled the terror and oppression of Edgefield, South Carolina, the town Elliott once represented. The fact that they moved to Alabama tells us that things must have been pretty bad. Life for blacks all over America got worse in 1883, the year before Elliott died, for it was in this year that the U.S. Supreme Court declared the Civil Rights Act of 1875 unconstitutional.

BOOK MARK

- *Black Reconstruction in America*, by W. E. B. Du Bois (1935)

- *Reconstruction After the Civil War*, by John Hope Franklin (1961)

- *Reconstruction: America's Unfinished Revolution, 1863–1877*, by Eric Foner (1988), who also wrote *Freedom's Lawmakers: A Directory of Black Officeholders During Reconstruction* (revised edition, 1996)

- *The Glorious Failure: Black Congressman Robert Brown Elliott and the Reconstruction in South Carolina*, by Peggy Lamson (1973)

- *The Trouble They Seen: The Story of Reconstruction in the Words of African Americans*, edited by Dorothy Sterling (1976)

Edward M. Bannister (1828–1901)

Among the events surrounding America's celebration of her one hundredth birthday was the Philadelphia Centennial Exposition's art show, in which a first-place medal went to a man who signed his paintings "EM Bannister." The award was for his oil painting *Under the Oaks.*

This painting is now lost, but we have a description of it in *Frank Leslie's Illustrated Historical Register of the Centennial Exposition.* According to this publication, *Under the Oaks* was "quite a startling representation of a grove of old gnarled oaks, beneath which a shepherd watches a small flock of sheep browsing on the slight declivity which leads to a quiet pool in the foreground. These trees are painted with such wonderful closeness to nature as to fairly stand out from the gray-and-white background of the sky as though in relief."

Under the Oaks bore witness to Bannister's attraction to the work of Jean-François Millet and other artists of the Barbizon school. The fact that an award was bestowed on a work that rebelled against the strict realism that dominated landscape painting was not insignificant. As Lynda Roscoe Hartigan noted in *Sharing Traditions: Five Black Artists in Nineteenth-Century America* (1985), it "signaled official recognition of American landscape painting's new direction and foretold its dominance among American artists and patrons until the 1890s." The award was also a big deal in black America. Edward Mitchell Bannister was the first of the race to receive an award from a national art show.

One of the oft-told stories about events surrounding this historic moment is what happened when Bannister went to verify that he was indeed a winner. It's one of those classic stories, to which many blacks have been able to relate, like the CEO or professor or whatever who shows up at some office for a meeting and is taken to be the messenger. Bannister recounted the incident to a white friend, fellow artist George Whitaker, who subsequently repeated Bannister's words in his "Reminiscences of Providence Artists."

I later learned from a newspaper . . . that "54" had received a first prize medal. I hurried to the committee room to make sure the report was true. A great crowd was there ahead of me, and as I jostled through this many resented my presence, some actually commenting within my hearing, in a most petulant manner asking, "Why is this colored person here?"

Finally I succeeded in reaching the desk where inquiries were to be made and endeavored to gain the attention of the official. He was very insolent. Without more than raising his eyes he demanded in a most exasperating tone of voice, "Well, what do you want here anyway? Speak lively."

"I want to inquire concerning 54. Is it a prize winner?" I replied.

"What's that to you?" he said.

In an instant my blood was up. The looks that passed between that official and the others were unmistakable in their meaning. To them I was a not an artist; simply an inquisitive colored man. Controlling myself I said with deliberation, "I am interested in the report that *Under the Oaks* has received a prize. I painted that picture."

The explosion of a bomb could not have created more of a sensation in that room. Without hesitation the official apologized to me and soon all were bowing and scraping to me.

Under the Oaks was sold to a white Bostonian for a handsome sum: $1,500, of which Bannister received $850. Like the award, this sale was a tremendous career boost, as it signaled that Bannister's talent was valued in the white art world.

Bannister's talent had long been prized by the black community, ever since he started pursuing art seriously in Boston in the 1850s. He had come to Boston from St. Andrews in New Brunswick, Canada, where he was born and where, as a boy, he developed a love for art. It was a passion applauded by his mother. "It was she," said Bannister, "who encouraged and fostered my childish propensities for drawing and coloring."

After his mother died in 1844 (his father had died in 1830), Bannister was hired out to Harris Hatch, a wealthy lawyer. In and around his chores, Ned, as he was known, spent time in his employer's library copying again and again two family portraits that hung on the walls, and later drawing "these two ancient faces" on barn doors, fences, and other places on Mr. Hatch's property. As he approached adulthood, Bannister left Mr. Hatch and became a seafarer. During stops at Boston and New York, he availed himself of opportunities to visit museums, galleries, and other places where art could be seen.

After he settled in Boston, Bannister took on various jobs, including barber. Some say that for a time he worked in one of the hair salons owned by Christiana Carteaux, one of the most prosperous black women in the northeast, and the woman he was later to marry. Others say Edward never worked for Christiana but met her at a drama club.

In any case, Carteaux was extremely supportive of her husband's desire to be an artist. She was, in a sense, the first patron of this practically self-taught man. The only formal training Bannister had was evening drawing classes at the Lowell Institute. So it was by dint of self-imposed discipline that he developed into a fine artist.

Bannister's first commission came in the mid-1850s. The purchaser was a friend and one of the most prominent members of Boston's black community, physician John V. DeGrasse. The painting was *The Ship Outward Bound* (also now lost). Other commissions followed, and soon Bannister was making quite a name for himself in Boston. One work that brought him kudos was a portrait of Robert Gould Shaw, who led into glory **William H. Carney** and others in the Massachusetts Fifty-fourth Regiment.

In 1870, Bannister and his wife moved to Providence, Rhode Island, where Christiana had opened a hair salon. Life was easy in Providence. The Bannisters fit in nicely with the black strivers in the area, and Edward fit in nicely with the area's white artists, too. It was with a group of them that he cofounded the Providence Art Club, formed in 1880. The club, which held its first meeting in Bannister's studio, is regarded as the genesis of the Rhode Island School of Design. By the time the Providence Art Club was launched, four years had passed since Bannister's first triumph. In the interim, he had received other awards, along with many commissions, particularly in Providence.

His subject hardly ever changed. Bannister was forever enthralled by nature. Among his later works are *Sabin Point, Narragansett Bay; In Morton Park, Newport Rhode Island, Looking Southward; Landscape with Man on a Horse; Approaching Storm; Sunset.* What was his work about? In *A History of African-American Artists, From 1792 to the Present,* by Romare Bearden and Harry Henderson (1993), we read, "Like most American landscapists in the nineteenth century, Bannister sought God in nature and tried to convey a moral sentiment in his work. . . . Along with his contemporaries, Bannister saw man as diminished in relation to the power and beauty of nature."

In terms of his technique, as Bearden and Henderson explain, in contrast to the Hudson River school that presented nature in meticulous detail, "in Bannister's painting, details are lost in massive but revealing shapes of trees, mountains, rocks, and trails. These shapes are developed through sharp contrasts of light and shade so that his work often appears to be based more on black-and-white values than on color relationships." Bearden and Henderson then quote Bannister's friend George Whitaker: "He was one of the few artists who knew the value of deep shadows as a foundation of his painting. His color was not of a voluptuous nature but rather a quiet kind that juggled with greys." This same man once summed up Bannister's work as "poems of peace."

Not all Bannister's work was peaceful, however. As Bearden and Henderson tell us, Bannister was "fascinated by conflicting, accidental effects in nature—what happens to clouds, light, trees in the wind or other varying weather conditions." The "poems of peace" were, by all accounts, more reflective of Bannister's temperament. Easygoing, solicitous, sweet: These are words that capture this man who loved reading (especially poetry) and fine music. Sadly, Bannister did not die with peace of mind. In his last years, he was sorely distressed, as interest in his work waned and then—poof! His health declined as well. Bearden and Henderson's comment that "lapses of memory made it impossible for him to stroll safely" makes you wonder whether he did not suffer from what's now known as dementia, such as that linked to Alzheimer's disease.

Bannister died shortly after offering up prayer at the Elmwood Avenue Free Baptist Church. Four months after his death, the Providence Art Club mounted a memorial exhibition of 101 pieces of his work. Later that year, a group of artists led by his friend Whitaker erected a monument on his grave. It was an eight-foot granite boulder with a palette inscribed with his name, and with a poem that remembered him as a "pure and lofty soul . . . who, while he portrayed nature, walked with God."

SOME OTHER NINETEENTH-CENTURY ARTISTS

- Robert S. Duncanson (c. 1821–1872), who was born free in Fayette, New York, made his living early on as a house painter. In 1841, he moved to Mount Healthy, about fifteen miles north of Cincinnati, Ohio. By 1842, his work was being exhibited in Cincinnati, where he, also a daguerreotypist, worked for a time with J. P. Ball. Duncanson's forte was landscape painting. A commission from an abolitionist in Pittsburgh, *The Cliff Mine, Lake Superior* (1848), brought his talent into view in a major way. In the early 1850s, he produced his best-known work, *Blue Hole, Little Miami River,* still regarded as one of the finest midwestern landscapes. By the early 1860s, some were hailing him as "the best landscape painter of the West." This acclaim came after the unveiling of *The Land of the Lotus Eaters,* inspired by Alfred Lord Tennyson's 1842 poem, "The Lotos-Eaters," about an idyllic island that moves Odysseus's warriors to study war no more. Duncanson was working on this painting when the Civil War broke out. Duncanson, who had two European tours, was the first African American artist to receive international attention. The last years of his life were tragic: He went insane.

- Grafton Tyler Brown (1841–1918), born free in Harrisburg, Pennsylvania, was living in San Francisco by the early 1860s. There, he worked as a drafter and lithographer, eventually opening his own business, G. T. Brown & Co. In the early 1870s, Brown sold his business and devoted himself to painting. His strength was faithful reproductions of the great outdoors of the West. *Grand Canyon of the Yellow Stone from Hayden Point* and *Mount Tacoma* are two of his best known works. In the 1900s, Brown was living in St. Paul, Minnesota, where he was apparently quite psychotic by 1914, and where he died in a state hospital.

- Charles Porter (c.1850–c.1923), born in Hartford, Connecticut, studied at the National Academy of Design in New York and, for a time, with the white portrait painter Joseph Oriel Eaton. Porter's forte was landscapes and still lifes. In 1878, he raised about $1,000 from sales of his work and used the money to study in Paris, where he stayed for about seven years (with some financial help from Mark Twain).

- Henry Ossawa Tanner (1859–1937), who grew up mostly in Philadelphia, Pennsylvania, was a member of an illustrious family. First off, his father was A.M.E. bishop Benjamin Tucker Tanner, editor of *Christian Recorder* and founder of what is considered the first African American scholarly journal, the *A.M.E. Church Review*. Henry's sister, Dr. Halle Tanner Dillon Johnson, was one of the first African American women to graduate from a medical school; and the achievements of his niece Sadie Tanner Mossell Alexander include being the first African American woman to receive a Ph.D. in economics (1921). Henry, who broke ground when he studied at the Pennsylvania Academy of the Fine Arts in the 1880s, became the most celebrated black artist of the late nineteenth and early twentieth century. His best-known works are two of the relatively few black-themed paintings he did: *The Banjo Lesson* (1893) and *The Thankful Poor* (1894). Early on, Tanner focused on landscapes and seascapes. Later in life, he devoted himself almost exclusively to renderings of Biblical events: *The Wise and Foolish Virgins*, *The Raising of Lazarus*, *Daniel in the Lions Den*, and *Christ and Nicodemus*, for example. Henry O. Tanner did not gain fame first in America, which he left in the early 1890s ("I could not fight prejudice and paint at the same time"), living almost all of the rest of his life in France. It was only after he received awards and honors in Europe that Tanner became acclaimed in the country of his birth.

 Lewis Adams (1842–1905)

Behind many a celebrated founder of an institution, there's often a forgotten spark. In the case of **Booker T. Washington** and Alabama's Tuskegee Institute, Lewis Adams was the school's first force.

Adams had become an able artisan during his attendance in the "peculiar institution." Tinsmithing, cobbling, and harness making were among his trades. He was also somewhat literate, the consequence of one of the kindnesses of his father–owner. When freedom came, "Adams proceeded to make the most of his opportunities," wrote

Arna Bontemps in his book *100 Years of Negro Freedom* (1961). Adams did this by becoming his own boss, with a shop in Tuskegee.

Soon, Adams became more than just a small-businessowner: He became a leader in his community. When he talked politics, people listened. When he urged listeners to vote Republican, many did. Adams's interest in politics wasn't all talk. One example of his involvement in the Republican Party is that in 1874, he was a representative to a Republican Negro convention in Montgomery. His support for the Republican Party never flagged—not until 1880, when, as Bontemps put it, "he was buttonholed by a Democrat."

That Democrat was former slaveholder and Confederate Army colonel W. F. Foster, editor and publisher of the *Macon Mail*. Foster was angling for a seat in the Alabama legislature, and the colored vote was a factor to be reckoned with if Foster was to fulfill his political ambitions. This made the support of a man such as Lewis Adams critical. Another Democrat, Arthur L. Brooks, also wanted Adams's help in the upcoming elections.

Adams would not be wooed to swing the colored vote to these Democrats in exchange for money or a new suit of clothes. Neither would intimidation have netted the desired effect. Adams would, however, be willing to bolt from his party in exchange for something quite concrete and potentially enduring: a school for his people.

A deal was struck, and the deal was kept. In early February 1881, Senator Foster and Representative Brooks introduced a bill that appropriated two thousand dollars "to establish a Normal school for colored teachers at Tuskegee." The deed was soon done: signed, sealed, and delivered up by Governor Rufus W. Cobb later that month. The money was earmarked for staff salaries only. For the physical plant, supplies, and other necessities of an educational enterprise, well, Heaven would have to help them—Heaven and a commission of three residents of Tuskegee charged with administering the funds and oversight of the nonexistent school. One of them was Lewis Adams.

Lewis Adams was there when a letter was sent to Union Army veteran and founder of Virginia's Hampton Institute General Samuel Chapman Armstrong, seeking a recommendation for principal. He was also one of the first to find out that Armstrong pitched a former pupil and his primary protégé for the job: Booker T. Washington. Lewis Adams was there, too, when the A.M.E. Zion Church on Zion Hill, where he was Sunday School superintendent, agreed to allow a shack beside the church and the church itself to be used as facilities for Tuskegee Institute.

Lewis Adams was definitely there during Booker T. Washington's rough early days: as a guide, booster, and hands-on helper. There was the time a Northerner gave the school a hundred dollars with the stipulation that it be used to buy a horse, and Washington entrusted Adams with the purchase. "I took that one hundred dollars," Adams was quoted as saying in *Tuskegee: Its Story and Its Work* (1901), "and made it go so far that when I came back to the school I had a good horse, a second-hand lumber wagon, a harness, a plow, and a sack of corn to begin to feed the horse on. That horse did all our work for a long while."

Adams did so much more for this school, from overseeing the construction of its first permanent building and managing its departments in shoemaking and tinsmithing for many years to serving on its board of directors for a good long while. Washington was no ingrate. In his autobiography *Up from Slavery,* he referenced Lewis Adams as one of the two men "upon whom I have depended constantly for advice and guidance."

 # Frederick Douglass (1818–1895)

There were Frederick Douglass dolls in the 1850s, and during his lifetime, no black person was painted, sketched, sculpted, and photographed more than he. Sometimes, he was even pictured in scenes in which he had been absent, as with the famous 1850 lithograph of Henry Brown being unboxed. (Incidentally, Douglass deemed the hoopla over this Virginia runaway folly: "Had not Henry Box Brown and his friends attracted slaveholding attention to the manner of his escape," he groaned, "we might have had a thousand *Box Browns* per annum.")

After Douglass's death came a plethora of tributes: from statues in miniature to those quite large; from an earthenware pitcher with his likeness on its belly to a silver spoon with his image embossed on the bowl and landmark dates in chain link climbing up the handle.

On and on, long after he was gone, he has remained always present: in biographies (scores), in essays (hundreds), and plays and more busts and statues—and in poems, such as "Frederick Douglass" by **Robert Hayden**:

> When it is finally ours, this freedom, this liberty, this beautiful
> and terrible thing, needful to man as air,
> usable as earth; when it belongs at last to all,
> when it is truly instinct, brain matter, diastole, systole,
> reflex action; when it is finally won; when it is more
> than the gaudy mumbo jumbo of politicians:
> this man, this Douglass, this former slave, this Negro
> beaten to his knees, exiled, visioning a world
> where none is lonely, none hunted, alien,

this man, superb in love and logic, this man
shall be remembered. Oh, not with statues' rhetoric,
not with legends and poems and wreaths of bronze alone,
but with the lives grown out of his life, the lives
fleshing his dream of the beautiful, needful thing.

Indeed, what a piece of work he was, this man bruted in conception (never did know for sure which white man raped his mother), bruted by bondage on Maryland's Eastern Shore, and in Baltimore where he served his owner Thomas Auld's brother, a ship's carpenter Hugh Auld, and in St. Michael's where he was hired out to farmer Edward Covey, who beat him beat him beat him until that epic day when the young man originally named Frederick Augustus Washington Bailey hit Covey back.

This striking back was not his first act of resistance. That had come years earlier, when he began to learn his letters on the sly. Then came the day, at age twelve, when with money saved up from bootblacking he made a prescient purchase: *The Columbia Orator,* a collection of great speeches by men who made history. In time, through newspapers, he schooled himself on that thing called abolition. He began a more serious study of his inherent worth, his preciousness, when he embraced Christianity, becoming a member of Baltimore's Bethel A.M.E. Church, and secretly engaging the Bible with the help of a free man. This is why absolute bruting had never set in. This is why sixteen-year-old Frederick struck back at the cruel Covey. Freedom is hot on his mind after that; he makes a break for it in January 1836; he gets caught; he listens to old Thomas Auld, who promises young Fred freedom at age twenty-five *if* he learns a trade and behaves himself; he learns a trade—becomes a caulker—but he doesn't behave.

With borrowed sailor's papers and money from a free woman, Anna Murray, with whom he has fallen in love, he slips away on September 3, 1838. He stops for a while in New York, where Anna joins him and they marry. The couple eventually settles in New Bedford, Massachusetts, where Frederick settles on a new surname.

The likes of Robert Burns, Shakespeare, Coleridge, Tennyson, Longfellow, and Alexandre Dumas *pere* become his delights, and he becomes, by the mid-1840s, star speaker for the Massachusetts Anti-Slavery Society. For more than a decade, in their home in Rochester, New York, Frederick and Anna shelter runaways bound for Canada. All the while, he is becoming the lion lecturer of the American Anti-Slavery Society, headed up by William Lloyd Garrison. Before Douglass reaches that final sleep, he will have lectured all across the nation and throughout the British Isles, with people every time, everywhere inspirited by his presence, his sound, his words, his being—as Elizabeth Cady Stanton said—"majestic in his wrath."

His fleshing out of his dream of the beautiful, needful thing meant railing not only against slavery, but also against segregation in the North and prejudice in England. It meant championing the black man as soldier in the Civil War—being chief recruiter for the first black regiment raised in the North (the glorious Massachusetts Fifty-fourth), pressing for equal pay for black soldiers, getting up in Lincoln's face (so to speak) over his do-nothingness about the Confederate Army's murder of black P.O.W.s. It meant calling for black suffrage and for women's suffrage. It meant calling for an end to discrimination in the trade unions and abuses against those "coolies" who had come to build railroads in an America they could not enjoy. It meant being opposed to capital punishment.

He was also a father: of Rosetta, Lewis, Frederick, Charles, and Annie; of the four-page weekly, *North Star,* launched in 1847 with the motto "Right Is of No Sex—Truth Is of No Color—God Is the Father of Us All, and We Are All Brethren"; of *Frederick Douglass's Paper,* the merger of the *North Star* and Gerrit Smith's *Liberty Party,* which came on strong in 1851 with its motto "ALL RIGHTS FOR ALL!"; of *Douglass's Monthly* (1858); and of *The New National Era* (1870), which he forged out of *The New Era* and turned over to his sons Charles and Lewis.

He sired books, too. *Narrative of the Life of Frederick Douglass* came out in 1845 and sold 4,500 copies the first three months. *My Bondage and My Freedom* came out in 1855. *Life and Times of Frederick Douglass,* which did not sell well, appeared in 1881. Once, he produced fiction as well: the novella *The Heroic Slave* (1852), his attempt to flesh out the bravery of Madison Washington, leader of the revolt aboard the slaver *Creole* in 1841. There are, too, all those short pieces of powerful prose, such as "What to the Slave Is the Fourth of July?" which we

Daguerreotype by an unidentified photographer of Frederick Douglass (circa 1850) in his late twenties/early thirties. (Courtesy of the National Portrait Gallery, Smithsonian Institution/Art Resource, NY)

wish we could read with his voice in our ears because we hear he could make prose song—this man who played well the violin.

And he bore scars. He became lonely and alien to many when he broke with his early benefactor William Lloyd Garrison because he could not abide Garrison's nod to colonization. Later, much to some people's chagrin, he chastised the great Garrison for believing that with emancipation a done deal, there was no more to do for the Negro.

Years earlier, Douglass had withheld support from his friend John Brown—what a grief! Douglass had knowledge aforehand of Brown's plan to take Harpers Ferry, and Douglass—superb in love and logic—told his fevered friend in so many words that he was out of his mind. So John Brown's body swung in a Virginia breeze, with Douglass unable to mourn properly because they said he had been a player in the

Frederick Douglass near the end of his life (circa 1890–1895), in the library of the home he purchased in Washington, D.C., in 1878 and named Cedar Hill. This house, which is now a museum, carries the address 1411 W Street, SE, Washington, D.C. (Courtesy of the National Park Service, Frederick Douglass National Historic Site)

plot—so he became hunted, forced to skip town, to leave his country and his family for a while.

He lost his daughter Annie—only eleven when she died in 1860; he was fifty-four when his home was consumed by a suspicious fire; and he was sixty-four when he lost Anna, that stalwart, but retiring wife of his youth, she who few thought was good enough for him, she who had helped him catch not only liberty but also his love for the violin.

He also risked the wrath of family and friends, of blacks and whites, when, in 1884, two years after Anna's death, he married a white woman, Helen Pitts. Papa Pitts would not have the hero in his house. Lots of power sisters had a fit, which made him cherish Ida B. Wells: She was nice to Helen. Yes, he knew just about everybody worth knowing in his era, and before his journey was over, he saw a lot of Europe and some of the Mediterranean, and he'd gone to Egypt, too. There was Haiti, as well. He was minister resident and consul general of that hot place from 1889 until 1891, when he resigned because his country was not about supporting the beautiful, needful thing in Haiti.

So busy busy busy, always, on behalf of the beautiful, needful thing: fighting something he felt would impede it or supporting something he felt could speed it. Maybe had he, at age seventy-seven, not attended the National Council of Women's meeting in D.C. on February 20, 1895, maybe—just maybe—had he stayed home with Helen and a book and his violin, maybe he would not have had a fatal heart attack that evening. Then again, maybe Frederick Douglass just had to die on the pulse of something relevant to the beautiful, needful thing.

PART II
SONS OF THE DAWN

Delivered but still not free—the strong men kept working hard, building communities and institutions, and protesting. They kept coming with dignity. They mastered in the sciences, and in arts—music, dance, film, painting, poems, precise-to-the-experience prose—and in sports. They came with brains that would open our eyes to black history, that would change skylines and insights, that would challenge Jim Crow and push for Black Power. All the while, we had times to cry over the price some paid for being a black man, who did nothing but be a black man or who did nothing but attempt to bring about good things.

With the passage of time, in the wake of some gains, some new opportunities, when the Second Reconstruction was in effect, it was carpe diem time for so many: They reached for things their forefathers never thought to dream, sometimes pushing into territory that was new for everyone.

❄️ W. E. B. Du Bois (1868–1963)

Late into the night of February 23, 1893—his twenty-fifth birthday—William Edward Burghardt Du Bois, once the precocious little Willie of Great Barrington, Massachusetts, was alone in his humble digs in Berlin, where he was taking graduate courses in sociology and economics at the university.

In the glow of candlelight and wine, writing in his diary, musings flowed—"I wonder what I am—I wonder what the world is—I wonder if life is worth the striving. I do not know—perhaps I shall never know." His determination roiled—"but this I do know: be the Truth what it may I shall seek it on the pure assumption that it is worth seeking—and Heaven nor hell, God nor Devil shall turn me from my purpose till I die. . . ." His will then gave utterance to a wild vow—"These are my plans: to make a name in science, to make a name in literature, and thus to raise my race. Or perhaps to raise a visible empire in Africa."

Highlights from the life of W. E. B. Du Bois reveal that it wasn't the wine talking.

- First black to receive a Ph.D. from Harvard University (in history, 1896), where he earned an M.A. and the B.A. the school required, even though he already had one from Fisk University, his Ph.D. dissertation *The Suppression of the African Slave-Trade to the United States of America, 1638–1870* being the first monograph in the Harvard Historical Studies series

W. E. B. Du Bois at age nineteen, soon to graduate from Fisk University. In his commencement address, he held forth on Germany's Otto von Bismarck. Du Bois later recalled, "Bismarck was my hero. He had made a nation out of a mass of bickering peoples. . . . This fore-shadowed in my mind the kind of thing that American Negroes must do, marching forth with strength under trained leadership." (Courtesy of Photographs and Prints Division, Schomburg Center for Research in Black Culture, The New York Public Library, Astor, Lenox and Tilden Foundations)

- Cofounder of the American Negro Academy (1897), led by the great activist–intellectual Reverend Alexander Crummell and dedicated to "the promotion of literature, science and art . . . the fostering of higher education, the publication of scholarly work and the defense of the Negro against vicious assault"
- Pioneer in urban sociology with *Philadelphia Negro* (1899), a study of a black ward in Philadelphia, based on interviews Du Bois himself conducted with more than three thousand families, commissioned by the University of Pennsylvania
- Cofounder of the Niagara Movement (1905) and first general secretary of this radical-integrationist organization, dedicated to the political and economic advancement of black America, the cofounders of which included editor of Atlanta, Georgia's, *Voice of the Negro*, J. Max Barber; A.M.E. bishop Reverdy C. Ransom; and **William Monroe Trotter**
- Cofounder of the National Association for the Advancement of Colored People (1909) and its director of research
- Organizer of the first Pan-African Congress (in Paris, 1919), with his call for unity among African peoples, drawing delegates from Africa, the Caribbean, Europe, and the United States; building on the legacy of Trinidad's Henry Sylvester Williams who spearheaded the Pan-African Conference in London in 1900, which Du Bois had attended, as he attended additional congresses in 1921, 1923, 1927, and 1945; by 1945, regarded as the "Father of Pan-Africanism"; by 1945, also had a great impact on Kwame Nkrumah, who would lead the Gold Coast out of colonialism and into the independent nation Ghana, the place Du Bois and his second wife Shirley Graham Du Bois made their home in 1961
- Founder of the Harlem theater group, Krigwa Players (1926)
- Founder of periodicals: *The Moon Illustrated Weekly* (1905–1906); *Horizon: Journal of the Color Line* (1907–1910); *Brownies' Book,* a monthly magazine for children (1920–1921); the *Crisis,* the organ of the NAACP of which he was editor-in-chief (1910–1934 and 1944–1948); and *Phylon: The Atlanta University Review of Race and Culture,* launched in 1940
- Member of the Council of African Affairs, led by Paul Robeson, formed in 1939 to increase awareness of the abuses suffered by black African people and to press in an organized way for decolonization (the only lobbying group for black Africa until the mid-1970s when **Randall Robinson** founded TransAfrica), and which, at various points, included as members Mary McLeod Bethune, Alain Locke, Louise Thompson Patterson (wife of William Patterson, counsel for the case of the **Scottsboro Boys**), and Adam Clayton Powell, Jr.

- Cofounder and chair of the Peace Information Center (1950), which worked to increase the number of supporters for the Stockholm Peace Appeal
- Teacher at several institutions: Wilberforce University (instructor of Greek and Latin, 1894–1896); University of Pennsylvania (assistant professor of sociology, 1896–1897); Atlanta University (professor of economics and history 1898–1909, and chair of the Sociology Department 1934–1944)
- Author, editor, coeditor of a mountain of books: Henry Louis Gates, Jr., captured how prolific Du Bois was with his reckoning that Du Bois wrote something scholarly every twelve days for fifty years. After *The Suppression of the African Slave-Trade to the United States of America, 1638–1870* and *The Philadelphia Negro*, Du Bois produced more than a dozen studies of black life in conjunction with the annual Atlanta University Conference of the Negro Problems, which he began heading up in 1896; the studies included *Morality among Negroes in Cities, The Negro in Business, The Negro Artisan, The Negro Common School, The Negro American Family*—all published by Atlanta University Press. Du Bois's longer works of nonfiction included the famed collection of essays *The Souls of Black Folk* and *The Negro in the South: His Economic Progress in Relation to His Moral and Religious Development* (a collection of his lectures and those of his then-future nemesis **Booker T. Washington**). There were also *The Gifts of Black Folk: The Negroes in the Making of America; Africa: Its Place in Modern History;* and the brilliant *Black Reconstruction: An Essay toward a History of the Part Which Black Folk Played in the Attempt to Reconstruct Democracy in America, 1860–1880*. Du Bois also wrote several plays and pageants, four novels (*The Quest of the Silver Fleece* and the trilogy *The Black Flame*), and three autobiographies, the first of which, *Dusk of Dawn: An Essay toward an Autobiography of a Race Concept*, should be as widely read as *The Souls of Black Folk*. Essays and articles by Du Bois number in the hundreds and covered just about every major issue of the twentieth century: "On Being Ashamed of Oneself: An Essay of Race Price"; "Japan, Color and Afro-Americans"; "Gandhi and the American Negroes"; "Negro Education"; "The Burden of Black Women"; "The Damnation of Women"; "Sex and Racism"; "A Lunatic or a Traitor" (about Marcus Garvey); "Socialism and the Negro Problem"; "The Pan-African Congresses: The Story of a Growing Movement"; Germany and Hitler"; and "The Real Reason behind Paul Robeson's Persecution." This list hardly does justice to his range. Du Bois's masterwork was to have been the *Encyclopaedia Africana*.

- Spark that ignited a demonstration, in mid-August 1963, on the U.S. Embassy in his final home, Accra, Ghana, as a show of support for the historic March on Washington for Jobs and Freedom, which took place the day after Du Bois died

"And I know that I am either a genius or a fool"—that's how he prefaced that vow he made on the night of his twenty-fifth birthday. Well, we know the answer to that—which is not to say that Du Bois didn't have his missteps. There was the "Close Ranks" article, urging black America to support the nation in its World War I work, which only netted black American deaths. There were the low blows on Marcus Garvey and participation in the persecution that resulted in Garvey's imprisonment and deportation. There was praise for Stalin, whose purges were among the worst crimes against humanity in the twentieth century. Du Bois could also be a snob.

Granted, Du Bois had good intentions when he championed the doctrine of the Talented Tenth, but it was unrealistic. To his credit, he did reexamine his thesis years later, and publicly so in the essay "The Talented Tenth: A Memorial Address" (1948). Just as many hold him to the Talented Tenth doctrine, many also hold him to the statement, "The problem of the Twentieth Century is the problem of the color line," something he wrote before he thoroughly processed issues of class and capitalism. Apparently, the notion that godlessness might be the problem didn't interest him. Also, why the hosannas for "One ever feels his twoness . . . "? Du Bois wrote this when he was acutely longing to be accepted by white people, when he thought integration would mean salvation. Why lay that angst on all African Americans when there are so many of us who feel no bifurcation, but accept ourselves as a peculiar, unique people, as "a brand new human being in this country," as Toni Morrison once said.

This is a roundabout way of pointing to the wonder-thing about Du Bois. He was not static. He *moved*. What a fine study of the evolution of consciousness. Du Bois was true enough and noble enough and sincere enough about social change to change his own mind as new information and new meditations came up on the screen. Integrationist . . . Talented-Tenthist . . . Pan-Africanist . . . Socialist . . . Communist—the movements of a mind trying to make real the better world he dreamed.

Because of his amazing intellect and fury of activities, we tend to forget that he was also a man who carried personal sorrows with him as he toiled to "raise the race." It couldn't have been easy to recall a childhood of poverty and a father who abandoned the family when he was an infant. Du Bois also had grief as an adult, having to endure the death of his infant son, Burghardt, from dysentery, which could have been treated if white doctors hadn't refused to help the baby. This

W. E. B. Du Bois on his ninety-fifth birthday, the day he received an honorary degree from the University of Ghana. (Courtesy of Special Collections and Archives, W. E. B. Du Bois Library, University of Massachusetts Amherst)

tragedy strained his marriage with Nina Gomer and gave us the poignant piece of prose, "Of the First Born." As for his second born, Yolande, Du Bois had to endure her unwise marriage to Countee Cullen, and years later, in 1961, he had the weightier burden of burying his beloved second born, whose mother had died in 1950.

Du Bois's sufferings also included two kidney operations. His sorrows included being fired from the NAACP in 1948 because of his leftist views twice, the second time being indicted in 1951, for not registering as a foreign agent (which he wasn't) and thereby violating the McCarran Act; being stripped of his passport; becoming persona non grata not only to the government but also to many erstwhile colleagues, friends, admirers—"The colored children ceased to hear my name."

It could not have been pleasant for him to find America so odious that he felt compelled to renounce his citizenship, which he did about six months before he died—still believing that life was "worth the striving," as he wrote in his diary on the night of his twenty-fifth birthday.

 John Merrick (1859–1919)

"John Merrick was essentially a man of action, a *doer.*" That's how Benjamin Brawley summed him up in *Negro Builders and Heroes* (1937).

Merrick, who was born in slavery in Clinton, North Carolina, and never had a day of formal schooling, began effectively *doing* at age twelve, at a brickyard in Chapel Hill, North Carolina. With his job as a helper, he was not only taking care of himself but also helping to support his mother and little brother. When the family moved to Raleigh in the late 1870s, the good son found work on the construction of Shaw University's first major building. When construction work dried up, young Merrick got a gig bootblacking. His job site was a barbershop, where he availed himself of the opportunity to pick up another trade.

Around 1880, Merrick and the barbershop's foreman, John Wright, decided to open a barbershop of their own in Durham. This city was not much to write home about at the time, but like other forward-thinking people, Merrick and Wright could see that it was a city on the rise, with Washington B. Duke's tobacco company paving the way for Durham's emergence as a major industrial city at the turn of the century.

In addition to their business enterprise, Merrick and Wright, both family men by now, teamed up for the purchase of a lot on Pettigrew Street, facing the railroad tracks, on which they each built modest three-room cottages. By 1887, Merrick and his wife were raising their children in a far more stately home on the famous street of black strivers, Fayetteville Street.

Merrick and Wright's partnership lasted twelve years, ending when Wright moved to Washington, D.C. Merrick, then in his early thirties, became sole proprietor of a very successful shop, where people could also purchase the dandruff cure he had created. He eventually opened four more barbershops, three of which served a white clientele. Among the prominent white men who patronized Merrick's barbershops was Washington B. Duke's son James.

Barbering was not Merrick's only line of business. He ventured into real estate, as well. Serving as his own contractor, main carpenter (and sometimes chief hauler), he built rental property in the black section of town—a wise move that was, what with loads of folks streaming into Durham for jobs at up-and-coming factories.

Merrick was also a *doer* for other people's endeavors. When Aaron McDuffie Moore, Durham's first black physician, decided to start a hospital, Merrick persuaded the Duke family to make very large donations to what became Lincoln Hospital. Merrick also served as president of the Board of Trustees of this hospital, which opened in 1901. Later, when Moore decided to fill the need for a library for his people, Merrick agreed to lease one of his properties for this purpose, and he later sold it at a hefty discount to firmly establish the Durham Colored Library, the cornerstone for what is today the Stanford L. Warren Library. (Moore and Merrick were to be further entwined in each other's lives: In 1916, Merrick's son Edward married Moore's daughter Lyda, cofounder of the *Negro Braille Magazine*.)

Giving back: John Merrick set a superb example, from giving money for the buildup of his church to giving money to various educational and social institutions in black Durham. At one point, he had a policy of returning to his tenants a week's rent at Christmastide, a time when he also handed out treats and necessities to the needy ("and many of his good deeds will never be known," wrote Brawley).

John Merrick's other doings include being an early shareholder and first vice president of the Mechanics and Farmers Bank, formed in 1908. He became the bank's president in 1910, the same year that the Merrick-Moore-Spaulding Real Estate Company was incorporated.

Every step of the way, Merrick was lifting as he climbed. Through his business ventures and affiliations, he became a beacon, a source of inspiration, a model of can-do. In the process, he was generating that most vital thing: jobs in which folks could rise.

Merrick's most enduring entrepreneurial effort was North Carolina Mutual and Provident Association. He was one of seven men (Aaron Moore among them) who put up fifty dollars for the company's start-up in 1898. The firm's first year was less than promising, and five partners pulled out. The other two hung in there. With Merrick as president and Moore as medical director, the company was reconstituted as North Carolina Mutual Insurance Company. In these days when white insurance companies would accept no black customers, like all black insurance companies, North Carolina Mutual was a precious, necessary thing. It became more vigorous after Merrick and Moore had the good sense to hire Moore's nephew, the legendary Charles Clinton Spaulding.

Spaulding joined the company in 1900. "General manager, agent, clerk and janitor" was Spaulding's famous line about his early days with North Carolina Mutual of which he became president in 1923, and which he had made the largest black-owned company in the United States by 1940. As C. C. Spaulding built up the company, surely he cherished the blessing he received from John Merrick back in June 1919. The occasion was North Carolina Mutual's twentieth-anniversary celebrations at White Rock Baptist Church. To the surprise of many, the gravely ill Merrick attended. In his remarks before an adoring crowd, he said, "As long as it is God's will I want this institution to move, for men to support their families; and God will let it live. That is what I am interested in, and God knows it. I want this institution to live, and she will. God bless you all." John Merrick died two months later.

"A loyal business partner," "a firm and loving friend," "a big-hearted sympathetic brother"—this is how C. C. Spaulding referred to Merrick in memoriam. "I never made an important decision without him," Spaulding said, "and always placed the utmost confidence in his judgment, because I knew he considered my interests his."

Stagolee

Ba-adest dude around, patron saint of gansta rap, a.k.a. Stack, Stack-olee, Staggerlee, Stag: He's the man unbound—no fear of the Lord or the law—no love for women, only sex. This native of Fatback, Georgia, was "so bad that the flies wouldn't even fly around his head in sum-mertime, and snow wouldn't fall on his house in winter." That's how Julius Lester tells it in *Black Folktales*—and dontcha know Stagolee was *ba-ad* from the very beginning. As Lester recounted,

> Stagolee grew up on a plantation in Georgia, and by the time he was two, he'd decided that he wasn't going to spend his life picking cotton and working for white folks. Uh-uh. And when he was five, he left. Took off down the road, his guitar on his back, a deck of cards in one pocket and a .44 in the other. He figured that he didn't need nothing else. When the women heard him whup the blues on the guitar he could have whichever one he laid his mind on. Whenever he needed money, he could play cards. And whenever somebody tried to mess with him, he had his .44.

Lester's sketch of Stagolee is for a general audience. In *Shuckin' and Jivin': Folklore from Contemporary Black Americans* (1978), edited by Daryl Cumber Dance, we find a choice example of the many R-rated re-membrances of this infamous fella. This ballad, collected in the Vir-ginia Penitentiary, reads in part,

> Back in thirty-two when times was hard,
> Stag had two forty-fives and a marked deck o' cards.
> He had a pinstriped suit and a old f——ed-up hat,
> He had a twenty-nine Ford and owed payments on that.
> Stag thought he'd take a walk down on Vampire Street,
> There where all them slick and *ba-ad* dudes meet.
> He wade through s—— and he wade through mud,
> He come to a crib they call the Bucket o' Blood.
> He called to the bartender for something to eat.
> Bartender gave 'im a muddy glass o' water and a stale piece o' meat.
> He say, "Bartender, Bartender, you don't realize who I am!"
> Bartender say, "Frankly speaking, Mister, I don't give a good
>   goddamn."
> But just then (the bartender hadn't realized what he had said)
> Stag had pumped two forty-five slugs in his m——f—— head,
> And in walked this ho and say, "Oh, no! Oh, no! He can't be dead!"
> Stag say, "Then you get back there, b——, and mend them holes in
>   his m——f—— head."

Stagolee's only virtue (if you can call it that) and the thing that makes some people cheer him is that he never has and never will take stuff offa white folks. So some boost him as the white man's worst nightmare, when really he's a sorrow—especially bad news for truly strong black men because he's so often spotlighted as the typical black man.

The reason Stagolee is popular with some white folks is because the brother preys mostly on his own people and is the most nonthreatening Negro of all: He lends zip—nothing—to efforts for social change; he builds no institutions, makes no plans, plants no family, leaves no legacy to treasure. Swagger and brags don't build no nation. Saddest of all, those who are so dispossessed as to see in him a hero and follow in his footsteps usually end up either in jail or in an early grave.

 # Johnson Chesnutt Whittaker (1858–1931)

In late June 1870, James W. Smith, Johnson Chesnutt Whittaker's fellow South Carolinian, wrote a letter to relatives about his days at the United States Military Academy at West Point. First off, he apologized for the delay in replying to their last letter, explaining that he'd been busy with exams and with "insults and ill treatment" of his fellow cadets. Smith then wrote,

> I passed the examination all right, and got in, but my companion, Howard, failed and was rejected. Since he went away I have been lonely indeed, and now these fellows appear to be trying their utmost to run me off, and I fear they will succeed if they continue as they have begun. We went into camp yesterday, and not a moment has passed since then but some one of them has been cursing and abusing me. All night they were around my tent, cursing and swearing at me so that I did not sleep two hours all night.
>
> It is just the same at the table, and what I get to eat I must snatch for like a dog. I don't want to resign if I can get along at all; but I don't think it will be best for me to stay and take all the abuses and insults that are heaped upon me. . . .
>
> If I complain of their conduct to the commandant I must prove the charges or nothing can be done.

In all likelihood, Whittaker knew what Smith went through at West Point. For one, Smith's letter was published in a newspaper. Smith was certainly a news story. He was one of the first blacks to receive an appointment to West Point. He entered in 1870, along with Michael Howard ("my companion, Howard"). There was no way for Whittaker not to know that Smith didn't make it through, that he'd been kicked out of West Point for breaking a coconut dipper over a cadet's head (never mind that he had been pounced on).

So when Johnson Chesnutt Whittaker entered West Point in 1876, surely he had to know it wouldn't be a cakewalk, and obviously he figured he was up for the challenge. "Maybe James and Michael were just weak"—could be that's what Whittaker concluded.

The first famous black West Point man, Henry O. Flipper, was there when Whittaker arrived, and Flipper (his roommate) was on the road to graduating in 1877. "If Henry could do it, so can I"—is that how Whittaker kept his courage high?

Flipper showed Whittaker the ropes, braced him for the cruel jokes and the silence Flipper had endured.

"I got it under control"—maybe that's what Whittaker thought after he survived the first year, the second year, the third year. "This can't be happening!" could have been the thought that grazed his mind on that April night in 1880 when he found himself being beaten by three masked men—legs tied to his bedstead, hands bound, and left to bleed like a pig from the blows, from the slashes to his hands and feet, from the slits to his ears.

"Justice will prevail"—was he that confident? If so, he must have been rocked nearly out of his mind when the Old Boys determined that he was the only guilty party. He had done it all to himself—that was the conclusion the commandant of cadets reached. Those who sat on the court of inquiry that Whittaker requested upheld the commandant's verdict in June 1880. What would possess a person to beat and mutilate himself? The Old Boys maintained that Whittaker's motive was to get sympathy.

The Whittaker affair made news bigtime. Given the support he received from influential blacks and whites, Whittaker was rather confident that he would be vindicated at the court martial he requested of President Rutherford B. Hayes, at the same time that he requested a leave of absence from West Point. The court martial commenced in January 1881. When it was over, Whittaker had been, for the third time, found guilty of perpetrating a hoax.

The Judge Advocate-General of the Army reviewed the case and rejected the decision: For one, there had been a misadmission of a piece of evidence—a threatening letter to Whittaker, which the Old Boys' handwriting experts claimed Whittaker had written himself. Eventually, the new President, Chester A. Arthur, declared the court-martial invalid. This was in the spring of 1882. Whittaker could be a West Point man again. "They dare not mess with me again," Whittaker might have declared but in short order, West Point gave Whittaker the boot. The reason was that he had done poorly on an exam—an exam taken shortly after the court of inquiry in June 1880.

Whittaker did not crawl into a cave. Once the dust settled, he embarked on what was to be a long career in education (teacher and administrator), and after he passed the South Carolina bar in 1885, he practiced law on the side.

Daniel Hale Williams (1856–1931)

Williams's most celebrated feat is what he did on a July evening in 1893 at Chicago's Provident Hospital: the first successful open-heart surgery (at least in modern times, for we don't really know all that, say, the ancient Egyptians had under the cap). If this surgery were all that Williams did, well, yes, that would have meant a lot—especially to the friends and family of James Cornish, the man who would have died of a stab wound to the chest, had the 37-year-old Daniel Hale Williams not operated. He even did so without benefit of blood transfusions, antibiotics, x-rays, and other medical wonders to come (not to mention prior experience).

The point is, Williams did so much more. Had it not been for Williams, Cornish would not have been rushed to Provident Hospital because it would not have existed. It existed because one day, Williams got sufficiently miffed that Chicago hospitals refused to have black physicians on staff and balked at offering training to blacks aspiring to be nurses. "We'll start a hospital of our own," Williams declared, "and we'll train dozens and dozens of nurses." A fund-raising campaign was underway in 1890. In 1891, in a building on Dearborn and 29th Streets, Provident Hospital opened. This institution, staffed with blacks and whites, was the first black-owned and -operated hospital.

Williams was able to raise support for this hospital because he had been a positive fixture in Chicago for several years. "Dr. Dan," as he was affectionately known, had a thriving private practice and a reputation as a very fine surgeon. Furthermore, in 1889, he had been appointed to the Illinois State Board of Health. A few years earlier, he had begun serving as a physician for the City Railway Company and at an orphanage. He'd also put in time as an instructor at Chicago's Medical College (now Northwestern University Medical School), where he had received his M.D. in 1883.

Williams's career in medicine owed a great deal to Henry Palmer, a prominent white physician in Janesville, Wisconsin, who served as that state's surgeon general for many years. Williams apprenticed with Palmer in the 1870s, and when Williams made up his mind to attend medical school, Palmer gave him both moral and financial support.

Williams, who was born in Hollidaysburg, Pennsylvania, had come to Wisconsin as a youth, following the death of his father. Before meeting

Henry Palmer, he supported himself in various ways, including his father's trade, barbering. Williams's eventual move to surgery is not such a leap when you think about the skills required to render sharp hair cuts and good, clean shaves. Too, once upon a time, barbers were known as "doctors of the short robe," because in addition to barbering, they also performed surgery (bloodletting mostly), which is why the once ubiquitous barber's pole is red (for blood) and white (for bandages).

Three years after Provident Hospital opened, and one year after Williams's historic surgery, President Grover Cleveland appointed him chief surgeon at Washington, D.C.'s federally funded Freedmen's Hospital (the seed of Howard University Medical Center). During his four years there, Williams lifted the hospital up a few notches, putting in place an internship program and a revamped nurses training course, among other things.

In 1898, Williams returned to Chicago. There, he resumed his private practice and rejoined the staff of Provident Hospital. In addition, he devoted a great deal of time and energy to getting people to care more about black health care. He did this through articles and lectures ("The Needs of Hospitals and Training Schools for the Colored People in the South," for example). He did it by helping others establish hospitals and by helping the few existing ones become stronger. Vital race work, indeed, since in those days, blacks were routinely refused admittance into hospitals run by whites.

Williams's very presence in the medical profession was a terrific encouragement for blacks pursuing careers in the field. It also made a strong case for the abilities of black-health care professionals, profoundly so in 1913, when he became the first black physician on staff at Chicago's largest hospital, St. Luke's, and the first black member of the American College of Surgeons.

NEWS BITS

In 1891, the year that Provident Hospital opened, . . .

- Isaac Murphy won the Kentucky Derby for the third time.

- Daniel Payne's *History of the African Methodist Episcopal Church* was published.

- Several colleges for blacks were founded, among them North Carolina Agricultural & Technical in Greensboro, the students of which later sparked a wave of sit-ins in the 1960s, which moved Bob Moses, among many others, to action.

In 1893, the year Williams performed that historic heart surgery, . . .

- Russell Webb founded the Oriental Publishing Company and started publishing *The Muslim World*.

- Paul Laurence Dunbar saw his first book of poetry published, *Oak and Ivy* (the kickoff of his becoming the most celebrated black poet of the day).

- A second Provident Hospital was founded in Baltimore, Maryland.

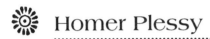 Homer Plessy

We do not know when Plessy was born, what were his aims, or how he frolicked. There's evidence to suggest that he may have been born in New Orleans, and that his trade (or at least one of them) was carpentry. What we know for sure is that he was an octoroon, and that though he could have passed for white, he did not—otherwise he would not have done what he did.

It was in New Orleans in June 1892 that Homer Plessy purchased a first-class ticket for the East Louisiana Railway train bound for Covington. When time came to ride, he took a seat in the coach designated for whites. How the conductor knew he was not white we do not know, but he did, and he ordered Plessy to remove himself to the coach for the colored.

The conductor was just doing his job, making Plessy abide by the 1890 Louisiana statute "to promote the comfort of passengers," which called for railway companies to provide "equal but separate accommodations" for whites and nonwhites. Not to sit in one's racially designated place was a crime.

When Plessy refused to move, he was forcibly removed from the train, then jailed and subsequently convicted of violating the law by Judge John H. Ferguson. So far, so good; things had gone just the way Plessy and his coconspirators had hoped.

Behind Plessy's defiance was the Citizens Committee to Test the Constitutionality of the Separate Car Law, formed in 1891. It had been waiting for such a moment as this, and when Plessy was arrested, the committee was ready. They had raised money (about three thousand dollars) for expenses. They had arranged for attorney Albion Tourgée (who charged no fee) to head up the litigation. Tourgée was one of the most outspoken white champions of black rights and author of the novel *A Fool's Errand*, a scold on the South during Reconstruction, which inspired **Charles W. Chesnutt** in his writing.

Plessy's conviction was appealed all the way to the U.S. Supreme Court, with arguments commencing in mid-April 1896. Plessy's attorneys contended that segregation violated the Thirteenth and Fourteenth Amendments and necessarily imposed inferiority on blacks. Justice John Marshall Harlan saw their point: "The arbitrary separation of citizens, on the basis of race, while they are on a public highway, is a badge of servitude wholly inconsistent with the civil freedom and the equality before the law established by the Constitution. It cannot be justified on legal grounds." Unfortunately, it was rationalized—if not justified—on legal grounds because Harlan was the lone dissenter in *Plessy* decision, handed down on May 18, 1896.

All of the other justices found that the separation of the races violated no one's rights. Furthermore, if blacks felt inferior, well, it was in their heads: "We consider the underlying fallacy of the plaintiff's argument," said Justice Brown, who delivered the majority opinion, "to consist in the assumption that the enforced separation of the two races stamps the colored race with a badge of inferiority. If this be so, it is not by reason of anything found in the act, but solely because the colored race chooses to put that construction on it." After all, the reasoning went, segregation cut both ways, and if separation from blacks didn't make whites feel inferior, then . . . you get the idea.

Jim Crow statutes had been cropping up since 1883 when the United States Supreme Court abolished the Civil rights Act of 1875.* The *Plessy* decision made the doctrine of separate-but-equal constitutional and thereby institutionalized, and it encouraged a plethora of laws that bred and fed racist behavior. It would be almost sixty years to the day before the *Plessy* decision was overturned, owing in large part to **Charles Hamilton Houston.** Until then, if a state so chose, African Americans would have to live with separate schools, separate water fountains, separate entrances to hamburger shacks, separate seating in movie theaters, separate parks and swimming pools—or no parks and swimming pools. They would have to contend with being refused admission into hospitals, with prohibitions against trying on clothes (not even a hat), with traveling in a railroad car that was usually quite ratty, for never was anything equal unless it was created and controlled by blacks.

As for Homer Plessy, as ordered, he paid the twenty-five dollar fine for his impertinence and then disappeared from history.

BOOK MARK

- *The Plessy Case: A Legal–Historical Interpretation*, by Charles A. Lofgren (1987)

*See **Robert Brown Elliot**

- *The Betrayal of the Negro: From Rutherford B. Hayes to Woodrow Wilson*, by Rayford W. Logan (1965, the revised edition of *The Negro in American Life and Thought: The Nadir, 1877–1901*)

- *The Thin Disguise: Turning Point in Negro History, Plessy v. Ferguson*, edited by Otto H. Olsen (1967)

- *The Origins of the New South, 1877–1913*, by C. Vann Woodward (1951)

- *The Strange Career of Jim Crow*, by C. Vann Woodward (1955)

 Robert Charles (d. 1900)

It's an all-too-familiar story: Two brothers just chillin', not stressing a fly, talking about what-we-don't-know. Trading bodacious lies? Parading earnest dreams for popcorn skies? Whatever it was, it all went goodbye when the two brothers just chillin' got hassled by the cops.

Such was the trigger of what befell Robert Charles the summer of 1900, a tragedy chronicled by the intrepid Ida B. Wells in her pamphlet *Mob Rule in New Orleans: Robert Charles and His Fight to the Death* (1900). It was on July 24, 1900, that, as Wells wrote,

> three policemen . . . observing two colored men sitting on the doorsteps of Dryades street, between Washington avenue and 6th streets, determined, without a shadow of authority, to arrest them. One of the colored men was named Robert Charles, the other was a lad of nineteen named Leonard Pierce. . . . They had not broken the peace in any way whatever, no warrant was in the policeman's hands justifying their arrest, and no crime had been committed of which they were the suspects. The policemen, however, secure in the firm belief that they could do anything to a Negro that they wished, approached the two men, and in less than three minutes from the time they accosted them attempted to put both colored men under arrest. The younger of the two men, Pierce, submitted to arrest, for the officer, Cantrelle, who accosted him, put his gun in the young man's face ready to blow his brains out if he moved. The other colored man, Charles, was made a victim of a savage attack by Officer Mora, who used a billet and then drew a gun and tried to kill Charles. Charles drew his gun nearly as quickly as the policeman, and began a duel in the street, in which both participants were shot. The policeman got the worst of the duel, and fell helpless to the sidewalk. Charles made his escape.

Some newspapers reported that Charles and Pierce, poised for a burglary, had instigated the hostilities, but as Wells pointed out, such accounts were at odds with Officer Mora's statement that the conflict started after he laid hands on one of the men. Mora had also stated that he and his fellow officers approached Charles and Pierce on the prompting of three black women who deemed them "suspicious types." If this was true, surely those women later rued the day they loosed their lips, considering all that transpired because of their tip.

The madness began when the New Orleans police department instructed officers to kill Charles on sight because he was a "desperate man." As Wells observed, "the only evidence that Charles was a desperate man lay in the fact that he had refused to be beaten over the head by Officer Mora for sitting on a step quietly conversing with a friend."

News of a dead-or-alive reward of $250 was soon in the streets, as were about one hundred of New Orleans's finest. The next day, Charles was found in his digs on Fourth Street. Long before sunrise, the block was ringed with cops. A shootout ensued in which Charles popped two cops and then evaded capture. Lots of others did not evade arrest: Dozens of black men were tossed in jail, as Wells reported, "upon the pretext that they were impertinent and 'game niggers.'" Later, for the crime of "not moving along" many more were given the choice of either a twenty-five-dollar fine or thirty days in jail.

Jail became a safer place to be as mob rule raged in New Orleans. Among those who suffered at the hands of vigilantes was George Meyers, who had been picked up for an offense classified as "insolence." During the thirty-minute mule-drawn wagon ride to the police station, Meyers was severely beaten by passersby, who assumed he was the desperado Robert Charles. No heroic efforts were made to disabuse the mob of this notion—nor did the police try to inform the crowd of about two hundred young toughs around the police station. Before Meyers could be brought into the station, reported the *Times-Democrat,* "he was punched, kicked, bruised and torn. His clothes were ripped from his back, while his face after that few minutes was unrecognizable." And it got worse. In a short time, gangs of white folks went off on black folks.

On the evening of July 26, some seven hundred "avengers" amassed at the square, where at one point they were addressed by the Mayor of Kenner, a town a tad northwest of New Orleans. According to the *Times-Democrat,* the mayor's remarks included the following:

> I have come down to New Orleans to-night to assist you in teaching the blacks a lesson. I have killed a Negro before, and in revenge of the wrong wrought upon you and yours, I am willing to kill again. The only way that you can teach these Niggers a lesson and put them in their place is to go out and lynch a few of them as an object lesson. String up a few of them, and the others will trouble you no more. That

is the only thing to do—kill them, string them up, lynch them! I will lead you, if you will but follow.

Mr. Mayor's recommendation for the first object lesson was Robert Charles's buddy Leonard Pierce.

They marched on the prison. When it proved impenetrable, the mob went after any black body they could find, from a newsie to an old man: Dragged from trolleys and beaten, shot down in the streets, their property—homes, businesses, schools—savaged, the mayhem stretched on into another day.

On Friday, July 27, Robert Charles was discovered in a house on Saratoga Street. His only ally was his Winchester rifle. With it, he did his level best to stave off the ever-growing crowd of cops and hooligans, killing and wounding more than a few. His surrender came only when the police torched the building. As Wells recounted,

> Finally, when the fire and the smoke became too much for flesh and blood, the long sought for fugitive appeared in the door, rifle in hand, to charge the countless guns that were drawn upon him. With a courage which was indescribable, he raised his gun to fire again, but this time it failed, for a hundred shots riddled his body, and he fell dead face fronting to the mob.

Robert Charles's death did not sate the mob. His corpse was dragged into the muddy road and riddled with more bullets. A container of kerosene was hustled over in response to cries of "Burn him! Burn him!" The police suppressed this act, but not the stomping of the body. After the mutilated remains of Robert Charles had been dumped into a patrol wagon, the violence continued, with sticks and whatever else came to hand. The following day, black New Orleans was to have more hell to pay: scores beaten, some thirty homes set afire.

Who was Robert Charles? Was he really "a daredevil and a fiend in human form" as many insisted? When a reporter for the *Times-Democrat* investigated his digs for clues to what manner of man Robert Charles was—*ecce*. What a treasury of terror he found:

> In his room were found negro periodicals and other "race" propaganda, most of which was in the interest of the negro's emigration to Liberia. . . . Well-worn text-books bearing his name written in his own scrawling handwriting, and well-filled copybooks found in his trunk showed that he had burnt the midnight oil, and was desirous of improving himself intellectually in order that he might conquer the hated white race. Much of the literature found among his chattels was of a superlatively vituperative character, and attacked the white race in unstinted language and asserted the equal rights of the negro.

Among the accursed propaganda were many copies of a magazine with editorials "anarchistic in the extreme." The reporter for the *Times-Democrat* suspected that this magazine was "the official organ of all haters of the white race." This dread publication was a product of the A.M.E. Church, *Voice of Missions*, edited by Bishop Henry McNeal Turner.

As for the man's burglaring, the only conclusion the reporter could come to is that he no doubt stashed his booty at another location because nothing of value was found in his room. His clothes were described as "little more than rags." Although the reporter unearthed nothing to support the casting of this man as a vast, vicious criminal, he titled his personality profile of Robert Charles, "The Making of a Monster."

What an all-too-familiar story.

Granville T. Woods (1856–1910)

Granville Woods had an attraction to things mechanical and a fascination with invisible fire. Put the two together in a creative mind, and out came a profusion of inventions. When Granville, a native of Columbus, Ohio, was ten years old, he began apprenticing in a machine shop that specialized in repairing railroad equipment. When he was sixteen, he was working for the Danville and Southern Railroad in Missouri, eventually becoming an engineer for this company. After a couple of other jobs and some side study of mechanical engineering and electronics, in 1878, Woods got a job with the British steamer *Ironsides*, starting as an engineer and rising to chief engineer.

By 1884, Woods was his own boss, running an electrical-engineering shop in Cincinnati, with his brother. This same year, he received his first patent: for a more fuel-efficient steam-boiler furnace. During the next two decades, he filed upward of sixty patents.

Among Woods' inventions of major significance are a telephone transmitter; an electromagnetic brake; a regulator for electric motors; the "troller," the little grooved wheel that allows streetcars (a.k.a. trolleys) to juice up from overhead powerlines; an "induction telegraphy," which enabled trains in motion to better communicate; the "third rail," so commonplace in subway systems around the world. These are just some of Woods' contributions to the early twentieth-century transportation and communications industries.

Sadly, Woods Electrical Company was never a financial success, not in Cincinnati and not in New York City, where he settled in 1890. When it came to marketing his products, he was stymied. Time and again, he was compelled to sell the rights to his inventions to companies with deep pockets, including American Bell Telephone and General Electric. What money Woods did accumulate was sapped toward the end of his life by legal fees he incurred while trying to keep big businesses from infringing on his patents.

INVENTORS OF WOODS' ERA

- Automatic engine lubricator — 1872, by Elijah McCoy, who inspired the term "the real McCoy" and was awarded more than forty patents, most related to machine lubrication
- Biscuit cutter — 1875, by A. P. Ashbourne, who also invented several coconut and coconut-oil processes
- Fire-escape ladder — 1878, by J. Winters
- Screw press — 1879, by Peter R. Campbell
- Carbon filament — 1882, by Lewis Latimer, who worked for Alexander Graham Bell in the 1870s and went to work for Edison Electric Light Company in 1884
- Shoe-lasting machine — 1883, by Jan E. Matzeliger
- Egg beater — 1884, by Willis Johnson
- Typewriter — 1885, by Lee S. Burridge and Newman R. Marsham
- Elevator — 1887, by Alexander Miles
- Fountain pen — 1890, by William B. Purvis, who invented a hand stamp
- Clothes dryer — 1892, by George T. Sampson
- Corn silker — 1894, by Robert P. Scott
- Bread-crumbing machine — 1895, by Joseph Lee, who also invented a bread-making machine
- Street sweeper — 1896, by Charles B. Brooks
- Lawn sprinkler — 1897, by Joseph H. Smith
- Train-car coupler — 1897, by Andrew J. Beard, who also invented a rotary engine
- Pencil sharpener — 1897, by John Lee Love
- Convertible settee and bed — 1897, by John H. Evans
- Galoshes — 1898, by A. L. Rickman
- Folding bed — 1899, by Leonard C. Bailey
- Modified Air Ship — 1900, by J. F. Pickering
- Self-feeding rapid-fire rifle — c. 1912, by Frederick M. Johnson
- Gas mask — 1914, by Garrett A. Morgan, who also patented the three-way automatic traffic signal in 1923, which he sold to General Electric for $40,000

William Drew Robeson (1845–1918)

> He had the greatest speaking voice I have ever heard. It was a deep, sonorous basso, richly melodic and refined, vibrant with the love and compassion which filled him.
>
> PAUL ROBESON, *Here I Stand* (1958)

William Drew Robeson, of Igbo lineage, had emancipated himself from Robersonville, North Carolina, at age fifteen, hitching a ride on the Underground Railroad. He had served as a laborer in the Union Army, had managed to get some basic schooling, and had made up his mind to get even more education. Like so many others, he wanted more out of freedom than survival.

Paying his way with farmwork, William Drew Robeson attended the Pennsylvania school that began as the Ashmun Institute in 1854, the first college expressly for blacks to be chartered in the United States. This school, originally purposed "for the scientific, classical, and theological education of colored youth of the male sex," became Lincoln University in 1866 and, in time, known as the "Black Princeton" because of its rigorous curriculum and because many faculty members had attended or taught at Princeton Theological Seminary.

At Lincoln, Robeson earned his A.B. in 1873 and his Bachelor of Sacred Theology in 1876. He displayed excellence not only in academics but also in character and awareness. A classmate, Nathan F. Mossell, would later describe him as "among the notable exceptions" to "the 'Uncle Tom' tendencies" of Lincoln students.

The Lincoln–Princeton connection probably accounts for William Drew Robeson's resettling in Princeton, New Jersey, where he became pastor of the Witherspoon Street Presbyterian Church in the late 1870s. By then, he was a married man. His wife was a former Philadelphia schoolteacher, Maria Louisa Bustill.*

Robeson's pastorate in Princeton was not a grand one; he'd never

---

*Maria Louisa Bustill's great-great-grandfather, the freedman Cyrus Bustill, a baker for the Continental Army and later proprietor of a prosperous bakery in Philadelphia, was a cofounder of the first black self-help organization in America, the Free African Society (1787) and a friend and mentor to **James Forten.** Among the other illustrious members of the Bustill clan: Cyrus's daughter Grace Bustill Douglass, a cofounder of the Philadelphia Female Anti-Slavery Society, and his grandsons Joseph Cassey Bustill, Underground Railroad agent, and David Bustill Bowser, artist. Maria Louisa's sister Gertrude Bustill Mossell was a prolific journalist and author of one of the first histories of black women, *The Work of the Afro-American Woman* (1894). Gertrude's husband was William Drew Robeson's college classmate Nathan Francis Mossell, the first black graduate of the University of Pennsylvania's School of Medicine and founder of Philadelphia's Frederick Douglass Memorial Hospital (1895), which later merged with Mercy Hospital.

live high off the hog. Many of his parishioners were farm laborers. A great many others were in service—as cooks and butlers, as gardeners and cleaners, as table servants and coachmen—at the university and in the homes of the wealthy ones in this town not at all benevolent to blacks. Princeton, as William's famous son wrote in *Here I Stand*, was "spiritually located in Dixie," having drawn "a large part of its student body and faculty from below the Mason–Dixon Line, and along with these sons of the Bourbons came the most rigid social and economic patterns of White Supremacy."

William Drew Robeson was not known to hold his tongue about racial injustices. His refusal to be the nice Negro that white Princeton wanted him to be was at the root of his ouster from Witherspoon Street Presbyterian Church in 1901, after some twenty years of dedicated service. At that time, Robeson was the father of five, the oldest of whom, William Drew, Jr., was around eighteen and the youngest, Paul, three years old. What's more, his wife was an invalid, almost blind.

Yes, he would be able to make money guest preaching, but there was no way he could support his family on that. Where others might have been broken and fled into madness, the bottle, or another town, Robeson kept being a man, doing what he had to do, which he could only do because he wasn't consumed with false pride:

> He got a horse and a wagon, and began to earn his living hauling ashes for the townsfolk. This was his work at the time I first remember him and I recall the growing mound of dusty ashes dumped into our backyard at 13 Green Street.

Reverend Robeson had a sideline, too: driving Princetonians hither and yon, around town and sometimes to resorts on the Jersey shore, to enclaves off-limits to blacks, except for the likes of a driver of a hack.

> Ash-man, coachman, he was still the dignified Reverend Robeson to the community, and no man carried himself with greater pride. Not once did I hear him complain of the poverty and misfortune of those years. Not one word of bitterness ever came from him. Serene, undaunted, he struggled to earn a livelihood and see to our education.

In 1904, Reverend Robeson suffered another blow: His wife died following the injuries she sustained when a piece of coal from the stove caught hold of her dress. Again, Robeson stood strong for himself, for his kids. Not long after the death of Mrs. Robeson, he sent his son Ben to a preparatory school in Charlotte, North Carolina, and then to Biddle University (now Johnson C. Smith University), and his daughter Marian to Scotia Seminary in Concord, North Carolina. William Drew, Jr., was already attending Lincoln University, and the son known as

Reed was working in Princeton as a cab driver. William's baby boy Paul was six years old.

When Paul was nine, his father returned to full-time ministry in a different denomination. His new church was the small congregation in Westfield, New Jersey, which became the Downing Street A.M.E. Zion Church. After a few years there, Reverend Robeson was transferred to St. Thomas A.M.E. Zion in Somerville.

With all the demands on his time and energy that came with being a pastor, the widower found time for his youngest, in need of a lot of attention now that he was in high school. Excellence was what he expected of his son. Reverend Robeson did not push Paul to best others but to do *his* best. If he was capable of earning a grade of 100, Paul recalled, his father was not jubilant over a 95. Reverend Robeson was also a devotee of that West African proverb, "Not to know is a misfortune, Not to want to know is anathema." As Paul later noted,

> A love for learning, a ceaseless quest for truth in all its fullness—this my father taught. . . . I do not know, in political terms, what stand my father took in the debate then raging in Negro life between the militant policy of **W. E. B. Du Bois** and the conservative preachments of **Booker T. Washington**—that clash of opposing ideas as to the path for Negro progress which was so largely expressed in terms of educational goals. But . . . he firmly believed that the heights of knowledge must be scaled by the freedom-seeker. Latin, Greek, philosophy, history, literature—all the treasures of learning must be the Negro's heritage as well.
>
> So for me in high school there would be four years of Latin and then in college four more years of Latin and Greek. Closely my father watched my studies, and was with me page by page through Virgil and Homer and the other classics in which he was well grounded. He was my first teacher in public speaking, and long before my days as a class orator and college debater there were the evenings of recitations at home, where his love for the eloquent and meaningful word and his insistence on purity of diction made their impress.

The father did indeed live on in the son.

 # Booker T. Washington (c. 1856–1915)

In all likelihood, the first time Booker appeared in print was in 1861, in the inventory of his late owner James Burroughs—"1 negro boy (Booker)." This boy of six or seven with no last name was valued at $400. Forty years later, Booker Taliaferro Washington appeared in print in a far more dynamic way with *Up from Slavery*, his own story of his sojourn from slave in Virginia, to master builder of Alabama's Tuskegee Institute.

When released in March 1901, *Up from Slavery* was an instant best-seller. "One of the great books of the year," proclaimed William T. Harris, the U.S. Commissioner of Education, adding that *Up from Slavery* was to the "problems left us by that civil war" what Harriet Beecher Stowe's *Uncle Tom's Cabin* was to its start. "Every white man in the South should read it, and every negro man should study it as an inspiration," stated C. P. J. Mooney, editor of Memphis Tennessee's weekly the *Commercial Appeal.* The book also received kudos from the white press up North. Over and over again, *Up from Slavery* was compared with *The Autobiography of Benjamin Franklin.* The "Horatio Alger myth in black" became its tag.

The root of the spectacular rise of this man born eight years before the Emancipation Proclamation was his childhood hunger for education. As we read in the early pages of *Up from Slavery:*

> I had no schooling whatever while I was a slave, though I remember on several occasions I went as far as the schoolhouse door with one of my young mistresses to carry her books. The picture of several dozen boys and girls in a schoolroom engaged in study made a deep impression upon me, and I had the feeling that to get into a schoolhouse and study in this way would be about the same as getting into paradise.

So it was that this lad, a few months free, began schooling himself with a used copy of Noah Webster's *Elementary Spelling-Book.* In and around his labors at a West Virginia salt furnace and later a coal mine, he snatched time to attend a makeshift school. Word of a "great school for the coloured people somewhere in Virginia" prompted him to leave home in 1872. With his meager belongings in a satchel and less than two dollars in his pocket, sixteen-year-old Booker T. Washington set out on a 500-mile trek to Hampton Normal and Agricultural Institute. He earned admittance by the vigor with which he cleaned a classroom, paid his way primarily through janitorial work, and graduated with honors in 1875.

Nothing at Hampton captivated him more than the school's founder, General Samuel Chapman Armstrong, a leading proponent of vocational education for black people and a firm believer that self-reliance and industry were the keys to the race's advancement. Advocacy for civil rights was foolish, Armstrong believed. No more faithful disciple did Armstrong find than Booker T. Washington.

After teaching a few seasons in his hometown of Malden, West Virginia, and then flirting with the study of law and with seminary, Washington returned to his alma mater to teach. With him came his hometown sweetheart, Fanny Norton Smith, whose studies at Hampton had been interrupted.

It was on General Armstrong's recommendation that in 1881 Washington was handed the job of starting a school in Tuskegee, Alabama, "in a broken down shanty and an old hen house," as he was so fond of saying. Tuskegee Normal and Industrial Institute's mission was to train up schoolteachers and masters of various crafts and trades. "The individual who can do something that the world wants done will, in the end, make his way regardless of his race," was one precept Principal Washington instilled in his students. "Nothing ever comes to one, that is worth having, except as a result of hard work" was another. Having students make the bricks with which they would construct their school buildings was just one way Tuskegee put into practice its preachments on industry and self-reliance.

Assisting Washington with this endeavor was his sweetheart Fanny, who became his wife in 1882 and who gave birth to their only child, Portia, in 1883. Also a tremendous help in fund-raising and other matters of Tuskegee's survival and growth was teacher and Lady Principal, Olivia America Davidson, whom Washington married about a year after Fannie's death, in 1885, and with whom he later had two sons.

Their marriage was an ideal match, but, sadly, it, too, did not last long: On a February night in 1889, when Washington was on the road fund-raising, a fire broke out in the Washington home, sending all therein out into the cold, and Olivia into collapse. Washington had her taken North, to Massachusetts General Hospital in Boston, but she never recovered, dying on May 9, 1889. "Olivia's death left [him] destitute, not only emotionally but financially," we read in volume one of Louis R. Harlan's *Booker T. Washington.* "He had spent so long at her bedside, forgetting all else, that he barely had money to bring her body home to Tuskegee for burial beside the grave of Fanny."

Though he was now a single father of three, Washington did not rush to remarry, but when he did take another wife, he made a logical choice: Margaret Murray James, Tuskegee's Lady Principal since 1890. They married in 1892.

One wonders how Washington coped with his personal griefs and family matters during Tuskegee's first decade, given the pressure he was under to make Tuskegee a viable institution. He knew the outside world was watching closely to see, as he wrote, "whether or not it was possible for Negroes to build up and control the affairs of a large educational institution." This was truly a feat in post-Reconstruction America, especially in the deep South, where with the 1877 withdrawal of federal troops, there ensued a most vicious reign of terror, with the wholesale theft of black property and white-on-black violence reaching all-time highs, and with the torching of schools for "nigras" a frequent night-riders' sport. Fully aware what savage reckoning could befall a black man tagged "uppity," Washington could do nothing but wear the mask as he worked tirelessly, ceaselessly, and with great success to procure white patronage and protection for his school. So it was that Tuskegee became a beacon, and Washington a Moses to multitudes striving to move up from myriad desolations rooted in the legacy of slavery. People such as these gained strength from the life story of Booker T. Washington, who became known as "the sage of Tuskegee."

The thing that endeared Washington to a great many white people was his implicit and explicit advocacy of accommodation. This philosophy earned him high praise from powerful white Americans on September 18, 1895, the opening day of the Cotton States and International Exposition in Atlanta, Georgia, where before an interracial and intersectional audience Washington delivered the address known as the "Atlanta Compromise."

In this speech, Washington pitched against the black emigration movement in general and black flight from the South in particular (which would have deprived the South of much cheap labor), saying, "Cast down your bucket where you are." Further along, he seemingly gave the okay to segregation with the now equally famous words: "In all things that are purely social we can be as separate as the five fingers, yet one as the hand in all things essential to mutual progress." (As many have pointed out, however, this statement was also cheered by many black nationalists.) Civil-rights activists abandoned all hope of help from Washington when they heard of his assertion that "the wisest among my race understand that the agitation of questions of social equality is the extremest folly."

The speech drew tremendous praise from diverse quarters. Washington's future rival **W. E. B. Du Bois** congratulated him by letter on his "phenomenal success," calling the speech "a word fitly spoken." People on both sides of the color line likened Washington to **Frederick Douglass,** who had died in February 1895. Not surprisingly, progressives found this comparison obscene, no doubt recalling Douglass's famous dictum, "Power concedes nothing without a demand." The A.M.E. Church Bishop Henry McNeal Turner's statement that Washington would "have to live a long time to undo the harm he has done to our race" was among the more subdued expressions of displeasure with Washington's Atlanta address.

What Bishop Turner or any other black person thought didn't much matter because with this address, influential white Americans summarily glorified Washington as *the* spokesperson for his race. "The speech stamps Booker T. Washington as a wise counselor and a safe leader," was the way an *Atlanta Constitution* editorial hailed Washington as a nonthreatening Negro. With this perception abounding, Booker T. Washington went on to become the most prominent and powerful black man in pre–World War I America.

In the wake of his Atlanta address, many urged Washington to write his autobiography, among them, Walter Hines Page, with the Boston publisher Houghton, Mifflin and Company. Washington needed little convincing that an autobiography was in order, but Walter Hines Page would not be the editor to acquire it. At some point in 1897, Washington sent a book proposal to a subscription house, J. L. Nichols, in Naperville, Illinois. To expedite things, he chose as his collaborator a black journalist, Edgar Webber.

The Story of My Life and Work (1900) was the autobiography that came of Webber and Washington's collaboration. It was not a fine piece of work, but flaws and all, *The Story of My Life and Work* sold briskly among blacks because of the huge hunger in the black community for books by anyone black, especially someone as idolized as Washington.

In his determination to get out a good autobiography, Washington engaged the services of Max Bennett Thrasher, a white journalist who became an ad hoc publicist for Tuskegee Institute. Washington was not an absentee author, however. According to Harlan, "manuscript fragments in Washington's own hand . . . suggest that [it] was largely the work of Washington's own mind and purpose."

Washington's mind was on Tuskegee Institute; his purpose, raising money. This came across loud and clear in a letter dated September 22, 1900, to J. L. Nichols's general manager, apparently written to halt a charge of breach of contract or trust. "The work which I am to do for the other people," wrote Washington, "will have as its main advantage the bringing of this institution before a class of people who have money and to whom I must look for money for endowments and other purposes." Near the end of the letter, Washington stressed that the book he was doing for "the other people" would not hurt *The Story of My Life and Work:* "In proportion as I can get money . . . and keep this institution in a prosperous condition, in the same degree will there be a sale for your book. If this institution were to go down tomorrow, your book would at once become dead property on your hands, so you see it is important that we work wisely and sympathetically together."

"The other people" were Doubleday, Page & Company, with "Page" being Walter Hines Page, who had left Houghton, Mifflin. Setting the stage for the book's triumph was its serialization in the November 3, 1900–February 23, 1901 issues of the *Outlook* magazine, which had a circulation of upward of 100,000. Installments of *Up from Slavery* appeared in very interesting company, including "An Interview with Count Tolstoy" by Edward Steiner and the short story "The Queen's Twins" by Sarah Orne Jewett.

Just as Washington had hoped, *Up from Slavery* did bring Tuskegee new benefactors. For instance, E. Julia Emery, an American living in England, cut a check for $1,000. A gift of $5,000 was the response *Up from Slavery* elicited from millionaire–inventor George Eastman, creator of roll film and of the Kodak camera. The biggest benefactor *Up from Slavery* attracted was industrialist Andrew Carnegie. Doubleday, Page & Company's cofounder Frank N. Doubleday coaxed Carnegie into reading *Up from Slavery* during a game of golf. After he did, Carnegie became a staunch supporter of Tuskegee. His early gifts included a Carnegie Library, $600,000 in U.S. Steel bonds, and the proclamation that "the serious race question of the South is to be solved wisely, only by following Booker T. Washington's policy."

Not so, said many members of the black intelligentsia, and those who deemed accommodation anathema likewise deemed *Up from Slavery* a disservice to the race. In the vanguard was **William Monroe Trotter,** publisher of the newspaper the *Guardian* and leader of the anti–Booker T. Washington faction in Boston. The book's most oft-cited criticism came from **W. E. B. Du Bois,** who had evolved quite a bit since he applauded Washington on his Atlanta address.

"It is as though Nature must needs make men a little narrow to give them force." This is how Du Bois opened his review of *Up from Slavery* in the July 16, 1901, issue of *Dial,* a lesser light among turn-of-the-century little magazines. As do many present-era readers of *Up from Slavery,* Du Bois took Washington to task for soft-pedaling on the horrors of slavery, for promoting stereotypes about blacks, and for being less than honest about the racism he had encountered. Du Bois's best known critique of Washington later appeared in his essay "Of Mr. Booker T. Washington and Others," collected in *The Souls of Black Folk* (1903). Here, Du Bois more firmly decried Washington's accommodationist propaganda as an abetment to black disenfranchisement, de jure segregation (as a result of the case of **Homer Plessy**), and the "steady withdrawal" of funds from predominantly black colleges and universities. As well, Du Bois asserted that Booker T. Washington's program "practically accepts the alleged inferiority of blacks" and absolves white America of all responsibility for the nightmare plight of so many among the nation's ten million black souls.

Reproach from a few intellectuals (a type Washington despised) had little to no effect on Washington's popularity. About six months after the publication of *Up from Slavery,* on October 16, 1901, Washington dined at the White House with President Theodore Roosevelt, who was anxious to consult with him on political appointments and assorted race matters. Though this infuriated many white people (North and South), ultimately it increased Washington's fame and power, enabling him to expand his network, dubbed "the Tuskegee Machine" by Du Bois, who may have been the one to dub Washington "the Wizard."

As the undisputed boss of black America, Washington could make or break people's careers and institutions. As an adviser to Theodore

Roosevelt and President William Howard Taft, he secured political appointments for black men loyal to his philosophy, as well as determined the fates of a few white men seeking an office. He steered philanthropists to dozens of black schools he deemed worthy and diverted funds from those of which he did not approve.

Some of the criticism of Washington was not well-grounded, however. For instance, he was falsely accused of being categorically opposed to higher education for blacks. Along with the fact that his own children went to college, tangible evidence that counters the myth is that he was a trustee of Fisk University and of Howard University and helped both institutions connect with major philanthropists.

Given his prominence, many activists were furious with Washington for not speaking out vociferously against white mob violence, Jim Crow laws and policies, and other injustices. Even today, there are those who cannot forgive him his silence on such things, though it is now more widely known that Washington secretly orchestrated and funded several test cases against Jim Crow laws and supported other efforts regarded as militant in his day.

Washington virtually controlled the black press—driving into ruination more than a few who published dissent and winning the allegiance of some newspapers and magazines through carrot, through stick, and even through secret ownership. He could also be most vicious against those who challenged his program. One notorious example followed what Washington called the "Boston Riot," which was more like a little ruckus, between pro- and anti-Bookerites in late July 1903, at a Boston church where Washington was speaking. **William Monroe Trotter** was there, but he had not instigated the trouble; nevertheless, Washington manipulated Trotter's arrest and conviction for conspiracy to disturb the peace, and Trotter spent thirty days in jail. After the "Boston Riot," Washington embarked on an intense persecution of Trotter and his supporters. **Du Bois**'s shutout from a job at Atlanta University is just one example. One standard in Washington's bag of dirty tricks was to plant spies in organizations he opposed. Among the organization's he kept tabs on and tried to sabotage in this way was one Du Bois helped found in 1909: the NAACP.

Washington's dastardly deeds were, for the most part, unknown to or overlooked by average black people, for Washington brought many blessings into their lives. There was the Tuskegee Negro Conference (started in 1892), an annual gathering of hundreds who, as Washington described it, "come to spend a day in finding out what the actual industrial, mental, and moral conditions of the people are, and in forming plans for improvement." There was the Jesup Wagon, an agricultural school on wheels, launched in 1904 for the purpose of going out into the countryside with news and information that would help small farmers increase their productivity. In 1900, Washington founded the National Negro Business League, an idea appropriated from Du Bois. Granted that this organization—over which Washington presided until his death—was yet another means of enlisting and controlling supporters (especially in the North), it did help foster black entrepreneurship. Another good deed was his sponsorship of National Negro Health Week (March 1915), designed to bring money and energies to bear on issues of sanitation, hygiene, and disease prevention among the poor.

All the while that Washington was being boss and benefactor of black America, he was attracting and maintaining tremendous backing for Tuskegee—John D. Rockefeller, Jr.; an early partner in Standard Oil, Henry H. Rogers; investment banker Jacob Schiff; the Phelps Stokes family; and Julius Rosenwald, president of Sears, Roebuck, and Company, among them. As a result, when Washington died in 1915, Tuskegee Institute had more than a hundred well-equipped buildings, a faculty of nearly two hundred men and women offering instruction in about forty trades and professions, and an endowment of roughly two million dollars. Considering what Washington started with, Tuskegee Institute had certainly come a long way.

What Washington accomplished took a tremendous toll on his health. Occasionally, he heeded the urging of his wife, close friends, and physicians to take a vacation, but he never really knew what it was to take it easy. Diabetes was just one of the many ailments he suffered in his later years. Exhaustion was another.

While up North in early November 1915, Washington could bear up no longer and was eventually admitted to St. Luke's Hospital in New

Booker T. Washington near the end of his life. (Courtesy of Photographs and Prints Division, Schomburg Center for Research in Black Culture, The New York Public Library, Astor, Lenox and Tilden Foundations)

York City. Among other things, his kidneys were in very bad shape and his blood pressure was dangerously high. When doctors advised him that death was imminent, Washington did not fight it. He did, however, resist dying in the North. To doctors' counsel that he would probably not survive the trip to Tuskegee, Washington responded, "I was born in the South, I have lived in the South, and I expect to die and be buried in the South." So it was that on November 12, Margaret Washington boarded a southbound train with her husband. They arrived at their home, "The Oaks," on the night of November 13. The next morning, a little before five, Booker T. Washington died.

 # Charles W. Chesnutt (1858–1932)

Chesnutt is regarded as the first African American master of the short story, but that's not all. As we read in the introduction to a sampling of his work in *The Norton Anthology of African American Literature* (1996), Chesnutt was the first writer "to make the broad range of African American experience his artistic province and to consider practically every issue and problem endemic to the American color line worthy of literary attention. Because he developed literary modes appropriate to his materials, Chesnutt also left to his successors a rich formal legacy that underlies major trends in twentieth-century black fiction, from the ironies of James Weldon Johnson's classic African American fiction of manners to the magical realism of **Charles Johnson**'s contemporary neo-slave narratives." As is often pointed out, the irony of this pioneer in black literature is that he was a "voluntary Negro." Like so many had (and do today), this son of freeborn mulattoes could have taken the presumed easy way out and passed for white.

Charles Waddell Chesnutt, who was born in Cleveland, Ohio, was bright in the other sense, too. In Fayetteville, North Carolina, where he spent most of his childhood, he was an excellent student at the Howard School, established by the Freedman's Bureau, and named after its chief, General O. O. Howard, founder of Howard University. At age seventeen, Chesnutt began teaching school. At age twenty-one, he was moving on from first assistant to principal of a normal school in Fayetteville. By this time, he had married Susan Perry and was starting a family. Also, by this time, he had his sights set on a literary life.

In an April 1879 journal entry, Chesnutt declared his plans to go to some large city and do his utmost to make it as a writer. "I will live somehow, but live I will, and work," he vowed. His hope was that his solid stenography skills would land him a job at a newspaper—"and then,—work, work, work! I will trust in God and work." His zeal was in large part sparked by a best-seller of 1879, a novel about Reconstruction in North Carolina (and not at all flattering to whites): *A Fool's Errand,* by Judge Albion Tourgée, who later made news as the lead lawyer for **Homer Plessy.**

Chesnutt tried to "work, work, work" in Washington, D.C., but was unsuccessful. His determination to be a professional writer, however, never waned. In a journal entry of March 26, 1881, we read, "I have just finished Thackeray's 'Vanity Fair,' his first great novel. . . . Every time I read a good novel, I want to write one. It is the dream of my life—to be an author! . . . It is a mixture of motives. I want fame; I want money; I want to raise my children in a different rank of life from that I sprang from." Chesnutt despaired of ever becoming prosperous working as a stenographer. As for other professions, well, that would just take too long: "In law or medicine, I would be compelled to wait half a life-time to accomplish anything. But literature pays—the successful."

There was also the sheer love of writing: "There is a fascination about this calling that draws a scribbler irresistibly toward his doom. He knows that the chance of success is hardly one out of a hundred; but he is foolish enough to believe, or sanguine enough to hope, that he will be the successful one." Though he knew the odds, Chesnutt was nevertheless going to stick with it and stay positive. Near the end of this entry, he wrote, "I am confident that I can succeed, in some degree, at any rate. It is the only thing I can do without capital, under my present circumstances, except teach. . . . 'Where there's a will etc,' and there is certainly a will in this case."

Back behind this hope for fame and fortune was a desire to make a contribution to American society. This is how he had expressed it in his May 29, 1880 journal entry:

> The object of my writings would be not so much the elevation of the colored people as the elevation of the whites,—for I consider the unjust spirit of caste which is so insidious as to pervade the whole nation, and so powerful as to subject a whole race and all connected with it to scorn and social ostracism—I consider this a barrier to the moral progress of the American people; and I would be one of the first to head a determined, organized crusade against it.

In 1883, Chesnutt went North again and found work as a stenographer and journalist in New York City. After a year of this, a less giddy and more pragmatic Chesnutt settled his family in the city of his birth, Cleveland, Ohio, where he established a legal stenography business. To this, after studying law and passing the Ohio bar (at the top of his class) in 1887, he added a law practice.

All along, Chesnutt had been submitting stories to little magazines and pint-sized periodicals. His big break came when two stories were accepted by the *Atlantic Monthly:* the now widely anthologized "The

Goophered Grapevine" (1887) and "Po' Sandy" (1888). Then, in 1899, *Atlantic Monthly*'s parent company, Houghton Mifflin, published Chesnutt's *The Conjure Woman*, a collection of beguiling stories about slavery days, which included "The Goophered Grapevine" and "Po' Sandy." The stories are narrated by a white Northerner, John, who has transplanted himself and his wife to a small estate in the South. The true storyteller, however, is the man from whom John got the tales: his gardener, the shrewd Uncle Julius MacAdoo. Uncle Remus he is not.

With sensitivity, wit, and craft, Chesnutt offered in *The Conjure Woman* a poignant portrait of what enslaved blacks endured and the ways many triumphed. This was significant, in light of the dumb-and-happy-darky stories that apologists for the South, such as Thomas Nelson Page, had been churning out. Chesnutt told it as it was: presenting slaveholders as cruel and inhumane, and presenting blacks as mentally and emotionally richer than most whites wanted to believe. Naturally, with Chesnutt being connected to the culture, his use of Southern black dialect and folklore was far more adept than that of white writers such as the creator of Uncle Remus, Joel Chandler Harris. *The Conjure Woman* sold very well, in large part, some say, because Chesnutt's publisher allowed the public to think the author was white.

The collection's success enabled Chesnutt to get other work published—and fast. *The Wife of His Youth and Other Stories of the Color Line*, which deals for the most part with the follies of light-skinned blacks (including their animus toward dark-skinned people) also came out in 1899, as did a short biography of **Frederick Douglass.** Soon, Chesnutt's racial identity was no longer a secret, and he actually be-

Charles Chesnutt in 1891, the year his first book, *The Conjure Woman*, was published. (Courtesy of Photographs and Prints Division, Schomburg Center for Research in Black Culture, The New York Public Library, Astor, Lenox and Tilden Foundations)

came something of a darling in the white literary world. In light of his success, he closed his business, convinced that he would be able to support himself and his family from book sales and speaking engagements.

His first novel to get published was *The House behind the Cedars* (1900). This story of a tragic mulatto, which treated passing with some complexity and not mere stereotypes, did not sell very well. Nor did Chesnutt's second novel, *The Marrow of Tradition* (1901), the story of the virtual obliteration of black life and property in the fictional town of Wellington. This novel was based on the events of 1898, in Wilmington, North Carolina, where, before white supremacists decided to "take back" the town, blacks were not only in the majority but also had a substantial business and professional class, with several occupying such important offices as deputy sheriff and police chief. After a cadre of leading white citizens issued a "Declaration of White Independence" in early November 1898, mobs tore into the black community—killing, burning, looting. By 1900, the year before *The Marrow of Tradition* was published, blacks held no offices in Wilmington, North Carolina, and the town was practically barren of black entrepreneurs and professionals. Chesnutt's recollection of the Wilmington Massacre did not do well. Chesnutt had not expected the novel to be embraced by the majority of white Southerners, but the thumbs down it received from most in the Northern white press was surprising, alarming. He had hoped his exposé on the nasty realities of post-Reconstruction South would "elevate" these whites to campaign for reform.

In 1902, Chesnutt reopened his stenography business and law practice, which turned out to be more financially rewarding than he had once imagined. Still, he wrote. He tried his hand at a piece of nonthreatening literature with a novel about romance among Boston's upper crust, but he was unable to interest a publisher in this work. He had better success with his short stories. One of his standouts of this period is "Baxter's Procrustes" (1904), which satirizes a snooty, all-white, all-male group of book collectors: the Rowfant Club in Cleveland, which had rejected Chesnutt's application for membership (but later admitted him).

In 1905, Chesnutt saw another novel published—*The Colonel's Dream*, another attempt to elevate, through the story of a redeemed ex-Confederate officer's unsuccessful efforts to make the small North Carolina town of his birth a more enlightened place. This novel sold poorly, and soon Chesnutt the literary artist was pretty much out of business.

Chesnutt did not stay out of the race business, however. He championed black ability and spoke out about discrimination in articles, in speeches, and through participation in events and programs of various organizations dedicated to racial uplift, including the Committee of Twelve, created by **Booker T. Washington** and the Niagara Movement, the cofounders of which included **William Monroe Trotter** and **W. E. B. Du Bois.**

In 1910, Chesnutt suffered a mild stroke, and poor health plagued him for the rest of his life. Though his literary work was neglected, it was not totally forgotten. In the early 1920s, there was renewed interest. The *Chicago Defender,* for example, serialized *The House behind the Cedars.* Then, in 1928, the NAACP honored the "voluntary Negro" with its Spingarn Medal, in gratitude for "his pioneer work as a literary artist in depicting the struggles" of African Americans. Long after Chesnutt's death readers would be reminded of his value through numerous books, including *Charles Waddell Chesnutt: Pioneer of the Color Line,* by the writer's daughter Helen M. Chesnutt (1952); *An American Crusade: The Life of Charles Waddell Chesnutt,* by Frances R. Keller (1977); *The Literary Career of Charles W. Chesnutt,* by William L. Andrews (1980); *The Short Fiction of Charles W. Chesnutt,* edited by Sylvia Lyons Render (revised edition, 1981); *The Journals of Charles W. Chesnutt,* edited by Richard Brodhead (1993), who also edited *The Conjure Woman and Other Conjure Tales* (1993), the "unexpurgated" conjure woman tales (i.e, the collection Chesnutt originally presented to Houghton, Mifflin).

 # William Monroe Trotter (1872–1934)

Trotter was very much under the weather on that early April day in 1934: Sleep eluded him that night, even after he'd taken his familiar constitutional up on the roof of the three-story Boston apartment building in which he was living. Back in his bed, he nagged sleep, and she refused him. Up to the roof again at some point closer to dawn than midnight—up to the roof to pace, to think, to find fatigue.

Perhaps he pondered his future, or perhaps the early April air whisked him back in time, way back, to the larks of his Boston boyhood in a sumptuous house in that swell suburb, Hyde Park. Fly in the buttermilk him and his family. Family. Inevitably, his father was the member most magnetic to memory. The famous James Monroe Trotter, veteran of the Civil War whose time with the Massachusetts Fifty-fifth included rising rapidly from a private to an officer and protesting vehemently for equal pay for black soldiers. The famous James Monroe Trotter became a man of means from his job as Recorder of Deeds and his real-estate business. Daddy was a real tiger when it came to race pride and progress, punching it out in politics and even writing a book about his people's achievements in music.

Perhaps on that early April day, James's only son wondered what course his life might have taken had he not absorbed Daddy's fire. Was

William Monroe Trotter as a young man. (Courtesy of Photographs and Prints Division, Schomburg Center for Research in Black Culture, The New York Public Library, Astor, Lenox and Tilden Foundations)

it love of learning or the need to prove himself as good as *them* (and fear of Daddy if he didn't) that made him excel at the predominantly white schools he attended and at Harvard College, where as a freshman he ranked third in a class of 376, where in his junior year he made history as the first black Harvard student elected to Phi Beta Kappa, where he graduated magna cum laude in 1895, earning a masters degree a year later? Or did brilliance just come easily to him?

Up on the roof all those years later . . . did he try to recapture the exhilaration of academic success? Maybe he strayed into why, during his Harvard days, he never pursued a friendship with that petite upperclassman with the ponderous name, who would one day simplify to W. E. B.?

If William Monroe Trotter was musing up there on the roof, surely he mused on his beloved Deenie, who once dated W. E. B. Geraldine Louise Pindell, of grace and charm and a prominent Papa, had been a catch, and she became his wife in 1899. Deenie and Monroe (as most called him) embarked on a whole life of their own in a lovely Dorchester house, ready to take their place among the bourgeoisie of Boston. There would be money enough for all the dainties with his inheritance and with the prosperity he'd generate through his real-estate business because, after all, the father was living on in the son.

Did he linger long on how sweet his life might have been had he not gotten involved with the founding of the Boston Literary and Historical Association, and gotten *so* involved with *so* many radical minds. For then, he might not have gotten *so* hot under the collar about that persistent peddler of accommodation, that "Benedict Arnold of the race!" **Booker T. Washington.** Why did Trotter have to make his disapproval a movement? Did he recollect the steps that led to his emergence as the leader of Boston's anti-Washington crowd? Was it simply because he had the biggest mouth, the sharpest tongue?

Had he not given into the obsession of bearding Booker, he never would have thrown in with George Forbes in starting a newspaper in 1901. Wasn't the *Guardian* supposed to be something he did on the side? Foolish thought that, when you give a paper the motto "For every right, with all thy might!"

The *Guardian* became his pulpit, his throne, his Sinai, from which he castigated the go-slow Negroes, from which he roused his readers to agitate! agitate! agitate! until racial justice became real.

Up on the roof, did he curse Booker T., imagining that if the Tuskegeean had not been so hell-bent on preaching against protest he would not have had to fight so hard, so long. Certainly that "Boston Riot," as Washington termed it, would never have occurred. "Are the rope and the torch all the race is to get under your leadership?" Trotter shouted out.

If Trotter and his allies had never attended Washington's address at a Boston church in late July 1903, he would never have uttered those words, there'd have been no fracas, and Washington would never have finagled Trotter's arrest and thirty-day jailing, never would have launched so vicious a campaign to destroy Trotter by financing rival papers, by sundry dirty tricks, including trying to dig up dirt—even on Deenie.

Oh, dear Deenie. When Forbes bailed out of the *Guardian,* dear Deenie, always rather physically fragile Deenie, came on board—associate editor, business manager, bottle washer.

If only making money and a crystal life with Deenie had been enough. . . .

He would not have gone through all the trouble of starting the Boston Suffrage League and then the New England Suffrage League, which worked for antilynching legislation, which worked for the death of Jim Crow, which worked for justice! justice! justice! He wouldn't have joined forces with that petite fellow with the ponderous name and some two dozen other black men of promise and prestige in forming the Niagara Movement in 1905. If he hadn't been so flinty and inflexible, he might have saved some energy and worked well within that organization instead of forming his own Negro Equal Rights League because the Niagara Movement was getting just a little too meek for him. Had he not been so insistent on black-led organizations for black people, maybe his league could have made merry with the Niagara Movement's reconstitution into the NAACP in 1909. Maybe he and W. E. B. could have become good buddies instead of contending forces.

Up there on the roof, maybe he regretted that he didn't shed some of his zeal in his forties. He could have spent time fishing, or raising begonias—instead of storming the White House in 1914 and raising hell, to Woodrow Wilson's face, about segregation in federal government offices.

Instead of spearheading a protest of *Birth of a Nation* in 1915—not a protest in rhetoric and petitions on paper, but the kind of protest the future would term "direct action," the kind with picket signs and bodies outside the movie house showing the offensive film.

Instead of masquerading as a ship's cook to get to France after the government denied him a passport for the must-make journey to the 1919 World Peace Conference, where he did all he could to broadcast his people's plight and to get some support for racial equality included in the Treaty of Versailles. He also wouldn't have been leading—in 1922, in 1923, in 1924, in 1926—delegations to the White House to press for desegregation and other things that would make life in America more bearable for blacks.

Up there on that flat roof, Trotter pondered, perhaps, how much more at ease he would have been right then had he not poured everything into protest and the *Guardian,* liquidating all his assets, spending his every penny. And Deenie, did she ruin her health standing by her man? Maybe she would not have succumbed to influenza if . . .

If only making money and a crystal life had been enough . . .

He wouldn't have found himself such an uninvited guest in the homes of most of the bourgeoisie of Boston. Did he fear he'd go down in history as a mere crank, as a footnote, if that?

During that early morning walkabout on the roof, he had no crystal ball, no way of knowing that the petite fellow with the ponderous name with whom he had so profoundly fallen out would proclaim that he "was a man of heroic proportions, and probably the most selfless of Negro leaders during all our American history," or that Lerone Bennett, Jr., would write that "Trotter laid the first stone of the modern protest movement," or that schools and libraries and more in Boston would bear his name.

Up there on the roof, sometime after five in the morning, William Monroe Trotter couldn't foresee any of this. Maybe he couldn't even see a tomorrow. Perhaps all he could see in the predawn light was that he was a sagging, powerless man without fame or fortune and with few friends. Did such ruminations push him to despair, or was it vertigo?

All we know is that around 5:30 A.M. on April 7, 1934, on the morning of his sixty-second birthday, William Monroe Trotter was found smashed on the pavement below the three-story Boston apartment building in which he was living.

Laurence C. Jones (1882–1975)

Jones's beginnings were humble, yet rich, because his parents held fast to all those ole-timey values such as hard work, honesty, and self-sacrifice. He was expected to be *somebody,* such as a lawyer, a doctor, or an entrepreneur.

His parents' high hopes were not at all moronic. The lad had a stout mind. It was a mind that had him reading like crazy and yearning for learning. It was a mind that made this boy of St. Joseph, Missouri, want to head up to Boston because he had heard it was a city of excellent schools.

As it turned out, he did not make it way North. He did, however, make it to Marshalltown, Iowa, where he boarded with kinfolks and attended Marshalltown High School, becoming the school's first black graduate. With his good mind still intact after all that, he went on to enroll in the University of Iowa, from which he graduated in 1907 with a bachelor's degree in philosophy.

What were his aims as a college student? How was he planning to be a somebody? For a time, he pondered a poultry business, but this dream grew no wings. It became mere memory during his sophomore year after a chance encounter—not with a person or place, but with a principle: noblesse oblige.

He had heard the college president use the phrase and had sought clarity on its depth and dimensions. A point of light and the apple of his eye the concept soon became. As his graduation drew nigh, Jones was fully convinced that he needed to make his life an expression of noblesse oblige. As he one day recalled,

> Although I had tempting job offers which ranged from the insurance business to a subsidized career in musical comedy, it seemed to me that if I used my education for selfish profit, [it] . . . would be a form of "willful waste." I decided to share my advantages with the neediest people of my race in the Black Belt of Mississippi. There was the most shocking waste of all: the waste of the human mind and soul. Men, women and children exhausted their bodies in the fields, making their living as farmers but having no knowledge of farming beyond the drudgery of chopping and picking cotton. Unable to read, write or figure, they had no way of knowing if what they were charged at the store was correct, or if their wages were paid in full. Winter diets were corn meal and dried peas because the women had never learned how to can or preserve the summer yield from their gardens or the wild berries that grew at their doors.

Jones accepted a teaching post at one of the "little Tuskegees," Utica Normal and Industrial Institute (later Hinds Junior College). Jones's life work would not be there, however, but a wee bit east in Piney Woods.

Jones wasn't looking for Piney Woods. Like the concept of noblesse oblige, it was something he stumbled upon after he accepted a Utica student's invitation to spend the Christmas holidays with him and his family in the Piney Woods community of Braxton. While there, Jones found out that for a long, long time, some people in the community had wanted to build a school, but hands and feet had never been put to the dream in any substantive way. Jones soon became the way.

He returned to Piney Woods in the Spring of 1909. His entry might not have been totally triumphal, but it was special: "The natives welcomed Dr. Jones, and immediately he went to work, visiting homes, churches, neighborhood gatherings under trees at noontime or anywhere he could get an audience." This quotation came from George Alexander Sewell and Margaret L. Dwight's profile of Jones in *Mississippi Black History Makers* (1984). "Sometimes astride a mule, sometimes in an ox-wagon, but more frequently afoot, walking eighteen or twenty miles a day, Jones travelled across Rankin and Simpson counties." Jones was on a mission to guide folks on small ways to improve their lot, from the how-tos and why-fores of whitewashing to the kernels of knowledge awaiting them in farm journals.

By the fall of 1909, Laurence C. Jones was fully determined to establish a school, even though the prospect of funds was pitiful. He did what Mary McLeod Bethune and so many others did who believed themselves called to some concrete work in uplifting the race from the very bottom: Laurence C. Jones stepped out on faith.

One fine Monday morning, Jones came together with a knot of boys and elderly men under the boughs of an old cedar tree. After singing the hymn "Praise God from Whom All Blessing Flow," reading scripture, and offering up prayer, Jones's school was officially in session. No place to go but up, that's for sure.

Jones's faith was not in vain. Close by the old cedar tree was an abandoned cabin that Jones thought would do nicely for a school. As it turned out, the cabin belonged to an old man with a kind heart. This man agreed to deed the property to Brother Jones, and he also pledged fifty dollars and forty acres. Soon, others were making donations to what became The Piney Woods Country Life School (not chartered until May 1913). Donations continued to come in. As we read in *Mississippi Black History Makers*, "In the second year of the school's existence, a friend sent money toward the purchase of a small hand press and type, and the school published a paper, *The Pine Torch*. . . . Little by little— or in the Jones tradition 'inch by inch'—the school prospered. Contributions came in the form of money, an old piano, a typewriter, tools for a blacksmith shop, farm implements, a mule, a plow, and an old broom-making machine."

Like most vocational schools of the era, the students paid their way with labor, and sometimes with donations from the folks back home. For example, Georgie Lee Myers's methods of payment included a pound of butter and a dime from Aunt Hester Robinson, four bits from Aunt Lucy McConnel, a chicken apiece from Grandma Willis and Sarah Pernell, a cake and a nickel from one woman and a dress from another, and two pecks of meal from a man. In the tradition of the Fisk Jubilee Singers, the school's Cotton Blossom Singers became a potent fundraising device.

Things were not all so fairy tale at the Piney Woods Country Life School, however. Twice, fire destroyed campus buildings. Once, the school, along with the whole of Braxton, was wiped out by a cyclone. There was also the day the school's founder was almost wiped out: Jones had journeyed to a neighboring state to lend a minister friend a little fire for his revival. One night, as Jones exhorted the congregation to wage a hot war against ignorance, poverty, and other evils, he was overheard by some white passersby. Soon the rumor mill had Jones's words misconstrued as nothing short of a call to riot and rebellion. The next day, Jones was snatched from his friend's home, noosed, and taken some distance to a tree, where a pyre had been prepared. Jones was thrown on top of the wood. Branches and sticks and wild gunshots came next. Then came a miracle: Jones was given a chance to address the crowd. After he explained the content and character of his speech and, yes, did a li'l scraping and bowing, he was released.

Jones went on with the buildup of his school, helped greatly every inch of the way by his wife, Grace Allen, with whom he had three children, and who died in 1928. Word of Jones's good work spread as he traveled around the nation seeking donations of money, clothes, building materials, equipment, seed, and supplies—you name it. The school's fortunes increased dramatically in 1954 when white Mississippians lobbied Ralph Edwards to honor Jones on his program "This Is Your Life." After the show aired, Jones received mounds of fan mail, as well as that most needed thing, money: Piney Woods received nearly $250,000 in a matter of days.

Laurence C. Jones died on a Sunday morning at the age of ninety-two. More than a thousand people were in attendance at his funeral, after which he was buried close by the old cedar tree where he started his school.

Oscar Micheaux (1884–1951)

Oh, Pioneer! Oscar Micheaux pushed the frontier via the silver screen, making upward of fifty flicks, only about a dozen of which have survived. Before venturing into filmmaking, this maverick, born in Metropolis, Illinois, did a mix of things to earn a living, including work as a Pullman porter. When he was pressing thirty, he managed to get a 160-acre homestead in South Dakota. It was there that one day he fancied himself a writer. *The Conquest: The Story of a Negro Pioneer* was his first work of fiction: a melodrama about a man named Oscar Devereaux, farming in South Dakota, who is so bold as to start a romance with a white woman. The book was published in 1913 by the Western Book Supply Company, for which the president, vice president, secretary, and treasurer was Oscar Micheaux. His first customers and stockholders were mostly white Midwestern farmers, though he did journey South for some sales.

In 1915 Micheaux came out with *The Forged Note: A Romance of the Darker Races,* the story of a homesteader in South Dakota who writes a book about his experiences and then journeys South to promote his work. (Daddy one-note could have been his nickname.) Two years later, he came out with *The Homesteader.*

The Homesteader (a reworking of *The Conquest*) held the attention of brothers George and Noble Johnson, owners of one of the first black movie companies, the Lincoln Film Motion Picture Company. Micheaux was eager to sell them the film rights, but only under one condition: that he be the film's director. The Johnson brothers didn't think so. Micheaux wasn't bluffing.

Fairly lickety split came the Micheaux Book and Film Company, for which the producer, director, publicity manager—you get the picture. By 1919, Micheaux was motoring from town to town shopping his film *The Homesteader* to movie-house managers. He managed to get enough showings (sometimes only one-night stands) to stayed pumped about his enterprise.

The Brute (starring the prizefighter Sam Langford), *Son of Satan, The Millionaire,* and *Wages of Sin* were among the films Micheaux made in the 1920s; these films played North and South in black theaters and at black-only matinees in white movie houses. These films had some life only because the tall, robust Micheaux, a real maven in the art of hype, was a dynamo when it came to marketing his work and rounding up investments. According to those who knew him, he could talk the shirt off your back and sell you ice in winter at the same time.

Black actors didn't need the hard sell to get involved with

Micheaux. His movies gave many a shot at stardom (albeit in a limited universe) that they might never have had otherwise. There was Lorenzo Tucker, the "Colored Valentino" (and after talkies, the "Colored William Powell"); Ethel Moss, "The Colored Jean Harlow"; Bee Freeman, the "Sepia Mae West"; and Slick Chester, "the Colored Cagney." It was in the 1924 Micheaux production *Body and Soul* that Paul Robeson made his movie debut.

As for the films themselves, even by his era's standards, they were pretty bad: melodramatic to the max; on the technicals, very flawed; and because every take was a wrap, viewers had to abide all the flubs. Too, there was the color thing.

Theophilus Lewis, writing for the *Amsterdam News,* about Micheaux's 1930 film *Daughter of the Congo,* captured the criticism many intellectuals lobbed at most of his films: "All the noble characters are high yellow, all the ignoble ones are black." Valid. Yet, some were and are inclined to cut Micheaux some slack on that, considering that in those days Hollywood rarely showed any shade of black as beautiful (except for the mulatto who was necessarily tragic), intelligent, or worthy of more than Stepin' Fetchit lines. (The first all-black cast film that white America produced in 1904, *The Wooing and Wedding of a Coon,* may have been out of sight but not out of mind.) Then here was Micheaux, patching together films that presented black life with some iota of complexity, and if not that, at least some glamour or grit—the stuff of escape, which is what the average person goes to the movies for anyhow. For workaday folks back then, it was a kick to see black people being educated, suave, and gangsta even.

As for the color thing, well, Micheaux was only in step with popular thinking at the time ("if you're light, you're alright, if you're brown . . ." and all that). Besides, how many late twentieth-century African American filmmakers can cast a stone on that account? Why did Micheaux have to pander to sick sensibilities? He didn't, but then, he wasn't out to be a revolutionary filmmaker. He was in the business of entertainment, pure and simple.

You also have to give him credit: He did hang on much longer than the few other independents of the Depression era. *The Exile* (the first all-black-cast talkie, 1931), *Harlem after Midnight, Underworld, The Notorious Elinor Lee,* and *Lying Lips* (coproduced by black star aviator Hubert Julian) are among his later films.

By 1940, Micheaux's stardust was fading, but he wasn't dead yet. He managed to turn out a few more novels: *The Wind from Nowhere* (1941), basically a recycling of *The Conquest* and *The Homesteader; The Case of Mrs. Wingate* (1944), about a black detective dealing with Nazi spies; *The Story of Dorothy Stanfield* (1946), about an insurance scam; and *The Masquerade* (1947), a rip-off of *The House behind the Cedars*

A poster for Micheaux's 1931 film *The Exile*, which made its debut at Harlem's Lafayette Theatre. "*The Exile* carries everything that a modern picture should have to hold the interest," proclaimed the *Pittsburgh Courier*. "There is a nice plot, a love story as gripping as it possibly can be and the portrayal of Negro life in a city that no one but a Negro, who has travelled and lived in cities, could tell." (Courtesy of Separate Cinema Archives ®)

by **Charles W. Chesnutt**, a novel Micheaux had once tried to get the film rights to.

Micheaux's final film offering came in 1948: *The Betrayal*, based on his novel *The Wind from Nowhere*. He was on a promotional tour for his work, in Charlotte, North Carolina, when he died three years later.

Not an outstanding artist, not a tremendous visionary—yet, most definitely, he was a pioneer. He *did* see the importance and potential profit of creating films that let black folks see something of themselves; he *did* have the guts to give it a try; he *did* lay a foundation for others to build on and do better (or worse). This is why, in 1974, the Black Filmmaker's Hall of Fame created an Oscar Micheaux Award. This is why many applauded when, in 1987, the maverick moviemaker became a star on Hollywood's Walk of Fame.

OTHER EARLY FILMMAKERS

- William Foster (1884–?), at one time a press agent for the famous duo of Walker and Williams, created the first black-produced, black-themed film. It was the comedy short *The Railroad Porter*, released around 1912. Foster later produced *The Fall Guy* and *The Barber*.

- Spencer Williams (1893–1969), a native of Vidalia, Louisiana, was a former intelligence officer in the U.S. Army who entered the movie business in the 1920s. He was first a writer for black-themed shorts for an affiliate of Paramount Pictures, and then an actor (starring in several black Westerns in the 1930s). It was in the 1940s that Williams, in partnership with Lester Stark, made a concerted effort to be a film producer. His commendable films, all of which he wrote, directed, and starred in, include *Marching On*, about blacks in the military; *The Blood of Jesus*, about a man who murders his wife; and the comedy *Juke Joint*. By 1950, Williams was finished with filmmaking and a year away from a new, controversial career: the role of Andy Brown in CBS's *Amos 'n' Andy*, which was canceled in 1953, but lived on in syndication until 1966.

 # Dave Dinwiddie (1891–1957)

Place nothing on earth before family. . . . When you help another you help yourself. . . . Education is the passport to freedom.

These are among the tenets for living that Dave Dinwiddie expounded more by deed than by word. This man of small stature with a giant soul was a rock for his family near and far, a rock for his fellow citizens in Taft, one of the roughly two dozen black towns established in Oklahoma between 1890 and 1910. These towns were seeded by flight from Southern sorrows and horrors that came in the wake of Reconstruction's destruction, towns rooted in territory once the domain of Cherokees, Creeks, Chickasaws, Choctaws, and other Native American tribes forced out of the eastern United States and onto the Trail of Tears beginning in the 1820s.

Dave Dinwiddie himself began on a prosperous farm in Clarksville, Texas, a farm pervaded by the notions of thrift and uplift. He himself began with family stories that gave him grit. His mother, Thursda, half Cherokee and half African, had walked with her family roughly four hundred miles from Alabama to Indian Territory in the late 1870s, a decade before it became Oklahoma Territory, and white settlers, the "Sooners" and then the "Boomers," rushed in. Finally, she made her way across the Texas border to meet and marry his father, Smith Dinwiddie.

Smith, in family solidarity, used some of his precious gold coins to help his nephew escape the threat of a lynching, then Smith lost his peace to irate locals. The sheriff, a white "cousin" Dinwiddie, urged Smith to sell his farm, a legacy from his white father (and former owner), and to move his family to the safety of Oklahoma. With fistfuls of dollars, Smith loaded farm implements and household goods onto a boxcar. Using his "inheritance" wisely, Smith Dinwiddie purchased 140 acres of farmland. On a smaller plot, he started a grocery store, at the back of which he built a pint-sized rock house so that his children, Porter and Dave, would be nearby as he ran the business.

While growing up, Dave worked in his father's store and on his father's land. He got some schooling, too: enough to enable him to attend what was then Wiley University, in Marshall, Texas, enough for him to teach school. Teaching never became his vocation, however. He kept the course Smith Dinwiddie walked: When his father was up in age, Dave Dinwiddie bought the store from him; after his father's death, he rented out his half of the 140 acres.

By this time, Dave Dinwiddie was a husband to Artemisia Elizabeth Baker from Klondike, Texas, a schoolteacher by trade. They started their life together in the little rock house. Soon came their son Merrill and then daughter Lorene. Three more children would come, but they would grow up in a far more substantial home, on fifty acres, up the hill from their father's store. Ever the enterpriser, when Dave Dinwiddie purchased these acres, he had more than a home in mind. Over the years, he rented out parcels for grazing and for farming. He used the land for collateral for many bank loans to support the needs of his family and community. He also built a small house on this land, which he rented out, eventually giving it to some longtime tenants.

Dinwiddie's Grocery & Market was a key constant for his community. It was where people purchased the horse feed, the cotton sacks, the tinned beef, the Holsum Bread, the meat, the cheese, the everyday everything they needed. It was where, during dusty-bright Saturday afternoons and long weekday evenings, menfolk gathered to reason together about the glooms and boons of the community, to discuss world news, and sometimes just to jawjack.

While Dave Dinwiddie was making his living, he was helping others keep themselves from hunger and miscellaneous pities. Many were the times he extended credit to a customer—the small farmer in between harvests and hard up for cash; the day laborer who could catch no hire for a week or more; the steady worker–sole breadwinner whose family was in jeopardy when sickness took him down. Many were the people who had tabs at the store for years. And this Dinwiddie did during the Great Depression, and never did he engage in usury.

He propped up his people in countless other ways, too. Giving handsomely to the Flipper Chapel A.M.E. Church for its various projects and programs is one for-instance. Getting the county commissioner to commit to town improvements such as graveling a road is another. He cosigned loans so a neighbor would not lose his farm or home. More than a few in Taft had him to thank for their jobs at the state-run institutions in their town, such as the Colored Insane Asylum; the Colored Home for the Deaf, Dumb, Blind and Orphaned; and the Colored Training School for wayward girls. Dave Dinwiddie also had a hand in securing the best

Dave Dinwiddie inside his grocery store around 1925. This photograph served as the verso of a postcard Dinwiddie used for advertising and for keeping in touch with kin in Kansas and Texas. (Courtesy of Elza Dinwiddie-Boyd)

qualified personnel for schools in his town. He was never a joiner, never holding or aspiring to any public office—just an everyday leader who labored behind the scenes in behalf of his people.

He was also forever there for his family. He was there for relatives and strangers who streamed into Taft in late May 1921, hasting away from the white wrath that had made of the black section of Tulsa a bonfire and a sore desolation. When his father-in-law died in the late 1920s, he was there for his mother-in-law and her two teenagers, taking them into his home, providing for them just as he did for his own wife and children, even putting his wife's sister through Langston University.

"Whenever there was a problem," his youngest daughter once said, "he was there with counsel and money." This youngest daughter is Elza Dinwiddie-Boyd, author of *Proud Heritage: 11,001 Names for your African American Baby* and *In Our Own Words: A Treasury of Quotations from the African-American Community.* Dinwiddie-Boyd's glad memories of her father include his coming home every evening with a special treat from the store—some Coca-Colas, some cheese and crackers, some sardines in tomato sauce—treats sipped or nibbled while Daddy talked, taught, and championed the souls of his children. "And he believed in children having fun," she recalled, citing, for example, how whenever they visited kin in Wichita, her father made sure there was ample time and loose change for a visit to that city's amusement park.

Precious, too, is the memory of being his helper in tallying up the store's receipts at the end of the day. He was teaching her not merely to count, but how paramount it was to save first—always stressing that when it came to the extras, if you couldn't plunk down cash, you ought to forfeit the purchase. He helped her practice the principle of saving by giving her pennies from the store's daily take and periodically taking her to the bank to make deposits in her bank account. Pennies became nickels became dimes became quarters became dollars became her college fund.

All his children would go to college—Dave Dinwiddie had been determined about that before they were born. So it was that Lorene became a special-education teacher; Odell, a schoolteacher and later a supervisor in a Chrysler plant in Detroit; Lily Jean, a social worker; and the baby girl, a teacher and writer. The only Dinwiddie child who did not go to college was the firstborn, Merrill—because he died when he was fifteen on a late August day in 1936. Bright and all a-beam over the bicycle he had bought with his earnings from his paper route and other odd jobs, Merrill was going to ride the short distance down and around to Daddy's store to help Daddy out. But there was a drunk driver between Merrill and the store, only a few feet from the Dinwiddie house. The driver was a doctor, a white doctor, who was never even charged with manslaughter. Dave Dinwiddie lost a little of his dance after that, but Dave Dinwiddie held up, stayed the rock.

 # Roland Hayes (1887–1976)

In 1917, Roland Hayes made history as the first black person to give a recital in Boston's Symphony Hall. The event did not make headline news across the nation, but it was a definite victory for this son of former slaves, born in a scrabbly cabin in Curryville, Georgia; this former choirboy for New Monumental Baptist Church in Chattanooga, Tennessee; this former member of the Fisk Jubilee Singers, which had made its fame with the spirituals.

Roland Willsie Hayes, with the rich rendering his tenor voice gave to the works of such composers as Beethoven, Brahms, and Mozart, soon became in his day the most renowned example that blacks could more than do justice to classical music. This was something that blacks had known all along, but which others had consistently turned a deaf ear to.

Not long after his recital at Boston's Symphony Hall, Hayes went to Europe for further study. A recital in London's Aeolian Hall in 1920, followed by a command performance at Buckingham Palace, was the beginning of a series of recitals with major European orchestras. As has been the case with so many black artists, it was only after he had been bravoed in Europe that Hayes gained some acceptance in white America.

In 1923, he had the triumph of performing at New York City's Carnegie Hall. His gift of song was such that he was able to get the for-whites-only rule suspended for his performance at Washington, D.C.'s Constitution Hall, where in 1942 the Daughters of the American Revolution would block his protégé Marian Anderson from performing.

Hayes was cherished not only for his fine voice, and not only for the doors he opened for other blacks seeking a career in classical music: Along with Henry T. Burleigh, Nathaniel Dett, and others, Hayes increased the acceptance and appreciation of one of the first types of music he learned, the spirituals. He did this by constantly including the spirituals in his repertoire and through his 1948 book *My Songs: Afro-American Religious Folk Songs.*

 James Edward McCall (1880–1963)

Say "The New Negro," and quite naturally, we remember Alain Locke, the Howard University philosophy professor whose anthology *The New Negro* "alerted the world in 1925 that something approaching a cultural revolution was taking place among blacks in New York, as well as elsewhere in the United States and perhaps around the world," as Arnold Rampersad put it in his introduction to the 1992 edition of the book. Say "The New Negro," and we also think of sociologist Charles S. Johnson, and founder of the National Urban League's magazine *Opportunity;* Jessie Fauset, literary editor of the NAACP's the *Crisis;* Arthur Schomburg, who urged blacks to dig up and into their past and whose personal library was the foundation of the Schomburg Center for Research in Black Culture in Harlem.

We remember so many others from that crew of electric minds and expectant hearts: people born for the most part after Reconstruction; people for whom slavery was history, albeit recent, yet history nonetheless; people who knew of black valor in World War I, of droves trekking North for opportunity, of more than ten thousand protesting white violence in that Silent March down New York City's Fifth Avenue. They were folks possessed with, as Rampersad wrote, "a growing sense of certainty that black America was on the verge of something like a second Emancipation—this time not by government mandate but by the will and accomplishments of people, especially the artists and intellectuals."

Some of the others who first come to mind when we remember the New Negro movement are Augusta Savage, Meta Vaux Warrick Fuller, and Aaron Douglas making all that rich art; Countee Cullen, Claude McKay, and Georgia Douglas Johnson making all those rich poems; **Carter G. Woodson** recording all that rich history; Van Der Zee capturing all that rich style and those great expectations; Duke doing new rhythms; Zora lifting up folklore and sharpening her oyster knife; Lang talking about tom-tom time; Garvey urging the race to get up, get mighty.

When we think of the New Negro movement, we should also remember James Edward McCall, a native of Montgomery, Alabama, who wrote a vital poem entitled "The New Negro," first published in the July 27, 1927, issue of *Opportunity:*

> He scans the world with calm and fearless eyes,
>   Conscious within of powers long since forgot;
> At every step, new man-made barriers rise
>   To bar his progress—but he heeds them not.
> He stands erect, though tempests round him crash,
>   Though thunder bursts and billows surge and roll;
> He laughs and forges on, while lightnings flash
>   Along the rocky pathway to his goal.
> Impassive as a Sphinx, he stares ahead—
>   Foresees new empires rise and old ones fall;
> While caste-mad nations lust for blood to shed,
>   He sees God's finger writing on the wall.
> With soul awakened, wise and strong he stands,
> Holding his destiny within his hands.

McCall's poem is a succinct expression of the essence of the New Negro movement, and his life, an arresting expression of the concept in action. This graduate of Alabama State Normal entered Howard University in 1900, headed for a career in medicine. Not long after he started Howard, however, he was stricken with typhoid fever, which left him blind. Nonetheless, his affliction did not leave him wanting to be a helpless, hopeless victim. He remained "conscious within" of his powers and turned to another interest, something he could do without sight: writing.

Mostly, McCall wrote poems at first, poems published in various periodicals, including Alabama's the *Montgomery,* which called him "The Blind Tom of Literature." This was a takeoff on "Blind Tom," the moniker given the pianist and composer Thomas Bethune of Georgia, a man born blind and enslaved. That Tom's incredible musical abilities were showcased all over the South (at one point to raise money for the Confederacy), and after the war, on concert stages all over the United States (to raise money for the people who became his legal guardians). The "Blind Tom of Literature" wasn't wanting to make it as merely some phenomenon, some act. Intent on "holding his destiny within his hands," he returned to school. With great assistance from his sister Annabel, he entered Albion College in Michigan in 1905, where he was the only blind student.

After he graduated from college, McCall returned to Montgomery, where he became a staff writer for a white paper before starting his own, *The Emancipator.* McCall also married, in 1914, and his wife was a steadfast help in all his endeavors. In 1920, the McCalls moved to Detroit, where James became city editor and editorial writer for the *Independent* and later, publisher and editor of the well-respected *Detroit Tribune.* Indeed, what a model of "The New Negro" he was.

Carter G. Woodson (1875–1950)

Many of the principles that govern the development of the Afrocentric idea in education were first established by Carter G. Woodson in *The Mis-Education of the Negro* (1933). . . . As Woodson contends, African Americans have been educated away from their own culture and traditions and attached to the fringes of European culture. . . . Woodson's alert recognition, more than fifty years ago, that something is severely wrong with the way African Americans are educated provides the principal impetus of the Afrocentric approach to American education.
MOLEFI KETE ASANTE, "The Afrocentric Idea in Education" (1991)

Carter Godwin Woodson, a son of former slaves, born in New Canton, Virginia, was the oldest of nine children in a family so poor that as a boy, he worked in West Virginia coal mines to help out. This meant going without schooling for a time, but Carter was determined to catch up, and was fierce about getting himself some education. He was nineteen when he enrolled in Huntington, West Virginia's Douglass High School, and he managed to complete the course of study in a year and a half. After high school came Berea College in Kentucky and study at the Sorbonne. Then came a master's degree from the University of Chicago, and then a Ph.D. in history from Harvard University (the second black person to get a Ph.D. from this institution). Throughout his student days, he largely supported himself by teaching.

The most important thing he learned from his studies and his teaching was how much of black history had been ignored and how much of what had been recorded was fallacious. He got hot and bothered about this distortion and neglect. He understood that knowledge was power, understood that the less blacks knew of their history, the weaker they would be; and early on, he held out a hope that if white people were more enlightened on the subject, they would not regard blacks as inferior. What made Carter G. Woodson a great man is not that he thought these thoughts, but that he did something about it: He devoted his life to researching and promoting the study of black history and culture.

In 1915, Woodson cofounded and went on to head up the Association for the Study of Negro Life and History in Washington, D.C. (now the Association for the Study of Afro-American Life and History). The organization's purpose was, as Woodson put it, "the collection of sociological and historical data on the Negro, the study of peoples of African blood, the publishing of books in the field, and the promoting of harmony between the races by acquainting the one with the other." The creation of the association laid the foundation for the treatment of black history as a serious subject.

One of the association's subsidiaries was Associated Publishers, which Woodson established in 1920, to publish books and materials on black history (especially his), which white publishers would not publish. Under the auspices of the association, Woodson also started two publications: the *Journal of Negro History* (1916) and *Negro History Bulletin* (1937). As historian John Hope Franklin wrote in his 1950 essay "Carter G. Woodson in American Historiography," "Dr. Woodson's founding and editing of two periodicals in the field of Negro history gave to scholars throughout the world a medium through which they could present their worthy efforts to a public that was becoming increasingly interested in the subject."

Woodson both sparked and sated this interest in history with roughly twenty books, among them his dissertation *The Education of the Negro Prior to 1861* (1915); *Negro Orators and Orations* (1925); *The Mind of the Negro as Reflected in Letters Written during the Crisis,*

Carter G. Woodson around age forty, about the time he launched the Association for the Study of Negro Life and History. (Courtesy of Photographs and Prints Division, Schomburg Center for Research in Black Culture, The New York Public Library, Astor, Lenox and Tilden Foundations)

1800–1860 (1926); *Negro Makers of History* (1928); *African Myths, To-gether with Proverbs, A Supplementary Reader Composed of Folk Tales from Various Parts of Africa* (1928); *The Works of Francis J. Grimké* (4 volumes, 1942); and *African Heroes and Heroines* (1944). One of his most widely read books was *The History of the Negro Church* (1921), the first in-depth chronicle of this major religious and social institution. Another was *The Negro in Our History* (1922), for years *the* textbook in high schools and colleges where black history was taught.

There was also that most essential book, his treatise on the mis-management of black potential and underdevelopment of the black mind: *The Mis-Education of the Negro* (1933) an outgrowth of an article of the same name published in the *Crisis* in 1931. Some of the chapters in *Mis-Education* are "How We Missed the Mark," "The Failure to Learn to Make a Living," "The Educated Negro Leaves the Masses," "Political Education Neglected," "The Loss of Vision," "The Need for Service Rather Than Leadership," and "Understand the Negro," in which we find the following:

> Looking over the courses of study of the public schools, one finds little to show that the Negro figures in these curricula. . . . Several mis-educated Negroes themselves contend that the study of the Negro by children would bring before them the race problem prematurely. . . . These misguided teachers ignore the fact that the race question is being brought before black and white children daily in their homes, in the streets, through the press and on the rostrum. How, then, can the school ignore the duty of teaching the truth while these other agencies are playing up falsehood? . . .
>
> Upon examining the recent catalogues of the leading Negro colleges, one finds that invariably they give courses in ancient, mediæval, and modern Europe, but they do not give such courses in ancient, mediæval, and modern Africa. Yet Africa, according to recent discoveries, has contributed about as much to the progress of mankind as Europe has, and the early civilization of the Mediterranean world was decidedly influenced by Africa. . . .
>
> A further examination of their curricula shows, too, that invariably these Negro colleges offer courses in Greek philosophy and in that of modern European thought, but they direct no attention to the philosophy of the African. Negroes of Africa have and always have had their own ideas about the nature of the universe, time, and space, about appearance and reality, and about freedom and necessity. . . . There were many Africans who were just as wise as Socrates.

The following passage from the chapter "The Seat of the Trouble" is just one example of why *Mis-Education* remains a must-read:

In the schools of business administration Negroes are trained exclusively in the psychology and economics of Wall Street and are, therefore, made to despise the opportunities to run ice wagons, push banana carts, and sell peanuts among their own people. Foreigners, who have not studied economics but have studied Negroes, take up this business and grow rich.

There's also this from the chapter "Higher Strivings in the Service of the Country":

The Negro should endeavor to be a figure in politics, not a tool for the politicians. This higher rôle can be played not by parking all of the votes of a race on one side of the fence as both blacks and whites have done in the South, but by independent action. . . . Any people who will vote the same way for three generations without thereby obtaining results ought to be ignored and disfranchised.

A hugely important part of Woodson's legacy is Negro History Week. He launched this annual celebration in 1926 to raise people's awareness of black contributions to civilization. Fifty years later, this endeavor became Black History Month; and for all his endeavors, Dr. Carter G. Woodson became known as the "Father of Black History."

Woodson was able to accomplish all that he did because it was all that he wanted to do. Forever a bachelor, he lived a very spartan life. In his essay "A Portrait of Carter G. Woodson," **W. E. B. Du Bois** remarked that Woodson "had very little outdoor life, he had few close friends. He cared nothing for baseball or football and did not play cards, smoke or drink." Practically everything Woodson established or produced was paid for out of his own pocket or through his own fund-raising efforts. He never snuggled up to philanthropists because he was, as Du Bois wrote, "fiercely determined to be master of his own enterprises and final judge of what he wanted to do and say. He pretty soon got the reputation of not being the kind of 'trustworthy' Negro to whom help should be given."

Woodson maintained his lone-wolf stance with whites and blacks alike, but his determination to avoid seeking help from white philanthropists was particularly acute. Over time, he had developed "a deep-seated dislike, if not hatred, for the white people of the United States and of the world," said Du Bois. "He never believed in their generosity or good faith. He did not attack them; he did not complain about them, he simply ignored them so far as possible and went on with his work without expected help or sympathetic cooperation from them."

In assessing Woodson's work, Du Bois did not refrain from criticism, describing him as "a big strong man with a good mind; not brilliant, not a genius, but steady, sound and logical in his thinking

Carter G. Woodson in his yonder years. Among the volumes soldiered between the busts of Frederick Douglass and Booker T. Washington are Woodson's *African Heroes and Heroines, The Story of the Negro Retold, The Negro in Our History, African Background Outlined, The Rural Negro, Negro Makers of History,* and *The Mis-Education of the Negro.* (Courtesy of Photographs and Prints Division, Schomburg Center for Research in Black Culture, The New York Public Library, Astor, Lenox and Tilden Foundations)

processes, and capable of great application and concentration in his work." Du Bois characterized Woodson's writing as "mechanical and unemotional." He stated that Woodson "had no conception of the place of woman in creation" and opined that "much of his otherwise excellent research will have to be reinterpreted by scholars of wider reading and better understanding of the social sciences, especially in economics and psychology; for Woodson never read Karl Marx."

Was Du Bois trying to tear down this man he'd known for more than forty years? No, not at all. This essay, which appeared two months after Woodson's death, in the June 1950 issue of *Masses and Mainstream,* closed with this: "The passing of Carter Woodson leaves a vacuum hard to fill. His memory leaves a lesson of determination and sacrifice which all men, young and old, black and white, may emulate to the glory of man and the uplift of his world."

NEWS BITS

In 1926, the year of the first Negro History Week, . . .

- Puerto Rico–born bibliophile Arthur Schomburg (1874–1938), who emigrated to the United States in 1891, donated his personal collection of black-interest books, pamphlets, photographs, and other memorabilia (some 5,000 items) to The New York Public Library's Division of Negro Literature. His donation was the seed of what is today Harlem's Schomburg Center for Research in Black Culture.

- Mordecai Johnson (1890–1976) became the first black president of Howard University.

- Langston Hughes (1902–1967) saw his first collection of poetry published: *The Weary Blues.* This book was the springboard for his celebrity as poet, novelist, essayist, and dramatist, and his everlasting popularity. The first and only issue of *Fire!*, the avant-garde literary magazine Hughes edited with Zora Neale Hurston, Wallace Thurman, and others, also came out in 1926.

- Charles Drew (1904–1950) graduated from Amherst Medical School and embarked on the medical career in which he'd make history for his work on blood plasma.

 # Thomas A. Dorsey (1899–1993)

"Precious Lord, take my hand, lead me on, let me stand, . . ."

Thomas accepted the Lord when he was a child, which isn't so surprising because his father was a preacher and his mother a devout Christian. His mother was also a church musician, who taught her son to play the piano. In time, he was good enough to play the organ for services his father preached.

When Thomas Andrew Dorsey was eleven, his family moved from the hamlet of Villa Rica, Georgia, where he was born, to Atlanta, where his father continued his guest preaching and worked odd jobs to make ends meet. In Atlanta, Thomas studied some with a local music teacher, firming up his fingering and learning the basics of music theory and composition. He also got a job hawking pop and popcorn in a movie house, where Ed Butler, the house pianist, taught him a thing or two; soon, he was good enough to fill in for Butler. Interest in popular music was nothing new. Dorsey's bootlegging and blues-guitar-playing Uncle Phil had sparked it years earlier.

By the time Dorsey was a young adult, he was seriously specializing in "the devil's music" at whorehouses and rent parties. Lowdown, down-home, slow, easy blues was his forte. By 1916, he had made a name for himself in Atlanta and its environs. Then, he left Atlanta to make a name for himself up North. He tried Gary, Indiana, for a while; after that, he took on Chicago, where he played in bars and honky-tonks that catered to the folks from 'Sippi, from 'Bama, and from other deep South states—folks who left sharecropping, piddlin' jobs, and terror after World War I, hoping for better jobs and dignity in the Promised Land. The old-style blues remained Dorsey's love, but like others, he found that to keep kicking as a musician, he had to get up to speed on the up-tempo type, "jassy" blues that were becoming all the rage.

Dorsey suffered a bad bout of the blues in 1920. It was a depression severe enough to make him return to Atlanta, where his mother helped him through his dark nights of the soul, exhorting him to come back home in the other sense, too—to devote his talents to the church. This Dorsey did, and in the process, he caught hold of a new sacred music. It was a music born in Pentecostal churches, a music that melded shout songs, the spirituals, and the city beats. It was a music that first gained some respect with the publication in 1921 of *Gospel Pearls,* edited by Willa A. Townsend and produced by the National Baptist Convention. Thomas A. Dorsey's first gospel song, "If I Don't Get There," was included.

Music for the Lord did not, however, remain Dorsey's sole preoccupation. By 1921, he was back in Chicago, back into secular music. By the mid-1920s, he had made a name for himself playing with various jazz bands and as a composer (his first hit was "Riverside Blues," recorded by Joe "King" Oliver in 1923). In 1924, Dorsey joined up with the "Mother of the Blues," Gertrude "Ma" Rainey, as composer, as arranger, and as leader of her Wildcats Jazz Band.

"I am tired, I am weak, I am worn, . . ."

Despite the success he had with worldly music (and a marriage to a good woman, Nettie Harper, in 1925), there was still a hole in Dorsey's soul. In 1926, he fell into another depression, this one lasting almost two years, pushing him to the brink of suicide on more than one occasion.

"Through the storm, through the night, lead me on to the light, . . ."

Again, Dorsey "came back home." "If You See My Savior, Tell Him That You Saw Me" and "How about You" were among the first fruits of his renewal.

Trying to make a living selling and playing his sacred songs was a trial. Several times, he was put out of a church for offering up what he once called "sacred blues": Though the lyrics were fit for songs holy, the sound was too close to the street for many churchgoers.

Dorsey ended up again with his feet in two worlds. Once again, he was making music of which the church would hardly approve. "It's Tight Like That" was a huge hit, which Dorsey recorded with lyricist Hudson Whitaker in 1928. As "Georgia Tom" and "Tampa Red," Dorsey and Whitaker collaborated on a number of songs Dorsey would never have played for his mother ("Pat That Bread" and "Somebody's Been Using That Thing," for example).

Dorsey's breakthrough in sacred music came in 1930, when Lucie E. Campbell, the "Mother of Gospel Music," included his "If You See My Savior" in one of the sessions of the National Baptist Convention's annual meeting. The song became a big hit on the Baptist church-choir circuit, and Dorsey was on his way to becoming the "Father of Gospel Music," for his prodigious promotion of this new music.

Starting the first publishing company devoted exclusively to gospel music in 1931 was one of Dorsey's contributions to the spread of gospel music. Equally important, he organized several dynamic church choirs, including Chicago's Pilgrim Baptist Church (in which James Cleveland grew up) and the National Convention of Gospel Choirs and Choruses.

Dorsey was organizing a choir in Indianapolis in 1932 when he received some heavy news: His wife had died in childbirth. Another blow was awaiting him when he returned home: The baby, a girl, was no longer among the living. For three long days, Dorsey was in the valley, and he asked the Lord to take his hand and lead him on. When Dorsey came out of his despondency, he had a song that became one of the most beloved in the Black Church:

Precious Lord, take my hand, lead me on, let me stand.
I am tired, I am weak, I am worn.
Through the storm, through the night, lead me on to the light,
Take my hand, precious Lord, lead me on.

Dorsey composed roughly five hundred gospel songs, with "The Lord Will Make a Way Somehow," "There'll Be Peace in the Valley for Me," "Walking up the King's Highway," "If We Never Needed the Lord Before, We Sure Do Need Him Now," and "Search Me Lord," among his most popular ones. His songs became the model for other composers of the music that would become *the* music of the Black Church.

What was Dorsey's gift? In his essay "Take My Hand, Precious Lord, Lead Me On," gospel music scholar Horace Clarence Boyer explained it like this:

It is a style in which imagery and metaphor are brought to unusual heights in poetry that expresses Christian aspirations in the language of the people, and in which the melody is so perfectly designed that it is singable by even the most inexperienced singer. It is set to a rhythm that follows the natural flow of African American speech and is supported by a harmony that, while simple and sparse, adds to rather than detracts from the message of the song. Lastly, it has an essence that testifies to the "good news."

So popular were his songs that for a time, gospel songs were called "Dorseys."

OTHER EARLY MUSIC MASTERS

- Scott Joplin (c. 1868–1917), born in Texarkana, Arkansas, published "Original Rag" in 1899, the year Thomas A. Dorsey was born. Not long after that, this piano player at the Maple Leaf Club in Sedalia, Missouri, came out with "Maple Leaf Rag." This tune, the first piece of sheet music to sell a million copies, spiked the ragtime craze and earned Joplin the crown "King of Ragtime." Joplin made a nice living from the roughly forty rags he composed; however, he, who had studied music at George R. Smith College in Sedalia, had his heart set on creating longer, more serious works and being famous for more than piano jigs. Joplin's greatest obsession was his opera about overcoming and uplift, *Treemonisha*. Joplin was never able to secure backers for the grand production he envisioned for this opera, and the trying took a toll on him. The ragtime craze died around the same time as Joplin (in a mental hospital). Some fifty years later, Joplin became famous again. One boost was that the theme song of the hit 1974 film *The Sting* was Joplin's 1902 rag "The Entertainer."

- W. C. Handy (1873–1958), born in Florence, Alabama, began playing the cornet when he was a child but later took to the trumpet. In his early efforts to make it as a musician, he met with some success, becoming the bandmaster of Mahara's Colored Minstrels. At the turn of the century, William Christopher Handy settled in Memphis, Tennessee, where he started Pace and Handy Music Company in 1908 with Harry H. Pace (who later launched the first black-owned recording company, Black Swan). It was also in Memphis, in 1909, that Handy wrote the song "Mr. Crump" for that city's mayor. This rag–blues tune caught on quick and was published in 1912 as "Memphis Blues." Handy's other hits include "Aunt Hagar's Children's Blues," "Joe Turner's Blues," the nonpareil "Beale Street Blues," and "St. Louis Blues." Handy was named "Father of the Blues" as much for his blues compositions as for the enormous work he did in collecting and promoting this folk music, first preserving it in print with *Blues: An Anthology* (1926). Handy's other books include *Book of Negro Spirituals* (1938) and his autobiography, *Father of the Blues* (1941).

- Jelly Roll Morton (1890–1941), born Ferdinand Joseph LaMothe in Gulfport, Mississippi, and raised in New Orleans, Louisiana, was known to crow that he had invented jazz. He didn't, but he did help give it wings, as one of the most accomplished jazz pianists, composers, and arrangers, and leader of a smashing band, Red Hot Peppers, which included the great trombonist Kid Ory. Among Morton's most treasured songs are "Wolverine Blues," "King Porter Stomp," "Black Bottom Stomp," and "Buddy Bolden's Stomp." In 1938, the flamboyant Morton recorded twelve albums' worth of jazz and jazz talk for the Library of Congress's Archive of American Folksong, one of the most significant oral histories of that music. More and more people became aware of Morton and his music due to the huge success of George C. Wolfe's 1992 Broadway musical *Jelly's Last Jam.*

- Duke Ellington (1899–1974), born in Washington, D.C., and named Edward Kennedy, came into the nickname Duke when he was young because of his penchant for carrying himself as if he were royalty. He became a musical monarch—"King of Swing," "The King of Jazz"—because of his genius as a pianist, as a composer, and as a manager of awesome talents, among them bassist Jimmy Blanton, saxophonist Harry Carney, trumpeter William "Cat" Anderson, drummer Sonny Greer, and composer and arranger Billy Strayhorn, whose most memorable composition for the Duke Ellington Orchestra is "Take the 'A' Train." Ellington, who wrote scores for several films and musicals, composed roughly one thousand songs. His greatest hits include "Black and Tan Fantasy," "Mood Indigo," "Satin Doll," "It Don't Mean a Thing If It Ain't Got That Swing" and the fifty-minute tribute to the African American will to triumph over tragedy, *Black, Brown and Beige,* the work his orchestra played at the 1943 debut of the annual concerts Ellington held at New York City's Carnegie Hall until the mid-1950s. Ellington's numerous awards include the Presidential Medal of Freedom, awarded by Richard Nixon in 1970.

 # Richard Samuel Roberts (1881–1936)

For nearly fifty years, from 1930 to the late 1970s, Roberts's legacy lay still and in darkness, catching dust, mildew, and tiny-creature cadavers in a crawl space at 1717 Wayne Street in Columbia, South Carolina. When his treasure was found—roughly three thousand glass-plate negatives—so was his world, a scant of which is forever on view in the nearly two hundred photographs collected in *A True Likeness: The Black South of Richard Samuel Roberts, 1920–1936* (1986), edited by Thomas L. Johnson and Phillip C. Dunn.

In 1920, the self-taught photographer Richard Samuel Roberts left Fernadina, Florida, for his wife's hometown because she, Wilhelmina Pearl Selena Williams, needed a less humid clime for her health's sake. When the Robertses arrived in Columbia, it was "an enigma and a contradiction at heart," wrote Thomas L. Johnson in his introduction to *A True Likeness.* "With a population of 37,524, Columbia was more an overgrown country town than an urban center," observed Johnson. "And yet, as the capital of South Carolina, as the seat of its university, and as a trading and distribution hub, it pulsed with the essential business of a state that in the 1920s was still basically rural."

Blacks made up about one third of the city's population, and like most everywhere else, they had only themselves to depend on for strength, solace, and a measure of grace. "Black Columbians could not live in certain sections of town," Johnson reminds us, "could not attend their state university, were denied access to all library, playground, and other public recreational facilities. . . . Blacks were not permitted to walk in certain areas of the university or state house grounds; black schoolteachers were paid less than white ones, and many black professionals had to double as skilled or semiskilled laborers or shopkeepers in order to make a living. The uneducated were relegated for the most part to menial, secondary, subservient jobs." It was in the midst of all this unreasonableness that Roberts did his art, that he made a simple, but powerful contribution to his community—providing a much-needed service in days when, by and large, blacks could only look to themselves for positive images of blackness.

Two years after the move to Columbia, Roberts purchased the house on Wayne Street where he and his wife raised their five children. The family's mainstay was Papa's work as a janitor at the post office. Photography was his moonlight, which he carried on in a little outbuilding on his property and later in a small second-floor space at 1119 Washington Street, in the city's black business district, its "Little Harlem."

"If you are beautiful, we guarantee to make your photographs just like you want them," promised a brochure for the Roberts Studio in the early 1920s. "If you are not beautiful, we guarantee to make you beau-

In *A True Likeness*, this photograph is captioned, "Robert Harper Kennedy (d. 1972) and his nephew, Hale B. Thompson, Jr. (b. 1922), ca. 1927. Kennedy was a chef at Columbia's Jefferson Hotel before moving to Binghamton, New York, where he became chef-cook in a hospital. The boy was the son of Margaret Kennedy Thompson, whose husband was a mathematics professor, vice president, and dean of the college at Allen University. Educated at Johnson Smith and New York University, [Hale] Thompson went on to become an educator and human resources administrator with the city of New York." (Courtesy of the Estate of Richard Samuel Roberts)

tiful and yet to retain a true and brilliant likeness of you." Three postcard-size portraits for $1.00, three small photographs "for identification, gift and album" for $0.50, or two small photographs and one 8 x 10 enlargement for $2.50: These are among the offerings found in a Roberts Studio rate book from the 1930s.

Some of the people who went to Roberts for a true likeness of themselves—for their wallets, mantlepieces, and albums, or for those of friends and relatives up North, out West, next door—included Joseph Williams, a former jockey and brother of Mrs. Roberts; Dr. Benjamin A. Everett, a physician; William Manigault, mortician and owner of a casket company; J. C. Artemus, Sr., a carpenter and insurance agent who became a union organizer; Cromer Ware, a shoeshine and porter who became a cabbie; John Taylor, wheelwright and blacksmith; Eddie Hoover Mosby, proprietor of a barbershop; Jessie Kennedy, a schoolteacher; Modjeska Monteith, the schoolteacher who became a warrior against tuberculosis in South Carolina and a civil-rights activist; William Augustine Perry, a graduate of Yale and Harvard who became principal of Columbia's Waverley School in the late 1920s; Reverend J. C. White, pastor of Zion Baptist Church; Martha P. Grier and her four grown daughters, one of whom, Malinda Bolden, later became the grandmother of astronaut Charles Bolden.

Roberts improvised a lot when it came to equipment. He mastered and refined his technique through study of books and magazines, developing his style over time through concerted effort and a commitment to perfection. As Johnson put it, like any good photographer, Roberts "was a craftsman who cared about beauty of image, grace of form, balance and line, tone and contrast, the quality of light and the shades of darkness." According to one of Roberts's sons, the man was a stickler for details, known to spend an inordinate amount of time during a posing session on something "as trivial or minute as a particular fold in a garment, or the flex of a reclining finger."

Roberts's work is precious for his artistry, as well as its insights into textures of black life in a South Carolina city during the Roaring Twenties and the Depression. During this time, he was Columbia's only black commercial photographer and, as such, pretty much the sole supplier of photographs for the city's black newspaper, the *Palmetto Leader.* This accounts for some of the street scenes and exteriors, as well as the portraits found in his work. Roberts was also the number-one picture-taking man for the special occasions of various institutions. This explains why his portfolio includes items such as a graduating class of Good Samaritan Hospital Nurse Training School, the football squad of the Booker T. Washington High School, and the Board of Deacons at Second Calvary Baptist Church.

Given all the history to behold in a photograph, it's sad that so many of the people Roberts photographed have yet to be identified in detail—a magician with his assistants, a soldier, a chauffeur, a maid, a plasterer and painter, a boxer, a dandy, a doll, newlyweds in wedding regalia, a father and infant, a mother and child, full families, a young man with a ukelele, a churchlady with her tambourine, a little girl on a tricycle, a little boy dressed as a cowboy. Anyone whose family tree has roots in Columbia, South Carolina, and its environs can't help but look into these faces, into these proud, defiant, expectant, eager, or wearied eyes, and wonder, Could he, could she, could they be kin? That's what I wondered when I saw the photographs of students at Brewer Normal School in Columbia's little neighbor, Greenwood, where my mother grew up, and where I spent some summertime as a child.

Had Roberts seen himself as the historian that he was, how much more we would know about his world: He would have catalogued all his work; he would have made provisions that after his death his handiwork be stored in a far better place than the crawl space under his home. Yet, we are grateful that he wanted to be an artist, that he wanted to portray his people in beauty and in truth.

OTHER PICTURE-TAKIN' MEN

- Cornelius M. Battey (1873–1927), who was born in Augusta, Georgia, received much of his training in photography with Underwood and Underwood in New York. The fine portrait work he did (mostly in New York and Cleveland) prompted Booker T. Washington to invite Battey to join the Tuskegee Institute faculty in 1914. Battey created a solid photography department at Tuskegee, and in the process, he did a huge amount of documentation of life at the school. Around 1917, Battey began work on a series of large-format photogravures of leading African Americans, which sold very well around the nation and was eventually titled "Our Master Minds." From the late 1910s until his death, many of Battey's photographs were used as covers of magazines, including the National Urban League's *Opportunity,* the NAACP's (and W. E. B. Du Bois's) *Crisis,* and A. Philip Randolph's the *Messenger.*

- Addison Scurlock (1883–1984), born in Fayetteville, North Carolina, was the official photographer of Howard University and *the* photographer of black Washington, D.C., in the early twentieth century. His sons George and Robert followed in his footsteps, and his work can be seen in *The Historic Photographs of Addison N. Scurlock* (Corcoran Gallery, 1976).

- James Van Der Zee (1886–1983), a native of Massachusetts, was one of Harlem's most prominent photographers. His huge legacy includes the work he did as Marcus Garvey's official photographer and the portraits he made of everyday and famous Harlemites, often experimenting wildly with photomontage assemblage. In the late 1960s, Van Der Zee was no longer in vogue and was living in poverty when a curator for the Metropolitan Museum of Art exhibit "Harlem on My Mind" happened upon him and his work. A considerable amount of Van Der Zee's work was used in this exhibit, which is why he is the best-known early twentieth-century black photographer, and why there are a number of books on him, including *The World of James Van Der Zee: A Visual Record of Black Americans*, by Reginald McGhee (1969); *James Van Der Zee: The Picture Takin' Man*, by Jim Haskins; and *Van Der Zee: Photographer, 1886–1983*, by Deborah Willis-Braithwaite (1993), who is also the author of *Black Photographers, 1840–1940: An Illustrated Bio-Bibliography* (1985), and *Black Photographers, 1940–1988: An Illustrated Bio-Bibliography* (1989).

- Marvin Pentz (1910–) and Morgan Sparks (1910–1993) Smith, twins born and raised in Kentucky, moved to New York City in the early 1930s. There, they began to focus their artistic bent on photography, eventually opening up M&M Studio on Harlem's famed 125th Street (next door to the Apollo Theater). In addition to doing portrait work for everyday people, the twins photographed many luminaries who lived in and passed through Harlem. They also shot a lot of what was going on in the streets, from street speakers and demonstrations to bread lines and Lindy hoppers at the Savoy Ballroom. In the 1960s, the Smith twins donated about two thousand photographs to the Schomburg Center for Research in Black Culture, which, in 1998, mounted a retrospective of their work, available in the book *Harlem: The Vision of Morgan and Marvin Smith*, with a foreword by Gordon Parks.

 The Scottsboro Boys

On March 25, 1931, a scuffle broke out among some young men copping a ride on a freight train bound for Memphis, Tennessee. It was a black–white thing, back of which was probably something petty: somebody stepping on somebody's toe, somebody invading somebody's space, a dirty look, a racial taunt, a boast.

At some point, some white guys alit from the train, and there would later be testimony that some black guys did, too. What the black guys went on to do, who knows. As for the whites, one of them got a message to a station up ahead that there were some blacks making mischief on the train. At Paint Rock, Alabama, the black guys got rousted from different parts of the train.

In one boxcar were Eugene Williams, age thirteen; Haywood Patterson, sixteen; Andy Wright, eighteen; and his little brother Roy, thirteen. The four, all from Chattanooga, were hoping to find riverboat work in Memphis. Buddies Clarence Norris and Charlie Weems, ages eighteen and nineteen, and both from Atlanta, were together in a car at the end of the train. Willie Roberson, seventeen, was by his lonesome, as were Ozie Powell, fourteen, and Olen Montgomery, also fourteen, and on his way to Memphis to a free clinic, hoping for some relief from whatever had rendered him almost blind.

Some white fellows got shunted from the train, too. The lot of them were charged with vagrancy and were probably just going to get a strong get-out-of-town as punishment, but everything changed when the sheriff discovered that two overall-clad white lads were young ladies. Soon, it wasn't about vagrancy, but a case of rape, gang rape.

Eugene, Haywood, Andy, Roy, Clarence, Charlie, Willie, Ozie, and Olen were hauled away and jailed in Scottsboro, Alabama. There, word spread fast of the fiendish crime of the nine, soon known as the Scottsboro Boys.

A crowd quickly formed outside the jail. It took the presence of more than a hundred National Guard to keep the throng from busting in and doing the Southern Whiteman's duty.

The nine were indicted for rape. There were four separate trials, each with an all-white jury. Start date: April 6, 1931, and all the trials were over four days later: Guilty, guilty, guilty, guilty.

It didn't matter that there were holes and contradictions in testimony against the Scottsboro Boys. It didn't matter that a medical examination revealed no evidence that rape had been committed against

The Scottsboro Boys outside the jail in Scottsboro, Alabama, on March 26, 1931. From left to right, Clarence Norris, Olen Montgomery, Andy Wright, Willie Roberson, Ozie Powell, Eugene Williams, Charlie Weems, Roy Wright, and Haywood Patterson. (Courtesy of UPI/Corbis-Bettmann)

the two young ladies: twenty-year-old Victoria Price and seventeen-year-old Ruby Bates, both dirt poor. It didn't matter that one boy was practically blind and another was suffering from a venereal disease that made it impossible for him to engage in sex. It didn't matter that the defendants had no attorneys until the day of their trials. It didn't matter that shouts of "Lynch the Niggers!" frequently broke in on the proceedings.

Roy Wright's case ended up a mistrial because some jurors, rebelling against the prosecution's request for life imprisonment only, held out for the death penalty, which is what the other eight were sentenced to, via the electric chair. Up to this point, none of the Scottsboro Boys had been allowed to contact Mama or Daddy or anybody.

The day of execution was set for July 10. The Scottsboro Boys would have to endure three more months of hell, for ever since the jailing, they had suffered all kinds of abuses: jailors' beatings and worse, deprivation of food in cells crawling with cockroaches.

The miracle was that their story was picked up, and they became a cause. The *Daily Worker* kept the story in public view, as did the *Amsterdam News* and other black papers. Many petitions were sent to President Franklin Delano Roosevelt, with signatures climbing to 200,000, by some accounts. There was a Harlem Scottsboro Parade and a Free the Scottsboro Boys March on Washington. Langston Hughes was inspired to write the one-act verse play, *Scottsboro Limited;* John Wexley, to script the drama *They Shall Not Die;* and Countee Cullen to pen the poem "Scottsboro, Too, Is Worth Its Song."

"We have been sentenced to die for something we ain't never done. Us poor boys been sentenced to burn up in the electric chair for the reason that we is workers—and the color of our skin is black." This is from the opening of a letter to the public, dated April 1, 1932, written by one and signed by all the Scottsboro Boys, then in Alabama's Kilby Prison, where they awaited the day of execution, where they endured a variety of torture, including being forced by "the boss-man" to "watch 'em burning up other Negroes on the electric chair." In closing, the Scottsboro Boys wrote, "Help us boys. We ain't done nothing wrong."

The outrage was international. There were demonstrations in more than twenty-five countries, with protests often aimed at the American Embassy. Albert Einstein, Maxim Gorky, Sinclair Lewis, Thomas Mann, Edna St. Vincent Millay, George Bernard Shaw, and Virginia Woolf were among the scores of prominent people who protested this legal lynching.

For control of the case, there was a power struggle between the NAACP and the International Labor Defense (ILD), an arm of the Communist Party. The ILD won and brought in criminal lawyer Samuel Leibowitz to serve as lead counsel. Working with him on legal strategy (as well as organizing political protests) was William Patterson, a member of the Communist Party, USA since the late 1920s, executive director of the ILD from the early 1930s until the mid-1940s, and the man who was later to edit the book *We Charge Genocide: The Crime of Government against the Negro People* (1951) and to title his autobiography *The Man Who Cried Genocide* (1971). Patterson had his work cut out for him. Though the trials of the Scottsboro Boys were clearly travesties, showing this to be so would be showing up the legal system in the South, would be showing up white Southerners as louts.

Appeals filed, appeals dismissed, appeals filed again, appeals granted, new trials—with Roy Wright thrown back into the mix. As a result, there were new convictions—even though Ruby Bates recanted her testimony, said the boys did not do anything, said she and Victoria were forced to tell a howling lie.

There were more trials and retrials, and through all the years the Scottsboro Boys stayed in jail, suffering things unspeakable at the hands of prison guards and inmates, and sometimes some of them tried to give as good as they got. The many beatings left wounds that would never heal. In 1936, during transport from one jail to another, a deputy sheriff gave Ozie Powell a blow upside the head, allegedly for sassing him. In response, Powell whipped out a shiv and slashed the deputy's throat, and the sheriff shot Powell in the head. Powell's brain was never the same after that.

In July 1937, four Scottsboro Boys had the charges against them dropped: Olen Montgomery, Willie Roberson, Eugene Williams, and Roy Wright. A few days earlier another four had received devastating news.

Charlie Weems, tried for the second time, was convicted and sentenced to seventy-five years. He was paroled in 1943.

Clarence Norris, tried for the third time, was convicted and sentenced to death but had his sentence commuted to life in 1938. He was paroled in January 1944, violated parole that September by leaving Alabama, and was reimprisoned the following month. He was paroled again in 1946, skipped out of Alabama again shortly thereafter (can you blame him?) and technically was a fugitive until 1976, when Governor George Wallace pardoned him.

Andy Wright, tried for the second time, was sentenced to ninety-nine years. He was paroled along with Norris, with whom he violated parole. He was reimprisoned in 1946 and paroled to New York in 1950.

The brain-damaged Ozie Powell received twenty years for assaulting the deputy sheriff and was paroled in 1946.

Only one of the Scottsboro Boys died in jail. That was Haywood Patterson, who was convicted for the fourth time in 1936 and sentenced to seventy-five years. Haywood escaped in 1947 and stayed on the lam for three years until the law caught up with him in Detroit. He got a reprieve when Detroit refused to extradite him to Alabama, but then, he was arrested in 1951 for stabbing a man in a barroom brawl, convicted of manslaughter, sentenced to six to fifteen years, and died in prison in 1952.

Although the Scottsboro nine never got justice, their case spotlighted racism in postslavery America like nothing before, as it spotlighted how hard it was for black people to come by justice in America. The Scottsboro Boys brought to the fore all the thousands of black men who had been lynched on the trumped-up charge of rape. The case of the Scottsboro Boys brought to light the common practice of excluding blacks from jury service solely because of race. It was in the case of the Scottsboro Boys that the United States Supreme Court declared that denial of competent legal counsel was a violation of the Fourteenth Amendment's due-process clause. It was because of these last two points that the Scottsboro Boys were able to get retrials in the first place.

Another good thing to come out of this horrible case was the NAACP's decision to mount a serious legal campaign against inequality and injustice. It was for this cause that, in the mid-1930s, the organization engaged the services of **Charles Hamilton Houston.**

Considering the case of the Scottsboro Boys, it is curious that some people regard the criminal trial of O. J. Simpson "the trial of the century."

BOOK MARK

- *The Last of the Scottsboro Boys,* by Clarence Norris and Sybil Washington (1979)

- *Scottsboro Boy,* by Haywood Patterson with Earl Conrade (1950)

- *Scottsboro: A Tragedy of the American South,* by Dan T. Carter (1976)

- *Stories of Scottsboro: The Rape Case that Shocked 1930s America and Revived the Struggle for Equality,* by James Goodman (1994)

 # Ernest Everett Just (1883–1941)

Just was in Europe during the worst of all times for anyone of color to be there, but he had abandoned all hope of America as a place he could heartily carry out his work. He was between a rock and a hard place because his appointed time (and funds) to do research in Italy was coming to an end. In a desperation letter, dated August 13, 1936, Just appealed to, of all people, il Duce,

> Your Excellency:
> Although I have, in accordance with regular procedure, presented a request to the office of your government to which such requests should be addressed, I nevertheless take the liberty to appeal to you personally because I am motivated by the thought that mine is such an unusual case that it merits your individual attention. As an American negro who for more than twenty-five years has contributed to the progress of biological science without having attained a place in America which such service deserves, I desire earnestly the opportunity to continue my labors in Italy and thereby co-operate in the ardent activity with which your energetic leadership accelerates Italy to a magnificent destiny. My scientific labors fructify in this moment and promise a new basis for both the investigation and the solution of fundamental problems of vital phenomena; they reveal a significance for medicine, for example, the elucidation of cancer, and they relate to the practical improvement of a natural food-resource in Italy—i.e., the piscatorial industry.
> I request that you grant me an audience that I may have the possibility to explain my purposes. I maintain myself at your disposal until August 29 when I must return to the U.S.A. Enclosed are my vita, a bibliography, and a separate of a recent publication of mine. I further enclose copies of two statements, translated into Italian, addressed to your Minister of Education, which presents my case in detail.
> I have the honor to remain, Your Excellency, with expressions of highest esteem,
>
> most sincerely Yours,
> E. E. Just

As Kenneth R. Manning put it in his 1983 biography of Just, *Black Apollo of Science* (where this letter is reprinted), "Mussolini was too busy building his Fascist machinery to be concerned with the problems of a lone black American scientist." Meanwhile, Just was too busy trying to stay a scientist to confront the fiendish goings-on in Italy. He had worked so long, worked so hard.

Just, a native of Charleston, South Carolina, had trekked to New York City when he was seventeen, to find work sufficient to save enough money to go to school; and he did, enrolling in Kimball Academy, where he worked so hard and was so brilliant that he completed the four-year course in three, graduating with honors. Dartmouth College came next. There, he majored in biology and minored in Greek and history, graduating magna cum laude in 1907. That fall, he began teaching at Howard University, first English and rhetoric. When Howard expanded its science curricula, biology, zoology, and physiology then became his domain.

Beginning in 1909, Just had the honor of spending twenty-something summers at the distinguished Marine Biological Laboratory (MBL) in Woods Hole, Massachusetts. He started out doing a lot of scut work and eventually became a research assistant to Frank R. Lillie, who was director of MBL and head of the zoology department at the University of Chicago. In 1916, Just earned his Ph.D. from that school. The year before, he had received the first NAACP Spingarn Medal, in recognition of his scientific endeavors and potential. For example, his paper "The Relation of the First Cleavage Plane to the Entrance Point of the Sperm" (1912) was widely regarded as an important study. All in all, he published some sixty research papers in important scientific journals. Cell life was Just's focus, and his hope was to learn everything he could about normal and abnormal cells so that he could penetrate the riddles of a host of diseases.

Just's quest was frustrated because, as he told Mussolini, he was unable to obtain strong continuous support for his work in America: large grants that would allow him to devote himself full-time to research, an appointment to a major university or research laboratory.

Just did receive some grants. In the late 1920s, for example, there was a grant from the Julius Rosenwald Fund, which allowed him to work abroad, where he was very much welcomed. In 1929, he spent seven months in Italy, carrying out research at the Stazione Zoologia in Naples. During the next ten years, for long and short periods of time, Just had the opportunity to work there again, as well as at other laboratories in Europe, including the Kaiser Wilhelm Institut für Biologie in Berlin.

When he wasn't abroad, Just was teaching at Howard, which he found stultifying. His patchwork, vagabond life put a strain on his relationship with his wife, Ethel Highwarden, a Howard instructor he married in 1912 and with whom he had three children. In time, like his marriage, Just's health was shaky.

Just was hoping things would improve when his masterwork *The Biology of the Cell Surface* was published in 1939. This book, which changed the way scientists viewed cells, was based on Just's pioneering thesis that the ectoplasm played as important a role in cell life as did the nucleus.

When his book came out, Just was in France at the Station Biologique in Roscoff, an appendage of the Sorbonne. By then, he had divorced his wife and married a graduate student he had met in Berlin. He was still in France and in failing health in June 1940 when the Germans burst in. Just was held in an internment camp for a time; his saving grace was that his new wife's father was able to pull some strings on his behalf. Just returned to the United States that summer. He died a little over a year later from a disease he had sought to elucidate: cancer.

Carl Murphy (1889–1967)

Carl followed in his father's footsteps, and when he reached the end of his road, black America said, Well done. His father was John Henry Murphy, a former slave who built a successful home-improvement company and, in the early 1890s, founded the Baltimore weekly, the *Afro-American,* born of a merger of three separate papers. One of the three was Murphy's own *Sunday School Helper,* which he started producing out of his cellar in 1890, as an offshoot of his work as Superintendent of Sunday School at Bethel A.M.E. Church.

The *Afro-American* was a true black enterprise from editorial to printing. It was a veritable school in every aspect of the newspaper business for bright young minds, including John Henry's many children, who started working at the paper as children and teenagers.

It was in large part because his father was ailing that in 1918, Carl Murphy, a graduate of Howard University and Harvard University who had been chair of Howard's German department, became the editor of the paper. When his father died in 1922, Carl became publisher. At the time, the *Afro-American* had a circulation of about 14,000.

On the foundation his father laid, Carl Murphy made the *Afro-American* one of the finest and most influential of the new-era black newspapers, one that eventually came out twice a week, had a circulation of more than 200,000 in its prime, and had subsidiaries in Washington, D.C.; Richmond; Philadelphia; and Newark.

What made the paper so dynamic and necessary was its coverage of not just local and national, but international news, as well. Also, there was the force with which it kept its readers informed about the pressing issues of the day—lynchings, the **Scottsboro Boys,** mistreatment of black soldiers, and the wins and losses in the civil-rights crusade. This was so because Carl Murphy was deeply committed to the advancement of his people, and he put his money where his mouth was. The *Afro-American* contributed handsomely to various court cases, including suits against the Southern Railroad for Jim Crow treatment of passengers heading South out of D.C., against University of Maryland and the Maryland Art Institute for exclusion of black students, and against Baltimore's public library system for hiring only whites.

Murphy, who served on the NAACP's Board of Directors, was instrumental in the growth of the NAACP's Baltimore chapter and a staunch supporter of the NAACP Legal Defense and Educational Fund's efforts, in Baltimore and elsewhere. Whenever the Fund was arguing a case in the Supreme Court, Carl Murphy was there, said Thurgood Marshall, who also recalled that whenever he needed money for lawyers, "Carl was always there." Murphy was also there for Morgan State College. As chair of its Board of Trustees from 1953 to 1967, he played an important role in its growth. The Carl Murphy Scholarship Fund established in 1963 is just one example.

In 1954, Carl Murphy was honored by the National Urban League. In 1955, he was awarded the NAACP's Spingarn Medal. These are just two of the ways he was thanked and applauded for many years of service to the race through his sideline endeavors and through the *Afro-American.*

OTHER NEW-ERA NEWSPAPERS

- *Black Dispatch.* This firecracker was launched in 1915 by one of Oklahoma's most indefatigable civil-rights leaders, Roscoe Dunjee (1883–1965), brother of historian Drusilla Dunjee Houston. (*The Wonderful Ethiopians of the Ancient Cushite Empire*). For Roscoe Dunjee, starting a newspaper was second nature: His father had published a small newspaper, *Harpers Ferry Messenger,* in West Virginia, where Roscoe was born. By midcentury, *Black Dispatch* had national readership, and its publisher was well-known for his stinging, winning editorials.

- *Chicago Defender.* This was the brainchild of Robert Sengstacke Abbott (1868–1940), who was born on St. Simon's Island, Georgia. Abbott, who had a trade (printing) and a professional degree (law), started the newspaper in 1905 in his landlady's kitchen with twenty cents and a little credit. A decade later, the paper had a circulation of about 250,000, with deep readership in the South.

- *New York Amsterdam News.* It was founded in 1909 by James H. Anderson, and in 1936, it was purchased by two doctors, Philip M. H. Savory and Clilan Bethany Powell (New York's first black radiologist), who became its editor-in-chief and the force behind the popularity of the "Dam News" outside its home in Harlem.

- *Philadelphia Tribune.* This, the oldest continuously publishing black newspaper, was founded in 1884 by Baltimore-born Christopher J. Perry, former journalist and editor of the "Colored Department" of the *Philadelphia Sunday Mercury.*

- *Pittsburgh Courier.* A man who made his living as a security guard, Edwin Nathaniel Harleston, started this paper in January 1910. Before the year was out, however, he pulled out of the enterprise. The *Courier's* new chief was the attorney who had handled its incorporation, Robert L. Vann (1879–1940), who made this newspaper the smart and extremely popular national institution that it was by the time he died.

Lorenzo Dow Turner (1895–1969)

Because the Yoruba wore *danshiki,* we have the dashiki. Because Tshiluba had *kingombo,* we enjoy gumbo. Because Wolof had *honq* (red, pink) and *dzug* (misbehave), rednecked whites (and blue-blooded ones, too) got called honkies and blacks let loose in juke joints. Because the Kimdundu had *mbanzo,* we've got banjo. Because the Mandingo said *o-ke* to convey the likes of "yes, indeed!" and used negatives to express positive supreme, we've got the ubiquitous *okay,* and we give a high compliment when we call a person, place, or thing *ba-ad.* Because in Bantu there's *jaja, mbubu, nyambi,* and *Ngola,* in English there's *jazz, booboo, yam,* and *Gullah.*

Lorenzo Dow Turner's decision to become a linguist has a lot to do with why we know these things and so much more about Africanisms in American English. It was Turner's 1949 book *Africanisms in the Gullah Dialect* that laid the foundation for understanding just how much of Africa her forced emigrants retained in their speech. As speech is such a central part of culture, Turner's work was a great contribution to the overall study of African retentions in the Americas. As for Turner's journey to linguist, it evolved out of a more general scholarly bent.

Turner, born in Elizabeth City, North Carolina, and raised in Maryland, earned his B.A. from Howard and his M.A. from Harvard (spending many summers playing for the Negro League's Commonwealth Giants of New York). After earning his master's degree, Turner taught English at Howard University for several years. During this time, he worked on his Ph.D. from the University of Chicago (his dissertation was *Anti-Slavery Sentiment in American Literature Prior to 1865*).

Turner eventually took a job at South Carolina State College in Orangeburg, where one day he overheard two students speaking Gullah. His curiosity, spiced by previous study with Melville J. Herskovits, prompted Turner to devote a string of weekends recording the speech on the South Carolina Sea Island of St. Helena. Through a series of grants (including ones from the Rockefeller Foundation and the Rosenwald Fund), Turner did intensive study of the language and culture of the Sea Island folks, mastering, in the process, a slew of languages. To the Latin, Greek, Italian, and German he had studied were added Kongo, Igbo, Yoruba, Mende, and many other African languages and dialects, as well as Portuguese, French, and Arabic.

In 1944, Turner started teaching English at Fisk, and he started turning out articles based on his study of the relationship between the language (and hence culture) of the people of the Sea Islands and their "cousins," the peoples of south-central and western Africa. These articles were the preset for his pioneering book.

What Turner showed through *Africanisms in the Gullah Dialect* was that, in contrast to the prevailing thought, many of the idiosyncracies of black folk speech did not arise from people's inability to grasp standard American English, that black commoner talk was not about lips too big and mind too slow, was not a corruption of English. Prior to Turner's work, for example, in "The English of the Negro," which appeared in *American Mercury* in 1924, American language maven Krapp, George Krapp, stated, "It is reasonably safe to say that not a single detail of Negro pronunciation or Negro syntax can be proved to have other than English origins." After the pioneering work of Lorenzo Dow Turner, fewer and fewer folks would believe this Krapp.

Turner's last academic base was Chicago's Roosevelt University, where he was professor of English and lecturer in African culture from 1946 until his death in the late 1960s. During this time, he produced scores of small gems, such as the essay "African Survivals in the New World with Emphasis on the Arts." In conjunction with his appointment as Peace Corps Faculty Coordinator at Roosevelt in the early 1960s, Turner also produced two more books: *An Anthology of Krio Folklore and Literature and Inter-linear Translations in English* (1963) and *Krio Texts: With Grammatical Notes and Translations in English* (1965). Turner had gathered a great deal of the raw material for these books during his 1951–1952 sojourn in West Africa (courtesy of a Fulbright Fellowship), where he collected hundreds of folktales and thousands of proverbs, along with loads of other kinds of folklore.

BOOK MARK

- *The African Heritage of American English,* by Joseph E. Holloway and Winifred K. Vass (1993)

- *Africanisms in American Culture,* edited by Joseph E. Holloway (1990)

- *The Bantu Speaking Heritage of the United States,* by Winifred K. Vass (1979)

- *Black English: Its History and Usage in the United States* (1972), by J. L. Dillard, who also authored *All-American English* (1975), *Black Names* (1976), and *Lexicon of Black English* (1977)

- *Black Names in America: Origins and Usage* (1975), by Newbell Puckett, offered the first deep chronicle of aboriginal, assigned, and created names (some 500,000, from 1619 to 1940)

- *Dictionary of Afro-American Slang* (1978; revised edition, *From Juba to Jive: Dictionary of African-American Slang,* 1994), by Clarence Major, best known as a poet, novelist, and playwright

- *Talkin and Testifyin: The Language of Black America* (1977), by Geneva Smitherman

 Jackson Jordan, Jr. (b. 1886)

So long a life, so far from an ol' fool, Jackson Jordan, Jr., a native of North Carolina, was near ninety when John Langston Gwaltney interviewed him in the 1970s. This interview ended up in Gwaltney's *Drylongso: A Self-Portrait of Black America* (1980), a collection of narratives of more than forty everyday people, such as Jackson Jordan, Jr. (not his real name), who in times past was a teacher of biology, music, and the out-of-Africa martial-art knocking and kicking.

Jordan's talk with Gwaltney indicated that over the years, Jordan had done a lot of thinking about race matters. His thoughts offer insight into how many black men survived on the inside, how they stayed steady in their heads, how they slipped the yoke. In this old man's ruminations, many of us hear echoes of grandfathers, granduncles, and other men not kin, yet family, who gathered on porches and in front rooms, in barbershops and pool halls, to talk about the ways of white folks and to trade strategies for surviving.

> The thing that makes us different is how we think. What we believe is important, the ways we look at life. . . . I have known stupid people of all colors. There seems to be more stupid white people because they talk more about everything than anyone else does. . . .
>
> . . . . White people are bolder because they think they are supposed to know everything anyhow. I have been a carpenter and it is common for white people to insist that you do something which is unsound, but they will not concede that they are paying me to do this job because they cannot do it themselves. They do not know enough about it to know what is sound or not. If they did know how to do my job, why pay me to do it?
>
> Then too, white people have the power. After all, they have the mojo and the sayso, as my father used to say. They are supposed to know what they are about. But it is not hard to tell that they don't really know everything, and this knowledge makes us think that because they don't know some things, they must not really know anything. . . .
>
> White people support their simpler brethren. They feel they must, so that makes our people say, "Well, if he supported him in that, then he must be just as stupid." So we feel a kind of contempt for them. But we admire their single-mindedness in helping their great personages. You would never get a group of black people to do that kind of thing. We try to do for ourselves and the few people we are close to

what white people do for their race. Now, they are able to do that because they are sure that inasmuch as they do it unto them that are
the greatest of them, they have done it unto themselves. . . . That is
why they will stand for leaders who are obviously lying to them and
cheating them. They hope that their sons might rise to such a place of
wealth, and they know that their power comes from deceit and force
and know that it can only be maintained by massive reliance upon de-
ception and force. It would be a matter of great concern to them if
they thought that they had put an honest man in charge of their business. Every now and then they make this mistake, but they are quick
to kill off that man before he can really do something decent. You see,
this country is basically an immoral enterprise. . . .

The business of white men is to rule. I did not make it so, but it is
so now. They want their children to rule, even to rule them. It pleases
them, no matter what they say, when their children are rude and
overbearing, because that is a sign to them that those children are
getting ready to rule as their parents have ruled. Now, our children
must bear the rule of the rude, weak, uncivil people, so they must always keep themselves to themselves. The white man must pretend to
know more than he does, but we must always show less than we
know.

He had also come to see white folks in power as people who "have
got to bluff it out," who were basically "very unsure of themselves," and
that those who became "great" were in denial about the edge their
whiteness gave them.

Every white person likes to think that he is what you used to hear
people refer to as "a self-made man." We used to read about all these
poor orphans who rose to be great men. Now, the reason they were
able to better themselves was that there was no huge weight of color
prejudice holding them down. But we are supposed to think that it
was their natural gifts which made them great. Now, back then, great
meant rich. People—white people, anyway—worshiped money then.
Rich men were supposed to be philosophers and great at everything
else because they had managed to get a great deal of money. We were
supposed to look up to the Mellons and the Morgans and people like
that. Now, white people, I think, did but we didn't, or we didn't in the
same way they did. For one thing, we knew that we would not be able
to be the kind of rich men that they were. We also knew that no matter how much money we had, we would still have to be careful.

Jordan maintained that another difference between blacks and
whites was that blacks rely more heavily on "mother wit and ordinary
common sense." To illustrate, he turned to humor, referring Gwaltney
to "that old street story" about the Massa who "misplaced his member"
and inquired of his servant where the thing usually was when not
being used. "Well," said Jordan, "there is a lot in that." Then he re-

turned to his point about the insecurity and immaturity that beset most white men as far as he could see.

> You see, in a very real sense white men never grow up. They make everything into schoolboy games. X has always got to mark the spot for them. The average white man is Dr. Watson and the leaders are all supposed to be the great Sherlock. . . . When I was a boy I used to think that only Southern white men did this, but now I know that it is a general habit with most of them. They are always waiting for orders. What they don't know is that their leaders are men just like themselves. There really are no people who know what to do without orders. Black people know this and make up their orders as they go along if they possibly can. . . . White men think that they can hide the fact that they generally do not know what they are doing. They think that because we don't tell them that, we don't know that they are meat men like all the rest. We don't tell them because we know that they are trying to convince themselves that they are what they would like to be. And so it proceeds. Of course, it is the rifle and the dollar which keep this game going.

What if black men had the mojo and the sayso? "When we have as much power as they have now, we will have to be the kind of people they are now," he said. He'd like to be wrong but "from what I can see after a number of years looking, most people are weak and greedy."

Jordan was clear about the fact that whites who oppose justice for blacks do so not out of ignorance or philosophical moorings, but because they don't want to give up the goodies.

> Those early white men were selfish, and now even the best of their grandchildren live in fear of justice. Black people love justice because it is denied them. White men say they love justice, which they fear worse than hell. If I were a good white man, I don't know what I would do. I would not want to see my children braggarts and cheats, but I would know that justice would be fatal for them.

Toward the end of the conversation, Jordan said something to Gwaltney he didn't think he had ever said outright.

> To me, the knowledge that I am morally superior to white men is important. No one has to mention it. . . . But I know it and they know it and there is nothing they can do—even improving themselves—which can change that fact. During all our history here we have been right and they have been wrong and the only man who cannot see that is a fool or a liar.

This clarity on race matters (or at least on his views) was part of what kept Jackson Jordan, Jr., from despair, nihilism, self-hatred. At the end of the interview, he said,

> I don't want you to think that I am in anywise tired of things down here. I've had my share of years, but I can use all they send me. I have

told you what I think. You know that I didn't make the world. . . . If I had, it would be different for everybody. Things are not all bad. I still get a good dinner and a good enough bottle and a conversation that makes sense every now and then. I am not a hopeful man or a hopeless man. I just go 'long drylongso, as they used to say.

Though you may not agree with all of Jordan's analysis, you cannot deny that there is a lot of wisdom in his words, and that he was hardly an ol' fool.

ABOUT THE INTERVIEWER

John Langston Gwaltney (1928–1998), who was born in Orange, New Jersey, received his B.A. from Upsala College, his M.A. in political science from the New School for Social Research, and his Ph.D. in anthropology from Columbia University, where he was a student of Margaret Mead. His first book *Thrice Shy* was his dissertation on river blindness among the Yolox Chinantec of Oaxaca, Mexico, for which he received Columbia University's Ansley Dissertation Award. No doubt, his sightlessness had something to do with his interest in this subject. As for his motivation for *Drylongso,* as he explained in the book's introduction, it stemmed from his "long-held view that traditional Euro-American anthropology has generally failed to produce ethnographers who are capable of assessing black American culture in terms other than romantic, and from my belief in the theory-building and analytic capacities of my people." Gwaltney's book *The Dissenters* (1986) is a collection of narratives of people from all walks of life, who rejected the status quo and took unpopular stands.

 The Black Boys of Summer

Oscar Charleston, Monte Irvin, Cool Papa Bell, Pop Lloyd.

They were among the few thousand souls whose talents and grit (and sometimes showmanship) kept their people from being shut out of America's favorite pastime.

Big Joe Green, Crush Holloway, Ankle Ball Moss, Cannonball Dick Redding, Home Run Johnson.

They were keeping on in the tradition of black baseballers that stretched back to the 1860s, and sometimes had blacks on teams with white boys, until the turn of the century, when professional baseball decided to strike black boys out.

Satchel Paige, Smokey Joe Williams, Josh Gibson, Buck O'Neil, Buck Leonard.

They were not boys at play but men at work. Most would have been laborers, waiters, drivers, or janitors, but for a good arm, flash speed, fetchin' catchin' that allowed them to make a living at something more pleasurable and better paying. True, they had grueling schedules, with all the barnstorming—sometimes three, sometimes four games a day—but working hard was nothing new for black men. Of course, the celebrity was real sweet: sweet for them, sweet for the black crowds hungry for chances to cheer for black men during the roar of the 1920s and the depressing days of the 1930s and on up deep into the 1940s.

Mules Suttles, Turkey Stearns, Jimmie Lyons, Larry Doby, Quincy Troupe.

The Homestead Grays at Forbes Field in Pittsburgh, Pennsylvania, in 1942. Standing, left to right: Jerry Benjamin (outfielder), Roy Partlow (pitcher), Josh Gibson (catcher), John Richard Wright (pitcher), Chester Williams (shortstop), Ray Brown (pitcher), John Leftwich (pitcher), J.C. "Ed" Hamilton (pitcher), Robert "Rab Roy" Gaston (catcher), and Walter "Buck" Leonard (first baseman). Kneeling, left to right: David "Speed" Whatley (outfielder), Jud "Boojung" Wilson (third baseman), Matther Carlisle (second baseman), Charles Gray (third baseman), Sam Bankhead (shortstop), Roy Welmaker (pitcher), Howard Easterling (third baseman), Vic Harris (outfielder). The Homestead Grays were organized by Cum and See, as the brothers Cumberland and Seeward Posey were known. This photograph was taken by the *Pittsburgh Courier*–based photojournalist Charles "Teenie" Harris. (Courtesy of the *Pittsburgh Courier* Photographic Archives)

They were proud of their progress from slingshot teams with scattershot schedules to leagues. Rube Foster, once a star pitcher for Philadelphia's Cuban Giants and founder of the Chicago American Giants, surely deserved to be called "The Father of Negro Baseball." Had he not put his good sense to launching the Negro National League in 1920, and making it a power, there might never have come the others, such as the Eastern Colored League, the Negro Southern League, and the much sturdier Negro American League.

The Kansas City Monarchs, the Newark Eagles, the Pittsburgh Crawfords, the Homestead Grays—shonuf somebodies and hotstuffs.

They had their own major and minors, their own world series. Some teams even had their own buses and trains; some, their own parks. Food and pop and paraphernalia and coverage in the black papers, a lot of people could profit. Yeah, so what if some owners were racketeers and white (and some white racketeers). How many blacks didn't ultimately work for The Man? How many entertainment entities didn't belong to men with ties to crime?

The Black Boys of Summer would despise all those soapsuds stories that made them out to be such pitiable vagabonds, naked to the winds of Jim Crow. As if any sane black person—and they were sane—would just go out on the road with no lookahead about where to eat, where to stay, where to use a bathroom. They negotiated the territory as all black folks had to.

The Memphis Red Sox, the Baltimore Black Sox, the Birmingham Black Barons.

They'd spit, too, at the stories of how sad it was that their talents were not on view—as if being seen by thousands of white people always and only was the measure of success for real. Plus, they knew the huge crowds their East–West Games drew—40,000, 50,000—some years far and away more than came out for the white boys' All-Star Game.

They didn't every day sweat the petty: Were they better than the white boys of summer? Who in black America, who accomplished anything, didn't have to be twice as good to get half as far? And how many times did they have to best the white boys in exhibition games to feel good about themselves? And look at how many from among the ranks of the black boys of summer became legends when they stepped onto white diamonds. Jackie Robinson and Larry Doby were only the first.

As more black boys of summer trooped into the white majors, there was no hip-hip hurrah everywhere and forever. The gain of a few was going to make a bust for the many as their people became more keen on seeing one black play with a team of whites over diamonds shining bright with all blacks—and so, their teams, their leagues did fade away.

As the black boys of summer faced the bottom of the ninth, never could they imagine that their rich history would be preserved in so wonderful a way as it is in the Negro League Museum in Kansas City. After all, the team that lasted the longest was the one that specialized in being a spectacle, the Indianapolis Clowns.

BOOK MARK

- *A Complete History of the Negro Leagues, 1884–1955*, by Mark Ribowsky (1995)

- *The Biographical Encyclopedia of the Negro Baseball Leagues*, by James A. Riley (1994)

- *The Negro Baseball Leagues: A Photographic History*, by Phil Dixon with Patrick J. Hannigan (1992)

- *Only the Ball Was White*, by Robert Peterson (1989)

 ## The Nicholas Brothers (1917– and 1921–)

Wouch! That's about what you think even after the second or tenth time you've seen the finale of the 1943 film *Stormy Weather* with the two brothers leapfrogging down the wide winding staircase—Wow!—doing full splits—Ouch!

Show biz came natural to these Philadelphia fellas: Their parents had their own band, working for vaudeville shows and, for a time, serving as a standard at Philly's Standard Theater. This meant that the kids spent a lot of time backstage. Fayard was the first to be fascinated by the fancy footwork he glimpsed, turning Harold on to the same as soon as little brother could walk. "The Nicholas Kids" was how they were first billed.

The name change came in 1932, when they made their debut at Harlem's legendary Cotton Club, where they were regulars for the duration of the 1930s, moving to the music of such bands as those of Jimmie Lunceford, Cab Calloway, and the Duke. Because they were just teens, they had the purported privilege of mingling with the club's white-only clientele between performances. Black boys as showpiece is probably what it really was.

Not long after their debut at the Cotton Club, the cute kids appeared in the minimovie *Pie Pie Black Bird*, with Nina Mae McKinney and Eubie Blake and his orchestra. On into the 1930s and 1940s, they were featured in a slew of films: *Kid Millions*, *Tin Pan Alley*, *Down Argentine Way*, and *Sun Valley Serenade*, with its precious "Chattanooga

The Nicholas Brothers in the film *Sun Valley Serenade*. (Courtesy of Donald Bogle)

Choo Choo" number with Dorothy Dandridge (to whom Harold was married for a while). There was also *Orchestra Wives* (1942), in which they did their most astounding stunt, which entailed running up a wall, doing a back flip and landing in a split (Wouch!), then rising lithely, blithely to their feet without missing a beat.

In and around their filmwork, the Nicholas Brothers did a nice amount of work in theater and in nightclubs. In the 1950s and beyond, their talent was viewed by millions through variety shows, including that show of shows—the really big one—*The Ed Sullivan Show*. Unfortunately, while the Nicholas Brothers had huge successes in Europe, they never made it really, really big in America, never got the big parts, though their talent was tremendous—better, many contend, than that of Kelly, Astaire, and other celebrated dancers in mid-century America. Superstars they should have been, would have been, had they not been black.

When the Nicholas Brothers were well past middle age, they were still doing dance. Fayard, for example, was choreographer for the 1980s Broadway hit *Black and Blue* (for which he received a Tony). Harold appeared in the 1984 movie *Tap*, in the 1985–1986 Broadway run of *The Tap Dance Kid*, and in the film *The Five Heartbeats*, which was released in 1991, the same year that the Nicholas Brothers received the Kennedy Center Honors for extraordinary contribution to American culture. Among the brothers' other honors are the American Black Lifetime Achievement Award, induction into the Black Filmmaker's Hall of Fame and the Apollo Theater's Hall of Fame, a star on Hollywood's Walk of Fame, and a *Dance* magazine award. In the summer of 1998, the

Nicholas Brothers received the Samuel H. Scripps American Dance Festival Award, which was established to honor those great choreographers who have dedicated their lives and talents to the creation of our modern dance heritage. One of the highlights of the ceremony was a performance by Fayard's granddaughters, the Nicholas Sisters.

OTHER BROTHER DANCE ACTS

- THE BERRY BROTHERS. Ananias (c. 1912–1951), James (c. 1915–1969), and Warren (c. 1918–?), who were raised in Hollywood, California, made a particularly hot item in the 1940s, with their stellar standard "flash act," which melanged tap, soft shoe, acrobatics, and a souped-up cakewalk. *Lady Be Good, Panama Hattie,* and *Boarding House Blues* are among the films in which they appeared. The bands of Count Basie, Cab Calloway, and Ella Fitzgerald are among those with which they toured.

- THE FOUR STEP BROTHERS. "Eight Feet of Rhythm" is how this acrobatic tap act was billed at one point. They appeared in nightclubs around the United States and Europe, as well as in many films, including *When Johnny Comes Marching Home, Rhythm of the Islands,* and *Shine on Harvest Moon.* The original quartet, formed 1929–1930, was composed of Maceo Anderson, Al Williams, Happy Johnson, and Sherman Robinson, none of whom were related by blood. By the time the group disbanded in the mid-1970s, there had been many changes in personnel.

 Jacob Lawrence (1917–   )

Street Orator, Ironers, Barbershop, The Seamstress, Shoe Shine Boys, The Cabinetmaker, The Family, Wounded Man: Jacob Lawrence has always made artworks that astounded the art experts and connoisseurs, yet his artworks have also inspired and been used by everyday people, too. Nothing wrong with some abstraction and surrealism, and there are days when some Dada will do nicely, but there are times when we African Americans want and need to see ourselves in ways we can relate to, connect with, without going through so many changes. In these moments, we truly savor some Lawrence. Thankfully, there's a lot of it to savor because, although not all his work is black-themed, a great deal of it is.

There are times when we want and need to behold some heroes, when we remember that there is power in the past, and a whole lot of role models are waiting for us back there. At times like these, we really appreciate the *Toussaint L'Ouverture* series, the *Harriet Tubman* series, the *Frederick Douglass* series. We review his *The Migration of the Negro* series when we want and need to remember not just the early twentieth-century Exodus, but our whole journey.

Jacob Armstead Lawrence's way to art began in Harlem when he was about thirteen. He had been born in Atlantic City, New Jersey, and had lived in Pennsylvania for a time, but when his parents separated, Mrs. Lawrence thought that New York City would have better opportunities for the only work she could probably get, domestic work. So that's where she moved herself and her three children, settling in Central Harlem.

To keep her children off the streets and out of trouble, Mrs. Lawrence enrolled them in an after-school program at Utopia House. This center had a strong arts component, and in it, young Jake found bliss. He also found a mentor in the sculptor and painter Charles Alston, who was the instructor of the arts and craft program. Alston saw Jake as a child of promise right from the start. When, in 1932, Alston established the government-funded Harlem Art Workshop, Lawrence became one of his pupils.

Charles Alston was not the only significant artist–intellectual Lawrence met in Harlem, where an extraordinary corps of writers and artists were still doing good brave work, even though the Negro was no longer "in vogue." Lawrence's circle of friends and associates included Langston Hughes, Aaron Douglas, Claude McKay, Romare Bearden, Augusta Savage, Alain Locke, and Gwendolyn Knight, whom Lawrence was to marry in 1941. Also, there was "Professor" Charles Seifert, the Barbados-born contractor "by day," who was in his real life a major bibliophile, an artist, and operator of the Ethiopian School of Research History on 137th Street. Seifert's school was a mecca for those hungry for information and insight on black history. As Lawrence recalled years later, in a letter to a gallery owner, one of Seifert's "projects" was "to get black artists and young people such as myself who were interested in art . . . to select as our content black history."

In 1937, when Lawrence was twenty, he saw his work exhibited for the first time, as part of a Harlem Arts Guild group show. Not long after that, his work was shown in another group exhibition at the American Artists School, which awarded him a scholarship to study there two years. At this point, Lawrence's work consisted of mostly interior and exterior scenes of Harlem life, but he had already begun work on his series about Toussaint L'Ouverture, and other series on historical figures were on the horizon.

In 1938, Lawrence had his first one-man show, at the Harlem YMCA. In that same year, owing to the influence of Augusta Savage, director of the Harlem Community Arts Center where Lawrence had taken classes, he secured a job with the Works Progress Administration (WPA) Federal Arts Project, which enabled him to earn money his mother and his siblings desperately needed *and* be an artist. Heretofore, Lawrence had helped his mother make ends meet through all sorts of jobs, including a paper route, delivering laundry, being a printer's go-fer, and digging ditches for a dam up in Middletown, New York, as a member of the WPA's labor corps, the CCC (Civilian Conservation Corps). With his new WPA assignment, Lawrence was to produce two paintings every six weeks for eighteen months. It was during this time that Lawrence created the thirty-three-panel *Frederick Douglass* series. Then came the one about Tubman.

In 1940, Lawrence applied for a Julius Rosenwald Fellowship for a project he'd had on his mind for a while. One of the people he approached for a reference was Alain Locke, who had included Lawrence's work in his book *The Negro in Art: A Pictorial of the Negro Artist and of the Negro Theme in Art.* "My proposed plan of work," he wrote Locke, "is to interpret in a sufficient number of panels (from 40 to 50—18 × 12) the great Negro migration north during World War I. I think this will make a colorful and interesting work, as any group migration is in itself."

Lawrence received the fellowship, which allowed him to set up a studio (in a loft on 125th Street) and dig deep into the research for his proposed "colorful and interesting work." Completed in 1941, the series turned out to be sixty panels long: "During the World War there was a great migration North by Southern Negroes. . . ." begins Lawrence's original text to the first panel.

"In every town Negroes were leaving by the hundreds to go North and enter into Northern industry. . . . They did not always leave because they were promised work in the North. Many of them left because of Southern conditions, one of them being great floods that ruined the crops, and therefore they were unable to make a living where they were. . . . Another cause was lynching. . . . The migration gained in momentum. . . . And the migration spread." This text is from a few of the next twenty-nine panels.

Lawrence's captions to the next thirty panels include: "They arrived in great numbers into Chicago, the gateway of the West. . . . The South that was interested in keeping cheap labor was making it very difficult for labor agents recruiting Southern labor for Northern firms. . . . They also made it very difficult for migrants leaving the South. They often went to railroad stations and arrested the Negroes wholesale, which in turn made them miss their trains. . . . They arrived in Pittsburgh, one of the great industrial centers of the North, in large numbers. . . . Housing for the Negroes was a very difficult problem. . . . Race riots were very numerous all over the North because of the antagonism that was caused between the Negro and white workers. . . . Among one of

"All other sources of labor having been exhausted, the migrants were the last resource." Panel 4 from *The Migration Series* (1940–1941; text and title revised by the artist, 1993). Tempera on gesso on composition board, 18 × 12" (45.7 × 30.5 cm). (Courtesy of The Museum of Modern Art, New York. Gift of Mrs. David M. Levy. Photograph © 1998 The Museum of Modern Art, New York)

the last groups to leave the South was the Negro professional who was forced to follow his clientele to make a living. . . . And the migrants kept coming."

The *Migration* series, regarded by many as Lawrence's finest work, became a sensation almost overnight. Alain Locke brought it to the attention of Edith Halpert, owner of the prestigious Downtown Gallery in New York City. Halpert was enthralled and laid plans for an exhibit in the winter of 1941. In her publicity campaign, she convinced *Fortune* magazine to publish some of the series, which it did in its November issue.

The show at the Downtown Gallery was a hit, even with the attack on Pearl Harbor occurring during its run. The series' next stop was at The Phillips Collection in February 1942. Then, in March 1942, two art patrons purchased the series for institutions: Adele Rosenwald Levy purchased the even-numbered works for The Museum of Modern Art in New York City; Duncan Phillips, the odd-numbered for The Phillips Collection. That same year, the entire series began a two-year fifteen-city tour. Not bad for a twenty-three-year-old fella.

Lawrence was on his way to becoming one of the premier twentieth-century American artists, producing, producing, producing. In the early 1940s, when he created the *Harlem* series, and after being inducted into the U.S. Coast Guard, the *Coast Guard* series . . . through the mid-1940s when he created the *War* series, and then, after a nervous breakdown, the *Hospital* series . . . and on into the 1950s when he gave us the *Theater* series and then, *Struggle: From the History of the American People* . . . and on through the 1960s, when he produced the *Nigerian* series and taught art at the New School for Social Research in New York City . . . and through the 1970s, when he began teaching at the University of Washington in Seattle and told the story of a black explorer of the Far West with his *George Washington Bush* series . . . into the 1980s when his works included the *Hiroshima* series.

And into the 1990s the art of Jacob Lawrence has kept coming.

BOOK MARK

There are dozens of extraordinary male artists of Lawrence's generation and the generation before, and there are books (many of them exhibition catalogs) on a number of these talents. Among them are these:

- For Romare Bearden (1912–1988), premiere collagist and cofounder of Spiral, a civil-rights-movement arts group—*Romare Bearden: His Life and Art,* by Myron Schwartzman (1990), and *Romare Bearden: His Life and Art,* by Ralph Ellison (1968)

- Aaron Douglas (1899–1979), "artist laureate" of the Harlem Renaissance and founder of the Carl Van Vechten Gallery at Fisk University—*Aaron Douglas: Art, Race, and the Harlem Renaissance,* by Amy Helene Kirschke (1995)

- For Palmer Hayden (1890–1973), known for his "caricature-like" celebrations of black culture (and the *Ballad of John Henry* series)—*Echoes of Our Past: The Narrative Artistry of Palmer C. Hayden,* by Allan M. Gordon (1988)

- For William H. Johnson (1899–1989), expressionist painter—*Homecoming: The Art and Life of William H. Johnson,* by Richard J. Powell (1991)

- For Hughie Lee-Smith (1915–), romantic–realist painter—*Hughie Lee-Smith Retrospective,* by New Jersey State Museum (1989)

- For Norman Lewis (1909–1979), abstract expressionist painter—*Norman Lewis: A Retrospective,* foreword by Milton M. Brown (Graduate School and University Center, City University, 1976), and *Norman Lewis: From the Harlem Renaissance to Abstraction,* by Kenkeleba Gallery (1989)

- For Archibald Motley (1891–1980)—*The Art of Archibald J. Motley Jr.,* by Jontyle T. Robinson and Wendy Greenhouse (1991)

- For Charles White (1918–1979), whose several murals include *History of the Negro Press* and *Contribution of the American Negro to American Democracy—Images of Dignity: A Retrospective of the Works of*

Charles White (The Studio Museum in Harlem, 1982) and all of the Fall 1980 issue of *Freedomways*

- For Hale Woodruff (1900–1980), founder of the art department at Atlanta University—*Hale Woodruff: Fifty Years of His Art,* by The Studio Museum in Harlem (1979)

 Chester Himes (1909–1984)

The titles of the autobiographies of Chester Bomar Himes, who was born in Jefferson City, Missouri, are quite apt: *The Quality of Hurt* (1972) and *My Life of Absurdity* (1976). How bad was it? As we read in Bernard W. Bell's *The Afro-American Novel and Its Tradition* (1987), Himes's "childhood was filled with the turbulence of a querulous, neurotic light-complexioned mother and a psychologically emasculated, dark-skinned father, whose marriage disintegrated under the stress of his wife's contempt for black people and the frustrations of Northern Jim Crow and unemployment." And that wasn't all.

When Chester was fourteen, his brother was blinded in a chemistry experiment, and he blamed himself for the accident. A few years later, Chester had his own terrible accident: He fell down the elevator shaft of a hotel in which he was working. The silver lining was a disability check, which he decided to use for a college education. Himes opted for Ohio State University in Columbus, got in, but dropped out. In no time at all, he went from being an aimless ex-student with a bellhop job to being a criminal.

Himes was pushing twenty when, in 1928, he was arrested for armed robbery and sentenced to twenty to twenty-five years in the Ohio Penitentiary. Things didn't totally fall apart. As Bernard Bell tells us,

> While in prison, which was incredibly free from racial conflict but rampant with homosexuality and violence, he became a professional gambler and writer. His apprenticeship stories were published in such black weekly newspapers and magazines as the *Atlanta World,* the *Pittsburgh Courier,* the *Afro-American,* and *Abbott's Monthly;* and his first professional story, "Crazy in the Stir," was sold to *Esquire* in 1934.* In 1936 he was released on parole, and he married the following year. In 1953, after the publication of his two most important novels, *If He Hollers Let Him Go* (1945) and *Lonely Crusade* (1947), and

*Another piece accepted by *Esquire* was "To What Red Hell" about the 1930 fire in Ohio State Penitentiary, which took the lives of more than three hundred inmates.

the failure in 1951 of his first marriage, and then, in 1952, of a torrid, ambivalent affair with a white woman, he became an expatriate in Europe, frustrated and embittered by his futile struggle with the absurdity of American racism. Driven by the absurdity and ambivalence of his experience as a black American, he sought desperately to reconcile his hope and despair, love and hatred, by turning to interracial sex, including two marriages to white women, and to writing.

Yep, the fella was pretty messed up and not much of a role model. Still, we applaud him. After all, he turned away from a life of crime. Also, in channeling his energies into writing, he gave us Coffin Ed Johnson and Grave Digger Jones, those two "tall, loose-jointed, sloppily dressed, ordinary-looking, dark-brown" bad-guy–good-guys who packed "long-barreled, nickel-plated .38 calibre revolvers" in their work as New York City cops with Harlem for their beat.

The duo was born while Himes was in France in 1956, where he was just about destitute: He was low on dough as well as hope that he'd ever know a sliver of the creative power (and celebrity) of his idol, that most famous black expatriate in France at the time, Richard Wright. Fortune smiled on Himes when Marcel Duhmel of Gallimard contacted him about producing a novel that would fit in with a series of crime thrillers.

Within three weeks, Himes came up with *For Love of Imabelle* (a.k.a. *A Rage in Harlem*), in which Coffin Ed and Grave Digger made their publishing debut, and for which Himes received the 1958 Grand Prix de Littérature policière. In rather rapid fashion, Himes produced nine more Coffin Ed–Grave Digger adventures, which were superb additions to the Dashiell Hammett–Raymond Chandler variety of detective fiction.

The Real Cool Killers, The Crazy Kill, All Shot Up, and *Blind Man with a Pistol* are among the books in the series. The one with the greatest name recognition was the one adapted into a film released in 1970, directed by Ossie Davis and starring Raymond St. Jacques (Coffin Ed) and Godfrey Cambridge (Grave Digger): *Cotton Comes to Harlem.* This action-packed uproarious film was a definite spark for the black movie boom of the 1970s and without a doubt increased Himes's fame and the popularity of his detective fiction. (Unfortunately, the 1972 film *Come Back, Charleston Blue,* based on Himes's *The Heat's On,* was a flop.)

While the Coffin Ed–Grave Digger series was the Himes work that most gripped the average Joes (and Janies), it was not the greatest prize as far as most scholars were concerned. Like Bernard Bell, many critics contend that Himes's "two most important novels" were *If He Hollers Let Him Go* and *Lonely Crusade.* The first is about a man named Bob Jones, who works in a World War II shipyard in Los Angeles. The second is the story of Lee Gordon, a union organizer also living in 1940s L.A. Both men feel the boot heel of racism, and both, like the author, get crazy caught up with white women. Both books are affecting meditations on the three R's that underline the black man's odyssey in America: Rejection, Rage, Rebellion. Himes explored these issues in several other works of fiction, each of which has its fans. There are *Cast the First Stone* (1952), a prison novel; *The Primitive* (1955), about the stormy relationship between a writer and his white lover, which one critic proclaimed as Himes's "most profound" novel; and *The Third Generation* (1954), the story of the nightmare life of a family made up of a light-bright, black-loathing mother, a dark-skinned husband, and their three sons. (Sound familiar?)

Himes had more fire in the belly. Three more novels were published in the 1960s: *Be Calm, Pinktoes,* and *A Case of Rape.* Yep, the fella was pretty prolific, but no great fame or fortune came his way. After he died in 1984 in Spain, there arose a new interest in him and his works, and many of his books were reissued. A variant edition of *The Primitive* was published as *The End of the Primitive* in 1990, the same year that *The Collected Stories of Chester Himes* came out, giving old and new fans of Himes a heavy dose of the genre he started out with.

 # Charlie Parker (1920–1955)

As a player, composer, and meditator on music, this native of Kansas City, Kansas, was primus inter pares in the new style of jazz that took flight in the 1940s: bop, bebop, or, rebop, if you prefer.

In *Down the Glory Road* (1995), Herb Boyd, journalist, historian, and musician, too, serves up a handy review of this phoenix who never arose from the ashes.

> "Bird," as Parker was known to intimates and eventually to the world, soared only a brief while over the jazz firmament, but his flight was majestic and unequaled. Parker was thirteen when he began studying the alto saxophone, and within two years he was already playing among the top musicians in the hotly competitive Kansas City area. In 1939 Parker made his first visit to New York City; he stayed for a year and began experimenting with different changes, playing, as he said, "on higher intervals of the chord as a melody line."
>
> From 1940 to 1942 he traveled with Jay McShann and took part in his first recording session in 1941 in Dallas. After serving a fruitful apprenticeship with McShann, Parker joined Earl "Fatha" Hines's band then went on to Billy Eckstine's famed bebop band, which in-

cluded Dizzy Gillespie, Gene Ammons, Sonny Stitt, Sarah Vaughan, Art Blakey, King Kolax, Linton Garner (Errol's brother), Miles Davis, and Fats Navarro. When Eckstine's band was in the New York City area, Parker and his cohorts would venture up to Harlem, where they polished their skills, and further experimented, at jam sessions held at Minton's Playhouse and Monroe's Uptown House.

The jam sessions, nights on the road, and relentless practicing made Parker the most talented and innovative of the emerging bebop giants. It was at this juncture that he and Gillespie began to front ensembles under their leadership. In 1945 Parker and Gillespie bopped to Hollywood with a scintillating sound, but this success was soon overshadowed by Parker's nervous breakdown and addiction to alcohol and heroin. Bird was on the horse, so to speak, and it would be a tortuous, endless ride, and considering the torment and horrendous side effects, it is simply amazing he left such a wealth of music behind.

By 1947 Parker had formed one of his most prolific bands, featuring Miles Davis (trumpet), Duke Jordan (piano), Tommy Potter (bass), and Max Roach (drums). Parker kept this band intact for about four years, recording such jazz standards as "Scrapple from the Apple," "Ornithology," "Round Midnight," "Donna Lee," "Parker's Mood," and "Yardbird Suite."

Parker was stripped of his New York cabaret license in 1951, and for two years his employment was hampered. Back in action in 1953, Parker was in poor physical and mental health. After two suicide attempts he was admitted to Bellevue Hospital in New York City. On March 5, 1955, Bird flew for the final time at Birdland, a club named in his honor.

Charlie Parker was dead before the month was out. His music, of course, survived, guiding, enlightening, mystifying generations of musicians, and bringing up that haunting question about genius: Why so often is it plagued by such demons?

ANOTHER CHARLIE PARKER

Charles Stewart Parker (1882–1950), a native of Corinne, Utah, was quite an innovator, too: not in music, but in botany. Parker, with many plants named after him (including *Lathyrus Parkeri,* a variety of the sweet pea), earned his bachelor's in botany from Trinity College, his master's from Washington State College, and his Ph.D. from Pennsylvania State College. He put down roots at Howard University in the mid-1920s, eventually becoming chair of the botany department, a position he held until his retirement in 1947.

❈ Benjamin J. Davis, Jr. (1903–1964)

In hindsight, we might say that Ben Davis was rather naïve. Yet, in hindsight, we must also cherish his courage. To be a Communist was to be outcast, scapegoat, target—anathema.

Benjamin Jefferson Davis, Jr., born in Dawson, Georgia, and raised in Atlanta, chose to walk a hard road, when he could have opted for ease. After all, he was the son of a powerful black politician (a big boss in Georgia), who ultimately became a member of the Republican National Committee (and who was also publisher of the rather militant weekly, the *Independent*).

Junior was on the track for high status from the beginning. This road took him to Amherst College, from which he graduated in 1925 (along with future scientist Charles Drew and William H. Hastie, the first black judge appointed to the U.S. Circuit Court of Appeals). Harvard Law School came next, and after that, it was back to Atlanta, where his father helped him set up a law practice.

Junior walked off the beaten path in 1932 after reading, as he put it, "a brief callous news account" of the troubles of eighteen-year-old Angelo Herndon. It was just a year after the railroading of the **Scottsboro Boys** that Angelo Herndon, a member of the Communist Party, was arrested and jailed as an inciter of insurrection under an 1861 statute created to deter slave revolts. Yes, very bizarre, and considerably so inasmuch as all Herndon had done was lead a biracial demonstration on Atlanta's City Hall. The point was to bring attention to the plight of the un- and underemployed. Herndon's plight so moved Ben Davis that he offered his services to the organization handling Herndon's defense, the International Labor Defense, an arm of the Communist Party.

Defending Herndon meant contending with gross disrespect from the judge (who often read the newspaper when Davis had the floor) and from the prosecution (never chastised for referring to Davis or Herndon as "darky" or "nigger"). There were death threats, too. Against formidable odds, and before an all-white jury, Davis battled hard and stayed fierce. When the trial was over, Herndon was sentenced to 18–20 years. For the next few years, Davis continued to work with the International Labor Defense on getting Herndon's conviction overturned. This finally happened in 1937, when the U.S. Supreme Court ruled 5–4 that Georgia's 1861 statute was unconstitutional.

By this time, Davis had relocated to New York and made Harlem his home. He had joined the Communist Party of the USA (CPUSA) shortly after Herndon's conviction. Advancing the CPUSA goals and objectives became his life's work.

Many thought him lunatic. Many thought him traitor. He, however, thought himself a crusader: He aligned himself with the only organization he felt offered real hope for his people. Davis explained himself eloquently in "Why I Am a Communist," an essay that first appeared in a 1947 issue of *Phylon*—two years after the end of the war supposedly waged to "make the world safe for Democracy," and the same year that one of Wisconsin's most infamous sons, Joseph McCarthy, entered the U.S. Senate and spearheaded the formulation of the House Un-American Activities Committee, which began proceedings in October 1947.

In presenting his reason for being a Communist, Davis said,

> As a Negro American, I want to be free. I want equal opportunities. . . . I want first-class, unconditional citizenship. I want it, and am entitled to it, now.
>
> I want to be free of discrimination, Jim Crow, segregation, lynch law; I want to be free of second-class citizenship. In short, I want, as an American citizen, to enjoy the four freedoms which were proclaimed by the late Franklin D. Roosevelt, and which the State Department is interested hypocritically in prating about for every place except America.

In elaborating on why he deemed communism the best hope for black people, Davis naturally pressed on the point that many have had a hard time understanding and accepting—namely, that, as was the case with slavery, the motor of racism is greed.

> The struggles of the Negro people are an inseparable part of the struggles of the working class of America, and of the workers, common people and colonials all over the world. . . .
>
> Racial, religious and other discriminations are weapons of capitalism to intensify its exploitation of certain sections of the population, to keep down the wages and working conditions of the working class, and to prevent the working people from uniting against the common foe—capitalism. Against the Negro people, capitalism has developed the so-called theory of "white supremacy" and "racial inferiority," against the Jews "anti-Semitism" on account of their religion, against Catholics "taking orders from Rome" on account of the central head of their church in the Vatican—and so on. Systematically, capitalism breeds and fans in Hitlerlike fashion religious, national, and racial antagonisms because these antagonisms can be used to coin gold.

By the time "Why I Am a Communist" was published, Davis had been quite busy, as an editor of the CPUSA's periodical the *Daily Worker,* as an organizer of the National Negro Congress, and as a mover-and-shaker in the Harlem Don't-Buy-Where-You-Can't-Work movement of the 1930s. Davis's activities brought him in close contact and collaboration with Harlem's legendary dragonslayer, the pastor–

politician Adam Clayton Powell, Jr. When Powell decided to run for Congress in 1942, he picked Davis to take his spot as New York City Councilman. Davis ran on the Communist ticket (with support from Paul Robeson) and won. Police brutality and substandard housing were among the issues he took on. Davis was reelected to the City Council in 1945, and hoped the same would happen in 1949, but he did not get his wish. By then, he was regarded as a serious national danger: He had climbed high in the party—member of the national committee, national secretary, chair of the Harlem region, chair of the National Commission on Negro Affairs, and chair of the New York State District.

In 1948, a year after the publication of "Why I Am a Communist," along with ten others in the CPUSA, Davis was indicted for violating the Smith Act, which prohibited advocacy of the overthrow of the government and membership in any organization engaged in such activities. The verdict was guilty; the sentence, imprisonment for five years and a ten thousand dollar fine; the appeal, unsuccessful. In the summer of 1951, Davis was sent to an Indiana penitentiary, where he stayed for three years, four months, during which time he began work on his memoirs.

When released in 1955, Davis resumed work with the CPUSA, and the persecution continued, culminating in an indictment (along with Gus Hall) in 1962 for violating the McCarran Internal Security Act, which required all agents of the Soviet Union to register as such. Davis was not found guilty in this case, but only because he died before the case went to trial. His autobiography, *Communist Councilman for Harlem*, was published five years after his death, in 1969.

ANOTHER BEN DAVIS, JR.

Benjamin O. Davis, Jr. (1912–), son of the U.S. Army's first black general, was very proud to be an American and was even willing to risk his life for this country. He began his military career when he entered West Point in 1932, where he endured heavy doses of the silent treatment for four long years. When he graduated in 1936, he was the first black to do so in the twentieth century; and he did it ranking thirty-fifth in a class of 276. His eye was on the Army Air Corps, but he was denied an assignment because black officers couldn't lead white units, and black units were nonexistent. Davis's dream was realized in 1941, with the formation of the first black flying unit, the 99th Pursuit Squadron. Davis distinguished himself as commander of this first troop of Tuskegee Airmen, as well as with the larger unit, the 332nd Fighter Group. Davis retired from the Air Force in 1970 as a three-star general. His autobiography, *Benjamin O. Davis, Jr., American*, was published in 1991.

A. Philip Randolph (1889–1979)

On May 6, 1969, well over a thousand people gathered together in the Waldorf Astoria's Grand Ballroom, where Eubie Blake and Noble Sissle were leading the band that played, among other things, "Happy Birthday." The honoree was A. Philip Randolph, who had recently reached his eightieth birthday.

Among those paying tribute to Randolph was the executive secretary of the NAACP, Roy Wilkins, who said,

> When I came along as a young man, you were my hero, my inspiration. You caught me at a time when every young college boy should be caught—when he is full of idealism and when he believes that the world can be changed. And here was a man changing it, who was confident it could be changed, who never faltered, who never gave his followers anything but the hope of victory. He is a man who has gained nothing out of the labor movement or the workers but the satisfaction of having been their savior, their advisor, their counsellor, and their inspiration.

There were thousands across the nation who could put an Amen to that, thousands who celebrated A. Philip Randolph, born in Cresent City, Florida, and raised in Jacksonville, Florida; this son of former slaves (his mother a homemaker and seamstress; his father an A.M.E. minister); this man named Asa, after a King of Judah who "did what was right in the sight of the Lord"; this man known as the consummate gentleman, a model of dignity, courtesy, and grace, with a fondness for horn-rimmed glasses, tweeds, and words such as "verily" and "vouchsafe."

Such touching words from Wilkins and others at that Waldorf dinner notwithstanding, by May of 1969, the octogenarian was on his way to being fairly well forgotten and very much unappreciated. Some Black Powerites even denounced him as an Uncle Tom.

Asa Philip Randolph an Uncle Tom? In 1911, at the age of twenty, he settled in Harlem with thespian dreams, but after some enlightening night courses in history, economics, and political science at City College, he declared himself a socialist, hooked up with the group of progressives known as "the Harlem radicals," and became one of the Mecca's most arresting street-corner speakers.

An Uncle Tom? In 1917, with Chandler Owen, Randolph launched the *Messenger,* a monthly magazine that spoke out boldly on a range of black burdens, from job and housing discrimination to lynching. The *Messenger* sharply criticized black leaders it deemed conservative. It took great issue with black support for America's participation in the Great War. Randolph's antiwar sentiments were a big part of the reason that in 1919, the U.S. Justice Department, which called Randolph "the most dangerous Negro in America," called the *Messenger* "by long odds the most able and the most dangerous of all Negro publications," and its officials tried to shut the *Messenger* down. Randolph still persevered in this and other radical endeavors, blessed with the stout and everlasting support of Lucille Green, whom he'd married in 1914. Lucille's thriving beauty parlor was the couple's sole source of income in the early years because Asa's activism (especially the *Messenger*) brought in naught but debt.

His fire brought a group of Pullman porters to his door. They wanted his help in mounting a fight against the mighty and highly exploitive Pullman Company. Randolph took up their cause, founding the Brotherhood of Sleeping Car Porters in 1925, and leading the long struggle for the union to be recognized and reckoned with. The struggle met with success in August 1937 when the brotherhood, which represented porters and maids, clenched its first contract with the Pullman Company. This contract—a wage increase, better working conditions—was a first between a large American corporation and a corp of black workers.

It was A. Philip Randolph who orchestrated the March on Washington movement, organized in December 1940, to move the government to do something about discrimination, especially in the defense industry. Randolph raised a lot of support for a demonstration set for July 1, 1941. As the day for the march drew nigh, he had President Franklin Delano Roosevelt convinced that around 100,000 dissatisfied black souls would be in his backyard soon. A few days before the march, F.D.R. issued Executive Order 8802, which outlawed discrimination in the defense industry and in government jobs on the basis of race, creed, color, or national origin, and he also created the Fair Employment Practices Committee to investigate complaints of discrimination. Randolph canceled the march. While some criticized him for accepting a half-step, many felt he had been most prudent, especially considering that his 100,000 was a bluff—and Asa kept stepping.

In 1948, he created the League for Nonviolent Civil Disobedience Against Military Segregation, a definite force in President Harry S Truman's Executive Order 9981, which desegregated the armed forces. In the early 1950s, as a vice president of the AFL-CIO, Randolph pressed this, the largest union in America, to contribute money to various civil-rights efforts. In 1959, he formed the Negro American Labor Council to spotlight discrimination in the unions. A. Philip Randolph was also the guiding light and the glue for the March on Washington for Jobs and Freedom of August 28, 1963, which was attended by more than 250,000 people from across the nation.

Asa Philip Randolph devoted more than fifty years of his life to enlightening his people to their condition, marshaling them to action, and laying a foundation on which younger backs could build. And "Uncle Tom" was all some young turks could come up with.

True, the elder had hard words to say about some of the tactics and the talk of the new militants (violence not viable, separatism stupid), but he also had some good things to say about those who denounced him. In a 1969 interview with a CBS reporter, he acknowledged that the young militants "had been instrumental in turning America around, and giving it a sense of the danger of the grave crisis in the cities." He went on to say, "I don't agree with their methods, but they have a romance in their heart for freedom. Victims of great oppression, youngsters who have dreams for a better future, they remind me of my own self in the '20s."

Paul R. Williams (1894–1980)

Williams, a virtuoso in the art of giving the traditional a modern accent and the modern a classic slant, was once known as "architect to the stars." His clients included Eddie "Rochester" Anderson, Lucille Ball and Desi Arnaz, Lon Chaney, Zsa Zsa Gabor, Betty Grable, Cary Grant, William Holden, Tyrone Power, Anthony Quinn, William "Bojangles" Robinson, and Frank Sinatra. Williams also designed homes for the rich and famous outside the entertainment industry. Automobile magnate E. L. Cord was one: Cord's Beverly Hills mansion, "Cordhaven," was quite the showpiece and talk of the town from the time it was built in the early 1930s until it was demolished in the early 1950s. Another millionaire customer was horse-racing bigwig "Overcoat Jack" Atkins, who wanted a home like the castle in his native Scarborough, England, and whom Williams did not disappoint. This 12,000-square-foot home lording on three-and-a-half Pasadena acres (and on which Atkins was intent on spending half a million dollars) has been used in a slew of films, from the late 1930s (*Topper*) to the 1990s (*Rocky V*), and in several television series, including *Batman and Robin* and *Murder She Wrote.*

Williams's other residential projects include Sunset Plaza Apartments in West Hollywood and the Compton-Imperial Housing Project in Los Angeles. The U.S. Naval Station in Long Beach was one of several commissions Williams received from the government during World War II. His commercial projects included the Palm Springs Tennis Club; Beverly Hills' Saks Fifth Avenue, W. J. Sloan Department Store, and MCA Building; and L.A.'s Golden State Mutual Life Insurance Company, Second Baptist Church, and 28th Street YWCA (which features portraits of **Frederick Douglass** and **Booker T. Washington** on its façade).

Williams left his mark on public and private space outside California: in Phoenix, Arizona; in Las Vegas and Reno, Nevada; in Washington, D.C.; in Yonkers, New York; in Bogotá and Medellín, Colombia; in

San Juan, Puerto Rico. All in all, from the time he opened up his office in the early 1920s in L.A.'s Stock Exchange Building until his retirement in 1973 (with offices on Wilshire Boulevard), Paul Revere Williams, the first black member (1923) and Fellow (1957) of the American Institute of Architects, designed some three thousand structures.

Williams's success strengthened those coming up behind him, who likewise wanted to make, as Goethe put it, "frozen music": people such as Harvey Gantt who had on his mind the design of structures such as First Baptist Church in his hometown of Charlotte, North Carolina, before politics called; and J. Max Bond, Jr., the New Yorker who designed the Martin Luther King Jr. Center for Nonviolent Change in Atlanta, and who received his master's in architecture from Harvard University in 1958, when Paul R. Williams was in his prime.

What was the key to Williams's success at a time when black architects hardly ever received commissions from whites and on into the days when he was not allowed to purchase property where most of his clients lived, even though he could afford it? For one, he was secure in his abilities as an architect. As he wrote in his 1937 essay "I Am Negro,"

> I came to realize that I was being condemned, not by a lack of ability, but by my color. I passed through successive stages of bewilderment, inarticulate protest, resentment, and, finally, reconciliation to the status of my race.
>
> Eventually, however, as I grew older and thought more clearly, I found in my condition an incentive to personal accomplishment, an inspiring challenge. Without having the wish to "show them," I developed a fierce desire to "show myself." I wanted to vindicate every ability I had. I wanted to acquire new abilities. I wanted to prove that I, AS AN INDIVIDUAL, deserved a place in the world.

This meant taking on small-fry projects and giving them his all. "I labored over the plans for a $15,000 residence as diligently as I do today on the plans for a huge mansion."

When a chance to do a major project came, Williams went above and beyond to secure the commission. Take, for example, what he did to land E. L. Cord's mansion.

> After we had gone over the building site, he warned me that he had already discussed plans with a number of other architects and demanded to know how soon I could submit preliminary drawings.
>
> "By four o'clock tomorrow afternoon," I answered.
>
> "Why, that's impossible!" he cried. "Every other architect has asked for two or three weeks!" He regarded me shrewdly for a moment. "Go ahead," he said.
>
> I delivered those preliminary plans by the scheduled hour—but I did not tell him that I worked for twenty-two hours, without sleeping or eating.

The accolades Williams received during his lifetime took many forms. In addition to the most obvious and important applause—referrals—he received dozens of awards from civic and professional organizations and educational institutions, as well as numerous government appointments, including to the National Monuments Committee (by President Coolidge in 1929), to the California Redevelopment Commission (by Governor, and later Supreme Court Justice, Earl Warren in 1947), and to the National Housing Commision and the Advisory Committee on Government Housing and Policies and Programs (by President Eisenhower in 1953).

Not bad for someone whose father made his living as a waiter in Memphis, Tennessee, and later, running a fruit stand in Los Angeles. Not bad for someone who lost both parents by age four. Not bad for someone who told his instructor at Polytechnic High School what he wanted to be when he grew up and was met with, "Who ever heard of a Negro being an architect?"

OTHER EARLY ARCHITECTS

- George Foster (1866–1923), who studied at Cooper Union in New York City, is believed to have worked on the Flatiron Building (1903). His great solo commissions include Mother A.M.E. Zion Church in Harlem. Foster collaborated with Vertner Woodson Tandy (described later herein) on several projects in Harlem, including St. Philip's Episcopal Church and Old Rectory, and the townhouse of hair-care millionaire Madam C. J. Walker.

- Robert R. Taylor (1868–1942), whom Booker T. Washington wooed to Tuskegee Institute in the early 1890s, was one of the first blacks to graduate from M.I.T.'s architecture program. Taylor designed many buildings on the Tuskegee campus, including Washington's residence "The Oaks." He also did a fine job of expanding the school's architecture program, which produced many superb architects, including Washington's future son-in-law William Sidney Pittman.

- John Lankford (1874–1946), who was born in Potosi, Missouri, opened one of the first black architectural firms in 1897, in Washington, D.C. Lankford is best known for the many churches he designed in Georgia, South Carolina, Virginia, D.C., and elsewhere in the South. The A.M.E. Church was his biggest customer, and he became this denomination's worldwide supervising architect in 1908.

- Julian Francis Abele (1881–1950), who was born in Philadelphia, graduated from the Pennsylvania School of Fine Arts and Architecture in 1904. Shortly thereafter, he went to work for that city's heretofore all-white firm of Trumbauer & Associates, which sponsored his studies at L'Ecole des Beaux Arts in Paris. By 1908, Abele was Trumbauer's chief designer, and his race was one of the firm's best-kept secrets. Among Abele's masterpieces are the Philadelphia Museum of Art and several buildings on the campus of Duke University in Durham, North Carolina.

• Vertner Woodson Tandy (1885–1949), a native of Lexington, Kentucky (and son of a contractor), was the first black person to graduate from Cornell University's School of Architecture (1908), where he co-founded the first black fraternity, Alpha Phi Alpha. Tandy's major commercial designs include the Children's Aid Society and the Abraham Lincoln Houses in the Bronx, New York. His residential masterwork is Madam C. J. Walker's mansion, Villa Lewaro, in Irvington-on-Hudson, New York.

 # Benson L. Dutton (1910–1992)

One Saturday during the winter of 1996, aboard an Amtrak train out of New York City, I found myself in the same car with my friend and agent, Marie Dutton Brown. I was headed to a book fair in Philly; she, to visit her mother in D.C.

The train was coming up on my destination (and her hometown) when Marie said, "Coming up are bridges Daddy won awards for." I had a vague recollection that her father had been an engineer but had never asked about his handiwork.

I grabbed the quick look the moving train allowed and saw what she was talking about: the Spring Garden Street Bridges over the Schuylkill River. I remember thinking, "We don't know the half of all the black history around us every day," and realizing that the man who designed these bridges was more than my friend's daddy.

Benson Leroy Dutton, born and raised in Philadelphia, was the youngest of three children of Bert Dutton, who worked at a Horn & Hardart cafeteria, and Beatrice, who often did domestic work. Young Benson became interested in engineering while a student at the predominantly white all-boys Central High. He knew he wanted to make it a career when he entered Penn State University. This was during the Great Depression; he had no scholarship, no student loan, just a few dollars his family scraped together and his earnings from dancing a mop at Horn & Hardart.

What Benson Dutton left home with in abundance was encouragement, from friends and near kin and, of course, from his parents. "We're proud of you, son." It was this kind of soul support that sturdied the young man to do what he had to do to make it through.

He paid his school fees mostly with the money he earned doing domestic work and childcare for the Bischoffs, the white family he boarded with. When time and opportunity permitted, he took on odd

Philadelphia's Spring Garden Street Bridges (built 1966), designed by Benson Dutton. In the background is the Philadelphia Museum of Art, designed by Julian Abele, one of the architects described in the sidebar to Paul R. Williams. (Courtesy of Marie Dutton Brown)

jobs on campus and around town. When he wasn't studying, he was working, and when he wasn't working, he was exercising his twin interests of boxing and track and field. All the while, he had to weave his way through the unpleasant things that came with the territory of being one of a handful of blacks at Penn State.

No moaning and groaning about the overwhelming whiteness of Penn State. No sighs and whines about alienation and isolation. Sure it was a challenge, but that's what being black in America is, and Benson Dutton knew it. He was hardly an aberration in this regard. In sharp contrast to later generations, for men and women of Dutton's generation, college was not where you went to "find yourself" and hang out until you grew up. Those attending predominantly white institutions knew better than to be heavily preoccupied with a social life. "We knew that we were there to get an education," said Dutton in the March/April 1989 issue of the *Penn Stater.* "I had to make it, for those who were sacrificing for me to be there, and for my own achievement."

Stories of the sacrifices others made for him inevitably became stories about keeping the faith. One such time he recounted in a letter dated July 25, 1985, to his daughter.

It was in 1931 when I was to go to Penn State's Summer Surveying Camp in Williamsport, Pennsylvania. It was a required 8 credit course for graduation for civil engineers. . . . I had no funds to pay the required $150. [My mother] told me to go up there (by train) and to wait in the train station at Williamsport and she would somehow get the money and send it. She said that prayer and faith would provide the reward. Well, that night I spent the time in the station waiting. But I prayed and had faith that my mother would do what she promised.

The money came the next morning. Later she told me that she went to a finance company and tearfully entreated the manager to let her have the money for her son's tuition.

Without this course I would never have graduated.

Dutton received his bachelor's degree in civil engineering in 1933. For the next seven years he held jobs with the government: chief of surveys in Philadelphia, construction engineer for the Naval Ammunition Depot, and a project engineer for the National Park Service. In 1940, he went into education, as an assistant professor in engineering at Hampton Institute (now Hampton University). After eight years there, he accepted a professorship at Tennessee State University, serving as the first dean of its School of Engineering from 1950 to 1956. By this time, he was very much a family man. In 1939, he had married the woman with whom he later had a daughter and two sons: Josephine Olivia Brown, a fellow Philadelphian, graduate of Temple University, and former schoolteacher in Winston-Salem, North Carolina.

During his years in academia, Dutton didn't just teach and advise on dead loads, elasticity, and I-beams. He instilled in all those who had ears to hear the vital necessity of a work ethic and of keeping the faith. And wasn't he a witness.

In 1956, Dutton moved the family back to Philadelphia, where he became this city's chief design engineer of bridges. The Lincoln Arc Welding Foundation's third-place prize for structures and the American Institute of Steel Construction's Award of Merit for Bridges were the honors he received for the Spring Garden Street Bridges. He later won other awards for other designs, and all the while that he was altering Philly's skyline, he was helping others push up. For decades, the YMCA was his special cause, as he helped boys become men at the core.

In 1965, Dutton went to work for the U.S. Office of Education, eventually becoming head of the operations branch of construction services. In 1971, he became director of construction for the U.S. Department of Health, Education and Welfare (H.E.W.), a position he held until his retirement in 1977.

The year Dutton went to work for H.E.W. was the year he received Penn State's highest award, the Distinguished Alumni Award. The citation reads,

> To Benson L. Dutton, a builder of bridges both structural and human, for his distinguished accomplishments in not one but three professions—engineering, education, and government service; and for his

award winning bridge designs; for his equally effective molding of young minds; and for his dedication and concern for his fellow man which have earned him respect and recognition from the community.

Benson L. Dutton is one of those who dared to aim high when low down was supposed to be what the black man had in sight. In defying the bind, Dutton had to be his own role model, pretty much. The steady strides of men like him helped expand the black middle class in mid-century America.

 # Charles Hamilton Houston (1895–1950)

"The engineer of it all." This was what Thurgood Marshall once said of Charles Hamilton Houston, the man who once declared, "a lawyer's either a social engineer or he's a parasite."

Charles Hamilton Houston, born in Washington, D.C., was following in his father's footsteps when he decided on a career in law. He entered this profession on firm footing as far as education was concerned. He was a graduate of D.C.'s prestigious preparatory school, the M Street School (later Paul Laurence Dunbar High School), and Amherst College, where he was inducted into Phi Beta Kappa and graduated magna cum laude in 1915. After teaching English for two years at Howard University and serving a stint as an officer in a black unit during World War I, he entered Harvard University, where he became the first black editor of the *Harvard Law Review*. There, he earned his LL.B. (cum laude) in 1922 and his J.D. a year later. A Sheldon Fellowship allowed study abroad: civil law at the University of Madrid.

In 1924, this New Negro started his law practice with his father: Houston and Houston. At the same time, he began teaching where his father had studied law, Howard University's law school, then an evening school and not fully accredited. Houston would change this situation.

The change began with a national study Houston conducted through a Rockefeller grant. There were too few black lawyers and too few versed in constitutional law—the sine qua non for civil-rights litigation. This was the seminal finding of his 1928 report, "The Negro and His Contact with the Administration of Law." Houston knew the deal before he did the study, but of course it's not enough to know, you have to show, have to produce paper.

The year after his report, Houston was made a vice dean of Howard and head of its law school. He was given room and resources to renovate the law school, which he did to spectacular effect. By 1932, Howard Law School was a full-time institution and accredited, approved by the American Bar Association and the Association of American Law Schools. From then on, Howard was virtually unchallenged as the chief training ground for the type of lawyers needed for the civil-rights crusade waged in the courts, with Charles Hamilton Houston the chief molder, shaper, and expander of a host of sterling minds, such as that of Thurgood Marshall, who entered Howard's law school in 1930. "First off, you thought he was a mean so-and-so," said Marshall, in recalling Houston's all-out press for excellence. Marshall went on to say,

> He used to tell us that doctors could bury their mistakes, but lawyers couldn't. And he'd drive home to us that we would be competing not only with white lawyers but really well trained white lawyers, so there just wasn't any point in crying in our beer about being Negroes. And I'll tell you—the going was rough. There must have been thirty of us in that class when we started, and no more than eight or ten of us finished up. He was so tough we used to call him "Iron Shoes" and "Cement Pants" and a few other names that don't bear repeating. But he was a sweet man once you saw what he was up to. He was absolutely fair, and the door to his office was always open. He made it clear to all of us that when we were done, we were expected to go out and do something with our lives.

In 1935, Houston took a leave from Howard to take the post as full-time special counsel to the NAACP, with Thurgood Marshall as his deputy. One of Houston's most important early NAACP cases was *Hollins v. Oklahoma*, which resulted in a death sentence being overturned because blacks had been excluded from the jury solely because of their race. This victory was to be echoed a few years later in *Hale v. Kentucky* (1938).

In black America's march toward freedom, discrimination in education was a critical place to attack, Houston believed. "These apparent senseless discriminations in education against Negroes," he stated, "have a very definite objective on the part of the ruling whites to curb the young and prepare them to accept an inferior position in American life without protest or struggle."

Houston also firmly believed that the civil-rights crusade would only be as strong as its support from everyday people. Of course, he also knew that for a people to give their support to a thing, they had to be informed. One of the ways Houston saw to this was through his columns in several black periodicals, including the *Afro-American*, which **Carl Murphy** had made one of the most intelligent newspapers of the day.

Among the cases Houston handled as special counsel to the NAACP was *Murray v. the University of Maryland* (1936). The plaintiff in the case was Donald Murray, who sought admission to the University of Maryland Law School, which had denied Marshall admission years earlier. Marshall was Houston's second on this case, which ended with the university being ordered to admit Donald Murray because there was no black law school in Maryland. Not to admit him was a violation of the equal-protection clause of the Fourteenth Amendment.

In 1938, Houston had his first triumph before the U.S. Supreme Court. The case was Lloyd Gaines's battle for admission in the University of Missouri's graduate school. The university had tried to keep in sync with the separate-but-equal doctrine born of the case of *Plessy v. Ferguson*** in 1896 by providing blacks with scholarships to attend an out-of-state school if there was no in-state black school that offered the desired course of study. In this case, *Missouri ex rel. Gaines v. Canada*, Houston effectively argued the wrongness of this policy, and in the end, the Supreme Court ruled that the university had to admit Gaines.

Houston resigned as NAACP special counsel in 1938 due to poor health (which included heart trouble). His primary protégé Thurgood Marshall took his place and institutionalized the work Houston had done by establishing the NAACP Legal Defense and Educational Fund. Houston's days in law were not, however, over.

Beginning in 1940, Houston worked on the labor front as general counsel of the International Association of Railway Employees and of the Association of Colored Railway Trainmen and Locomotive Firemen. In 1944, he was appointed to the Fair Employment Practices Committee, one of the concessions President Truman made in the face of the March on Washington **A. Philip Randolph** threatened. Houston's appointment came as the committee was about to hold hearings on discrimination in the railway industry. Houston did not stay long with the committee, resigning in 1945, when Truman declined to make D.C.'s Capital Transit Company cease racial discrimination.

During his years outside of the NAACP Legal Defense and Educational Fund, Houston stayed very much involved with it, serving as sounding board and late-night counselor. More than a few times, his help was also hands on. For instance, in the late 1940s, he played a part in two successful cases challenging racially restrictive housing covenant's in D.C.: *Shelley v. Kraemer* (he helped write the brief) and *Hurd v. Hodge* (he argued the case).

The last NAACP case Houston was involved in was *Bolling v. Sharpe* (1950), which challenged segregated schooling in D.C. It was Houston who filed the brief for this case, which was among the several subsumed in *Brown v. Board of Education,* where the U.S. Supreme Court ruled that separate was inherently unequal, and in so doing overturned *Plessy v. Ferguson.* When, on May 17, 1954, the Supreme Court

*See **Homer Plessy.**

handed down this landmark decision, Charles Hamilton Houston had been dead four years.

After the *Brown* decision, the astute, unflinching Thurgood Marshall, who had served as the case's lead attorney was hailed as a Moses who parted a sea, as a master builder of a great legal weapon in the civil-rights crusade, as "Mr. Civil Rights." Marshall, however, never wanted to take all the credit. Not only had other bright minds done a whole lot of work, but Marshall also knew that he might never have been heading up the NAACP's legal arm, never would have been the lead attorney on *Brown*, never would have become a legal eagle had he not been mentored by the man he came to call "Charlie," the indefatigable man who established legal precedents on which Marshall built. This is why Marshall insisted that Charles Hamilton Houston be remembered as "The First Mr. Civil Rights." That's why he looked back in wonder at the work of Houston and proclaimed him "the engineer of it all."

Vernon Johns (1892–1965)

Johns was something of a lone one crying out in something of a wilderness: for the racist to repent of their ways; for the complacent among the oppressed to get busy. Definitely, he was preparing the way for a King.

Casting James Earl Jones as Vernon Johns for the 1994 television movie *The Vernon Johns Story* was a good move. Jones was perfect: for the fortitude he exudes, for his height and his breadth, for that handsome voice. Yes, Jones was just right to capture the erudite yet very rooted Johns, who grew up outside Farmville, Virginia, on a farm: son of the soil at birth, son of the soil forever.

Vernon Johns's story was full of much that was mythic. There is the story of his paternal grandfather, who was hanged for cutting his master in two. There are the stories about his exquisite memory (as a youngster, he memorized the entirety of Apostle Paul's letter to the Romans). There's the story, too, of his getting kicked out of Virginia Seminary for insubordination. The granddad of them all concerns Vernon Johns's unorthodox admittance into Oberlin Seminary.

Having received a letter of rejection from Oberlin, the B.A.-less Johns barreled into the dean's office one day. "I want to know whether you want students with credits or students with brains," he boomed. The dean thought he'd get rid of this apparent country bumpkin quick-quick when he handed him a book in German and asked him to read from it. Johns obliged without pause. The flabbergasted dean shuttled

Johns to the dean of the Seminary, the renowned Edward Increase Bosworth, who tossed Johns another test: Scripture in Greek. Again, Johns delivered. Not only did Bosworth let Johns enroll in Oberlin Seminary, but he also became a mentor of the bold young man and helped him secure part-time preaching work that would help pay the bills.

After Oberlin, Johns attended the University of Chicago's Graduate School of Theology, a heaven for proponents of the social gospel. By the time he graduated in 1918, Johns had a reputation as a superb orator–preacher: much sought after as a pastor and a teacher. His temperament, however, made him something of a misfit, so he lectured and guest preached, mostly in the mid-Atlantic states. When he was away from the pulpit or the lectern, he farmed on his homeplace in Virginia, probably composing sermons and orations at the plow.

In 1927, Johns married the daughter of a college president, Altona Trent, with whom he was to have three daughters. Marriage (and one into the middle class at that) did not, however, steer Vernon Johns into a more predictable life. He remained his iconoclastic self. In *Parting the Waters* (1988), Taylor Branch captures Johns's vagabond life with this:

> During the Depression his eccentricities carried him beyond maverick status into more or less the life of a bohemian. He would jump into the car with a friend and leave the family for months at a time, preaching here and there, hawking old books at ministers' conventions, selling subscriptions to fledgling magazines. Most of the people he saw on these tours knew nothing of his intellectual attainments. Among those who did, Johns did not bother to answer when they wondered why he eschewed the relative security of a college for a life on the road. Johns loved to travel. Because Negroes had trouble finding motels and restaurants to serve them in the segregated South, he would pack blocks of cheese and quarts of milk in ice and take off on drives of non-stop poetry recital. Fellow travelers knew him to finish all of Keats in Alabama and get through Byron and Browning before hitting Farmville. Johns calculated distances in units of poetry, and if he tired of verse he waded into military history.

Even when Johns was a guest at a place prone to pomp, still he kept it plain, arriving with all his necessities in a brown paper bag.

Vernon Johns appeared to be ready to settle down, toe the line, be a proper cleric, when in 1948 he accepted the pastorate of the Montgomery, Alabama, Dexter Avenue Baptist Church, a historically hinkty host. But it wasn't long before Johns was rocking the boat.

He fought for the inclusion of the spirituals in worship service, which many pooh-poohed as low-class. He spoke out boldly on the Bible's obvious condemnation of oppression, denouncing white and black ministers alike who did not see and teach this light. He rallied victims of white terror to speak up, speak out. He tried to get served at the counter in a restaurant that only allowed blacks takeout. "Segregation after Death," "When the Rapist Is White," "It's Safe to Murder Negroes in Montgomery": These were the kinds of titles he gave some of his sermons.

His congregation had conniptions when Johns started selling produce and notions behind the church. It was a sin and a shame, many contended, to have your minister clad in overalls and work boots, hawking fruits, vegetables, fish, pencils, stockings. It was a sin and shame, Johns contended, to buy where you are blatantly disrespected and cannot work.

On several occasions, Johns moved to resign from Dexter. Each time, a small corps convinced him to change his mind. There came a day, however, when he became too much of an embarrassment and a pinch. When, in 1952, Johns offered his resignation, it was accepted.

When Vernon Johns took his clod-hopping, belly-laughing, turnip-selling, "Go Down, Moses"–singing self out of town, many at Dexter Avenue Baptist Church sighed, hallelujah. No more maverick, no more mischief maker, no more minister with protest in his veins. That's what some were probably thinking when Johns's successor, Martin Luther King, Jr., took the pulpit.

Emmett Till (1941–1955)

Now, all these years later, it seems that young Emmett Till didn't do anything: didn't proposition that white lady, didn't say, "Hey, baby," didn't wolf-whistle. Even if he had, would he have deserved what they did to him?

He was snatched from Uncle Moses's home and beaten, beaten, beaten, and shot in the head. His slashed, bashed body was dumped into a river, with a gin-mill fan barbwired around the neck for anchor.

He was a fourteen-year-old boy from Chicago on holiday in Money, Mississippi. His savaged body, his gone potential, lay in the Tallahatchie River for three-going-on-four days. That naked, decomposed corpse hauled up from the watery grave was the history of the black man in America, the history of white-on-black violence never fully told. It was the trouble we've seen, again and again, and now again in late August 1955.

He was a fourteen-year-old boy from Chicago on holiday in Money, Mississippi. No place to hide, sighed so many mothers, so many fathers and granddads and grandmas and sisters and aunts and uncles of teenaged black boys. What a weight to be black and male in America.

This time, the world would know: The open-casket viewing lasted four days, with 100,000 people coming to see him—the pictures in *Jet* and then in the *Chicago Defender* and then in other newspapers, black and white. Despite the watchful eyes of the world—or perhaps to spite them—an all-white all-male jury caused Mamie Till's grief to grow, when her only son was lynched again with the trial's outcome. After about an hour of deliberations, the jury found Roy Bryant and J. W. Milam, that white lady's husband and brother-in-law, not guilty of murder. This was despite evidence to the contrary, including Uncle Moses's positive identification of the two men as the ones who snatched Emmett Louis Till from his house.

Shock became outrage became the catalyst for thousands to join the civil-rights crusade: He was a fourteen-year-old boy from Chicago on holiday in Money, Mississippi.

Bob Moses (1935–   )

There was a movement going on, a struggle for justice, dignity, the freedom to be an American, going on in a part of the nation fairly foreign to Bob Moses. Soon, there came a day when he couldn't shake the images of students' daring lunch-counter sit-ins and more for this cause. He was a student, too, but a student on hold.

This young man, born Robert Parris Moses, grew up in Harlem projects and whizzed through one of New York City's special high schools, Stuyvesant, and had graduated from Hamilton College in New York, where he had been drawn to Quaker philosophy and to the American Friends Service Committee. That's how he came to spend two summers abroad, helping the distressed communities build up (doing construction work on shelter for homeless miners in France and working in a mental institution in Japan, for example). In his spiritual quest, he also was involved, for a time, with a group of young Pentecostals who took the Word to the streets, and he explored Zen Buddhism and French existentialism.

After college, in 1956, the soft-spoken, nimble-minded, bespectacled Bob Moses entered Harvard with plans for a doctorate in philosophy. Not long after he earned his master's degree, his mother died, which took a terrible toll on his father's mental health. These twin traumas greatly complicated the son's life, compelling him to quit his graduate studies and return to New York City.

Back home, Moses eventually began teaching math at Horace

Mann, a private all-boys school up in poshy Riverdale, while down South, people, many younger than him, were enlarging a movement. The Montgomery Bus Boycott had ended in 1956, the Southern Christian Leadership Conference (SCLC) had formed in 1957, and the Civil Rights Act of 1957, with its protection of voting rights, had passed, a month before the Little Rock Nine were brave. A steady stream of civil-rights actions and initiatives followed. One of the most riveting occurred on February 1, 1960, when Ezell Blair, Franklin McCain, Joseph McNeil, and David Richmond, all freshmen at North Carolina A&T, ordered coffee and doughnuts at the lunch counter of an F. W. Woolworth's in Greensboro. When the four were refused service, they refused to leave, staying at the lunch counter until the store closed. This act of civil disobedience inspired a series of sit-ins at that Woolworth's. Then came sit-ins elsewhere in North Carolina, and then in Nashville, Tennessee. Then came sit-ins, kneel-ins, and swim-ins elsewhere in the nation. This was the year that Bob Moses, this Northern boy, this pacifist to the core, whose Baptist grandfather had supported Marcus Garvey, left his teaching post for the movement.

Early on, he did clerical work and whatever else in Atlanta, Georgia, for Bayard Rustin, protégé of **A. Philip Randolph** and cofounder of SCLC, which was sharing office space with the Student Nonviolent Coordinating Committee (SNCC). SNCC was formed in Raleigh, North Carolina, in the Spring of 1960, with an emphasis on grassroots organizing. Through his work in SCLC's Atlanta office, twenty-five-year-old Moses came to be mentored by Ella Baker, SCLC's executive secretary and "mother" of SNCC. It wasn't long before Moses joined SNCC and became its first full-time voter-registration worker in the South—and in Mississippi, at that.

"Like South Africa, only a little better." That's how Allard Lowenstein, a progressive New York Congressional Representative and a Moses ally, once summed up the Magnolia State, where in the 1960s, blacks (40% of the population) had a yearly income of a little less than $1,500, where less than 10 percent of blacks graduated from high school, where the state spent four times as much on white students as on black students, and where the first cell of the White Citizens Council, a group sometimes called the country-club Klans, formed in the mid-1950s. That group was the power behind the election of the fierce segregationist Ross Barnett as Governor of Mississippi, where hordes of whites were predisposed to violence when the subject was black progress—neck and neck with Alabama, where in May 1961, Freedom Riders were beaten in Anniston and then in Birmingham and then in Montgomery, after which they set out for Jackson, Mississippi, where they were arrested and jailed. Their arrest occurred two months before Moses established his first voter-registration camp in this state, where a mere 5 percent of blacks eligible to vote were registered.

Moses, this meek man—power under constraint, not weak—started his civil-rights crusade in McComb, Mississippi, daring rednecks and risking everything to help blacks claiming citizenship get ready, and to buck up those so long scared, so long thinking politics and such was white-folks business. Moses went door-to-door to advise people of their rights. He held meetings in churches and other allegedly safe places to raise volunteers to register. He went about talking softly about freedom, bolstering blacks, infuriating whites.

"Poor Bob took a lot of beatings," said Ernest Nobles, a small-business owner in McComb. "I just couldn't understand what Bob Moses was. Sometimes I think he was Moses in the Bible. He pioneered the way for black people in McComb. . . . He had more guts than any man I've ever known."

One beating occurred when Moses walked to the McComb courthouse with farmer Curtis Dawson and Preacher Knox, who had volunteered to register to vote. Three men halted their progress: two were cousins of the sheriff and one, the sheriff's son. At the end of the confrontation, Moses, who never even so much as swore at the thugs, was on the sidewalk with blood pouring from three deep gashes in his head. "We've got to go on to the registrar," Moses whispered as his attackers fled. He, Dawson, and Knox did just that, only to have the registrar tell them that he was closing the office for the day.

Moses not only survived beatings himself, but he also survived the beatings and deaths of people who worked with him. One horror of his early days in McComb was the murder of Herbert Lee, one of Moses's first guides and "fathers," the man who drove Moses all around town, introducing him to other brave souls and getting the timid to give Moses a hearing. Lee, a farmer and father of nine, was shot in the head in broad daylight, at a cotton gin in Liberty, by Mississippi State Representative E. H. Hurst.

By the fall of 1962 (the same season the U.S. Supreme Court ordered Ole Miss to admit James Meredith), Moses was managing nearly two dozen fieldworkers in half a dozen offices in Mississippi, with his headquarters in the home of another brave Mississippi man, Amzie Moore, a World War II veteran and head of the NAACP chapter in Cleveland, Mississippi, not too far from Money, where **Emmett Till** was murdered in 1955.

Moses and his lieutenants made great progress in raising both black courage and black awareness of their rights as citizens. For every victory, however, for every soul brought into the crusade, there had been a pain. Back in February 1962, the SNCC office in Greenwood was threatened with arson, and Moses's colleague Sam Block was arrested for breaching the peace when he reported this threat to the press. There was also more hell ahead—such as the night that Moses, Randolph Blackwell, and Jimmy Travis, upon leaving a meeting at the Greenwood office, were chased down a back road by three white men in a Buick, with Travis catching a bullet in the back; such as the day Sam Block and three other SNCC workers miraculously escaped death from a shotgun blast at the car they were in, parked out front of the SNCC office; and the time when that SNCC office was torched in late March, two days before the home of an activist family, the Greenes, was shot up.

With former Freedom Rider, now SNCC officer, James Forman, Moses led a demonstration to Greenwood's city hall to protest the violence. During this demonstration, Moses and another demonstrator were attacked by a police dog, and along with a slew of others, they were arrested and sentenced to four months in jail.

Moses seemed never to weary. As much as he inspired, he also unnerved some of his colleagues with his constant composure, with his quiet intensity.

Moses's work became more intense when he became the coordinator of a coalition of Mississippi chapters of the Congress of Racial Equality (CORE), NAACP, and SNCC: the Council of Federated Organizations—COFO, for short. Not long after, Medgar Evers, the head of the NAACP in Mississippi, was assassinated, Moses, as the head of COFO, became the architect of the Mississippi Freedom Summer Project: the mobilization and coordination, in the summer of 1964, of nearly a thousand men and women, most of whom were white college students from the North, into a disciplined nonviolent army on missions to dramatically expand black voter registration and preparation for the upcoming November elections. The previous summer, Moses had organized a make-pretend gubernatorial election, the "Freedom Vote," with "Freedom Ballots" and "Freedom Candidates" and a "Freedom Party." Now, more Mississippians would be readied for the real thing.

The centerpiece of Freedom Summer was the freedom schools. By summer's end, more than two thousand children and adults with pitiful skills had attended more than forty freedom schools. These schools majored in community leadership and community-relevant lesson plans, and offered not only literacy education, but also political education, including black history. Moses's soldiers also established community centers where the truly disadvantaged could get legal, medical, and other kinds of help.

Another core objective of Freedom Summer was to build up the Mississippi Freedom Democratic Party (MFDP), formed in Spring 1964, to challenge the all-white delegation that would be representing Mississippi at the Democratic National Convention in Atlantic City, New

Jersey, in August. By the time of the convention, some eighty thousand people had joined the MFDP, the supreme delegate of which was the sharecropper from Sunflower County, Fannie Lou Hamer, one of the finest grassroots leaders of the civil-rights movement.

The righteous gains made during Moses's Freedom Summer came at a price. Freedom Summer had just started when, on June 21, CORE's Michael Schwerner, Andrew Goodman, and James Chaney went to inspect what was left of Longdale's Mount Zion Methodist Church, torched because it had offered its facilities for a freedom school. The young men, all in their twenties, ended up in a shallow grave on a farm in nearby Philadelphia, Mississippi: They had been shot in the head, and Chaney, the black one and a native of Meridian, Mississippi, had been savagely beaten, to boot. These murders were the ones that received the most media attention, but they were not the only ones connected with Freedom Summer, during which nearly a hundred freedom workers were beaten, and more than a thousand jailed, and some sixty churches, homes, and businesses affiliated with the movement were torched or bombed.

Out of this terrible glorious time in Mississippi came building blocks for future work. For one, the freedom schools, themselves modeled after the citizenship schools started in South Carolina in the 1950s, became the model for Head Start. Many leaders of the upcoming Black Power, peace, and women's movements were alums of Freedom Summer. As Freedom Summer changed the consciousness of black Mississippians, it also changed youth culture: Had denim pants and overalls not been part of the SNCC uniform, blue jeans would never have moved from workers' clothing only to casual wear for the middle- and upper-income folks. There were some other things that came out of Freedom Summer that now seem to many of dubious value, including experiments in interracial romances and "free" love.

At the end of Freedom Summer, Bob Moses was a bit weary—and then came the tiffs and rifts within SNCC: Some women were fed up with the dominance of men; some blacks were fed up with the prevalence of whites. The discord led Moses to quit SNCC.

He became an invisible man, disappearing from the media and from civil-rights work. He became Robert Parris. Then, when his claim of conscientious objector was ignored and he was drafted, he became Robert Parris in Canada.

Before 1968 was out, he was in Tanzania, teaching math. In 1976, he returned to the United States and resumed his graduate studies at Harvard. By this time, he was a husband (for the second time) and a father of several children. One aspect of his self-assigned homework was pumping up one of his daughters' math skills because he was dissatisfied with the instruction she was receiving at the Martin Luther King Jr. School in Cambridge, Massachusetts. Out of this came a concern that thousands of kids, especially black kids, were receiving inadequate education in math (too little, too slow). Why not give these kids a leg up by introducing algebra and the critical-thinking skills that come with it in the middle grades? Soon, Moses's graduate studies were again put on the back burner. After receiving a Genius Award, as the MacArthur Award is often called, in 1982, Bob Moses founded The Algebra Project, an innovative way to develop math skills and power thinking, based on the principle that the curriculum and approach should be in sync with students' environments and sociocultural experience. After The Algebra Project proved workable in Massachusetts (adopted in many schools and raising scores on standardized tests in the process), the program was adopted in cities across the nation—Chicago, Milwaukee, Los Angeles, Oakland, San Francisco. By 1992, The Algebra Project had helped some nine thousand inner-city youths and had garnered great praise from the National Science Foundation. This same year, Moses launched The Delta Algebra Project in the place of his greatest trials and greatest triumphs: Mississippi.

NEWS BITS

In 1964, the year of Freedom Summer, . . .

- The 24th Amendment was ratified in January, outlawing the poll tax often used to keep blacks from voting.

- Between February and April, hundreds of thousands of black children were absent from schools in Harlem, Cleveland, Cincinnati, and Chicago, as part of a boycott protesting de facto school segregation.

- Joseph E. Jackson, head of the largest black organization in the world, the National Baptist Convention, publicly condemned boycotting as a tactic for social change.

- Malcolm X left the Nation of Islam, and soon cofounded (with John Oliver Killens) the Organization of Afro-American Unity. Subsequently, he made a pilgrimage to Mecca, returning as El-Hajj Malik El-Shabazz.

- Congress passed the Civil Rights Act of 1964, which prohibited discrimination in employment, public accommodations, and voting.

- Congress passed the Economic Opportunity Act, which allowed one billion dollars for Head Start, Upward Bound, work–study programs for college students, and a number of other programs in the "War on Poverty."

- In mid-July, an off-duty white police officer shot a fifteen-year-old black boy in Harlem, sparking a five-day riot that ignited a riot in the Bedford-Stuyvesant section of Brooklyn. That same summer, there were racial clashes in several Northern cities, including Jersey City, Chicago, and Philadelphia.

- Amiri Baraka (then LeRoi Jones) founded the Black Arts Repertory Theatre, considered the kickoff of the Black Arts Movement.

- Cassius Clay became world heavyweight champ (when he KO'd Sonny Liston) and shortly thereafter announced his conversion to Islam and his new name, Muhammad Ali.

- President Lyndon Johnson presented two blacks with the Presidential Medal of Freedom: Leontyne Price and A. Philip Randolph.

- James Baldwin's *Blues for Mister Charlie* opened on Broadway.

- Martin Luther King, Jr., received the Nobel Prize for Peace and donated the prize money to several organizations, including the NAACP, SCLC, and SNCC.

Malcolm X (1925–1965) and Martin Luther King, Jr. (1929–1968)

Martin said, "Well, Malcolm, good to see you."

Malcolm said, "Good to see *you.*"

They met once: on March 26, 1964, in Washington, D.C. The two had come to the nation's capital separately to hear United States Senators prate, skate, debate on the Civil Rights Bill. On the edge of this critical moment, the two had a brief meeting, seeing face-to-face how they were different, how they were the same. These are things we think about all these years later, especially those of us who were youngsters when they were men.

One born in the month of flowers, and dead in the shortest month. One born in the month of New Years, and dead in the cruelest month. Both assassinated at age thirty-nine.

"I have a dream that one day this nation will rise up and live out the true meaning of its creed, 'We hold these truths to be self-evident, that all men are created equal.' I have a dream that one day. . . ."

"And I see America through the eyes of the victim. I don't see any American dream; I see an American nightmare!"

Either/Or? That way lies madness, for we needed them both—to speak truth to power, to tower, to help us rise. We needed them both.

Malcolm X and Martin Luther King, Jr., at the U.S. Capitol on March 26, 1964. (Courtesy of AP/Wide World Photos)

We needed the one who came up the threadbare way in the Midwest, whose father was a big, strapping Georgia-born Baptist preacher, with an ironic name (Little, Earl Little). This boy-child was awed by his father—so black by birth and so proud by choice, such a champion of Marcus Mosiah Garvey; and this boy-child treasured his mother, Louise, who colabored with her husband for Garvey's UNIA, who tried to hold the family together after her husband's death, who ultimately went mad.

We needed the one born into a measure of plump and ease down South, whose father, pastor of Atlanta, Georgia's Ebenezer Baptist Church and head of the NAACP Atlanta branch, wanted his name to proclaim his faith, his bond with the Protestant Reformation leader Martin—"Here I Stand I Can Do No Other"—Luther. So Michael King became Martin Luther King, whose first-born son looked up to him as much as he looked up to his mother: stalwart, tireless, churchworking Alberta, a stern, exacting woman, who helped groom her son to be a preacher—not only like his daddy but also like her daddy, Albert Daniel Williams, cofounder of the Georgia Equal Rights League and the NAACP's Atlanta branch, and master builder of Ebenezer Baptist. Heavy family.

Yes, we needed this princely King who, as a young man, did typical petit bourgeois slick, and who trained a marvelous mind at Morehouse College, at Crozer Seminary, at Boston University—just as we needed the one who was an East Coast (Harlem heavy) hustler, thief, and pimp, and who trained a marvelous mind behind bars.

We needed the tall, slim, yalla one with almost auburn hair. We needed the short, stocky, brown one raised on Auburn Avenue. We needed them both in their man-tailored hats, narrow ties, cool white shirts, dark serious suits.

Malcolm Little to Detroit Red to Malcolm X to Minister of Harlem's Temple Number Seven to El-Hajj Malik El-Shabazz and head of the Organization for Afro-American Unity—as Ossie Davis said, "our own black shining prince."

Michael, Jr., to Mike or M.L. to Martin Luther King, Jr., to Pastor of Montgomery, Alabama's Dexter Avenue Baptist Church and head of the Southern Christian Leadership Conference—drum major/prophet/dreamer/agape in action.

We need not choose between the two who rallied hundreds of thousands, the two who riled hundreds of thousands, the two who handled the media with aplomb, the two who uttered words of thought-out thoughts: not sound bites, not quick fixes, not whine-baby-whine, but ideas coming from a deep place, from the journeys they had dared—one moving beyond white-man-is-devil doctrines to international vision; one moving up South and into international vision. Both eschewing lick-spittle ways and not pimping their people's pain.

Both were treated to homes bombed, fools funneling death threats through the phone, bullets massacring their lives.

No time for Malcolm to say "goodbye and stay strong" to Betty and their children—Attallah, Qubilah, Ilyasah, Gamilah, and to Malaak and Malikah, their twins on the way. No time from Martin to say "goodbye and stay strong" to Coretta and their children—Yolanda, Martin III, Dexter, and Bernice.

By the time they were ripped away, Malcolm and Martin had long since been strong men, with frailties and silent questionings all strong men have; yet, they were still questing. Neither was finished. Both were still becoming.

In Harlem, what was 125th Street has become Martin Luther King, Jr. Boulevard, and what was Lenox Avenue has become Malcolm X Boulevard. When standing where these two streets meet, when close by any sign and symbol of their legacies, or when anywhere thinking about their testimonies, their testaments, many are moved to wonder what Malcolm and Martin might have become had they had the time to come together, to help us walk together, children, and not get weary.

Two streams, same source—and same hope: a waterfall of freedom. Freedom from outside oppression. Freedom from self-indulged ignorance. Freedom from materialism. Freedom from spiritual wasteland. We needed them both—and we still do.

Martin said, "Well, Malcolm, good to see you."

Malcolm said, "Good to see *you*."

Woody Strode (1914–1994)

Sidney Poitier: competence. James Earl Jones: deep dignity. Richard Roundtree: chocolate-drop cool. Bill Cosby: good-guy and apple pie. Lou Gossett, Jr.: snap. Also, of course, before and after these actors, there were hundreds who projected the black man as fool. As for the native of Los Angeles, born Woodrow Strode, who came to acting after football (at UCLA, and for the Cleveland/L.A. Rams), he projected the black man as a regal force.

In *Blacks in American Films and Television: An Illustrated Encyclopedia* (1988), **Donald Bogle** offers a review of this captivating man:

> Once he pursued an acting career, Strode—6'4" and 205 pounds—was a commanding presence. Admittedly, sometimes he seemed stiff and ill at ease with his dialogue. Other times his silence added to his appeal. Always, though, his flat-out, rather straight-arrow masculinity and physical strength won him a significant following among black males in the 1950s and early 1960s. During this period when black moviegoers rarely saw an assertive, physical black man of action, Strode was so powerfully built in such films as *Pork Chop Hill* (1959) and *The Last Voyage* (1959) that he looked as if he could overcome almost any opponent or physical adversity. Even in his brief appearance as the King of Ethiopia in Cecil B. DeMille's *The Ten Commandments* (1956), Woody Strode was a towering, muscular sight to behold as he confidently entered the court of the Egyptian palace. And certainly when he was cast in *Spartacus* (1960) as the gladiator Draba who is locked into physical combat with the film's hero, black audi-

Woody Strode in the film *Black Jesus.*
(Courtesy of Donald Bogle)

ences yearned for this slave rebellion epic to focus less on its star Kirk Douglas and more on its supporting player Woody Strode.

In the 1960s, Strode appeared in several films directed by the legend John Ford, including *Sergeant Rutledge, Two Rode Together*, and *The Man Who Shot Liberty Valance*. As Bogle noted, whereas the black presence in previous Ford films gave us little to cheer about, in the aforementioned films, Ford "used his camera to bring out Strode's innate power and nobility, his gallantry and unexpected gracefulness. Woody Strode often looks like a prince from another land, stranded in an alien world that does not see his beauty."

In the late 1960s, Strode sought more open eyes in Europe. The Italian film *Black Jesus,* one of the pictures he made there, met with some success when released in the United States in 1971, when black-themed movies were about to have a heyday. Woody Strode was still pretty much an invisible man, though. One of his most memorable appearances in later years was as "Yank" in the 1987 television movie about a group of men in Louisiana who stand up to white power, *A Gathering of Old Men,* based on the novel of the same name by Ernest J. Gaines.

☼ Berry Gordy (1929–   )

The music of Motown Records is a challenge and an inspiration to anyone making pop records. Because, quite simply, the musical achievements of Berry Gordy's company have been monumental. The talented people that flowed through Motown, both the performers on stage and the writers and producers behind the scenes, broke down the barriers between black and white, between the R&B world and the "mainstream," letting everyone see the beauty of black music.

Trying to compete with Motown in the 1960s while I was an A&R executive at Mercury was a study in frustration. Mercury was a major label based in Chicago. Yet just up the road in Detroit this little company was enjoying hit after hit. But they weren't just hits. They were hits with a signature, a sound that denoted quality and soul.

Quincy Jones, foreword to *Where Did Our Love Go?: The Rise and Fall of the Motown Sound* (1986), by Nelson George

The Four Tops . . . The Temptations . . . Mary Wells . . . Marvin Gaye . . . Tammi Terrell . . . Stevie Wonder . . . The Spinners . . . The Marvelettes . . . Junior Walker and the All Stars . . . Smokey Robinson and the Miracles . . . Martha and the Vandellas . . . Gladys Knight and the Pips . . . Diana Ross and the Supremes . . . The Jackson Five.

These are some of the voices that made majestic music, voices served so well by songwriter-producers Norman Whitfield, Valerie

Simpson and Nickolas Ashford, the prolific H-D-H (brothers Eddie and Brian Holland and Lamont Dozier), and the versatile Smokey, among others. Earl Van Dyke, James Jamerson, and Benny Benjamin were among the dozens of inspired musicians working the notes. Working every which way was Harvey Fuqua—writing, coaching, talent-scouting, producing, promoting. Teaming in to give the acts polish and ultra sheen was modeling school CEO Maxine Powell and dancer-choreographer Cholly Atkins, creator of The Temptations Walk.

The driven, demanding, dictatorial Berry Gordy was the force behind it all. No doubt about it: He was a self-made man. His will to captain his own ship, lord over his own castle, be his own boss—this he came by honestly: The entrepreneurial spirit was a family tradition. It started with his grandfather Berry, born in 1854, child of planter Jim Gordy and an enslaved woman, Esther Johnson. With his helpmeet, Lucy Hellum, who endured more than twenty pregnancies for a net of nine children, this first Berry Gordy made a name for himself south of Athens, Georgia, in Oconee County. He had close to three hundred bountiful acres, with cotton the primary crop; he had a smithy; he had a general store; he had a handsome house. When he died in 1913, he left quite a legacy, and the second Berry Gordy didn't drop the ball. He so multiplied the family fortune that ugly manifestations of white envy seemed a definite possibility. So in 1922, he and his wife Bertha decided to make themselves and their children members of the great migration.

Detroit, Michigan, was the patch of the Promised Land the Gordys chose. After some false starts and setbacks, Berry Gordy made his way nicely in the world, diversification his trick: the Booker T. Washington Grocery Store, a contracting business, a printing shop, real estate, and various seasonal gigs, such as selling evergreens at Christmastide.

It was on Thanksgiving Day 1929, a month after the stock-market crash, that there entered the world the Berry who would bring the Gordy name to major fame.

He was an unpromising kid—not an ace student, often misbehaving—but he had pluck. There was no escaping the ethic of hard work, however, not with his pops for a father, not with his moms in view, a woman who juggled her home work (eight children!) with business classes at Wayne State University and the University of Michigan, who one day graduated from the Detroit Institute of Commerce, and who cofounded the Friendship Mutual Life Insurance Company.

Working in his family enterprises loaded Berry Gordy III (a.k.a. Jr.) with a multiplicity of talents and business basics, but he had no plans to follow in his parents' footsteps directly. His first goal was to be a boxer, in the pursuit of which he buddied up with fellow pugilist Jackie Wilson, who'd later hang up the gloves to work his voice.

Though Gordy did go pro, he soon found that he didn't have what it took to be a champ. After a two-year stint with Uncle Sam, in 1953, Gordy bounced back with another dream, a record shop—*only jazz spoken here*—only it went bust. By now, 1955, Gordy was in his midtwenties and a married man and father; plus, he and his wife Thelma were expecting again. To take care of business, Gordy pushed it on an assembly line at one of the automobile plants that made Detroit the Motor City, a.k.a. Motor town.

One of the ways Gordy endured the monotony of his job at Ford was by composing songs. Songwriting was something he'd been doing since he was a kid (once winning a talent contest for his "Berry's Boogie"), something that was really his first passion. After doing his time on the assembly line, Gordy often haunted the most happening Detroit nightspots, hoping to hook up with singers, trying to sell his songs (and get some release from a marriage on the rocks, as well).

Gordy caught a break when Etta James recorded a song he'd written with his sister Gwen and his friend Billy Davis, "All I Could Do Was Cry." Another break came when his old chum Jackie Wilson recorded a song he wrote with Davis: the snappy "Reet Petite," number eleven on the R&B chart two months after its release in the fall of 1957. Another Gordy-Davis-Gordy collaboration became another hit for Jackie Wilson when released in 1958: the ballad "To Be Loved."

Gordy wrote and produced several more songs for Wilson and for others. One of the songsters was Barrett Strong, who recorded the song Gordy cowrote with Janie Bradford, "Money (That's What I Want)." "Money," released in 1959 by Anna Records (a short-lived Gwen Gordy–Billy Davis enterprise), was a big hit, and money was what Gordy was determined to make. Helping him along was the woman who was to become the second Mrs. Gordy, singer and musician Raynoma Liles, with whom Gordy formed the Rayber Voices, backup singers for hire. Another person in his corner was the young William Robinson, Jr., with the wistful voice and the nickname Smokey. Robinson was seventeen and a member of the Matadors when he met Gordy in late 1957. It was Gordy who prodded the group into a name change and who wrote the song that would be The Miracles's first single: "Got a Job" (1958). It was Smokey Robinson who nudged and cheered Gordy on to cease being a vagabond songwriter and producer, to dare to be a master of a musical universe. With a loan of $800 from his family, Gordy got ready, got busy.

Jobete Music Publishing . . . Tamla Records . . . Gordy Records . . . International Talent Management. These are some of the moves Gordy made in building what became Motown Record Corporation. His first HQ was at 2648 West Grand Boulevard, the two-story house he paid down on in 1959, and bodaciously named—"What are you going to call it?" an acquaintance asked Gordy. "This was something I'd been thinking hard about, wanting to come up with the perfect name," recalled Gordy in his autobiography *To Be Loved* (1994). "Standing there looking at that unique picture window, I came up with it."

"Hitsville" is what Gordy proclaimed. When his acquaintance laughed and said, "You're joking," Gordy said, "No, I'm serious. That's the only name I can think of that expresses what I want it to be—a hip name for a factory where hits are going to be built. That's it, Hitsville."

At Hitsville, U.S.A., Gordy wrote songs. Gordy cowrote songs. Gordy produced songs. Gordy pressed his growing staff and performers for excellence, for perfection in everything. Gordy harnessed every ounce of shrewd in his bones, and this Svengali entranced so many young talents to see Motown as their world and as their first family to whom all allegiance and honor was due. Wisely, Gordy had his own family all up in his business. For one, Pops was a key consultant and confidante. At various times, all his siblings were Motowners, with, for example, Esther becoming a vice president and overseer of the management arm, Loucye keeping an eye on accounts payable and receivables, and Robert (who briefly recorded as Bob Kayli) learning to be an engineer. In the mix, Anna Gordy married Marvin Gaye, and Gwen married Harvey Fuqua.

Among Motown's early hits was "Please Mr. Postman" by The Marvelettes, released in 1961, the same year of Motown's first million-copy seller, the Berry Gordy–Smokey Robinson collaboration, "Shop Around." In 1962, years before record companies routinely engaged in "tour support," Gordy put his gold on the road with the company's first revue. Soon, all across the nation, there was a growing crowd of fans for a distinct sound coming out of the Motor Town.

According to cultural critic Nelson George, 1964 marks the spot. This was the year The Four Tops hit with "Baby I Need Your Loving," Martha and the Vandellas with "Dancing in the Street," The Temptations with "The Way You Do the Things You Do," the Supremes with "Where Did Our Love Go?", "Baby Love," and "Come See about Me"— and Mary Wells had "My Guy."

"Drumsticks pounded the skins on every beat, a beat accentuated by tambourine, guitar, and often vibes, while the bass rolled forward like a speeding locomotive." This is how Nelson George commenced his painting of the Motown sound in *Where Did Our Love Go?* "Guitars and pianos and organs all squeezed into a cluttered mid-range while blustery horn charts and weirdly arranged strings lingered in the background." The lyrics George assessed as "all right." Their strength, he allowed, was the chorus—"and man, sometimes these songs seemed to be all chorus and no verse." So at the end of the day—"the words burned into your brain"—and your soul.

The hits kept coming.

1965: "Shotgun," "I Can't Help Myself (Sugar Pie, Honey Bunch)," "Nowhere to Run," "My Girl," and the Supremes's four-for-four triumph "Stop! In the Name of Love," "Back in My Arms Again," "Nothing but Heartache," and "I Hear a Symphony."

1966: "You Can't Hurry Love," "Reach Out I'll Be There," "Function at the Junction," "Don't Mess With Bill," "Get Ready."

1967: "I Heard It through the Grapevine," "I Second That Emotion," "I Was Made to Love Her," "You're My Everything," "Jimmy Mack," "Bernadette," "Ain't No Mountain High Enough."

1968: "Ain't Nothing Like the Real Thing," "I Wish It Would Rain," "Love Child."

1969: "I'm Gonna Make You Love Me," "I Can't Get Next to You," "What Does It Take (to Win Your Love)"—and this was the year The Jackson Five made their Motown debut, with "I Want You Back."

These are just some of the year-after-year hits of Motown's glory days. The Motown sound wasn't the only thing happening in black pop music (Aretha was around and James Brown, too, for starters) but nowhere else was so much memorable music to be found in one place. For many, the Motown sound was the number-one escape during a most tumultuous time: with the civil-rights movement moving into Black Power, with the Vietnam War tearing families asunder. Though its mainstay was tunes about love and roses and honey chile, Motown did dip into the deeper things. There was the label Black Forum, which released albums by Stokely Carmichael, **Amiri Baraka,** Elaine Brown, and others who stood up for Freedom Now and for Black Power. Also from Black Forum came the album *The Great March to Freedom* with **Martin Luther King, Jr.**'s speech, "I Have A Dream" and King's *Why I Oppose the War in Vietnam,* which won a Grammy in 1970, the same year Edwin Starr hit with "War," asking "Good God, y'all, what is it good for?" and answering "Absolutely nothing." In 1971, the tortured Marvin Gaye asked us to stop the madness with "What's Going On?" a song Gordy was initially far from keen on.

By the early 1970s, Berry Gordy was presiding over a company grossing $40 million per annum. A decade later, the figure topped $100 million. In these pre–Reginald Lewis days, Motown was for many the number-one role model for black capitalism. Paradoxically, Gordy was regarded as a number-one demon by some. Stories of the many artists he ripped off, lied to, and crushed were out there in spades. His use of whites to handle sales in the early days was another piece of old dirty laundry folks paraded. His foray into film, which included disasters such as the Diana Ross prop-ups *Lady Sings the Blues, Mahogany,* and *The Wiz,* garnered him more ridicule and scorn. It didn't help that he was rumored to have a painting of himself as Napoleon in his Bel Air mansion.

In 1988, the year Gordy was inducted into the Rock 'n' Roll Hall of Fame, he sold Motown (then the fifth largest African American-owned company) to RCA for $61 million (with RCA selling it to Polygram in 1993 for $325 million). Many were angry when Gordy made that move. They felt the sale was a sellout, that it was downright treachery to release the source of the Motown sound from black hands. All this notwithstanding, folks still maintained a measure of gratitude for Berry Gordy as the master builder of a majestic music, of the Motown sound that would grace the soundtrack of scores of films, that would inspire waves of singers and instrumentalists, that would never go out of style.

 # John Oliver Killens (1916–1987)

Not one of Killens's novels is a waste of a reader's time. The first one, *Youngblood* (1954), is a deep-reaching story of a Georgia family struggling against infamies inherent in Jim Crow. *And Then We Heard the Thunder* (1962), which was nominated for a Pulitzer Prize, barreled into racism in the military during World War II. Capturing the battle for voting rights in the state Nina Simone (among others) damned was the objective of *'Sippi* (1967), after which came *Slaves* (1969). Then Killens had us laughing (through tears, at points) with the send-up on wannabes that was *The Cotillion; Or, One Good Bull Is Half the Herd* (1971), also nominated for a Pulitzer Prize. In 1989, two years after his death, we saw the publication of his musing on the octoroon who was the Father of Russian Literature, *Great Black Russian: A Novel on the Life and Times of Alexander Pushkin.*

John Oliver Killens also gave us books to build up the young: *Great Gittin' Up Morning: A Biography of Denmark Vesey* (1972) and *A Man Ain't Nothin' but a Man: The Adventures of **John Henry*** (1975). He wrote and cowrote several screenplays and plays, among them, *Ballad of the Winter Soldier, Odds Against Tomorrow,* and adaptations of his novels *Slaves* and *The Cotillion.* Killens was versatile, for sure.

A great-grandmother planted in him the seeds for a love of storytelling. During his growing up in Macon, Georgia, she inspired him with stories about slavery days and the first days of freedom. She puffed a corncob pipe, he said. Added to Granny was Killens's mother being president of the Dunbar Literary Club and his father ritually reading him a weekly newspaper column by Langston Hughes.

The idea of being a writer was cotton candy when John started wearing long pants. After studies at Edward Waters in Jacksonville, Florida, and Morris Brown in Atlanta, Georgia, he was aiming to be a lawyer. He moved to Washington, D.C., in the late 1930s. There, he worked for the National Labor Relations Board and finished up on the B.A. through night classes at Howard University. This done, he entered Robert Terrell Law School, but after a time lost interest in law and entered the U.S. Army, doing duty in the South Pacific. After World War II, Killens returned to a job at the National Labor Relations Board and later worked for the Congress of Industrial Organizations (CIO) and became active in the Progressive Party.

The idea of being a writer was more than cotton candy in late 1940s, by which time Killens was in New York. There, he took writing classes at Columbia University and New York University and came under the heavy influence of Langston Hughes, **W. E. B. Du Bois** and Paul Robeson. He also wrote for the leftist magazine, *Freedomways,* among other periodicals.

Killens's politics necessarily informed his vision of fiction. Writers either produced works that advanced liberation or they produced works that hindered it. There were no two ways about it. To foster and keep alive literature that liberated, along with Walter Christmas, Rosa Guy, and **John Henrik Clarke,** Killens formed a writing workshop in Harlem, known by the early 1950s as the Harlem Writers Guild. *Youngblood* was the first published novel by a member of the guild, which over the years came to include Maya Angelou, DorisJean Austin, William Banks, Jr., Arthur Flowers, Joyce Hansen, Paule Marshall, Julian Mayfield, Terry McMillan, Walter Mosley, Walter Dean Myers, and Brenda Wilkinson.

Killens's activism went beyond the realm of literature. For one, in 1964, he cofounded the Organization of Afro-American Unity with **Malcolm X.** It was a year later that Killens's enlightening collection of essays appeared: *Black Man's Burden,* with meditations and manifestos on a range of issues, from manhood to the flaws of nonviolence as a liberation tactic. Like his fiction, screenplays, and books for young adults, *Black Man's Burden* is not a waste of a reader's time.

ALSO WORTH READING

There are scores of black male writers of Killens's generation whose books will always merit our attention, among whom are

- James Baldwin (1924–1987), who was born in Harlem and died in France, made his fiction debut with Go Tell It on the Mountain (1953). After this, he published eight more books of fiction, among them, the short-story collection Going to Meet the Man (1965) and the novels If Beale Street Could Talk (1974) and Just Above My Head (1979). Baldwin also produced a book of poems Jimmy's Blues (1983) and several plays, the most famous of which is Blues for Mister Charlie, first produced in 1964. It was with nonfiction that many contend Baldwin was at his best brilliance—for example, *Notes of a Native Son* (1955) and *The Fire Next Time* (1963). A resplendent assortment of the essays by this mid-century witness can be found in *The Price of the Ticket: Collected Nonfiction 1948–1985* (1985).

- Cyrus Colter (1910–), who was born in Noblesville, Indiana, and eventually made Chicago home (teaching at Northwestern University), is one of the most neglected writers who produced quite good work. (This neglect is in part because his work was never overtly racial.) Colter's novels are *The River of Eros* (1972), *The Hippodrome* (1973), *Night Studies* (1979), and *The Chocolate Soldier* (1988). His short stories have been collected in *The Beach Umbrella* (1970), winner of the Iowa School of Letters Award for Short Fiction, and *The Amoralists and Other Tales* (1988), which includes some stories from *The Beach Umbrella*.

- Ralph Ellison (1914–1994), who was born in Oklahoma City and lived in Harlem for the last forty years of his life, is most remembered for his only novel, the perennially in print *Invisible Man* (1952), which won the 1953 National Book Award for Fiction. Ellison was also applauded for his nonfiction: *Shadow and Act* (1964) and *Going to the Territory* (1986). These works, along with other essays and speeches, are in *The Collected Essays of Ralph Ellison* (1995), edited by John F. Callahan, who also edited a collection of Ellison's short fiction, *Flying Home and Other Stories* (1996).

- Albert Murray (1916–), who was born in Nokomis, Alabama, and eventually made Harlem his home, has tackled both fiction and nonfiction to superb effect. His nonfiction includes the essay collection *The Omni-Americans: New Perspectives on Black Experience and American Culture* (1970 and rereleased in 1983 as *The Omni-Americans: Some Alternatives to the Folklore of White Supremacy*); a meditation on black music *Stomping the Blues* (1976); the "as told to" *Good Morning Blues: The Autobiography of Count Basie* (1985); and more meditations on music, *The Blue Devils of Nada* (1996). His novels are *Train Whistle Guitar* (1974), the story of a boy named Scooter growing up in 1920s Alabama, nutshelled as a "blues version of Mark Twain's *Tom Sawyer*," its sequel *The Spyglass Tree* (1991), called a "riff on James Joyce's *Portrait of a the Artist as a Young Man*," and *The Seven League Boots* (1996), with part three of Scooter's life.

- John A. Williams (1925–), who was born in Jackson, Mississippi, and had as his first career broadcast and print journalism, is one of the most prolific post–World War II writers. His eleven novels include *The Angry Ones* (1960); *Night Song* (1961); *Sissie* (1963); *The Man Who Cried I Am* (1967), which brought him international acclaim; *Captain Blackman* (1972); and *!Click Song* (1982), winner of the 1983 Before Columbus Foundation American Book Award. Williams's many books of nonfiction include *This Is My Country, Too* (1965); *The Most Native of Sons: A Biography of Richard Wright* (1970); *The King God Didn't Save: Reflections on the Life and Death of Martin Luther King, Jr.* (1970); and *If I Stop I'll Die: The Comedy and Tragedy of Richard Pryor* (1991), written with his son Dennis A. Williams. In addition, John A. Williams has edited or coedited several anthologies. Among them is *The Angry Black* (1962; second edition, *Beyond the Angry Black*, 1966).

 Gordon Parks (1912–   )

How will he go down in history? Let us count the ways:

1. PHOTOGRAPHER. In 1941, he became the first person to receive a Julius Rosenwald Fellowship for photography, which paved the way for him to work with photographer Roy Stryker at the Farm Security Agency. This New Deal agency's projects included documenting in black and white the plight of the truly disadvantaged in urban and rural America. It was while at this work that Parks produced his best-known photograph: Ella Watson, a cleaning lady in a government building standing before an American flag with mop and broom in hand and a stony weariness upon her face. "American Gothic" is the title of this piece, which Parks later called his "indictment of the government."

Through a combination of luck and the sense to seize opportunity, Parks managed to secure assignments with *Glamour* and *Vogue*. Then, in 1948, he received his huge break: becoming a staff photographer for *Life* magazine. It was a position he stayed with until 1970. By this time, he was an internationally renowned photojournalist, one whose portfolio contained incredible range: crime, art, poverty, fashion, celebrities, the civil-rights movement.

2. WRITER. When someone suggested that he tell about his life, he took the challenge. The result was the autobiographical novel *The Learning Tree* (1963), which became a best-seller. This was not his first book: In the late 1940s, he had produced two books about photography, *Flash Photography* and *Camera Portraits: Techniques and Principles of Documentary Portraiture. The Learning Tree* was his first attempt at literature, however, and it would not be his last. His other books include a collection of essays and photographs, *Born Black;* another novel, *Shannon;* three autobiographies—*A Choice of Weapons, To Smile in Autumn,* and *Voices in the Mirror;* four collections of poetry and photography—*Gordon Parks: A Poet and His Camera; Gordon Parks: Whispers of Intimate Things; Gordon Parks: In Love;* and *Moments without Proper Names.* In 1996 came *Glimpses toward Infinity,* a collection of poetry and paintings. So that makes. . . .

3. PAINTER.

4. FILMMAKER. His first film, *Flavio* (1964), was a documentary on

Flavio da Silvia, a desperately poor, ailing Brazilian boy, whose story Parks had told in *Life* in the early 1960s. Another early documentary was *Diary of a Harlem Family* (1968), for which he won an Emmy. In the late 1960s, Parks made history as the first African American to produce, direct, and script a film for a major Hollywood studio (Warner Brothers). The film was an adaptation of *The Learning Tree*, released in 1969 and named one of the twenty-five most significant films in America, according to the National Film Register of the Library of Congress in 1989. After *The Learning Tree*, Parks directed several more films. There was the very commercial, very successful, trend-setting *Shaft* (1971), which featured Richard Roundtree as the law-unto-himself detective John "Shut Yo' Mouth" Shaft. Then came *Shaft's Big Score* (1972, the same year his son Gordon Parks, Jr., directed *Superfly*) and *The Super Cops* (1974). Parks also directed noncommercial films: first, *Leadbelly* (1976), a portrait of the folk and blues singer Huddie Ledbetter; then another biography, *The Odyssey of Solomon Northup* (1984), about the freeborn New Yorker who was kidnapped in 1841 and suffered through twelve years of bondage. Parks's documentary on himself, *Gordon Parks: Moments without Proper Names*, premiered on PBS in 1988.

5. COMPOSER. Many of his films carry his music: the score to *The Learning Tree* and "Don't Misunderstand" in *Shaft's Big Score*, for example. *Concerto for Piano and Orchestra*, *Piece of Cello and Orchestra*, and *Celebrations for Sarah Ross and Andrew Jackson Parks* (his parents) are among his long works that have been performed by symphony orchestras in the United States and abroad. Parks also composed the music and libretto for *Martin*, a five-act ballet that aired on national television in 1990, on the birthday of the man it saluted: **Martin Luther King, Jr.**

This Renaissance man, this man obviously born with a genius curiosity is a reminder that we all can probably do more than we think we can. He is all the more an inspiration considering that he was born in Fort Scott, Kansas, where racism was raw, where he was the youngest of fifteen children of very poor farmers, and where he never finished high school (there or anywhere else).

His accomplishments become all the more extraordinary when you consider that he almost wasn't born. "When summoning up the past," he wrote in *Voices in the Mirror*, "I take into account the luck, which first touched me at my birth. Our family doctor, having pronounced me dead, was wrapping me for disposal when his young assistant asked to try something on his own." The doctor's response was, "but the child's dead," and the young assistant was persistent, "Please—let me try," he said. When the doctor consented—"I was swished about in a tub of cold water like a slab of beef. Suddenly I started yelling, and they say I kept up the yelling for an hour." In this first hour of yelling was a fierce clinging to life, and perhaps the taproot of the zest and zeal for life that enabled Gordon Parks to do so much.

Robert Hayden (1913–1980)

He was born Asa Sheffey, Jr., to a couple who split up shortly after his birth. He was rechristened Robert Earl Hayden by the couple who adopted him: Sue Ellen and William Hayden, dutiful, fine people who gave the boy love and a decent home in a far-from-Edenic section of Detroit: Paradise Valley.

A serious sight impairment cramped young Robert's social life, but he could freely read, and he did with heat, with literature becoming his beauty place—poetry, his song.

One day he came up with a collection of poems (most about black history), which he hoped was good enough for publication, but the publisher he queried, Harper Brothers, didn't think so. This was in 1931, when Hayden was eighteen. Around the same time, he did get a boost: when *Abbott's Monthly* published "Africa"—"In thee I take undying pride—/ Dark cradle of a race denied!" This poem, this echo of Countee Cullen's "Heritage," was evidence of the young poet's "tie to the waning Harlem Renaissance," noted Pontheolla T. Williams in *Robert Hayden: A Critical Analysis of His Poetry* (1987).

Next up on Hayden's horizon was college. In 1932, he entered Detroit City College (now Wayne State University), where he majored in Spanish, hung out with a group of writers that included Marxists, and spent a fair amount of time involved in theater productions. When he was close to the finish, financial difficulties forced him to leave college. The good news is that he got a job with the WPA's Detroit Writers Project, as a writer and researcher on black history and folklore. In 1939, he became this agency's Director of Negro Research, a post he held until 1940, the year he married Erma Morris. Also in 1940 his first collection of poetry was published, *Heart-Shape in the Dust*. These "proletariat poems" had received the Jules and Avery Hopwood Award of the University of Michigan, where Hayden had resumed his education and studied with W. H. Auden, the person whom he credited more than anyone else with helping him sight the weaknesses and strengths of his verse.

Hayden began graduate studies at the University of Michigan in 1942, the year of the birth of his daughter Maia, and the year he won another Jules and Avery Hopwood Award. This award exalted "The Black Spear," a selection of poems he planned to expand into a full-scale collection about the antebellum liberation struggle and black action in the Civil War. Then, in 1944, shortly before receiving his master's degree, Hayden became a teaching assistant at the University of Michigan. Two years later, he took a job as an assistant professor in English at Fisk University in Nashville, Tennessee. He remained at Fisk for twenty-three years, becoming a full professor along the way. Then it was back to the University of Michigan in 1969, where he was a professor of English until 1980, the year he died.

He taught, he once said, so that he could write a poem or two now and then.

Across the years, Hayden produced pages and pages of poetry, for the making of more collections, among them: *The Lion and the Archer* (1948); *Figure of Time* (1955); *A Ballad of Remembrance* (1962), winner of the World Festival of Negro Arts grand prize; *Words in the Mourning Time* (1970), which was nominated for a 1971 National Book Award; *The Night-Blooming Cereus* (1972); and *Angle of Ascent: New and Selected Poems* (1975).

Writing poetry was a way of "coming to grips with inner and outer realities." It was, he said, "a spiritual act, really, a sort of prayer for illumination and perfection."

Among Hayden's most treasured lights is "Middle Passage," which sprang from meditations on Cinque of the *Amistad* revolt, and which begins with the urgent

> *Jesús, Estrella, Esperanza, Mercy:*
> Sails flashing to the wind like weapons,
> sharks following the moans the fever and the dying;
> horror the corposant and compass rose.

> Middle Passage:
> voyage through death
> to life upon these shores.

Another star is "Runagate Runagate," a tribute to souls who said no to enslavement. Hayden wrote poems about **Crispus Attucks,** Phillis Wheatley, Gabriel Prosser, **Nat Turner, Frederick Douglass,*** Paul Laurence Dunbar, Paul Robeson, **Malcolm X,** and "Homage to the Empress of the Blues," to tribute Bessie Smith. There's also the gazing "[American Journal]," with an alien concluding his report on his American experience with this:

---

*His tribute to **Frederick Douglass** appears on pages 116–117 of this book.

> confess i am curiously drawn   unmentionable   to
> the americans   doubt i could exist among them for
> long however   psychic demands far too severe
> much violence   much that repels   i am attracted
> none the less   their variousness their ingenuity
> their elan vital   and that some thing   essence
> quiddity   i cannot penetrate or name

Hayden wrote poems about Bahá'í, the faith he embraced in the early 1940s. He wrote about Jews, Mexicans, the Vietnam War. He mined the lore of ancient Greeks and ancient Africans. He wrote about deaths and resurrections, shadows and starbursts, shouts and whispers, crazies and sages, the human heart, the soul's search.

Whatever his subject or voice, Hayden was nearly always superb in his craft and logic. Across the years, his gift was honored. In addition to awards already cited, there were these: In 1970, he received the National Institute of Arts and Letters Russell Loins Award for distinguished poetic achievement; in 1975, he was elected a Fellow of the American Academy of Poets; in 1976, he became the first black Consultant in Poetry to the Library of Congress, and was reappointed to the post the following year.

O, black and unknown bard: This could fit Robert Hayden, absolutely one of the finest modern poets, yet not as known/remembered/ recited as he merits, this poet's poet. Pity. For, as Margaret Walker recalled in a memorial poem, Hayden gave us "across the years/ a multiplicity of Jewelled words/ taken from the casket of memory/ like a magician with legerdemain." Hayden gave us "all the books/ all the years/ all the songs/ still shining in our ears."

John Henrik Clarke (1915–1998)

Those who have no truck with shadow listened up and learned from John Henrik Clarke. They are grateful for his long presence on the planet, for all his years of showing that there is deliverance in knowing history, that there is power in the past. "History is not everything . . . but it is a starting point," he told us. "History is a clock that people use to tell their time of day. It is a compass they use to find themselves on the map of human geography. It tells them where they are, but more importantly, what they must be."

John Henry Clark, born in Union Springs, Alabama, and raised (from age four) in Columbus, Georgia, began the journey into history when he was young—long before he added an "e" to his surname, long before he changed his middle name from Henry to Henrik because as he said he liked the "spunk" of the Scandinavian "rebel playwright" Henrik Ibsen. He started his journey when he was a little kid called "Bubba" by most folks. "I looked at the world around me, and tried to understand what it was all about." This is how he summed it up in his essay "A Search for Identity." His first guide was his great-grandmother Mom Mary, who had first been enslaved in Georgia and then in Alabama. One of the memories Mom Mary frequently recounted—a story that stayed vivid in Clarke's mind—was of the great grief of being separated from her first husband, Buck, who was sold to a stud farm in Virginia. Mom Mary profoundly loved Buck, a man with whom she'd had three children, a man for whom she searched, in vain, when freedom came.

Mom Mary told her great-grandson not only about her personal history, but also bits and pieces of the race's history. When he became a grown man, Clarke came to understand that his Mom Mary was essentially what his ancestors had classified as a griot.

> Years later when I went to Africa and listened to oral historians, I knew that my great grandmother was not very different from the old men and women who sit around in front of their houses and tell the young children stories of their people—how they came from one place to another, how they searched for safety, and how they tried to resist when the Europeans came to their lands.
>
> This great grandmother was so dear to me that I have deified her in almost the same way that many Africans deify their old people. I think that my search for identity, my search for what the world was about, and my relationship to the world began when I listened to the stories of this old woman. I remember that she always ended the stories in the same way. . . . It was always with the reminder, "Run the race, and run it by faith." She did not rule out resistance as a form of obedience to God. She thought that the human being should not permit himself to be dehumanized, . . . and she thought that anyone who had enslaved any of God's children had violated the very will of God.

As a child, Clarke prized literacy as much as the oral tradition. He recalled that he, one of nine children, learned to read by "picking up signs, grocery handbills, and many other things that people threw away, and by studying signboards. . . . I would read the labels on tin cans to see where the products were made, and these scattered things were my first books." His first major bound book was the Holy Bible, which he knew well enough for the grown folks to let him teach the children's Sunday School before he was ten. In his reading of the Bible, he couldn't overlook certain incongruities. For one, he wondered why Jesus was blonde and blue-eyed in all the representations he saw, when clearly the Bible described Jesus not so.

In his thirst for knowledge, Clarke found ready love from one teacher

John Henrik Clarke in 1996, at a tribute to him and his good friend and fellow historian Yosef ben-Jochannan ("Doc Ben"), hosted by a coalition of activists at Boys and Girls High in Brooklyn, New York. (Courtesy of Herb Boyd)

in particular: Evelena Taylor, who one day "took my face between her hands and looking me straight in the eyes, said, 'I believe in you.'"

His family did, too. From her work as a laundress, his mother saved fifty cents a week for his education, "hoping that eventually she would be able to send her oldest son to college. Her hopes did not materialize; she died long before I was ten."

Clarke paid tribute as well to the menfolk who invested in his promise.

> We lived just outside of the city limits. Children living beyond the city limits were supposed to go to country schools because the city schools charged country residents $3.75 each semester for the use of books. This was a monumental sum for us because my father made from $10.00 to $14.00 a week as a combination farmer and fire tender at the brickyards. In order to get the required $3.75 each semester, my father and some of my uncles had to put their money together. It was a collective thing to raise what was for us a large sum of money not only to send a child to a city school instead of to a country school but also to make certain that the one child in the family attending the city school had slightly better clothing than the other children. So I had a coat that was fairly warm and a pair of shoes that was supposed to be warm but really were not. As I think about the shoes, my feet sometimes get cold even now, but I could not tell my benefactors that the shoes were not keeping me warm.

By hook, by crook, Clarke kept on his search for knowledge. He borrowed books from some of the whites for whom he did odd jobs. He also engaged in what he called "illegitimate book borrowing" from the for-whites-only Columbus public library: That is, just as Richard Wright and so many others who grew up in Jim Crow America did, Clarke would go to the library with bogus notes from prominent white people that directed the librarian to give the little colored boy such-and-such a book. The librarians fell for the ruse, convinced that the little colored boy was simply serving as a delivery boy for the white Sir or Ma'am. "I accumulated a great many books that way," Clarke recalled. He also recalled the sting that came in response to his asking a lawyer for whom he worked if he had anything in his library on the accomplishments of black people in ancient history. This "kind man" who had permitted Clarke to borrow many of his books explained that blacks in antiquity had no history, and that even closer to their day, blacks hadn't done very much that was noteworthy.

Clarke was soon to find out that the kind lawyer had been so wrong about blacks having no history. His great day came when he had the honor of safeguarding the belongings of a guest speaker at his high school (where there was no cloak room, he remembered). Among the speaker's things was a copy of Alain Locke's anthology *The New Negro*. The piece that blew Clarke away was "The Negro Digs Up His Past" by Arthur A. Schomburg. "From this essay I learned that I came from a people with a history older than the history of Europe," Clarke remembered. "It was a most profound and overwhelming feeling—this great discovery that my people did have a place in history and that, indeed, their history was older than that of their oppressors." Clarke was now, more than ever, ready from within to run the race.

Where else to start than in the capital of Black America, Harlem, where Clarke arrived at age eighteen in 1933. One of the first things he did was to search out Arthur A. Schomburg at the 135th Street branch of The New York Public Library. When he finally met with the bibliophile, Clarke told him that he wanted to know his history—"and I wanted to know it right now and in the quickest possible way."

"Sit down, son," said Schomburg, "What you are calling African history and Negro history is nothing but the missing pages in world history. You will have to know general history to understand these specific aspects of history." Schomburg continued patiently, "You have to study your oppressor. That's where your history got lost." Clarke set about doing what Schomburg advised. His studies of ancient European history brought him to the discovery of how indebted early European civilization was to the "dark" continent. This journey led to other discoveries that led to Clarke's learning about the how and why of the slave trade.

Soon Clarke would have deep context for the lives of Mom Mary and

Buck, because soon he'd discover the works of such people as **William C. Nell** and **Carter G. Woodson** and the worlds of Willis Huggins, founder of the Harlem History Club and Africanist William Leo Hansberry (uncle of "Sweet Lorraine"). Clarke found other mentors in various organizations committed to social change, including the National League of Negro Youth, and for a time, the Young Communist League.

Clarke's search for identity was slightly jagged in the early 1940s, due to his service in U.S. Air Force. After his release, he returned to New York City, where he renewed the search with vigor. Along with prodigious self-study, Clarke engaged in formal schooling at various institutions of higher learning, in New York (New York University and the New School of Social Research) and in West Africa (Nigeria's University of Ibadan and the University of Ghana). This determined student of black history soon became a dynamic, pioneering teacher himself.

In the mid-1950s, Clarke was an occasional teacher of African and Afro-American History at the New School of Social Research. Beginning in the early 1960s, and for more than two decades, Clarke taught at various community centers in Harlem (where from 1964 to 1969 he was director of the Heritage Teaching Program of the antipoverty agency HARYOU-ACT). He also trained others to teach and teach well the history of African peoples at various institutions (including Columbia University), developing curricula, study guides, and other teaching material in the process. In 1965, eight years before he earned a Ph.D. from Pacific Western University, Clarke became a professor of Black and Puerto Rican Studies at Hunter College in New York City (becoming professor emeritus when he retired from full-time teaching in 1988). Over the years, he held visiting professorships at an array of colleges and universities, becoming a Distinguished Visiting Professor of African History at the Africana Studies and Research Center at Cornell University. He lectured widely, across the United States and abroad, and served as a consultant to many print and broadcast history projects.

Clarke played a critical role in several organizations. He was **Malcolm X**'s key adviser on the Organization of Afro-American Unity. He also helped found the Black Academy of Arts and Letters and, with **John Oliver Killens,** the Harlem Writers Guild. From 1949 to 1955, he was vice president of the Association for the Study of Negro Life and History, founded by **Carter G. Woodson.** He was one of the founders and the first president (1969–1973) of the African Heritage Studies Association, the mission of which was to preserve, interpret, and disseminate information about the history and cultures of Africa and the diaspora.

Not to be forgotten is Clarke's impact in print. From his "The Lives of Great African Chiefs," serialized in the *Pittsburgh Courier* in the late 1950s, to the countless articles he contributed to *Negro History Bulletin, Chicago Defender, Journal of Negro Education, Phylon,* and *Présence*

Africaine, among other periodicals. He served as associate editor of *Harlem Quarterly* (which he cofounded) from 1949 to 1951 and for a number of years, beginning in 1962, as associate editor of *Freedomways.* Among the many books he edited are *Harlem U.S.A.: The Story of a City within a City* (1964); *American Negro Short Stories* (1966); *William Styron's Nat Turner: Ten Black Writers Respond* (1968); *Malcolm X: The Man and His Times* (1969); *Marcus Garvey and the Vision of Africa* (with Amy Jacques Garvey, 1973); and *New Dimensions in African History: The London Lectures of Dr. Yosef ben-Jochanan and Dr. John Henrik Clarke* (1991), which contains the essay "A Search for Identity." Among the books he authored are *Africans at the Crossroads: Notes for an African World Revolution* (1991), *Christopher Columbus and the African Holocaust* (1992), and *My Life in Search of Africa* (1994). Clarke also composed verse (*Rebellion in Rhyme,* 1948) and many short stories, with "The Boy Who Painted Christ Black" being perhaps his most precious and certainly his most widely anthologized short story, and one made into an HBO film (1996), starring a former student of Clarke's, Wesley Snipes.

By the mid-1990s, Clarke's eyesight was in deep decline, but as one of his persistent protégés, Herb Boyd, put it, "Clarke had not lost his vision, nor his perspicacity." Clarke, not only nearly sightless but also way up in age, kept teaching, kept lecturing, kept mentoring, too. Sadly, he was not able to literally see the worthy documentary *John Henrik Clarke: A Great and Mighty Walk.* This film, which premiered in New York City in Spring 1997, was directed by St. Claire Bourne and executive produced and narrated by Wesley Snipes. "What makes this film so remarkable," wrote Joan H. Allen in the May 31, 1997, issue of the *New York Amsterdam News,* "is that it not only traces Clarke's roots from his early childhood . . . to his becoming one of the leading authorities on African-American history, but also traces 5,000 years of African and African-American history." Another marvelous thing about the film is that proceeds from its premiere were earmarked for the cataloging and preserving of Clarke's papers (The John Henrik Clarke Collection), which Clarke donated to the institution seeded by the man who gave him that sterling advice so long ago, the Schomburg Center for Research in Black Culture.

When the eighty-three-year-old John Henrik Clarke suffered a fatal heart attack in the summer of 1998, there was deep grieving around the nation, around the world among people who knew his work, knew his worth. At a six-hour Service of Commemoration, and the Initiation into Eternity on July 21, 1998, at Harlem's Abyssinian Baptist Church Reverend Calvin O. Butts, III, applied Apostle Paul's words in 2 Timothy 4:7 to Clarke: "I have fought the good fight, I have finished the race, I have kept the faith." Four days later, the master griot was funeralized again and buried in Columbus, Georgia, where all those years ago he began heeding Mom Mary's advice.

Robert H. Lawrence, Jr. (1935–1967)

Robert Lawrence believed he could fly. This native of Chicago, Illinois, had, as his mother once said of both her children, "a discipline that must have come from within." Such discipline enabled young Robert to master Rachmaninoff's pieces for piano, train his brain for chess, and tackle a succession of chemistry sets. Another hobby was building model airplanes.

After graduating from high school in the top 10 percent of his class, Lawrence attended Bradley University in Peoria, Illinois, where he earned a bachelor's degree in chemistry and the rank of cadet lieutenant colonel in his campus's Air Force ROTC, of which he was also cadet commander. With an Air Force reserve commission of second lieutenant, Lawrence took on the assignment of flying instructor in Germany. During this time, he married fellow Chicagoan Barbara Cress (sister of activist-psychiatrist-scholar Frances Cress Welsing). He and Barbara later had a son, Tracey.

Following his tour of duty in Germany, and on the Air Force's nickel, Lawrence continued his education in the sciences at Ohio State University. There, he managed a GPA on the up side of 3.5, in pursuit of his Ph.D. in physical chemistry, which he received in 1965.

By then, he was Captain Lawrence, a senior pilot and seasoned teacher, who had logged in about 1,500 jet hours and had worked for a time as a research scientist in an Air Force weapons laboratory in New Mexico. Things were looking up for him, and he was looking up, too, eager to move on from an aviator to a star sailor.

NASA said, "Nein," several times after Lawrence's first application for its astronaut training program in 1961. Undaunted, Lawrence pursued another avenue: the Air Force's astronaut Manned Orbital Laboratory Program, which would send two men up in a *Gemini B* capsule to conduct a range of experiments. This program accepted Lawrence, and he became a major.

Hate mail, death threats—all because he was poised to become the first African American astronaut. There was also the ghost of the Dwight Affair: Air Force Captain Edward Joseph Dwight, Jr., the first African American astronaut candidate, left the space program in 1965, after much controversy about his qualifications and treatment, and strong evidence that his career had been sabotaged by the legendary test pilot, Colonel Charles "Chuck" Yeager, commandant of the Aerospace Research Pilots' School (ARPS) at Edwards Air Force Base in California.

Robert H. Lawrence, Jr., in 1957, at Webb Air Force Base in Big Springs, Texas. The aircraft is a T-33, the jet trainer of that era. (Author's collection)

When Lawrence arrived at Edwards Air Force Base in 1967 to begin his astronaut training, Yeager was gone. No doubt Lawrence knew he would still have to be twice as good. Determined to make the grade and make it into space, he did what he had always done: He braced himself and stayed disciplined for all the training he'd have to do. Naturally, this included flying—such as the practice session on December 8, 1967, with Major Harvey J. Royer in command and he the copilot of a F-104D *Starfighter*.

In *They Had a Dream: The Story of African-American Astronauts* (1994), J. Alfred Phelps, who served in the U.S. Air Force for more than twenty years, set the scene with this:

> The F-104D *Starfighter* crouched silently on the Edwards Air Force Base ramp. A proud century series fighter aircraft, its lines evoked images of speed, even though it sat stock-still, casting angled shadows across the tarmac in the desert sun. It was a bullet with wings. Jazzy. Fighter pilots loved the *Starfighter*. . . .
>   The *Starfighter* was fun to taxi. When you jiggled the throttle out of idle and pulled it back, that juiced-up, crazy engine would go *woooooh*—like the Super Chief riding a straightaway. Some pilots liked to shock people around the flightline that way. They would sneak up on them at idle, then goose the throttle and make the engine roar—just to see them jump!

Phelps guessed that Lawrence and Royer indulged in this runway frolic and then got stone serious once *Starfighter* was cleared for take-off. Once airborne, Phelps tells us, "they climbed like a rocket until, within a matter of seconds, they were twenty-five thousand feet above the Edwards runway centerline on a heading of 130 degrees." He goes on to explain,

> What they were about to practice had been used as a training tool in the ARPS program since 1961. At that time, planners had sought a way to simulate the in-flight mechanics of space and reentry vehicles. The skills and experience required to master those mechanics were considered necessary for test pilots and astronaut trainees. Early on, while training pilots—to fly the X-15, instructors noted that the F-104 *Starfighter* in "dirty" configuration (i.e., with landing gear extended, speed brakes down, and drag chute to increase aerodynamic drag) closely approximated the X-15 in unpowered flight.

For all its zap and jazz, the *Starfighter* could be, said Phelps, "an unforgiving rascal under certain conditions." Such was the case on this day.

> Royer and Lawrence were on a standard ARPS lift/drag mission. The plan called for them to make two simulated X-15 approaches until fuel depleted to 3,500 pounds or less, two "clean" (i.e., wheels up) lift/drag approaches until fuel burned to 2,500 pounds or less, and two dirty lift/drag approaches. . . .
> As they went through the drill that afternoon, things went horribly wrong for Lawrence and Royer. An approach that was probably too low. That sudden, gut-wrenching lift pilots feared. . . . No one will ever know for sure why, but the F-104 smacked into the runway left of the centerline, twenty-two thousand feet from the approach end, its underbelly blossoming fire. Both main landing gear collapsed on first contact. The canopy shattered. The F-104's fuselage dragged along the runway for over two hundred feet, then took to the air again, sailing madly down the runway for another eighteen hundred feet.

Both pilots ejected, but only one survived. "Lawrence's shattered body landed seventy-five feet from the wreck," Phelps wrote. "He was still strapped in his ejection seat. His chest was crushed; his heart lacerated."

Had things not gone so horribly wrong that day, Lawrence would surely have made it through the astronaut-training program. Would he have been aboard the flight of *Apollo 11,* however, with which the United States first touched down on the moon in 1969? It would have been very risky business for NASA to include him on that mission. Among those gung-ho for this nation to have a man on the moon were many who had a serious problem with a black man playing a role in that dream. As one such person put it in a letter to Lawrence's widow: "I'm glad he's dead. We don't want no coon on the moon!"

Nearly thirty years after the crash of the *Starfighter,* the U.S. Air Force officially recognized Lawrence as an astronaut, which is how black America had always regarded him. Once his official status changed, the Astronaut Memorial Foundation board of directors voted to include his name on the Kennedy Space Center's Space Mirror, a memorial to astronauts who died in the line of duty. The ceremony was held on December 8, 1997, the thirtieth anniversary of his death.

Amiri Baraka (1934–)

"MY POETRY is whatever I think I am. . . . I CAN BE ANYTHING I CAN. I make poetry with what I feel is useful & can be saved out of all the garbage of our lives." This passage from the essay "How You Sound??" (1959) is most telling and typical of the electricity, eccentricity, and wit of Amiri Baraka, one of the most prolific writer–provocateurs: His writings include more than forty plays and screenplays, some twenty-five volumes of poetry, and six collections of essays, on top of editing about a dozen books. This passage, as well, speaks to the man's mutability, captured in the title of an essay by cultural critic Greg Tate, "Growing Up in Public: Amiri Baraka Changes His Mind."

Amiri Baraka was born Everett LeRoy Jones in Newark, New Jersey. This son of a middle-income family graduated with honors from Barringer High School in 1951. After a brief stint at Rutgers University—during which time he frenched his name to LeRoi—he enrolled in Howard University. After he was expelled in 1954, he propelled himself into the Air Force. Looking back on this period of his life, he would one day write, "the Howard thing let me understand the Negro sickness. They teach you how to pretend to be white. But the Air Force made me understand the white sickness. It shocked me into realizing what was happening to me and others."

After his discharge ("undesirably") from the service in 1957, the twenty-three-year-old headed for New York's Bohemian enclave, Greenwich Village, and into the literary lair of avant-garde Beat poets Allen Ginsburg, Frank O'Hara, and Charles Olson, among others. Under the influence of the Beatniks and their anti-white-middle-class mentality and mores, he began work on his first book of experimental poetry, *Preface to a Twenty Volume Suicide Note* (1961).

A trip to Cuba in 1960 was a (re)defining moment for Jones. There, through his encounter with artists–revolutionaries, he awakened to the concept of art as agent of change, as political weapon. Thus began his disenchantment with his circle of liberal white and integration-minded black rebels without a cause. As he wrote in his essay "Cuba Libre," "The rebels among us have become merely people like myself who grow beards and will not participate in politics. Drugs, juvenile delinquency, complete isolation from vapid mores of the country, a few current ways out. But name an alternative here."

For all his angst, his break with the Beats was not immediate, but its imminence was evident in the more racially focused and high-voltage writings of what has been termed his "Transitional Period" (1963–1965), during which time he produced two of his best known works: *Blues People: Negro Music in America,* a seminal study of black music from slavery to the 1960s, and *The Dutchman,* which won the 1964 Obie Award for best Off-Broadway play. He wrote the play in a blaze. "Yeah, I wrote [*Dutchman*] in one night," he said in an interview with William Jelani Cobb, which appeared in the November 1994 issue of *Quarterly Black Review of Books.*

> I think I came home at maybe 10 and wrote to about four or five in the morning and just put it down on the desk. When I woke up, I read it again. I didn't really understand a lot of it. It was a kind of laser from the inner mind. It was something I was releasing. It turned out to be very, very critical to my understanding of where I was at the time. I remember the night that the play was produced. About two in the morning I went to this store that stayed open all night. At the time there were a lot of newspapers in New York and I stood there reading all of them. In every one of them they were saying how crazy I was. Sick. But what I could see is that they were really concerned about this. Whoever this Negro was, he was saying some dangerous things. I said "I see, they're going to make me famous." This is very story-like but it's very true. At that point it came to me. I said if they make me famous, I'm going to make them pay for all the stuff I know. Up to that point I had been an anonymous little Negro blood living in the Village, hanging out and being irresponsible. But now that they're going to make my name known, I'm going to say all the things I think need to be said for all the people I know. People very close to me like my grandfather, grandmother. People think they can bring you up to a level and make you compromise your world view, but it had the opposite effect on me.

In the mid-1960s, this brilliant man found the "alternative" for which he'd been searching. Its name was cultural nationalism. His radical change of mind-set was triggered by the assassination of **Malcolm X** (1965), following which he left the Village (and his Jewish wife) and moved up to Harlem (and shortly thereafter, back to Newark) to set about the business of nation building. He emerged as one of the chief architects of the Black Arts Movement and, as critic William J. Harris put it, "the main artist–intellectual responsible for shifting the emphasis of contemporary black literature from an integrationist art . . . to a literature rooted in the black experience." Among his numerous concrete contributions to this cause was his founding in 1965 of the Black Arts Repertory Theatre and School in Harlem, the catalyst for scores of community black theaters around the nation. There was also the anthology *Black Fire* (1968), coedited with Larry Neal; *Black Magic* (1969), his first collection of black nationalist poetry, and *Raise Race Rays*

Raze (1971); among other literary productions. The most obvious declaration of his nationalist stance was his taking (in 1967) of the Bantu-ized Muslim name Imamu (spiritual) Ameer (blessed) Baraka (prince), amended to Amiri Baraka.

In the mid-1970s, Baraka split the nationalist scene, deeming it misguided. As he now saw it, the primary enemy of his people, and by extension all the wretched of the earth, was not the white man per se, but the thing that makes oppression a sine qua non: capitalism. On the heels of this revelation, Baraka converted to "the science of Marxist–Leninist–Mao Tse-tung thought," a.k.a., Third World Socialism. Despite his change of politics, Baraka continued to write primarily to and about his people because he continued to believe in their great revolutionary potential. Through all Baraka's changes of mind, he has been consistent in this: He's remained maverick; he's remained boundless—one of the most captivating and complex works-in-progress.

A huge chunk of Baraka's life can be reviewed in his 1984 book (called "brilliant" by Arnold Rampersad) *The Autobiography of LeRoi Jones.* For a rich taste of his poetry, there's *Transbluesency: The Selected Poems of Amiri Baraka/LeRoi Jones (1961–1995),* edited by Paul Vangelisti.

Tommie Smith (1944–)
and
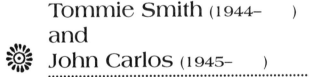# John Carlos (1945–)

Whether they articulated it or not, whether they fully believed it or not, African Americans who competed in the Olympics have had the entire "nation within a nation" behind them. When they won gold, silver, and bronze medals, the whole race felt crowned.

George Coleman Poage made us victors in St. Louis in 1904 and John Baxter Taylor in London in 1908. Six others did it in 1924 and in 1932. In Berlin, in 1936, Jesse Owens stole the show with his four golds, overshadowing the other nine African American winners (eight in track and field, one in boxing), and annoying the hell out of Hitler. Who knows how many medalists we would have had but for the war. After that, however, weight lifter John Davis and Floyd Patterson, Bill Russell, Cassius Clay, Joe Frazier, Bob Hayes, and Hayes Jones were among the nearly ninety African American Olympic medalists of 1948–1964.

In 1968, at the Nineteenth Olympiad, in Mexico City, Mexico, track stars Tommie Smith, a native of Texas, and John Carlos, a Harlemite, were among black America's champions. Smith won the gold and John

Carlos the bronze in the 200-meter-dash finals. These two brothers gave the more militant something else to hurrah. As Smith later described it,

> I wore a black right-hand glove and Carlos wore the left-hand glove of the same pair. My raised hand stood for the power in black America. Carlos' raised left hand stood for the unity of black America. Together they formed an arch of unity and power. The black scarf around my neck represented the brutal lynchings of people who gave their lives for such an opportunity as this. The black sock with no shoes stood for black poverty in racist America. The totality of our effort was the regaining of black dignity.

This was in October of 1968, the year of the student takeover of an administration building at Howard University to protest certain administrators and to push for black studies. It was the year that students at South Carolina College in Orangeburg peacefully protesting a segregated bowling alley were killed (three) and wounded (many) by police. It was the year Ralph Abernathy led the Poor People's March because King had been assassinated weeks before. It was the year that Huey P. Newton was convicted of manslaughter in Oakland; that James Baldwin, at the World Council of Churches convention in Geneva, Switzerland, took clergy to task for doing nothing about the black plight; and that Albert P. Cleage's *The Black Messiah*, Eldridge Cleaver's *Soul on Ice*, and Julius Lester's *Look Out Whitey! Black Power's Gon' Get Your Mama* were published. It was also the year folks first heard James Brown's "Black Is Beautiful: Say It Loud, I'm Black and I'm Proud."

The year before had been just as full. It was in 1967 that King went public with his opposition to American involvement in the conflict in Viet-

Tommie Smith and John Carlos taking a stand at the 1968 Olympics. (Courtesy of Photographs and Prints Division, Schomburg Center for Research in Black Culture, The New York Public Library, Astor, Lenox and Tilden Foundations)

nam; that riots and rebellions rocked Detroit, Chicago, and Newark; that a Black Power Conference was convened in Newark; that Muhammad Ali was stripped of his heavyweight title for refusing draft induction; and that John A. Williams's *The Man Who Cried I Am* was published.

It was also in 1967 that Harry Edwards, professor of sociology at San Jose State, where John Carlos was a student, formed the group that became the Olympic Committee for Human Rights. The point was to get black athletes to boycott the 1968 Olympics to protest racism in sports, racism in America. There was no groundswell of support for the boycott, but various individuals managed symbolic gestures—like standing on the victory stand in black-socked feet, and bowing their heads as they raised arms at the end of which were clenched fists in black gloves—and this, during the singing of the national anthem.

Tommie Smith and John Carlos could forget about ever again competing in the Olympics, and you can bet no contracts for product endorsements came their way. Back home, they were hounded, pilloried, and suffered deep personal losses, including their wives (Carlos's to suicide). Still, they rose. After earning his master's degree in sociology, in 1972 Tommie Smith joined the faculty of Oberlin College, as assistant athletic director and physical education instructor. In 1978, he joined the physical education department (as a teacher and track and field coach) at Santa Monica College. As for John Carlos, he had a brief career in professional football and worked for the International Track Association from 1973 to 1975. In 1984, he had another taste of the Olympics as a special assistant for the United States Olympic Committee.

NEWS BITS

In 1968, the year Smith and Carlos took a stand, . . .

- According to a *New York Times* poll, 59% of "Negroes" polled said they preferred to be called "Afro-American" or "black" to being called "Negro."

- Nine blacks, the most since Reconstruction, were elected to the U.S. Congress.

- President Lyndon B. Johnson signed the Fair Housing Act (the Civil Rights Act of 1968).

- Arthur Ashe became the first black man to win the U.S. Open and was ranked the number-one tennis player in the world.

- O. J. Simpson won the Heisman Trophy.

- A total of thirty-two African Americans won medals at the 1968

Olympics. These included Bob Beamon (a gold for long jump with his leap of 29' 2-1/2"), a world record not broken for years); the 1964 winner of a gold and a silver in track, Wyomia Tyus (three golds), and members of the U.S. basketball team, Calvin Forbes, Spencer Haywood, James King, Charlie Scott, and Jo Jo White.

 ## Curt Flood (1938–1997)

Curt Flood had been passionate about America's favorite pastime ever since his boyhood days in Oakland, California. Truly, he dearly loved baseball. It became his vocation in 1956 when, straight out of high school, he signed with the Cincinnati Reds. There came a day when the bondage became unbearable, however.

In early October 1969, Curt Flood found out that his team, the St. Louis Cardinals, was trading him to the Philadelphia Phillies. At that point, this spectacular outfielder had been with the Cardinals for more than a decade, and he'd won seven consecutive Golden Glove Awards and had been a major factor in the team's three National League pennants and two World Series victories. Truly, he had served the St. Louis ball club very well. Despite his outstanding outfielding, he was now being shipped out, with no say whatsoever. The thing was, what the St. Louis Cardinals team was doing was perfectly legal because of the reserve clause in players' contracts, which made them the exclusive property of a team, to do with as it pleased.

Flood had been traded before; that's how he got from the Reds to the Cardinals. He was older now, however, and he was stronger now, and living in 1969, when increasing numbers of people had freedom on their minds. "After twelve years in the major leagues," wrote Flood to baseball commissioner Bowie Kuhn, "I do not feel that I am a piece of property to be bought and sold irrespective of my wishes."

In January 1970, Flood filed a suit against Kuhn, the heads of the National and American Leagues, and the twenty-four clubs under their wings at the time. The core contention was that the reserve clause was a violation of antitrust laws. Flood got a great deal of support from his fellow baseball players, but not all of them had the courage to go public with it. Among those who did was Richie "Dick" Allen, who said, "Curt Flood's doing a marvelous thing for baseball, and many people don't know it." The legendary Jackie Robinson, by then retired from baseball fourteen years and quite sour on his once-beloved sport, remarked, "I think Curt is doing a service to all baseball players in the major leagues."

Curt lost his suit, appealed, lost again, appealed again—to the United States Supreme Court, losing again, in a 5-to-3 decision (with Thurgood Marshall among the dissenters).

Flood really did do "a marvelous thing" for baseball and a "service to all baseball players," however. His suit was a catalyst for Major League baseball's first general strike in 1972 (while Flood's case was with the Supreme Court). His suit impelled others to protest the reserve clause. Its nullification in 1975 created the free agency (and the crazy money) players enjoy today. Not surprisingly, Curt Flood, who told about it in his autobiography *The Way It Was* (1971), became a major persona non grata in baseball.

When Curt Flood died in 1997, his fans waited for a corps of superstar ball players to, in some stellar way, pay their respects to the man who paved the way for their financial success. The wait was, however, in vain.

Fred Hampton (1948–1969)

Four gunshot wounds—two to the head—he never knew what hit him, never got out of bed. A menace to society, rabble rouser, cur—that's how Chicago cops saw the twenty-one-year-old who was killed on an early December morning in 1969. The five-thousand people who attended Fred Hampton's funeral and the thousands who mourned from afar knew better, however. They knew, too, that his death was a loss for the liberation movement.

Fred Hampton, who was raised in the Chicago suburb of Maywood, had shown signs of being a prize early on. In high school, he was a stellar student and athlete who had plans to cap his education with law school. That was the course he was charting when he entered a junior college in Illinois in 1966.

His community called, however, and he became president of the NAACP's youth chapter in Maywood, proving himself a whip when it came to raising membership and campaigning for better educational and recreational opportunities for disadvantaged young people. Soon, another organization attracted Hampton: the Black Panther Party for Self-Defense, organized in 1966 by Huey P. Newton and Bobby Seale, students at Merrit Junior College in Oakland, California.

"We want freedom. We want power to determine the destiny of our Black Community. . . . We want full employment for our people. . . . We want an end to the robbery by the white man of our Black Community. . . . We want decent housing, fit for shelter of human beings. . . . We want education for our people that exposes the true nature of this decadent American society. We want education that teaches our true history and our role in the present-day society. . . . We want an immediate end to POLICE BRUTALITY and MURDER of black people. . . ." These are some of the lead-ins to the Black Panther Party's ten-point Platform and Program.

In the fall of 1968, Fred Hampton organized the Illinois chapter of the Black Panther Party. Under his leadership, this chapter was soon bearing good fruit, including a truce among black, Hispanic, and white street gangs in Chicago, intended not just to stop the violence but also to transform toughs into agents of social change. Like other Black Panther Party chapters, the Chicago chapter established a health clinic, a free breakfast program for children, and other needed operations for the poor.

All that was good about the Panthers was shoved into shadow by negative press. In the minds of many, it was nothing but a posse of thugs. Good works and good intentions were sabotaged by the FBI's COINTELPRO: from misinformation on the group to instigating riffs among members through its planted agents. The FBI's efforts to destroy the Panthers were aided by police harassment, which included frequent raids on their headquarters.

Fred Hampton's headquarters (and home), a first-floor apartment at 2337 Monroe Street on Chicago's Southside, was subjected to several police raids. The ultimate assault came on December 4, 1969, around 5 A.M., when Hampton and five others were asleep. Search and seizure of illegal guns was allegedly the police officers' only intent, but the police claimed that their knock on the door was met by shots from within, leaving the corps of Chicago's finest no recourse but to shoot back, and with fury. An investigation later revealed how false a report this was.

Ballistic tests showed that only one shot had been fired from within the apartment, while some one-hundred slugs found inside and outside the apartment had come from the guns of police officers. Not one police officer suffered a bullet wound, but every one of the Panthers did. Blair Anderson, Verlina Brewer, Ronald "Doc" Satchel, and Hampton's pregnant girlfirend Brenda Harris, who ranged in age from seventeen to nineteen, were seriously wounded and all shot more than once. Mark Clark, a Panther from Peoria, was shot to death—as was Fred Hampton: four gunshot wounds, two to the head.

The reason Fred Hampton never knew what hit him, never got out of bed, came to light in the late 1970s during the civil suit that survivors of the raid brought against the police department. The same African American FBI informant, William O'Neal, who had provided the police with floor plans of the apartment had slipped Fred Hampton a heavy sedative the night before the raid.

✺ Blood

By the time the United States had both feet in another military monstrosity that was technically never a war, loads of brothers were convinced that no matter how heartily they served Uncle Sam, they'd never get their due on the home front. "Man, I ain't got no quarrel with them Vietcong," declared heavyweight boxing champion of the world, Cassius Clay/Muhammad Ali. "Solid," said other brothers, and many lit out for Canada and Mexico and America Underground, some advancing Black Power plans, others just watching weeds.

Blood, however, he went to boot camp. He, Blood, hardly knew what was going on: no connections, no raised consciousness, no equal opportunities at home. A high school diploma and maybe a 'fro was about all he had. He was seventeen or eighteen when he went: from Harlem, Chicago, Roxbury, Detroit, Houston, East St. Louis, L.A., Nashville, Newark.

Then one day he's Manchild in Asian Jungle, spending more time doing menial stuff and frontline fighting than white grunts did. He had to stomach cross burnings and Confederate flags and Yahoos when news came that **Martin Luther King, Jr.** was dead. He faced enemies on all sides, with the VC taunting, "Soulman, is you crazy, why you doing the white man's bidding, don't you see who's filling up so many bodybags?"

Blood had to commingle with all that gutsy grenade and bullet stuff, to riddle old folks and children, too, on command, out of fear. *You're in the army now.* He probably did not know how to spell the word *celibacy*, let alone contemplate the concept, so he found himself groping for catch-as-catch-can foreign poontang, risking VD and the seeding of a life that would be called "Freak."

He lost an arm or a leg or got shrapnel in his face. Touches of his mind clipped away, too. What a friend he had in opium. Maybe. Is this what manhood has to offer, baby?

He came home with a limp in his soul, a loving feeling for a gun, and the need for camouflage. Too many nightmare memories: Private Calloway's half head, Private Johnson's blown-away johnson, Private Wilkins somewhere tortured—and the children's screams, and the blood and guts splattered on the trees, and—

He came home to not much: piece o' job, here and there, school's a balloon, and girlfriend or wife saying, "Blood, you bugged."

"But, baby, I didn't mean to knock you outta the bed. Least I didn't grab my gun this time."

His girlfriend or wife says, "Blood, I'm outta here," and—

He came home to be spit upon and labeled a louse by dungaree-wearing mini-intellectuals pseudoconversant in Marx and Mao and Timothy Leary, who had spent spring days making love (not WAR!) while he was dragging bloodied, muddied brothers and hillbillies to the rear in the rain, without rhetoric.

Not every black man had Blood's experience. Many who served in Vietnam (Colin Powell, most notably) went on to have glorious careers in the military and others to successes in civilian hires or self-started enterprises. However, thousands were way less fortunate. Thousands were Blood, filing into the ranks of the homeless.

BOOK MARK

- *A Hero's Welcome: The Conscience of Sergeant James Daly versus the United States Army*, by James Daly (1975)

- *Bloods: An Oral History of the Vietnam War by Black Veterans*, by Wallace Terry (1984; updated edition, 1992)

- *Brothers: Black Soldiers in Nam*, by Clark Smith (1985)

- *GI Diary*, by David Parks (1968)

- *Just Before Dawn: A Doctor's Experiences in Vietnam*, by Fenton Williams (1971)

- *Memphis—Nam—Sweden: The Autobiography of a Black American Exile*, by Terry Whitmore (1971)

- *The Courageous and the Proud*, by Samuel Vance (1970)

- *Thoughts about the Vietnam War*, by Eddie Wright (1984)

- *Yet Another Voice*, by Norman A. McDaniel (1975)

 # Arthur Ashe (1943–1993)

"If one's reputation is a possession, then of all my possessions, my reputation means most to me." This is how Arthur Ashe opened his memoir *Days of Grace*, co-authored with Arnold Rampersad and published not long after the tennis great passed away.

Reputation. This son of Richmond, Virginia, this son of a loving mother who died when he was six and a father he described as a "strong, dutiful, providing man," Arthur Ashe did indeed cherish a good thing—and grace is the centerpiece of his reputation.

Grace: on the court and under that palpable pressure of daring to play "a white man's game," daring to dream of winning, winning, winning, and doing just that so many times—and in the top tournaments of tennis: the U.S. Open in 1968 (a first for a black man); the Australian Open in 1970; Wimbledon in 1975. Not a clown or peacock did he become. This man with a degree in business and a love for poetry and fine art comported himself as a gentleman.

Grace: when, in 1979, a heart attack followed by a quadruple bypass operation forced him to say farewell to competing. Not a lazy, sad sack did he become, lounging on past laurels. He stayed with the game as he could, as a journalist, as a commentator, as captain of the U.S. Davis Cup Team from 1981 to 1985.

Grace: when in 1983 he had to have a second heart operation.

Grace: when in 1988 he discovered that through blood transfusions administered during this second surgery he had contracted the HIV virus, and in fact had full-blown AIDS. There was also brain surgery in 1988.

Grace: when in April 1992 the merciless in the media decided that the public *had to know* about Arthur Ashe's illness, and he was faced with having *USA Today* tell his business or—so it was that on an April afternoon in 1992 the curious, the concerned, and the confused watched the news conference he held. As Ashe recounted in *Days of Grace*, after plainly confirming that, yes, he had AIDS, he addressed the next pressing question: Why hadn't he gone public when he discovered this four years earlier?

> The answer is simple: Any admission of HIV infection at that time would have seriously, permanently, and—my wife and I believed—unnecessarily infringed upon our family's right to privacy. Just as I am sure that everybody in this room has some personal matter he or she would like to keep private, so did we. There was certainly no compelling medical or physical necessity to go public with my medical condition. I have had it on good authority that my status was common knowledge in the medical community, and I am truly grateful to all of you—medical and otherwise—who knew but either didn't even ask me or never made it public. What I actually came to feel about a year ago was that there was a silent conspiracy to assist me in maintaining my privacy. That has meant a great deal to me and Jeanne and Camera.

At this point, Ashe could feel his "emotions bubbling and surging to the surface," all the more when his thoughts turned to his daughter Camera, then just a child. So he asked his wife, photographer Jeanne

Moutoussamy-Ashe, to finish the statement. Picking up where he left off, his wife read his comments about their daughter, which included, "Even though we've begun preparing Camera for this news, beginning tonight, Jeanne and I must teach her how to react to new, different, and sometimes cruel comments that have little to do with her reality."

Arthur Ashe is not remembered as a tennis champion who died of AIDS, but as a man possessing a grace larger than mere graciousness. During his celebrity and during his sufferings, he gave his time, energy, and money to an array of solid causes. The American Heart Association and the United Negro College Fund are among the organizations he supported. For many years hence, he served as cochair of TransAfrica Forum, the fund-raising arm of TransAfrica, the advocacy organization for Africa and the Caribbean founded by his boyhood friend **Randall Robinson.** In 1983 (the year of his second heart surgery), along with Harry Belafonte, Ashe founded Artists and Athletes Against Apartheid to rally people not to grace South Africa with their presence until that country stopped apartheid. It wasn't long after he found out that he had AIDS that Ashe began work on a comprehensive history of black athletes: the three-volume *A Hard Road to Glory* (a revised edition of which was published several months after his death). In 1992, the same year he began work on *Days of Grace,* he founded Safe Passage Foundation, an organization devoted to building up disadvantaged youth in the Newark, New Jersey, area, the highlight of which was a tennis program. Shortly after his press conference in April 1992, he founded the Arthur Ashe Foundation for the Defeat of AIDS, which was to be global in its endeavors.

These are just some of the ways that Ashe, in days of triumph, in days of defeat, gave back, lifted up, and motivated others to do likewise. These are some of the reasons that multitudes around the world who do not care a flick for tennis regard Arthur Ashe as a champion in the most meaningful sense of the word.

 # Reginald F. Lewis (1942–1993)

Reginald Francis Lewis, born on the first anniversary of the "day that will live in infamy," embodied the Zeitgeist of the 1980s, captured so well in the film *Wall Street,* particularly when the character played by Michael Douglas proclaimed "Greed is good!" Money, money, money was the mantra of the decade, and this business-savvy son of East Baltimore's working-class made lots of it—for himself and legions of others.

Straight out of Harvard Law School in 1968, Lewis joined a prime New York law firm, Paul Weiss Rifkind Wharton & Garrison. A few years later, he formed Lewis & Clarkson, the first black law firm on Wall

Street and one that was to specialize in raising venture capital for small and midsize companies. A decade later, Lewis created the investment firm The Lewis Company, soon known as TLC (and given the CEO's style, no one could think the acronym stood for tender loving care).

The purchase of the McCall Pattern Company for close to $23 million in 1984 really put TLC on the map. After TLC refashioned McCall and sold it in 1987 for $65 million, Lewis was proclaimed a genius and became a god to many who worshiped at the altar of Mo' Money—but the best was yet to come.

The $985 million leveraged buyout of Beatrice International Foods, a conglomerate with upward of sixty companies in some thirty nations, was Lewis's deal of deals, which he masterminded in 1987 with help on the financing from Drexel Burnham Lambert's Michael Milken, who soon after made news as a criminal. With the acquisition of Beatrice (with annual revenue in excess of 1.5 billion), Lewis was serious major news and clearly the leader of the pack of a new breed of black entrepreneurs: those who re-created, as opposed to created, entities the very old-fashioned way and in so doing were able to turn a profit more quickly, highly, boldly. TLC became the largest black-owned company in the United States, giving more than a few Fortune 500 companies a run for their money.

By the early 1990s, Reginald Lewis's personal worth was an estimated $400 million. Through The Lewis Foundation, several of these millions went to a range of charities, social and civic organizations, and educational institutions, a good deal of them black. The donation that made the most news was the $3 million to Harvard Law School for the establishment of the Reginald F. Lewis Fund for International Study and Research. With this gift, Lewis became the donor of the largest single gift Harvard had ever received, and The Lewis Center became the first Harvard building to bear the name of black person. These Lewis landmarks filled a lot of black people with great pride, as it symbolized, they thought, that "we" have arrived. Lewis's fortunes could do nothing but keep rising, everyone was sure. The wheeling and dealing came to an end, however, when he was seized by brain cancer, dying a month after his fiftieth birthday. Prior to his death, Lewis had been working on his autobiography, passages of which were incorporated into Blair S. Walker's authorized biography of the titan, *"Why Should White Guys Have All the Fun?": How Reginald Lewis Created a Billion-Dollar Business Empire.*

Lewis's death was quite a shocker, a huge loss for black America. The way the media controlled by white people handled Lewis's death was, as Ishmael Reed pointed out, a reminder, a wake-up call about the way it is. Reed expressed these thoughts in the essay "Reginald Lewis," collected in Reed's *Airing Dirty Laundry* (1993). Wrote Reed,

I was waiting for these [major] networks to comment about the death of Reginald Lewis—the richest black man in America and head of a multinational corporation. . . . His death, however, was virtually ignored. I found this strange, because blacks are always getting a scolding from places like the *New Republic* and the *New York Times* op-ed page about their lack of the work ethic. Yet when a man who epitomized stable Protestant ethics died, the network shows typically handed black children buffoonish entertainers and athletes as role models, while ignoring Reginald Lewis, who gave millions of dollars to cultural and educational enterprises. . . .

Reginald Lewis is a hero, not only for scaling the heights of the business world—going where no black man had ever gone before (it must have been lonely)—but also for showing abundant generosity toward Americans both black and white, and for revealing a very important truth: that the powerful white Americans who control the equipment upon which most Americans rely for information don't want blacks to lose and don't want blacks to win. Another reason **Chester Himes** was right-on when he said that to live in a racist society is to live in a situation of comic absurdity—and, I might add, a situation of irony and paradox.

NEWS BITS

In 1987, the year that Reginald F. Lewis bought Beatrice International, . . .

- Brigadier General Fred A. Gorden became the first black commandant of cadets at West Point, where Johnson Chesnutt Whittaker was savaged a little more than a hundred years earlier.

- Bo Diddley was inducted into the Rock and Roll Hall of Fame.

- Willie D. Burton became the first black to win an Oscar for Sound, for *Bird,* about the jazz innovator Charlie Parker.

- Walter E. Massey became the first black president of the American Association for the Advancement of Science.

- Ben Carson, who at age thirty-three became director of pediatric surgery at Johns Hopkins Hospital in Baltimore, Maryland, became an internationally known miracle worker for the major role he played in the five-month planning and twenty-two-hour execution of the first successful separation of Siamese twins joined at the back of the head.

- Kurt Schmoke became the first black elected mayor of Baltimore.

- Harold Washington was reelected mayor of Chicago but died of a heart attack six months into his second term.

- Jesse Jackson announced that he would once again seek the Democratic Party's nomination for president.

- August Wilson's *Fences* won the Pulitzer Prize for Drama and four Tonys: for best play, best director, best performance by an actor (James Earl Jones), and best performance by a featured actress (Mary Alice).

 # Matel Dawson, Jr. (1921–   )

"Here's her Oseola McCarty"—that's what my friend Ronda Racha Penrice said she was thinking one late fall 1997 day as she clipped an article about Matel Dawson, Jr. Ronda, then a graduate student at the University of Mississippi, had been on the lookout for interesting subjects for the book you are now reading. A big fan of Oseola McCarty, the eighty-seven-year-old washerwoman from Hattiesburg, Mississippi, who donated $150,000 to the University of Southern Mississippi in 1995, Ronda had always known there were lots of McCartys out there. The article about Dawson was terrific affirmation—and I am so glad she mailed it to me.

"An Extraordinary Ordinary Gentleman" was the headline of the article on Matel Dawson, Jr., by the award-winning journalist Wallace Terry, author of *Bloods: An Oral History of the Vietnam War by Black Veterans.* This piece, which appeared in the November 9, 1997, issue of *Parade* magazine began,

> "As soon as you see someone in need of a helping hand, you should come to his rescue," says Matel Dawson Jr. "Somebody had to help me one day. Why shouldn't I return that help to someone else? If you only have a little to help others, give what you can. Sharing money, giving my help, makes me feel good. And it gives me peace of mind."
>
> Matel Dawson Jr. is an extraordinary ordinary gentleman. Now 76, he has worked at the Ford Motor Co. since 1940—long past the time he could have taken a 30-year retirement. On the salary of a rigger–forklift driver, he has managed to donate more than $800,000 to colleges, churches and charities since 1991.

How did this blue-collar brother come up with enough money to have $800,000 to give away? An inheritance? The numbers? No, buddy, he did it by saving and investing his savings in strong stocks.

Investing came relatively late in his life (in 1977), but saving was something this son of cotton farmers in Shreveport, Louisiana, had been doing all his life. As Terry reported, when Dawson, the fifth of seven children, was seventeen, he had forty bucks in the bank—no pittance in 1938, and no small feat considering that he was employed as a drugstore's delivery boy for $7.50 a week and that a chunk of his earnings went into his family's pot. His family's poverty was the reason he had dropped out of school after the eighth grade and had entered the work world.

It was from his parents, Bessie and Matel, Sr., that Dawson learned about industry and thrift. "His mother made her children's clothes and was taking in laundry well into her 60s," wrote Wallace Terry. "His father built their home, raised vegetables and chickens, and worked several jobs to keep his family together through the Depression." Said Dawson of his father: "I had a lot of respect for him." And we are in awe of Junior, are we not?

When Terry interviewed the 76-year-old working man, Dawson was on the 7 A.M.–3 P.M. shift, and doing lots of overtime, clocking no less than forty-eight hours a week and sometimes sixty, with his wages at about $23 an hour. The divorcé of twenty years was living in a modest one-bedroom apartment in Detroit. His leisure pursuits were low budget: watching television (especially baseball and movies), reading books (especially history).

Since the day he started at Ford in 1940 (earning $1.15 an hour), Dawson had been giving back: standing in the gap when his parents, siblings, or other kin were in need. In time, strangers became his family. "I wanted to give back to society." That's how he explained the impetus of his first five-figure gift: $30,000 to the Detroit office of the United Negro College Fund, with another $20,000 soon to follow. "Some say I'm crazy for giving this kind of money away," Dawson told Terry, "but we need to support black students, black colleges. Education is the key to success. What else could I do as a black man?"

As Terry reported, not all Dawson's giving is color coded. In 1996, for example, he donated $200,000 to Wayne State University's scholarship fund, with no stipulation about race or region or anything. At the same time, he also gave $30,000 to that university's Keith Collection, a repository of information on black lawyers and judges. The $100,000 he gave to Louisiana State University (in honor of his parents) in 1997 was earmarked simply for scholarships. When Terry interviewed Dawson, this man had plans to double that gift to LSU.

What drives Matel Dawson, Jr., to such generosity? "I'm on a mission to fulfill my parents' dream," he told Wallace Terry. "They wanted me to be something, to stand for something."

☸ Tom Feelings (1933–   )

Art was always on his mind, ever since his boyhood days in the Bedford-Stuyvesant section of Brooklyn, New York. At George Westinghouse Vocational School, he concentrated on graphic art. At the School of Visual Arts, his focus was cartooning and illustration. There was a hole in his education from 1953 to 1957, time he spent in the Air Force, but even there, he stayed with art, serving as a graphic artist.

In 1958, two years before Feelings graduated from the School of Visual Arts, the *New York Age* began running his comic strip "Tommy Traveler in the World of Negro History," and people went traveling along with a boy hungry for history, and whose reading led to dreamtime encounters with history makers. (This bright boy was to have his own book in 1991: *Tommy Traveler in the World of Black History,* where he'd meet **Frederick Douglass, Crispus Attucks,** and Joe Louis, among others.)

Traveling into his culture and history was always on Feelings's mind, more keenly later on than before. During his years of freelancing in America, he was awake and alive to the hopes and prides of the civil-rights movement and became more absorbed in the challenge and the rapture of portraying the beautiful truths of his people. His horizons broadened during the two years in the mid-1960s he spent in Ghana, where he worked as an illustrator for Ghana's Government Printing House and for the *African Review.* The bounties of the black world made a deeper impression on his soul in the early 1970s, during the few years he spent in Guyana working for its Ministry of Education as an art instructor and director of a children's book project.

Yes, children were always on his mind, black children who saw so little of themselves, their cultures, in books. Among the books for young readers Feelings illustrated in the 1970s and 1980s (and which

One of the paintings from *Middle Passage,* rendered in pen and ink and tempera on rice paper. (© 1995 Tom Feelings)

garnered him numerous awards and honors) are *Zamani Goes to Market, Mojo Means One,* and *Jambo Means Hello,* all written by his first wife, Muriel Feelings; *To Be a Slave,* written by Julius Lester; and *Daydreamers,* by Eloise Greenfield.

Along with illustrating more books for young readers, Feelings gave us books for readers of all ages. Take, for example, *Now Sheba Sings the Song* (1987), a collection of more than eighty sepia-toned portraits of girls and women, drawn from life on the spot in Africa, and in South and North America, portraits connected by a poem by Maya Angelou. Take *Soul Looks Back in Wonder* (1993), a selection of vibrant paintings featuring girls and boys—knowing, piercing, daring, dreaming, seeking—each artwork accompanied by a gem from a poet (Lucille Clifton, Mari Evans, Darryl Holmes, and Eugene B. Redmond, among them).

There's also the book immediately hailed a masterpiece when published in 1995: *The Middle Passage: White Ships/Black Cargo,* composed of more than sixty wide, inescapable black-and-white paintings. The scenes from the nightmare include a raid on an African village by bearded, white-robed men with rifles and men akin to the villagers with spears . . . coffles trudging, stumbling, dying in a drive to the coast, with scavengers circling above in an African sky the Africans will never see again . . . a fat, self-satisfied African king, savoring his compensation . . . black life crammed in the hideous hold of a ship . . . black bodies topside being aired, being bludgeoned, being force-fed, being whipped, and resisting the ship's ghastly crew.

"What happened to all of you when you were taken away from here?" This, wrote Feelings in his opening statement to *Middle Passage,* was a question from a Ghanaian friend in the mid-1960s. "As he continued to speak, muted images flashed across my mind. Pale white sailing ships like huge birds of prey, plunging forward into mountainous rising white foaming waves of cold water, surrounding and engulfing everything."

These and other images that flooded Feelings's mind led him to some daunting questions. For one, "Who would want to force himself emotionally in that horrible time to tell this story and risk the loss of sanity stepping back into what had to be the most agonizing experience for any black person alive?" It would take Feelings some twenty years to make the journey. Twenty years of watching the world turn as he went about making a living as an artist and a teacher of art.

Sketches here and there, fact-finding, bracing his soul, fighting fear of failure, drawing, redrawing, questioning, doubting, revising, fatiguing.

"Get up, go back to it, and start over again . . . because you are not doing this just for yourself." These words from his maternal grandmother came to Feelings in a feverish half-sleep.

Then one night I sat down and thought about all those artists and writers that I truly respected, like **John O. Killens,** Margaret Walker, Charles White, Paule Marshall, John Biggers . . . the ones who took the time, a long time, to finish their work in the only way they could . . . in their best way, even when it meant staying on the edge for long periods of time. And that calmed my fears.

What was the moral of the story? Feelings's statement in *Middle Passage* closed with this:

My struggle to tell this African story, to create this artwork as well as live creatively under any conditions and survive, as my ancestors did, embodies my particular heritage in this world. As the blues, jazz, and the spirituals teach, one must embrace all of life, both its pain and joy, creatively. Knowing this, I, *we,* may be disappointed, but never destroyed.

Randall Robinson (1941–   )

As was the case with many of his generation, Randall Robinson's early sightings of Africa were not pretty. As he recalled in his memoir *Defending the Spirit* (1998), "Africa when mentioned at all in my childhood, was almost invariably in a humiliating context. Yet it was the fountainhead of our people. Like it or not, we were indissolubly bound up with it by blood and history. But every white reference to Africa—in films, books, newspapers, and television—was negative, grossly and meanly so. Edgar Rice Burroughs saddled us with Tarzan, D. W. Griffith with *Birth of a Nation.* A tortured and damned people from a ridiculed continent. This was the lesson of my childhood South."

There were other lessons, too, however—lessons about pride and dignity, lessons that saved this Richmonder from deep self-hatred. These lessons were instilled through the words, deeds, and comportment of his parents: Maxie Cleveland, a history teacher and basketball coach at his school—"dutiful, rectitudinous Daddy"— and Doris Alma—"Mama of brilliance and academic achievement. Mama who lived an ethical and Christian life. Mama who loved her husband and children. Mama of grace and beauty."

Mr. and Mrs. Robinson constantly told their two daughters and two sons to think better of themselves than the white world did, and to strive. This, their children did, with the eldest, Maxie, Jr., becoming a journalist and making history as the first black network anchor, when in 1978 he joined ABC's *World News Tonight,* by which time he was known as Max Robinson. Randall would also do his parents proud after an exasperating period of aimlessness, which came to a head when he dropped out of college and opened himself up for induction into the army.

Robinson was posted at Fort Jackson, South Carolina, in the winter of 1963, and in the summer of 1965, Fort Benning, Georgia. It was there, in the fort's library, the place he often went "to escape the olive drab regimented hell," that he happened upon a book that would begin his epiphany. The book was E. R. Braithwaite's account of his journey to Africa, *A Kind of Homecoming,* "the first positive thing I had ever read about the continent that had produced everyone I loved and trusted."

After his discharge from the service (luckily with no time in Vietnam), Robinson completed his college education at Virginia Union and then entered Harvard Law School, where **Reginald F. Lewis** was plotting his course for the corporate world. On his way to earning his J.D., Robinson became increasingly "political." He also developed a greater curiosity about Africa.

A grant from the Ford Foundation enabled him to spend a year in Tanzania, where he conducted research on the Africanization of European law and its social impact on the population of Dar es Salaam. This was in 1970–1971. Being in the Tanzania of the noble Julius Nyerere was a watershed time. This kind of homecoming filled Robinson with a wider sense of pride. It also seeded the notion of devoting himself to helping Africa—and so he would, indefatigably.

Before he devoted himself to Africa, however, first came work as a civil-rights attorney for the Boston Legal Assistance Project in Roxbury, then the directorship of the community-development division of the Roxbury Multi-Service Center. In 1975, Robinson moved to the nation's Capital to work for Missouri Congressional Representative William L. Clay and then for Michigan's Charles Diggs, Jr., whom he accompanied to South Africa in 1976, as a member of a congressional delegation. Pretty soon after this trip, Robinson founded TransAfrica.

Since its inception in 1977, TransAfrica—a lobby for Africa, the Caribbean, and Latin America—has worked assiduously for a humane U.S. foreign policy toward dozens of nations and, in the process, greatly increased the American people's awareness of the First World's insensitive and sometimes criminal actions toward the Third World.

TransAfrica's accomplishments include mobilizing opposition to U.S. support of apartheid so successfully that the Anti-Apartheid Act of 1986 was passed despite then-President Reagan's veto. TransAfrica also helped to establish and coordinate the Free South Africa Movement and organized a yearlong protest in front of the South African Embassy, where more than five-thousand people were arrested, including Robinson's childhood friend **Arthur Ashe.** TransAfrica also spearheaded the struggle to maintain economic sanctions against

The resolute Randall Robinson. (Courtesy of Randall Robinson)

Rhodesia (now Zimbabwe) and mounted the largest speak-out against human-rights violations in Liberia, Zaire, Kenya, Haiti, Somalia, Sudan, and Ethiopia, among other nations.

The work that TransAfrica has done arose from the sorrows absorbed and risks taken by Randall Robinson. Here are a few such memories from *Defending the Spirit:*

> In May 1981, as Secretary of State Alexander Haig sat with South African foreign minister Roelof Botha on the seventh floor of the State Department to discuss a new era of friendship between the United States and South Africa, twenty-eight million black South Africans were completely without rights. . . .

> In December 1993, I had lunch at the White House with a high-ranking Clinton administration foreign policy official. "Randall, if we don't do something soon about Rwanda, it's going to blow sky-high. . . ."

> [April 1994]: I am in the nineteenth day of the hunger strike I have undertaken to protest American treatment of refugees fleeing Haiti. . . .

> It was a warm late spring day in 1995. I opened my fourth-floor Dupont Circle office window to catch the breeze. "Robinson! Mind your own business and stay out of Nigeria's!" Down below, a placard-bearing crowd of at least a hundred people circled in front of our building. . . . This was one of many demonstrations conducted at TransAfrica's headquarters by mercenaries whom the Nigerian mis-

sion to the United Nations gave a stipend of up to $300 per person for a day's work. . . .

On March 1, 1996, Congresswoman Maxine Waters and I held a meeting of African-American leaders and Caribbean ambassadors with Mickey Kantor, the U.S. trade representative, to discuss the growing threats to vital markets abroad for Caribbean agricultural exports. . . .

"Where does a black soul go to rest?" Robinson asked near the end of his memoir.

 # Jesse Jackson (1941–)

To my grandmother, Matilda, who in her lifetime will never read this book because she can neither read nor write—but who gave *me* encouragement to do so. To my mother, Helen Jackson, who, along with my grandmother, took me to church. To Charles Jackson who adopted me and gave me his name, his love, his encouragement, discipline, and a high sense of self-respect—who has since gone to be with God, but whose presence in my life assures me that heaven smiles upon our sincere efforts. Their love, concern, affection, sacrifice, and discipline helped, in my formative years, to shape my values.
Dedication to *Straight from the Heart* (1987)

When, in his hometown of Greenville, South Carolina, rheumy-eyed Mr. Sir or silver-haired Miss Ma'am needed a pair of sturdy eyes to read them the paper or a pair of strong limbs to run an errand or tote a bag or box, he was there.

When his family needed a child to do them proud, needed to show that growing up poor and branded "illegitimate" did not mean you could not be somebody—oh, yes, he was there: making the grades in grade school, being a junior achiever in junior high school, being a sterling student at Sterling High School, getting a football scholarship to the University of Illinois, having the guts to pass on this institution and transfer to North Carolina A&T, where he would have equal opportunity to play quarterback.

When, in the early 1960s, the student sit-in movement in Greensboro, North Carolina, needed another foot soldier, when the Congress of Racial Equality needed another braveheart, when **Martin Luther King, Jr.,** needed a youngblood to head up the Chicago Branch of SCLC's Operation Breadbasket, he, a student at Chicago Theological Seminary, was there.

He was there in Memphis, Tennessee, in 1968: there to help King help black sanitation workers; there at the Lorraine Motel when Martin was martyred. In the aftermath, he was there and there and there with King's blood still on his shirt—being dramatic when drama was the need of the hour.

In the early 1970s, at the onset of acute meism in America, when this nation needed a push in the progressive direction, needed people to get united to save humanity, he was there with Operation PUSH, and this:

> I am somebody
> I may be poor,
>   but I am somebody.
> I may be uneducated,
> I may be unskilled,
>   but I am somebody.
> I may be on welfare,
> I may be prematurely pregnant,
> I may be on drugs,
> I may be victimized by racism,
>   but I am somebody.
> Respect me. Protect me. Never neglect me.
> I am God's child.

He was there with more than singsong. As with Operation Breadbasket, with PUSH, he orchestrated boycotts of companies that wanted black dollars but wanted neither black bodies in their employ nor business relations with black businesses. Just as he had gotten A&P, Country Delight Dairy, and others to change their racist ways in the 1960s, now with PUSH, he got more companies to get on the good foot—Burger King, KFC, Coca-Cola, and General Foods, among others. Just as with Breadbasket, so with PUSH, he rallied for black business development, building on his initiation of the first Black Expo in 1969. PUSH also pressed for enrichment programs for youths underserved by public-school systems, pressed for corporations to make their Affirmative Action programs more than scraps of paper, pressed for justice abroad, especially in South Africa.

When, in the early 1980s, "the boats stuck at the bottom" needed somebody to make waves and needed to get reengaged with the political process, he was there to run for the presidency: there to raise voter registration, there to elevate the debate.

"What does Jesse want?" the snide or stupid asked, when the answer was there all along, and elementary: ABC—a better chance for the trammeled and marginalized. He made this so plain during his campaign, summing it up most memorably in his speech at the 1984

Democratic National Convention: "My constituency is the damned, the disinherited, the disrespected, and the despised." Before he said that, he said this:

> Tonight we come together, bound by our faith in a mighty God, with genuine respect and love for our country, and inheriting the legacy of a great party—the Democratic Party—which is the best hope for redirecting our nation on a more humane, just, and peaceful course. This is not a perfect party. We are not a perfect people. Yet we are called to a perfect mission: to feed the hungry, to clothe the naked, to house the homeless, to teach the illiterate, to provide jobs for the jobless, and to choose the human race over the nuclear race. We are gathered here this week to nominate a candidate and write a platform which will expand, unify, direct, and inspire our party and the nation to fulfill this mission.

He was there in the running again in 1988: this time with his Rainbow Coalition; this time garnering twice as many votes—seven million— as in 1984; this time being taken more seriously; this time capturing some concessions for his constituency from the Democratic Party and its contender William Jefferson Clinton.

In the 1990s, he didn't slow down. He kept on being there everywhere: for D.C. statehood; for hostages in Iraq (echoing his 1983 rescue of Robert Goodman from Syria); for victims of a fire at a rogue chicken-processing plant in North Carolina; for needy Gulf War veterans; for the Democratic Party; for **The Million Men;** for the dissed at Texaco; for Ebonics—yes, for him there is a there.

Blunders, bungles, goofs, stumbles—indeed, he has committed his share. Yet, given all that he has voiced and dared on behalf of millions he will never know, how could he not have a few blots? Plus, he's human. As to the claims that he has used causes as a causeway to personal gain and glory, are there not less dangerous, less trying ways to reach that endgame?

When the future retrospects on the late twentieth century, his presence will be greatly remembered, and folks will be hard-pressed to name a black man who has been more there for the lost and losing, in America and abroad, than Reverend Jesse Louis Jackson—and like heaven, they will smile broadly upon the abundance of his sincere efforts.

 Molefi Kete Asante (1942–   )

It is not enough to know; one must act to humanize: This is one of the principles that has long guided the man born Arthur L. Smith, Jr., the fourth child and the first son of Arthur and Lily Smith of Valdosta,

Georgia. His efforts to humanize the world include serving as president of the Student Nonviolent Coordinating Committee (SNCC) at UCLA, where he earned his Ph.D. in Communication in 1968. He continued his efforts by becoming an educator. For twelve years, he shared what he knew as a professor of Communication and African Studies at the State University of New York at Buffalo. Then in 1984, he took a professorship at Philadelphia's Temple University, where he established the first Ph.D. program in African American Studies and has since served as chair of the Department of Africology.

It was during a visit to Ghana in 1972 that Arthur L. Smith, Jr., changed his name. There, the paramount king of Asante, Opoku Ware II, gave him the last name Asante. Arthur took as a middle name Kete—"One Who Loves Music and the Dance." For his first name, in solidarity with the South African liberation struggle, he took a name from the Sotho language of southern Africa, Molefi—"Keeper of the Traditions."

Molefi Kete Asante is as much a keeper of the traditions as a creator of them, for he, one of the most prolific scholars of the late twentieth century, is the founder of the Afrocentric school of thought.

Afrocentricity is one of the most misunderstood and abused concepts in the world of ideas (along with *republic* and *democracy*). Contrary to what some well-intentioned, seeking souls think, Afrocentricity is not about merely casting off one's "European name" and wearing *kente* cloth. "The Afrocentric school of thought," says Asante, "places Africans at the center of any analysis of ideas, concepts, or people."

Molefi Kete Asante relishing African glories and potent possibilities. (Courtesy of Molefi Kete Asante)

This gives a handle to the concept, but some elucidation is still in order. One place to find it is in a conversation Asante had with Kim Pearson, professor of journalism and professional writing at The College of New Jersey. In this interview, which first appeared in the fall 1994 issue of *Quarterly Black Review of Books,* Pearson began with a very necessary question.

Q: What is Afrocentricity?

A: It's very simple. Afrocentricity is an orientation to data, which says that African people are ancient, and should be seen as agents, as subjects, in history, instead of as marginal players on the fringes of Europe. . . .

   If you don't see yourself as agent, you will always be a beggar people.

Q: What constitutes agency?

A: We have a number of ways of determining whether Africans are being seen as agents. For example, when evaluating texts, we can locate a writer easily. In classes, I have had students count: How many references to European writers are there? How many African sources? How does the writer critique and value these sources? In a novel, what figures of speech does a writer use? Are there flattering references to a character's "sharp" profile or to someone being, "as white as snow"?

   Or let's take a historical situation. Ray Winbush . . . says that when he studies the [U.S.] Constitutional Convention he doesn't just want to know what Thomas Jefferson was saying. What were the Africans who were there saying? What were Jefferson's horsemen, the cooks, etc., saying?

Q: In your writings, you make reference to the African cultural character. What is that?

A: We can look at either historical or contemporary accounts. When Europeans talk about their cultural character, they refer back to the Greeks, whom they associate with rationality, or Rome, for its laws. I and others contend that the African cultural character has historically included a reliance on ancestors, love of children—we see this in Kemet [ancient Egypt], in Ghana among the Yoruba. There is also the notion of fertility, the earth—the relationship between humans and the earth, a search for harmony [Ma'at]. There is a great deal about this in the works of [Cheikh Anta] Diop and [Theophile] Obenga . . .

Q: How has this experience of being in America affected African Americans?

A: Part of our reality is that we were not operating on our own terms. We were operating on everyone else's terms. That is why we see,

among African Americans, a revival of ancestralism with the growing popularity of the rites of passage movement. We are tapping into
what African people have felt ever since we were moved off our center. It is only by knowing to whom you are connected that you know
who you are and where you are going. . . .

   Although I'm not a Republican, the one part of [journalist and
commentator] Tony Brown's philosophy I agree with is that we
shouldn't ask anybody for anything. I don't ask anybody for anything, including ideas.

Q: How is Afrocentricity similar to or different from cultural nationalism?

A: Cultural nationalism is a political philosophy, while Afrocentricity
   is a theoretical orientation. It is perfectly legitimate to choose to be
   both an Afrocentrist and a cultural nationalist, but they are not the
   same thing. The Afrocentric perspective is not a racial perspective.
   We have had students from Japan and China who have conducted
   research from an Afrocentric perspective, for example. But being in
   African-American Studies doesn't make you an Afrocentrist. . . .

Q: What do you think about melanin theory?

A: We do not teach melanin theory. We do not believe in biological de-
   terminism. The media is always trying to connect us with that. Yes,
   we have more melanin. So what?

Q: What are the biggest misconceptions about Afrocentrism?

A: There are many, but one of the biggest is that Afrocentricity is
   about trying to raise the self-esteem of black people by trying to create a romantic ideal of history. Another is that Afrocentricity is
   about specific facts. It's not about specific facts, but about orientation to facts. Given any subject, we ask, "What is it in terms of
   African agency?" People say that we're concerned, for example,
   about whether Cleopatra was black. That's not the issue. In fact,
   she was probably Greek. The issue is, was she important? The answer is no. Our study of history does lead many of us to certain fac-
   tual conclusions. We do claim, for example, that the first Queen in
   human history was a black woman.

Q: You argue that Afrocentrism and Eurocentrism differ in the ways in
   which they answer the question, "What do we know, and how do we
   decide that we know it?" Specifically, you say that European intellectual tradition excludes African ways of knowing.

A: The way European writers conceptualized the world is to say that
   you can only know things through sense experience [observation—a
   tradition called positivism]. We say that all human experience is ra-
   tional, in that it comes out of the brain. For example, I can go into a
   meeting and say, "There's a whole lot of soul in this room." I can feel
   it, but it's not tangible. . . . The notion of the classification of knowledge, for example, is deeply rooted. Of course, we use observation as

well. When I wanted to know whether the ancient Egyptians were black, I went to Egypt and I looked at the paintings. I looked at the people of Egypt today.

Q: If we become Afrocentrists, what changes? What do our lifestyles, our customs, our economics and our politics look like?

A: We create a new world. My wife [Professor Kariamu Welsh Asante] and I talked about this when we visited our [12-year-old son's] school. We asked, "If most of the students here are of African descent, why isn't that reflected in the school curriculum, the food served in the cafeteria, the atmosphere?" My son studies to music most of the time, and he's a very good student—why not have music in the halls and jubilee choirs? . . .

Even our architecture would be different. David Hughes's book, *Afrocentric Architecture,* points out that a 90-degree angle is a Western invention. As for economics and politics, as with everything else, we go back to the question that Haki [Madhubuti] asked: "Is it in the best interest of African people?" Our interest and the best interests of America coincide.

Asante has enlightened people about Afrocentricity and increased our knowledge of the history and culture of Africa's people through his lectures, through his work as a consultant to several school systems interested in adopting Afrocentric education methods, and through upward of two hundred scholarly articles. Added to this are the nearly forty books he has authored or edited, among them *Afrocentricity: The Theory of Social Change* (1980; second edition, 1983); *African Culture: The Rhythms of Unity* (edited with Kariamu Welsh Asante, 1985); *Afrocentricity* (1988); *Umfundalai: Afrocentric Rite of Passage* (1989); *Kemet, Afrocentricity and Knowledge* (1990); *Malcolm X as Cultural Hero and Other Afrocentric Essays* (1993); *African American History: A Journey of Liberation* (1995); *African Intellectual Heritage: A Book of Sources* (edited with Abu S. Barry, 1996); *The Afrocentric Idea* (revised edition, 1998) and *The Stream of Blood: Desettlerism in Southern Africa* (1998).

When Molefi Kete Asante isn't busy sharing what he knows and humanizing the world, he can be found not only loving music and the dance, but also gardening, writing poetry, playing basketball, and gazing at the stars as an amateur astronomer.

 Charles Johnson (1948–   )

Charles Richard Johnson had just hit a half-century when, in June 1998, he received a John D. and Catherine T. MacArthur Foundation

Award, popularly known as the "Genius Award." This award came nearly twenty-five years after he made his full-length fiction debut. The year was 1974, and Johnson, age twenty-six, was a student at the State University of New York at Stonybrook, working on his Ph.D. in phenomenology and literary aesthetics. The novel was *Faith and the Good Thing,* the story of a young Southerner, Faith Cross, who, on the advice of a one-eyed grotesque, The Swamp Woman, kicks it to Chicago to find herself and in the process loses innocence and illusions. Johnson's next novel, *Oxherding Tale* (1982), patterned after early black narratives (the first autobiography of **Frederick Douglass,** in particular), turns on the adventures and misadventures of a mulatto in South Carolina bondage, Andrew Hawkins, who is trying to make sense of himself and his world.

Johnson's fascination with the universe of literary form became more apparent with the publication of *The Sorcerer's Apprentice: Tales and Conjurations* (1986). This collection, which was nominated for a PEN/Faulkner Award, contains eight profoundly philosophical stories, each spun from a different genre. Among them are "Menagerie, A Child's Fable," hardly about kid stuff; a piece of sci-fi, "Popper's Disease," about a sad and searching doctor's encounter with an ailing E.T.; and a horror story, "Exchange Value," in which two brothers who thought they'd lucked onto an easy robbery learn a stiff lesson about greed.

Johnson's next book was not fiction, but about fiction: *Being and Race: Black Writing Since 1970* (1988). Then came the novel *Middle Passage* (1990), in which Rutherford Calhoun, a very learned recently freed slave and petty thief finds himself on a weird journey when he stows away on the *Republic,* a decrepit clipper captained by a crazy philosophizing dwarf, Ebenezer Falcon, bound for Africa to pick up no ordinary cargo: forty members of an ancient tribe of wizards, the All-museri—and not only them, but their god, as well. This rousing adventure was a long journey for Johnson. "I spent six years, literally, reading every sea story that I could get my hands on," he said in a 1993 interview in *The Seattle Review.* "I looked at nautical dictionaries. I looked at ship's logs. I looked at one book on Cockney slang . . . for the sake of getting the sailors' idiom right." Johnson's hard work paid off: *Middle Passage* received the 1990 National Book Award for Fiction. Not since 1953, when one of Johnson's inspirations (Ralph Ellison) won this award (for *Invisible Man),* had a black male writer received it.

In his next novel, *Dreamer* (1998), Johnson moved way ahead in time and into the inner life of **Martin Luther King, Jr.** In an interview with William Jelani Cobb, which appeared in the June 1995 issue of *Quarterly Black Review of Books,* to the question "What is the King book about?" "Unconditional love," was Johnson's reply. "The book allows me to get a lot of things out about King in terms of minutia that I don't think people talk about, in terms of biography, but also to really look at the man as a philosopher, a Christian philosopher within a tradition of philosophers and to see what that vision is all about, to ask for our time, how one lives the nonviolent way of life. Not just as a method of social protest, but as a way of life, in every aspect of life. That's why [King] is interesting to me because I look at him as a philosopher."

A few months after *Dreamer* came out, there was more of Johnson's fiction to be had in the companion book to the PBS series *Africans in America: America's Journey through Slavery,* which first aired in October, 1998. Weaving through Patricia Smith's narrative on the black experience from the days of **Jiro** to the Civil War, are Johnson's twelve luminous short stories, among which are "The Transmission" about the meditations and observations of a young Allmuseri enduring the middle passage aboard the slave ship *Providence;* "Confession," about the Stono Rebellion in Charleston, South Carolina, in 1739; "Poetry and Politics," where Phillis Wheatley frets that the future will abuse her for not writing antislavery verse; and "A Lion at Pendleton" where we meet **Frederick Douglass** in the fall of 1843, willing himself to keep a speaking engagement after suffering a terrible beating at the hands of the white mob that busted up an antislavery rally in Pendleton, Indiana.

As for what makes Johnson tick, we find a lot of clues in an interview in the *African American Review* Winter 1996 issue, devoted to Johnson. The interviewer is scholar, poet, and fiction writer Michael Boccia, whose first question was, "Is there any little-known or unknown autobiographical information that would help us better understand your fiction?" In response, Johnson talked about his first passion, cartoons, which he began to get published when he was seventeen. He studied with cartoonist Lawrence Lariar and published steadily for seven years. "This career consumed me," Johnson told Boccia, "leading to over 1,000 published drawings in dozens of publications." *Black World* and the Chicago *Tribune* were among Johnson's outlets. His other cartooning work included scripting for Charlton comic books; creating, coproducing, and hosting a fifty-two-part public television series on cartooning, *Charlie's Pad* (1971); and two books of comic art, *Black Humor* (1970) and *Half-Part Nation-Time* (1972). Cartooning is something Johnson continues to do, drawing regular features for *QBR* and *Literal Latte.*

Soon, Johnson moved on from talking about cartooning, and then came more good questions by Michael Boccia, opening up on the writers who did it for Johnson when he was a young adult—"mainly the authors who would appeal to a lover of philosophy—Sartre and Camus, Mann and Hesse, Hawthorne and Melville, etc." Jean Toomer, Richard Wright, and Ralph Ellison were the black writers he found most engaging. As for what was on his mind when he began writing: "I began writ-

ing novels in earnest in 1970 with one specific goal in mind, that of expanding the category we might call black philosophical fiction; i.e.,
opening up black literature to the same ethical, ontological, and epis-
temological questions—Western and Eastern—that I wrestled with as a
student of philosophy." Informing this striving is his mastery of martial
arts (three traditional karates and three kung-fu systems) and his belief, Buddhism, to which he was drawn when a teenager.

Before the martial arts, the Buddhism, the cartooning and early
scribbling (his first six attempts at novel writing were, he freely admits,
mud-awful), before the high education and phenomenology, there was
family, some of whom we've met in Johnson's fiction.

> On my mother's side of the family (all deceased now), I can trace back
> my ancestors to a New Orleans black coachman born in the 1820s. I
> think his name was Jeff Peters. My father's people come from rural
> South Carolina near Hodges and Abbeville. My dad was one of twelve
> kids—six boys, six girls—born to a man who was a farmer and a
> blacksmith. What brought my Dad North to Evanston, Illinois, where
> he met my mother, was a promise of work from his uncle, William
> Johnson, who'd moved to Illinois in the 1920s. There, he started his
> own milk company to serve the black community (whites didn't
> deliver to them). . . . Uncle Will's milk company went belly up during
> the Depression. He started another company, the Johnson Construc-
> tion Co., and once it was going (it continued into the 1960s), he in-
> vited his brother's sons in the South to come to work for him. So Dad
> and his brothers traveled north to work for my great-uncle. . . .
>
> As a kid I remember riding around Evanston and my father point-
> ing out to me places Uncle Will had built—Springfield Baptist Church,
> apartment buildings, and residences. He erected architecture all over
> the North Shore area, so I always had a sense that my family mem-
> bers had created parts of the world in which we lived. . . .
>
> My mother and father were a complementary pair. Both were qui-
> etly pious, and Ebenezer [A.M.E.] Church in Evanston . . . was a valued
> part of our lives. . . . She, an only child (like me), had always wanted to
> be a school teacher, but health problems (asthma) prevented this. Still,
> her interests ran toward books—she belonged to numerous book clubs
> in the 1960s—which we often shared, and toward whatever was un-
> usual, exotic, unique. She was a Democrat, a passionate woman with a
> wicked sense of humor who encouraged my childhood passion for
> drawing, and she was someone my father relied on completely. As for
> my father, there is simply this to say: He is the hardest working, most
> moral man I've ever known. In the South he went as far as the fifth
> grade before his parents needed him full-time to help with farmwork
> during the Depression. After moving to Evanston, he often worked two
> jobs a week—construction and as a night watchman—as well as odd
> jobs for an elderly white couple in the suburbs on the weekends.

Evanston was integrated long before Johnson was born: "My
friends from kindergarten through high school were white as well as

black. Bigotry, as we understood it then, was simply 'uncool.'" When Boccia asked, "Did your idea of your cultural identity change over the years?" and "How would you say this has shaped you and your work?" Johnson replied,

> Given my childhood, I think I can safely say that I was a child of integration. I never questioned its validity until I went away to college and met other black students more affected by Black Power than integration, by **Malcolm X** than **Martin Luther King, Jr.** The ideology of "blackness" was something I learned in the late 1960s and early 1970s on campus. . . . A part of me sympathizes with black nationalist concerns, such as economic self-sufficiency—remember, my Uncle Will was a black businessman devoted to helping his own. But I never bought into black cultural nationalism. It always struck me as naïve (all cultures we know about are synthetic, a tissue of contributions from others). The way its proponents portrayed other races—whites, for example—had nothing to do with the supportive people I knew when I was growing up. In the end, black cultural nationalism only served to remind me of how thoroughly American my family and I have always been.

When the interview returned to writing, Boccia remarked that Johnson's work had touched on "issues ranging from entropy to Asian philosophies." Boccia then asked, "What are the central themes that run through all your work?" "The investigation of the nature of the self and personal identity." This is what Johnson sees as the crux of his fiction. "As a phenomenologist, I cannot help but believe that consciousness is primary for all 'experience'—that the nature of the *I* is the deepest of mysteries, and that all other questions rise from this primordial one, What am I?"

One of Michael Boccia's last questions was, "What has happened to you as a human and as an artist that marks you as distinctly of our historical period?" Johnson's reply is something many of his generation and preparation can identify with:

> Obviously, the Civil Rights Movement was of central importance in shaping the lived-world (Lebenswelt) of my young manhood. I came of age at a time when America was still "the land of opportunity" but also fluid during the 1960s. As one of my friends during that time put it, "I'm a nigger, I can do anything!" That was the sense of life that I soaked up around me—there were no artistic or intellectual restrictions. If I wanted to be a cartoonist, a philosopher, a fiction writer, a college professor, an essayist, a screenwriter, a martial artist, all I needed to achieve any or all of these things was my own talent, disciplined labor, and the blessing of God. In other words, the self was a verb, not a noun—a process, not a product. You defined your life through action, deeds; or, as Sartre might put it, "Existence preceded essence." In the late 1960s, you did not see yourself or your essence—your life's meaning—as defined wholly by the past, or by race or class.

As an artist, you were not confined to any single tradition; rather, you could creatively cross genres and in doing so bring something fresh in the way of meaning and form into existence. Whether we are talking about the arts, politics, or the art of living, the one word—the single driving idea—of this historical period is *freedom.*

All the time that Johnson has been exercising his freedom to be phenomenological with the pen, he has been teaching in Seattle (where he and his wife have raised their two children) at the University of Washington, where he became a professor of English in 1976, and then Director of Creative Writing, and then the S. Wilson and Grace M. Pollock Endowed Professor of Creative Writing. Also, over the years, Johnson has written more than twenty screenplays, including *Booker* (PBS, 1985), winner of a Writers Guild Award. Johnson has contributed essays and short stories to numerous anthologies and, with John McCluskey, Jr., he coedited a collection that explores the experiences of present-era African American men, *Black Men Speaking* (1997), with art by **Jacob Lawrence.**

ANOTHER CHARLES JOHNSON

Charles Spurgeon Johnson (1893–1956), who was born in Bristol, Virginia, did great and mighty things for his people in many capacities. First off was his work in sociology, in which he earned a Ph.B. from the University of Chicago in 1918, by which time he was already serving as director of the Chicago Urban League's division of research and records. In 1919, in the wake of the race riot in Chicago (one of the roughly two dozen of the summer of 1919 that led James Weldon Johnson to tag the period "Red Summer"), Charles Johnson was appointed to the Chicago Commission on Race Relations, for which he co-authored *The Negro in Chicago: A Study of Race Relations and a Race Riot* (1922). When this report was published, Johnson was living in New York, serving as director of the National Urban League's department of research and investigation.

In 1923, Johnson launched this organization's journal *Opportunity: A Journal of Negro Life,* which gave scores of now legendary writers and artists an outlet for work, and which, among other things, prompted Langston Hughes to later call Charles Johnson one of the three "midwives" of the Harlem Renaissance. In 1927, Johnson moved to Nashville, Tennessee, to become chair of Fisk University's Department of social sciences, and twenty years later, he became this university's first black president. During his Fisk days, Johnson produced several important books, among them, *Shadow of the Plantation* (1934), a pioneering study of the modern South, which delineated the relationship between economic oppression and racial discrimination; *The Negro College Student* (1938); *Growing Up in the Black Belt* (1941); and *Patterns of Negro Segregation* (1943).

☀ Donald Bogle (1952–   )

Donald sure was one inquisitive lad:

> As a kid sitting in movie theaters transfixed by the giant figures I saw on the big screen or sitting glued to the television set intrigued by its tiny, flickering images, I was always, from the very beginning, fascinated by the black faces I saw come and go. Black performers in movies and television cast a beguiling spell over me . . .
>
> Even during those early years of my moviegoing and TV-watching experience, I think I was struggling to sort out incongruities of what I viewed, to clear up the disparities. Always my curiosity and thirst for information led me to the library in search of some comment on a particular film, character, or personality. Usually, I returned home empty-handed, without any answers to some basic questions. For instance, I wondered, as I watched on television a broadcast of the original 1934 version of *Imitation of Life,* what effect this movie had had on the black community when first released. Moreover, what had happened to the actress Fredi Washington, who had touched a national nerve when she hadplayed Peola—a light-skinned black girl who passes for white? Why, too, had Paul Robeson appeared in so many films made abroad? . . . Had there really been a black director named **Oscar Micheaux**? . . . Why was it that Dorothy Dandridge, after her great success in *Carmen Jones,* did not appear in another film for almost three years?

When Donald Bogle grew up, he turned his curiosity into a vocation, becoming one of the nation's foremost authorities on African Americans in American popular culture, with an emphasis on motion pictures and television. Bogle has shared what he knows as an educator: at Rutgers University, at the University of Pennsylvania, at New York University's Tisch School of the Arts. He has also lectured at various forums around the nation and has written countless articles and reviews for *Freedomways, Essence, Spin,* and *Film Comment,* among other periodicals. He has served as a commentator for several specials, including HBO's *Mo Funny: Black Comedy in America* and the American Movie Channel's documentary on African Americans in the movies, *Small Steps, Big Strides.* Curating and cocurating a number of major film series in New York City is another way Bogle has contributed to the culture: a retrospective on Sidney Poitier at the American Museum of the Moving Picture, and the Film Forum's *Black Women in the Movies: Actresses, Images, Films; Blacks in the Movies: Breakthroughs, Landmarks and Milestones;* and *Blaxploitation, Baby!* are among his credits on this account.

Donald Bogle's books represent his greatest contribution to our

Donald Bogle with movies on his mind, photographed by Frank Stewart. (Courtesy of Donald Bogle)

knowledge about blacks in movies and television (in front of and behind the camera). His first book was the best-seller *Toms, Coons, Mulattoes, Mammies, & Bucks: An Interpretive History of Blacks in American Films,* which prompted Spike Lee to say, "Mr. Bogle continues to be our most noted black-cinema historian." This book received the Theater Library Association Award for Best Film Book of the Year when it came out in 1973 (with the third revised and updated edition published in 1994). There's also *Brown Sugar: Eighty Years of America's Black Female Superstars* (1980), adapted into a four-hour documentary for PBS by Bogle, who was also head of the film-research team and executive producer for this series, named one of the best documentaries of 1987 by the Association of American Women in Television and Radio.

Another prize is *Blacks in American Films and Television: An Illustrated Encyclopedia* (1988), which contains a host of entries on motion pictures in which blacks have appeared since the early twentieth century, plus more than one hundred entries on television shows (series, miniseries, made-for-TV movies) and profiles of a slew of performers. (It's also the source of his reminisce, quoted earlier.)

Bogle's first work on a single performer is *Dorothy Dandridge* (1997), which Mel Watkins, writing for the *New York Times Book Review,* hailed as "an ambitious, rigorously researched account" and stated that Bogle "has fashioned a resonant history of a bygone era in Hollywood and passionately documented the contribution of one of its most dazzling and complex performers."

Bogle's "short works" include the lengthy foreword on the jazz artist in the movies for Spike Lee's *Mo' Better Blues*, the introduction to *A Separate Cinema: Fifty Years of Black-Cast Posters*, and to the new edition of Ethel Waters's autobiography *His Eye Is on the Sparrow*.

Thanks to Donald Bogle, a whole lot of people, young and old, who are curious about the history of African-American actors, producers, and directors, do not have to search high and low for substantive information and analyses. Through mixed methods, Bogle has helped us understand the way Hollywood has shaped the world's perception of African Americans and the way African Americans have complied with and defied Tinseltown.

 ## Neil deGrasse Tyson (1958–   )

Fourteen-year-old Neil deGrasse Tyson put one and one together: He needed money, and many people in the Bronx, New York, complex where he lived could use someone to walk their dogs. "So I made a whole lot of money walking other people's dogs," Tyson told photographer Bruce Caines in an interview for Caines's book *Our Common Ground: Portraits of Blacks Changing the Face of America* (1994).

A leather jacket, eight-track tapes, taking a date down to Manhattan for a movie and dinner at Tad's Steakhouse, some spending money for other run-of-the-mill puerile pursuits? Nope, that's not what young Tyson wanted the money for. His eye was on a telescope. Tyson got his telescope, and he got to take special classes at the Hayden Planetarium in Manhattan, and he got to be a member of the Amateur Astronomers Association, and to be editor of the *Physical Science Journal* at Bronx High School of Science, and to go on two scientific expeditions through special scholarships (one to Africa to behold a total solar eclipse).

This faithful reader of *Scientific American* also got to go to Harvard for his bachelor's degree in physics, to the University of Texas at Austin for his master's degree in astronomy, and to Columbia University for his Ph.D. in astrophysics. After his learning journey, Tyson became a research associate in Princeton University's Department of Astrophysics, and in 1994, a visiting research scientist and lecturer in this department. Concurrent with his work at Princeton, Tyson has held a series of positions with the institution that was his favorite haunt as a child: the American Museum of Natural History's Hayden Planetarium.

Tyson started with the planetarium in 1994, as staff astronomer. In 1995, he became its acting director and, a year later, its newly created Frederick P. Rose Director. Also on his plate: project scientist for the planetarium's $100-million reconstruction, which began in the spring of 1997—a few months after Tyson became acting chair and associate

Neil deGrasse Tyson in 1989 in the Dome of the Rutherford Observatory, Columbia University, New York City. In Tyson's hand is a 16" hand-painted "Celestial Sphere," an educational tool for astronomy labs. In the background is a 9" Refracting Alvin Clark Telescope. (Courtesy of Bruce Caines)

astronomer of the American Museum of Natural History's new Department of Astrophysics.

Yep, he's definitely one smart, capable brother, who has quite naturally contributed numerous research papers to scientific publications, such as "On the Possibility of Gas-Rich Dwarf Galaxies in the Lyman-α Forest," in *Astrophysical Journal.* Throughout his sojourn in the sciences, this latter-day **Benjamin Banneker** has been primarily interested in dwarf galaxies, exploding stars, and the chemical-evolution history of the Milky Way. If all that gave you vertigo, you can get some understanding in the books Tyson has put out for a general audience: His *Universe Down to Earth* (1994) is a collection of essays that "uses creative 'household' analogies to help bring complex topics of the universe to the lay reader"; his Q&A book *Merlin's Tour of the Universe* (1997) is based on the column he did (with the pen name "Merlin") for the University of Texas magazine *Stardate*.

As one of the most highly regarded astrophysicists on the planet, Tyson has made a host of television appearances when the subject has been space. There was a PBS interview for a program on the development and role of large telescopes for cosmic discovery; an *ABC World*

News Now interview with Peter Jennings, on the discovery of ice on the Moon and on Mars probes; and an interview on *Charlie Rose* about the Mars Pathfinder mission.

Of course, Neil Tyson has had to deal with double takes, but it's something he knew to expect since he was a teenager. In that interview for Bruce Caines's *Our Common Ground,* Tyson talked about the contrast in reactions to his involvement in sports and his involvement in the sciences. "Yes, I was good at basketball, and, yes, I could slam dunk in ninth grade," said Tyson, who was also captain of his school's wrestling team. "I was sort of your quintessential black athlete. As expected. It was easy. And why was it easy? I'm convinced it was because all the forces in society *allowed* it to happen." When Tyson became editor of the school's science journal, however, "people started murmuring, 'Well, how did *he* get to be . . . ?' 'What did *he* do . . . ?' All this sort of undercurrent. But no one questioned my athletic achievements. No one questioned that at all."

Over the years, Tyson learned to take the "undercurrent" in stride. "Yeah, there are struggles," he told Caines. "And to overcome them I had to say to myself, I'm running this race and I have more hurdles, and my hurdles are higher. My whole profession is based on the challenge of problem solving. That challenge has had to be applied to my path in life."

Tyson is determined to keep taking it in stride and allowing himself no illusions as he continues to make contributions to the exploration of the universe, reaching for breakthrough discoveries all the time. "I'll just have to jump higher and faster to get to that finish line at the same time, or before anybody else."

The Million Men

They came to the city **Benjamin Banneker** helped lay out, the city **A. Philip Randolph** threatened to march on in 1941 and did in 1963, the city where **Charles Hamilton Houston** designed the legal campaign of the civil-rights crusade, the city for which **Paul R. Williams** designed buildings. They came to say we are not what they project.

On October 16, 1995, they came, despite the divisions, wanting the support of all their sisters and brothers, trying to forget that some in the family preferred to traffick in spite, knowing that this march was beyond Louis Farrakhan, its convener.

They did not hail from every place, but they came from everywhere: from the Harlems and the Highland Parks. As Archbishop George A. Stallings declared, as part of his prayer, "We, as proud black men, black

Two who were among the million on October 16, 1995. (Courtesy of Christopher Griffith)

men from the rural South and the industrial North, we as struggling black men, from the heart of America and the gleaming shores of the West, we as accomplished black men; black men from the East Coast to the West Coast, have all sojourned to this gateway of the Promised Land to take ownership and control and lay claims to our destiny."

Artists, activists, physicians, attorneys, journalists, teachers, preachers, former gang members, construction workers, civil servants—they came with the dawn, by train, plane, car, bus, bike, truck, RV, two feet.

"I am just caught up in the mood, the movement of our people," said Winston Williams III, a magazine publisher from Milwaukee. "I'm just feeling good about being black. . . ."

They came with friends and family and entourage. They came to brother–brother with Al Sharpton, Marion Barry, Jim Brown, Cornel West, **Jesse Jackson,** Leonard Jeffries, Dick Gregory, Stevie Wonder, Chuck D., Ice T., Prince D'Jour, Brother Beel.

They came to smile at the sisters who came to cheer. "I already see brothers walking taller," said Woody Henderson, an interior designer from New York.

They came to say it was okay to come to the nation's capital and not ask others for a darn thing. 1.2 million came to see who would be there and who cared and who would dare.

Thousands, thousands, thousands more watched from home, barbershop, bar, pool room, schoolroom, corner office, and the pen.

"When you stop making excuses, when you start standing with our mothers, when you stick it out with your family, when you start mentoring our young, when you start teaching us to be humane, then we can build a new nation of strong people," declared the Chicago teen Ayinde Jean-Baptiste.

They came to go home with a story, with a memory, and a thousand words. And for the picture of the Million Men, we find a fitting caption in the essay Herb Boyd wrote for the 1996 edition of the anthology he coedited with Robert Allen, *Brotherman: The Odyssey of Black Men in America.* Recalled Boyd,

> The Million Man March was a special moment of rare epiphany for men who had endured the effects of chattel slavery, racism, and humiliation, who have been pushed to the margins of society, bruised by an ensemble of negative stereotypes, alienated from affection and respect, and, for the most part rendered invisible.
>
> But for this brief, affirming moment, we were not invisible, no longer isolated in our own despair, but asserting our manhood in the nation's capital for all the world to see.

Frederick Douglass and **Henry Highland Garnet** and **David Walker** and **William Monroe Trotter**—they all would have been so proud. **Nat Turner,** too. And **High John the Conqueror** was singing with his drum.

Long after the Million Men disbanded, there were ardent prayers that they would all do better or keep being good, courageous, brilliant, aware, and would be more vigilant in teaching the future that there is no freedom in victimhood, and that, yes, America never wished us well, never meant us any good—yet, African Americans, a tribe created out of mad thievery, we are a people who have stayed determined to survive and perpetually produced strong men.

INDEX

Abbott, Robert Sengstacke, 193
Abele, Julian Frances, 220, 222
Abernathy, Ralph, 264
Adams, Lewis, 114–16
African Civilization Society, 52
African Free School #2 (N.Y.C.), 36, 38, 49, 59, 60
African Grove Theater (N.Y.C.), 36–37
Africanisms in Gullah Dialect (Turner), 194–95
Afro-American, 192, 193, 225
Afrocentricity, 172, 285–88
Aldridge, Ira, 36–38
Algebra Project, 235
Ali, Muhammad, 236, 264, 269
Allen, Richard, 32
Alston, Charles, 205
American Anti-Slavery Society, 32, 75, 117
American Colonization Society, 29–31, 45
American Negro Academy, 124
American Revolution, 15, 16–17, 32, 65–66, 107
Anderson, Caroline Still, 70
Anderson, James H., 193
Anderson, Jourdon, 93–94
Anderson, Marian, 170
Anderson, Osborne P., 82
Andrews, Charles C., 38, 39
Appeal (Walker), 44–45, 46, 47, 51
Aptheker, Herbert, 36
Armstrong, Samuel Chapman, 115, 145, 146
Asante, Molefi Kete, 172, 284–88
Ashbourne, A. P., 141
Ashe, Arthur, 25, 26, 265, 270–72, 280
Ashford, Nickolas, 241
Association for the Study of Afro-American Life and History, 173, 256
Atlanta Compromise (1895), 147
Atlanta University, 125, 150
Atlantic Monthly (magazine), 153–54
Attucks, Crispus, 15–16, 66
Auden, W. H., 250
Augustine Society, 31
Auld, Thomas, 117

Bailey, Leonard C., 141
Baker, Ella, 231
Baldwin, James, 236, 246–47, 264
Ball, J. P., 70–72, 113
Banneker, Benjamin, 20–25, 297, 298
Bannister, Edward M., 110–13
Baraka, Amiri, 236, 244, 261–63
Barber, J. Max, 124
Bates, Ruby, 187, 188
Battey, Cornelius M., 184
Battle of Bunker Hill (1775), 16, 17

Beamon, Bob, 265–66
Beard, Andrew J., 141
Bearden, Romare, 112, 113, 205, 208
bebop, 211–12
Beckwourth, Jim, 62–64
Bell, Philip A., 61
Bennett, Edward, 7, 8
Bennett, Lerone, Jr., 159
Beran Building and Loan Association, 70
Berry Brothers, 204
Bethune, Mary McLeod, 124, 161
Bethune, Thomas, 171
Bevins, James, 42
Bibb, Henry, 39
Black Academy of Arts and Letters, 256
Black Arts Movement, 236, 262
Black Boys of Summer, 199–202
Black Dispatch, 193
Black English (Dillard), 195
Black Forum, 244
Black Panther Party, 267–68
Black Power, 234, 244, 264
Blacks in American Films and Television (Bogle), 239–40, 295
Blackwell, Randolph, 233
Blair, Ezell, 231
Blake, Eubie, 216
Block, Sam, 233
Blood, 269–70
Blow, Peter, 72, 73, 74, 75
Bogle, Donald, 239–40, 294–96
Bolling v. Sharpe (1950), 226–27
Bond, J. Max, Jr., 219
Bonner, Thomas D., 64
Bontemps, Arna, 114–15
Boon, James, 75–78
Boston Literary and Historical Association, 157
Boston Massacre (1770), 15, 16, 66
Boston Riot (1903), 150, 158
Bosworth, Edward Increase, 228
Bowser, David Bustill, 142
Boyd, Herb, 300
Bradford, Janie, 242
Branch, Taylor, 228
Brawley, Benjamin, 106, 127
Bridges, Robert, 32–33
Brooks, Arthur L., 115
Brooks, Charles B., 141
Broteer, 11–14
Brotherman (Boyd and Allen), 300
Brown, Caesar, 16
Brown, Elaine, 244
Brown, Grafton Tyler, 113–14
Brown, Henry Box, 58, 116
Brown, James, 264
Brown, John, 81, 119
Brown, Katie, 27–28
Brown, Marie Dutton, 221

PERMISSIONS

The author is grateful to those listed below for granting her permission to use the following material. All possible care has been taken to trace ownership of material and to make full acknowledgment. If any errors or omissions have occurred, they will be corrected in subsequent editions, provided that notification is sent to the publisher.

Excerpt from *Darktown Strutters*. Copyright © 1994 by Wesley Brown. Used by permission of Wesley Brown.

Excerpt from "High John de Conquer" by Zora Neale Hurston. Used by permission of the Estate of Zora Neale Hurston.

"Frederick Douglass," copyright © 1966 by Robert Hayden, opening stanza of "Middle Passage," copyright © 1962, 1966 by Robert Hayden, and last stanza of "[American Journal]" copyright © 1978, 1982 by Robert Hayden, from *Collected Poems of Robert Hayden* by Frederick Glaysher, editor. Reprinted by permission of Liveright Publishing Corporation.

Adaptation of "About Booker T. Washington" by Tonya Bolden for The New York Public Library Collector's Edition *Up from Slavery and Other Early Black Narratives* published by Doubleday. Copyright © 1998 by The New York Public Library, Astor, Lenox and Tilden Foundations. Used by permission of Doubleday, a division of Bantam Doubleday Dell Publishing Group, Inc.

"The New Negro" by James Edward McCall. Copyright © 1927 by *Opportunity: A Journal of Negro Life*. Used by permission of the National Urban League.

Lyric excerpts from "Take My Hand, Precious Lord," by Thomas A. Dorsey © 1938 (Renewed) Warner-Tamerlane Publishing Corp. for U.S.A. All Rights outside the U.S.A. Controlled by Unichappell Music Inc. All Rights reserved. Used by permission of Warner Bros. Publications U.S. Inc., Miami, FL 33014.

Excerpts from "Jackson Jordan, Jr." by John Langston Gwaltney in *Drylongso: A Self-Portrait of Black America* by John Langston Gwaltney. Copyright © 1980 by John Langston Gwaltney. Used by permission of J. L. Gwaltney.

Text only excerpt pp. 128–130 from *Down the Glory Road: Contributions of African Americans in United States History and Culture* by Herb Boyd. Copyright © 1995 by Herb Boyd. Used by permission of Avon Books, Inc.

Excerpt from "A Conversation with Amiri Baraka" by William Jelani Cobb, which appeared in the November/December 1994 issue of *Quarterly Black Review of Books*. Copyright © 1994 by William Jelani Cobb. Used by permission of William Jelani Cobb.

Excerpts from "African as Agent: Molefi Kete Asante on Afrocentricity" by Kim Pearson, which appeared in the Fall 1994 issue of *Quarterly Black Review of Books*. Copyright © 1994 by Kim Pearson. Used by permission of Kim Pearson.

Excerpts from "An Interview with Charles Johnson" by Michael Boccia, which appeared in the Winter 1996 issue of *African American Review*. Copyright © 1996 by Michael Boccia. Used by permission of Michael Boccia.